The Race for Paradise

The Race for Paradise

An Islamic History of the Crusades

Paul M. Cobb

OXFORD

UNIVERSITY PRESS

OXFORD

UNIVERSITY PRESS

Oxford University Press is a department of the
University of Oxford. It furthers the University's objective
of excellence in research, scholarship, and education
by publishing worldwide.

Oxford   New York

Auckland   Cape Town   Dar es Salaam   Hong Kong   Karachi
Kuala Lumpur   Madrid   Melbourne   Mexico City   Nairobi
New Delhi   Shanghai   Taipei   Toronto

With offices in

Argentina   Austria   Brazil   Chile   Czech Republic   France   Greece
Guatemala   Hungary   Italy   Japan   Poland   Portugal   Singapore
South Korea   Switzerland   Thailand   Turkey   Ukraine   Vietnam

Oxford is a registered trade mark of Oxford University Press
in the UK and certain other countries.

Published in the United States of America by
Oxford University Press
198 Madison Avenue, New York, NY 10016

Library of Congress Cataloging-in-Publication Data
Cobb, Paul M., 1967–
The race for paradise : an Islamic history of the crusades / Paul M. Cobb.
pages   cm
Includes bibliographical references and index.
ISBN 978-0-19-935811-3 (hardback)
1. Crusades.   2. Islam—Relations—Christianity—History—To 1500.
3. Christianity and other religions—Islam—History—To 1500.
4. Muslims—Mediterranean Region—History—To 1500.   I. Title.
D157.C58   2014
909.07—dc23   2013040040

3 5 7 9 8 6 4 2
Printed in the United States of America
on acid-free paper

For Emily,
who overtook me

Contents

Acknowledgments

It need hardly be stated of a book such as this that it takes a village to get it done. That it is done at all, overweight and well past due as it is, merits my thanks to three people possessed of near geological patience. These are, first of all, Timothy Bent, my editor at Oxford University Press USA—a more judicious and intelligent interlocutor would be hard to find inside or outside the world of publishing; Matthew Cotton, my understanding editor at Oxford UK; and Jeffrey Gerecke of G Agency, my literary agent. I thank them collectively for their shared enthusiasm for my project and their gentle reminders and continued support as life periodically intervened to delay this book.

Various residents of my village contributed their support of this project in intangible ways. I would particularly like to thank Caitlyn Campbell, Brian Catlos, Remie Constable, Sarah Davis-Secord, Malika Dekkiche, Bree Demers, Don-John Dugas, Taef ElAzhari, Nahyan Fancy, Yehoshua Frenkel, Cecilia Gaposchkin, Bill and Connie Gillen, David Giovacchini, Jessica Goldberg, Robert Goulding, Rebecca Guay, Lisa Harteker, Konrad Hirschler, Jeanne Jacques, Jeffrey Kallberg, Anne Lester, John Meloy, Margaret Meserve, Matthew Mitchell, Suleiman Mourad, Stephennie Mulder, Megan Reid, Marina Rustow, Devin Stewart, and Richard Zettler. My colleagues at Penn, in particular Roger Allen, Jamal Elias, Renata Holod, Joseph Lowry, and Heather Sharkey, make my work environment the delight that it is. Ed Peters, now retired from Penn, taught me much about the Crusades and Penn's place in crusades studies in the United States, and flattered me by taking an interest in my own contributions to it. Niall Christie took time off from his own important work on Muslim perspectives on the Crusades to save me from many errors, and Mark Stein reliably showed me how little I really know about Ottoman history. Elisabeth Alba created the two hand-drawn maps for chapter 1 at short notice (see more of her work at www.albaillustration.com). Keely Latcham at Oxford USA exuded calm and order as she helped me wrangle with the dreaded details of maps and illustrations at the last minute. In Amherst, Sunset Farm and its denizens provided me with lessons about the value of real work. And all the Cobbs, especially my late mother, Patricia, kept me moving forward.

But here I must particularly acknowledge two people to whom I owe everything that allowed me to complete this book, and to do much more besides. They are Emily Gillen, who saved my life, and Beatrice Ballou, who makes it worth living.

Maps and Illustrations

A Note about Names

Despite the eagerness of readers to learn more about Islamic history, medieval Islamic naming practices can confuse and deter even the most determined of us. Medieval Muslims, particularly those with a noble lineage, might be known by any number of names or titles or their combinations. Here is an example of a perfectly ordinary medieval Muslim name in all its glory: Majd al-Din Muhammad ibn Khalid ibn ʿAbd Allah al-Tamimi.

That can be broken into its component parts as follows: **Majd al-Din** is an example of a fancy formal title, usually bestowed by the state authorities. These titles generally are constructs having to do with "al-Din" (the Religion, i.e., Islam) or "al-Dawla" or "al-Mulk" (the State, Kingdom). In this case, Majd al-Din means "The Glory of Religion," but since these are largely empty titles, it doesn't necessarily mean the bearer was particularly glorious or religious. **Muhammad** is this person's given name, used only in the most intimate settings; **ibn** means "son of" (**bint** in women's names means "daughter of"; **Banu**, often used in tribal names, is the plural, meaning "sons of"), so his father was named **Khalid** and his grandfather was named ʿ**Abd Allah**. His grandfather's name is one of those common Arabic names that describes the bearer as the servant (ʿAbd) of God (Allah). Very often "Allah" is replaced with one of His attributes—hence ʿAbd al-Rahman ("Servant of the Merciful"). Genealogy was very important to the medieval Arabs (and others), and this is reflected in their names, which can extend back many generations, linked by series of "ibns" and "bints." Finally, **al-Tamimi** is what is known as a *nisba*, an adjective that can describe a number of attributes, such as a person's birthplace, profession, sect, or tribe (as in this case, indicating that the man hailed from the tribe of Tamim). It is common for modern authors to drop the "al-" prefix of *nisbas* like this, so al-Tamimi might equally be encountered as Tamimi. Additionally people might be known by an array of nicknames. Men, most typically, were known by the name of their eldest male child, say, "Father of Yusuf," in Arabic Abu Yusuf ("Abu" meaning "father"; in women's names, "Umm" means "mother").

Most of the Muslim figures in this book bear Arabic or Turkish names of varying degrees of complexity. Since this book is intended for readers with no background in Arabic or Islamic history, I have tried whenever possible to simplify and regularize these names. However, as the reader can see, by mustering some patience with them, one can yield precious information about the bearer's background and lineage.

For similar reasons, I have not used the daunting dots and dashes and other scholarly conventions used in academic circles for representing non-Latin alphabets like Arabic in the Latin alphabet. The exceptions are the symbols ʿ and ʾ, which represent two Arabic letters (*ʿayn* and *hamza*, respectively) that have no close equivalent in English. Finally, if a commonly accepted English version of a name or term exists, I have used it. Thus I use Mecca, not the scholarly form, Makka, and Saladin, not Salah al-Din.

Principal Historical Figures and Dynasties

'**Abbasids**: Sunni dynasty of caliphs in Baghdad, 750–1258. During the period covered in this book, the power of these caliphs was largely symbolic.

'**Abd al-Mu'min**: First caliph of the **Almohad** Empire in al-Andalus and the Maghrib, 1147–63.

Al-'Adil: Also Saphadin, etc. **Ayyubid** sultan (1200–1218). He died while on campaign against the Frankish invasion of Damietta.

Al-Afdal: A title borne by a number of individuals in this book, principally the **Fatimid** vizier (1094-1121), who led Egyptian campaigns against the Franks during and after the First Crusade, and the son of **Saladin**, who served his father as a commander and reigned as **Ayyubid** amir of Damascus, 1193-96.

Afonso Henriques: King Afonso I of Portugal, reigned 1139–85, active foe of the Muslims of western al-Andalus.

Alexios Komnenos: Emperor of Byzantium, reigned 1081–1118. His appeal to the West for military assistance against the Turks on his eastern frontier contributed to the calling of the First Crusade.

Alfonso I of Aragon: King of Aragon and Navarre, reigned 1104–34. Nicknamed El Batallador, "The Battler," due to his many campaigns against the Muslims of al-Andalus, among them the conquest of Zaragoza in 1118.

Alfonso VI: King of Leon and Castile, reigned 1077–1109. Nicknamed El Bravo, "The Brave." Conqueror of the Muslim city of Toledo in 1085, among many other places.

Almohads: The second of the two great Berber dynasties of the Maghrib and al-Andalus, following the **Almoravids**, whom they opposed and ousted.

Based usually in Marrakesh, from 1130 until (with greatly reduced power) 1269.

Almoravids: The first of the two great Berber dynasties of the Maghrib and al-Andalus, preceding the **Almohads**, who supplanted them. They ruled from their capital of Marrakesh from ca. 1040 until 1147.

Alp Arslan: Sultan of the Great **Saljuq** Turks, reigned 1063–72. The first Turkish sultan to cross into Syria, which he claimed for the Saljuqs before marching north to defeat the **Byzantines** at Manzikert in 1071.

Amalric I: Also known as "Amaury." King of Jerusalem, reigned 1163–74. He ruled over the Frankish kingdom of Jerusalem at the height of its power.

Artuqids: Also "Ortoqids," etc. Turcoman dynasty ruling in many branches throughout northern Mesopotamia, northern Syria, and eastern Anatolia in the eleventh and twelfth centuries.

Al-Ashraf Khalil: **Mamluk** sultan, reigned 1290–93. He succeeded his father, the sultan **Qalawun**, and oversaw the conquest of Frankish Acre and the expulsion of the last of the Franks from the Near East.

Atsiz: Atsiz ibn Uwaq, a Khwarizmian mercenary in the employ of the **Saljuqs** and **Fatimids**. While pursuing Fatimid goals in Palestine, he brought much of central and southern Syria under his control in the 1070s, before being toppled and killed by the Saljuq general **Tutush**.

Ayyubids: Dynasty founded by **Saladin**. The Ayyubids were centered in Egypt, but goverened most of the Near East, including Syria, northern Mesopotamia, western Arabia, and Yemen, at various points between the dynasty's founding in 1171 and its effective extinction in 1250 at the hands of the **Mamluks**.

Al-Bakri: Geographer from al-Andalus (ca. 1014–94), notable for his coverage of Rome and for preserving the much earlier European travelogue of **Ibrahim ibn Ya'qub**.

Baldwin: Also Baudouin. A common name among Frankish rulers in the Near East, principally Baldwin of Boulogne, who founded the Frankish State of Edessa and later became the first King of Jerusalem (reigned 1100–18), succeeding his brother Godfrey, who had refused to bear the title of king; Baldwin II of Jerusalem, his successor, also known as Baldwin du Bourcq, who replaced Baldwin I as Count of Edessa (1100–18) and then succeeded him as King of Jerusalem (1118–31); Baldwin IV of Jerusalem also known as Baldwin the Leper (reigned 1174–85), an early Frankish foe of **Saladin**.

Barkiyaruq: Sultan of the Great **Saljuqs** from 1094 to 1105. He came to power after a bitter succession struggle following the death of his father, **Malikshah**.

Baybars: Also known as al-Malik al-Zahir, "The Conquering King." **Mamluk** sultan who began his career as a commander in the service of the **Ayyubid** sultan **al-Salih Ayyub**. During his reign (1260–1277), Baybars conquered much of what was left of Frankish territory in the Near East after **Saladin's** reconquests.

Beyazid: Also known as Beyazid I Yildirim, "The Thunderbolt." Sultan of the **Ottoman** Empire in its early years, 1389–1402. Beyazid was constantly occupied with extending Ottoman control into the Balkans and eastern Europe.

Boabdil: Also known as Muhammad XII of Granada. Last ruler of Muslim Granada (1487–92), the seat of the **Nasrid** dynasty in al-Andalus. He was thus the last Muslim to rule independently in the old territory of al-Andalus.

Bohemond: A common name among Frankish rulers in the Near East, principally Bohemond I of Antioch, also known as Bohemond of Taranto. Son of the Norman warlord **Robert Guiscard**, he became prince of Antioch (1098–1111), whose capture he had secured, and was a prominent leader of the first Frankish invasion of the Near East; Bohemond VI of Antioch-Tripoli, the two Frankish States having fallen under his rule in from 1252 to 1268. He had openly sided with the Mongols during their confrontation with the **Mamluks** in 1260 and was ruler of Antioch when it fell to the **Mamluks** in 1268. He continued on as ruler of Tripoli until his death in 1275.

Byzantines: The Christian, Greek-speaking continuation of the Roman Empire, sometimes called the Eastern Roman Empire. Its capital was located in Constantinople, founded by Constantine the Great in 330, until its capture by the **Ottomans** in 1453.

Conrad III of Germany: King of Germany, 1138–52, first of the Hohenstaufen dynasty to bear this title. With Louis VII of France, he was the principal leader of the so-called Second Crusade.

Constantine XI: Last of the Byzantine Emperors. He took the throne as a member of the Paleologos dynasty in 1449 and ruled from Constantinople when it captured by the **Ottoman** Turks in 1453. He died during the final siege of the city.

Danishmendids: A Turcoman dynasty that ruled in north-central and eastern Anatolia during the eleventh and twelfth centuries. They were rivals and occasional allies of the **Saljuqs** of Rum.

Duqaq: Also Shams al-Muluk, etc. **Saljuq** prince of Damascus, 1095–1104. Son of the mighty Saljuq general **Tutush**.

El Cid: Rodrigo Díaz de Vivar, a Castilian nobleman and mercenary who made his fortune fighting for Christian and Muslim princes on the Iberian Peninsula. He ruled as Prince of Valencia from 1094 until his death in 1099.

Fakhr al-Mulk: Judge (*qadi*) and independent ruler of Tripoli before it was captured by Franks in 1109. During the siege of his city, he moved first to nearby Jabala and then to Damascus and finally Baghdad, where he sought the aid of the ʿ**Abbasid** caliph in ousting the Franks.

Fatimids: Ismaʿili Shiʿite dynasty. Originally based in the Maghrib at the city of Mahdiya, the Fatimids moved the center of their caliphate to Cairo, which they founded shortly after their conquest of Egypt (969–1171). They quickly expanded into southern Syria and Palestine and Yemen, and were the nominal overlords of Jerusalem when the Franks appeared before its walls in 1099.

Frederick II: Holy Roman Emperor of the Hohenstaufen dynasty, 1220–50. Frederick had also been King of Sicily from 1198 to 1250, brutally crushing a Muslim uprising there even as he portrayed himself as an Islamophile and reluctant crusader to the **Ayyubids** of the Near East.

Guy of Lusignan: King of Jerusalem, 1186–92, through his consort, Sibylla of Jerusalem. Reigning king of Jerusalem during **Saladin's** great conquests in the Near East, he was captured at the Battle of Hattin and later ransomed. He later became king of Cyprus from 1192 until 1194 and founder of the Lusignan dynasty there.

Harun ibn Yahya: Arab, possibly Christian, captive of the **Byzantines**, captured in the ninth century. He left an eyewitness account of Constantinople and Rome, among other places in Christendom.

Hülegü: Mongol prince and commander of the great Mongol conquests of Iran, Iraq, Anatolia, and parts of Syria, 1256–65. He laid the foundations for the Mongol **Il-Khanate** in the Near East.

Ibn ʿAbbad: Leader of a Muslim revolt against Norman rule in Sicily in the early decades of the thirteenth century. Proclaimed amir of Sicily. Arguably the last Muslim leader to hold power on the island.

Ibn ʿAsakir: Syrian theologian, jurist, and historian (1105–75), his work was patronized by **Nur al-Din** of Damascus. This work includes his most famous book, the massive *History of Damascus*.

Ibn al-Athir: Arabic chronicler from northern Mesopotamia (1160–1232). His chronicle, *The Perfect Work of History*, is considered to be one of the standard chronicles of Islamic history.

Ibn Jubayr: Andalusi pilgrim who passed through Sicily and Syria, including Frankish lands, during his travels (between 1183 and 1185).

Ibn al-Thumna: Independent Arab warlord on Sicily. To assist him in his wars against his rivals on the island, he made an alliance with Norman mercenaries under **Robert Guiscard**, who eventually conquered all of Sicily for themselves.

Ibrahim ibn Yaʿqub: Tenth-century Andalusi traveler of Jewish origin. Excerpts of his description of western and central Europe were preserved by the geographer **al-Bakri** many years later.

Il-Ghazi: Also known as Najm al-Din, etc. Turcoman ruler from the **Artuqid** dynasty, he was involved in much of the earliest Muslim campaigns against the Franks and led his troops to a spectacular victory at the battle of the Field of Blood in 1119.

Al-Idrisi: Maghribi geographer and scientist, 1099–1161. He served in the court of Roger II, Norman king of Sicily, and composed a detailed geographical treatise for him, known commonly as the *Book of Roger*.

Il-Khanate: The Mongol "sub-khanate" representing those parts of the Near East under Mongol suzerainty (1256–1335), ruled by a line of *il-khans* loyal to the Great Khans in China.

John Hunyadi: A leading Hungarian lord and crusader. One of the leaders of the Crusade of Varna in 1444, which resulted in an **Ottoman** victory. He died in 1456.

Joscelin: A common name among Frankish rulers in the Near East, principally Joscelin I of Edessa, also known as Joscelin of Courtenay. Count of Edessa during its heydey, 1119–31; Joscelin II, count of Edessa, 1131–59 ruler of the Frankish county of Edessa when **Zangi** took the city; he died in prison in 1159.

Al-Kamil: **Ayyubid** sultan, 1218–38. Became sultan while the Franks occupied Damietta and later arranged a treaty with **Frederick II**, ceding control of Jerusalem to him.

Karbuqa: Also Kerbogha, etc. **Saljuq** atabeg of Mosul, sent to relieve the city of Antioch, which was under siege by the Franks during their first invasion of the Near East. Disgruntled former colleague of **Yaghi-Siyan** of Antioch.

Louis IX: Also St. Louis, etc. King of France, 1226–70. Led an invasion of **Ayyubid** Egypt in 1249 and of Tunis in 1267, where he became ill and died.

Malikshah: Sultan of the Great **Saljuqs**, 1072–92. He oversaw the final Saljuq subjugation of Syria, appointing his brother **Tutush** as its governor.

Mamluks: Dynasty of military men of slave origin that ruled over Syria and Egypt from 1250 to 1517. Their most active sultans, notably **Baybars**, were responsible for spectacular victories against the Mongols and the Franks, and led the campaign that ousted the last of them from the Near East.

Mawdud: **Saljuq** atabeg of Mosul, 1109–1113. He led many (ultimately unsuccessful) campaigns against the Franks of the Near East, some in concert with his colleague **Tughtakin** of Damascus.

Mehmed II: Also known as Fatih Sultan Mehmet, "Mehmed the Conqueror," etc. Ottoman sultan, 1451–81 (his earlier reign having been interrupted by the return of his father, **Murad II**, to the throne). Conqueror of Constantinople in 1453.

Al-Mu'azzam: **Ayyubid** lord of Damascus, 1218–27.

Muhyi al-Din: Also Ibn al-Zaki. Prominent preacher and religious scholar whom **Saladin** chose to give the first Friday sermon in Jerusalem after the city was returned to Muslim rule.

Al-Muqtadir: **Taifa** king of Zaragoza in al-Andalus, 1049–82.

Murad: The name of two **Ottoman** sultans: Murad I (1362–89), who expanded Ottoman control of the Balkans and died in battle at Kosovo; and Murad II, who reigned twice, in 1421–44 and 1446–51. He was involved in the prolonged Ottoman invasion of the Balkans and eastern Europe, including the Battle of Varna.

Naser-i Khusraw: Also Naser-e Khosrow, etc. Persian poet, philosopher, and traveler, 1004–88. Wrote a description of Muslim lands during his travels from 1046–52.

Nasrids: Last Muslim dynasty of al-Andalus, based in their capital of Granada (1232–1492).

Nizam al-Mulk: All-powerful vizier of the early Great **Saljuq** sultans, 1063–92.

Nizar: **Fatimid** prince and imam of the Nizari Isma'ilis who followed him, 1045–97.

Nur al-Din: Son and successor of the atabeg **Zangi** in the Near East, 1146–74. United Aleppo and Damascus and extinguished the **Fatimid** caliphate.

Orhan: Son of Osman Ghazi and **Ottoman** sultan, 1326–62.

Osman Ghazi: Founder of the **Ottoman** Empire, 1299–1326.

Ottomans: Dynasty founded by Osman Ghazi, eventually claiming Constantinople/Istanbul as its capital. Ruled one of the greatest Muslim empires in history, which lasted from 1299 to 1922.

Philip Augustus: Also Philip II, etc. King of France, 1180–1223. With **Richard** the Lionheart, led an invasion of the Near East after **Saladin's** reconquest of Jerusalem.

Qalawun: Also Qalavun, etc. **Mamluk** sultan, 1279–90.

Qilij Arslan: Also Kilij Arslan, etc. The name of many of the sultans of the **Saljuqs** of Rum. Of particular note are Qilij Arslan I (1092–1107), who faced the brunt of the first Frankish invasions of Anatolia; and Qilij Arslan II (1156–92), who was unable to stop a Frankish invasion under the German emperor Frederick Barbarossa.

Ramiro I of Aragon: First king of Aragon in Spain, 1035–63.

Raymond: The name of various Frankish rulers in the Near East. Most prominent among them are Raymond of St.-Gilles, also Raymond IV of Toulouse, ca. 1042–95, Provençal leader during the first Frankish invasions of the Near East; he died besieging the city of Tripoli, which was added to his family's domain; his descendant, Raymond III, count of Tripoli in 1152–87, regent for Baldwin IV of Jerusalem.

Reynald of Châtillon: Also Reynaud, etc. Prince of Antioch, 1153–60; lord of Transjordan, 1177–87. Relentless nemesis of **Saladin**.

Richard the Lionheart: King of England, 1189–99. With **Philip Augustus**, led invasion of the Near East in the wake of **Saladin's** recapture of Jerusalem.

Ridwan: Son of **Saljuq** general **Tutush**, he was Saljuq lord of Aleppo, 1095–1113.

Robert Guiscard: Norman duke of Apulia and Calabria, 1057–85. Mastermind of the Norman conquest of Sicily.

Roger of Salerno: Regent of Antioch, 1112–19. Defeated and killed at the Field of Blood.

Roussel de Bailleul: Also Urselius, etc. Norman mercenary and adventurer who alternately served and opposed the Byzantines from his bases in Anatolia. He died in 1077.

Saʿid al-Andalusi: Precocious Andalusi jurist, historian, and scientist, 1029–70. Author of, among other things, *The Book of the Categories of Nations*.

Saladin: Also Salah al-Din, etc. Founder of the **Ayyubid** dynasty, which he ruled as sultan from 1174–93. Renowned Muslim leader and warrior against the Franks, from whom he reconquered Jerusalem.

Al-Salih Ayyub: Also Najm al-Din, etc. **Ayyubid** sultan, 1240–49, supported in his contests with his kinsman **al-Salih Ismaʿil** by allies from among Khwarizmian mercenary troops.

Al-Salih Ismaʿil: **Ayyubid** lord of Damascus, 1237–45.

Saljuqs: Family of Turkish sultans who ruled most of the Near East in two branches: the Great Saljuqs, who generally ruled from Iran, from 1016–1157; the Saljuqs of Rum, who ruled Anatolia from their capital of Konya, 1060–1307.

Sibt ibn al-Jawzi: Firebrand preacher, jurist, and historian. He died in Damascus in 1256.

Al-Sulami: Syrian jurist and philologist who was the first Muslim to preach against the Frankish invasions whose account has survived. He died around 1106.

Taifa Kings: Also "Party Kings." Term used to describe the various rulers who emerged as independent sovereigns of their own petty kingdoms in al-Andalus after the collapse of **Umayyad** central authority in 1031.

Timur: Also Tamerlane, etc. Turco-Mongol warlord, 1370–1405. From 1399 to 1402 he was engaged in campaigns against Muslim rulers in the Near East.

Tughtakin: Also Toghtekin, etc. Powerful atabeg of Damascus, 1104–1128. Founder of the Burid dynasty.

Al-Turtushi: Also Tartushi, etc. Andalusi jurist and political philosopher who lived and worked in Fatimid Egypt, 1059–1127.

Tutush: Also Taj al-Dawla, etc. Powerful **Saljuq** general and governor of Syria, 1079–95.

Umayyads: Dynasty of caliphs who first ruled in Syria in early Islamic times, 661–750; a branch of the dynasty subsequently ruled as caliphs in al-Andalus from Córdoba, 929–1031.

Usama ibn Munqidh: Muslim warrior-poet and diplomat from Shayzar in Syria, 1095–1188. He served many of the Muslim lords of the Near East and wrote a collection of autobiographical reflections called the *Book of Contemplation*.

Vladislav: Also Wladislaw III of Poland, etc. Ruled also as King of Hungary, 1440–44. Killed by the **Ottomans** at the Battle of Varna.

William II: Norman king of Sicily from 1166 to 1189.

Yaghi-Siyan: **Saljuq** lord of Antioch, 1090–98. A favorite of **Tutush**, he was in command of Antioch when it fell to the Franks during their first invasion of the Near East.

Yusuf I: Also Abu Ya'qub, etc. **Almohad** caliph in the Maghrib and al-Andalus, 1163–84.

Zangi: Also 'Imad al-Din, etc. Turcoman warlord in the service of the **Saljuqs**. Atabeg of Mosul and Aleppo (1127–46) and father of **Nur al-Din**. Reconquered Edessa from the Franks.

Zirids: Berber dynasty that ruled in Tunisia from 973 to 1148, occasionally involved in Sicilian affairs.

The Race for Paradise

Prologue: Damascus Crossroads

B Y A QUIRK of contemporary traffic patterns, he takes the visitor
to Damascus by surprise. Suddenly a large modern bronze
statue looms up just outside the walls of the old city, beneath
the redoubtable towers of the citadel used by his descendants: this is
Saladin, or Salah al-Din, as he is known in Arabic, perhaps the best
known of the many Muslim rulers who rose to prominence during the
historical events generally called "the Crusades."

His is a remarkable story, one of a meteoric rise from humble beginnings. Though he came to rule as sultan of the Ayyubid dynasty of
Egypt and Syria, Saladin started out as an ordinary Kurdish soldier in
the army of a local potentate in Syria. He grew to become the most
powerful military leader of his day, legendary for his victory at the
Battle of Hattin in 1187 that allowed him to retake Jerusalem and
much of Palestine after nearly a century of Crusader occupation. In
both the Middle East and the West he remains admired, a symbol of
statesmanship and chivalry.

The bronze statue of him in Damascus proves that Saladin can
stand for other things too. Erected in 1992 to mark the 800th anniversary of his death, it shows Saladin, accompanied by three armed companions, on horseback, his cloak trailing in the wind. Behind him kneel
two Crusader prisoners, the expression on their faces abject and defeated. One hand holds the reins of his galloping horse; the other is
tightened around his scimitar, as he gazes intently at the West (Fig. 1).[1]

This statue depicts a leader with both worldly and spiritual concerns, a triumphant monarch who was also a pious Sunni Muslim; his companions include a Muslim mystic, or Sufi, a personification of Saladin's Islamic credentials. And yet it stands in the capital of Syria, a secular Arab socialist republic inspired by Western models, and now deep in a civil war made all the more tragic by the sectarian violence between Sunnis and Shi'ites that has colored it. Saladin's heroic pose, evoking Victorian etchings, has no roots in Islamic art; its very medium—statuary—would likely have been condemned as idolatrous by the man it depicts. But maybe we shouldn't be surprised by these ironies. After all, the statue stands just up the hill from Syria's modern nationalist memorial at Martyrs' Square and around the corner from the medieval gates of Old Damascus. This is the Syrian capital's Sharia al-Thawra, "Revolution Boulevard": a kind of no-man's land of historical memory.

For those seeking the Arabic perspective of the Crusades, Saladin has long been the focus, no less so in the region where those events took place. Syria is certainly not alone in claiming him. Streets named after him appear in many Middle Eastern cities, including Jerusalem and the former Crusader bastion of Acre. Schools too. There is an entire Salah al-Din province in Iraq. In the provincial Jordanian town of Kerak, whose castle dates from the Crusader period, another statue of Saladin can be found, much smaller than the one in Damascus. Here he is depicted as a lone rider, his steed rearing and his unsheathed scimitar slicing the air. In Cairo, which was also the capital of Saladin's Ayyubid dynasty, the city's magnificent citadel, bristling with nineteenth-century Ottoman minarets, is usually called "Saladin Citadel."

Many see Saladin as a unifier or liberator, a Middle Eastern Simón Bolívar or George Washington. In the Middle East today it is not uncommon for someone to quietly express a wish that his or her country had a leader like Saladin. Middle Eastern politicians, already keen to gain a bit of Saladin's glamour for themselves, have been quick to take advantage. Saddam Hussein rarely missed the opportunity to remind people that he had been born in Saladin's hometown, Tikrit; he even altered his date of birth by two years to coincide with the 800th anniversary of Saladin's birth. In public art and state propaganda, Saddam was often described as a new Saladin or, as in one Iraqi children's book, "Saladin II Saddam Hussein."[2]

Saladin's revered status in the Middle East is not a recent thing, concurrent with the rise of "political Islam" or with anti-Western sentiment accompanying the "war on terror." Muslim authors from the thirteenth century onward kept alive the memory of Saladin and his accomplishments, especially in original works devoted to the history and religious sites of Jerusalem and the Holy Land, to say nothing of their constant copying and reuse of earlier works about him.[3]

Nonetheless it is modern nationalism that has made him something like a household name.[4] The first biography devoted purely to Saladin after the Middle Ages was published in Ottoman Turkey in 1872 by the prominent Turkish nationalist and intellectual Namik Kemal. Significantly it was later edited and published with biographies of two Ottoman sultans whom Kemal also cast as warrior-heroes pitted against the empire's foes. Other works devoted to Saladin soon followed, many under the foreign influence of Sir Walter Scott, whose popular romance *The Talisman* (1825), set during the Crusades, depicts a palatably noble and chivalric Saladin. This version of the sultan was picked up during the nineteenth-century Arab literary renaissance known as the *Nahda* (Awakening), which added intellectual fuel to emerging Arab nationalism.

The "branding" of Saladin by various intellectual subcultures in the Middle East has been reflected in the West, where he is best known as the "Saracen" who was more knightly than the knights of Christendom. This is best exemplified in Ridley Scott's 2005 film, *Kingdom of Heaven*, which received almost exclusively positive acclaim in the (largely secular) Arab press. In Scott's film, a tolerant Saladin is played by the Syrian actor Ghassan Massoud, who grants the sultan an enigmatic cool.

Today's Saladin is, as a result, protean, capable of being all things to all people. The twenty-first-century Saladin naturally has a Facebook page and, as of this writing, boasts nearly ninety-five thousand Facebook friends—far above the twenty thousand–odd followers he brought with him to his great victory at Hattin. Saladin has gone global. Millions have at least heard of him, whereas few, even in the Middle East, know about, say, the sultans Nur al-Din or Baybars, men who also had spectacular military and diplomatic successes against the Crusaders to their credit and whose stories deserve to be told.

Saladin's global embrace is also coincidental to growing interest in the Crusades, which have become a subject of keen interest, shaped by a growing cadre of experts, some trained and others not. Most of their works retain none of the messiness and nuance evident in the medieval sources and are inevitably spun as tales of heroes versus villains. Who are the heroes and who the villains has tended to shift, according to fashion. For example, well into the twentieth century the Crusades were seen in the West as a triumphal story, an epic moment in the ineluctable rise of the West that showcased values of nobility, faith, bravery, and ingenuity taking on the indolent, corrupt, and barbarous East. Traces of this triumphal narrative still persist, especially when the Crusades are trotted out in discussions of foreign policy. Today, however, the dominant narrative about the Crusades is what we might call, adapting a term from Jewish history, the "lachrymose narrative." In this version, which has its roots in the Enlightenment, the Crusades are not a noble European adventure but a savage attack by a fanatical, intolerant, and hypocritical Christian West, a precursor to European colonialism inflicted upon a hapless Islamic East, sublimely supine in its high civilization of tolerance and wisdom, caught unawares by what one historian suggested could be called "the last of the barbarian invasions."[5] To most people, in the East and the West, this is what the Crusades mean today. Osama bin Laden, in an extreme version, saw the world he operated in as divided between Muslims and a global Crusading movement directed against them. In its clumsiness this view has much in common with the triumphal narrative it has supposedly replaced.

This book offers neither triumphal nor lachrymose narratives. The story it tells is based almost entirely on the original Islamic sources and therefore aims to show how these events were perceived by medieval Muslims themselves. There is a wealth of material, and yet it has never been used consistently, as the basis for its own story, in part because many scholars could not read it.

While the value of Arabic sources for Crusades history has been recognized since the Enlightenment and few works devoted to the Crusades these days avoid them altogether, at least in translation, historians of the Crusades tend to be trained in the history of the medieval West, do not know Arabic, and therefore have trouble navigating the rather sophisticated historiographical traditions of the medieval Islamic world. And historians active in the Middle East, who do of course use (and publish) Arabic sources, are much thinner on the ground and not widely read in the West. The Egyptian Saʿid Abd al-Fattah ʿAshur (or Said Ashour), certainly the dean of Crusades studies in the Arab world, for example, wrote more than twenty books over his long career (from 1946 until his death in 2009), yet none of them have been translated. Much the same can be said of his Syrian counterpart, Suhayl Zakkar (himself Western-trained).[6]

The question is ultimately one of perspective. Most histories of the Crusades, triumphal or lachrymose, tend to be written from what we might call the "traditional perspective." Although this perspective itself embraces many different approaches, it tends to address the Crusades solely as a part of medieval or European history and so, unsurprisingly, relies very heavily on medieval European sources (to which some pungent anecdotes from a few translated Islamic or Eastern Christian sources might be appended).[7]

In the traditional perspective, the crusading movement begins in 1095 at Clermont in France, where Pope Urban II began a preaching tour, urging his assembled audiences to embark on an armed pilgrimage to come to the relief of their fellow Christians in the East and to liberate the Holy City of Jerusalem from Muslim occupation. After some fits and starts, the armies of this First Crusade managed to create four Crusader kingdoms in the Middle East out of land they conquered from their Muslim enemies: the county of Edessa (in 1097), the principality of Antioch (in 1098), the kingdom of Jerusalem (in 1099), and the county of Tripoli (in 1109). After chronicling the greatly varied fortunes of these states, with Saladin's victories starting a period of deep decline, the traditional perspective generally ends with the last crusaders being ousted from the Middle East with the Mamluk reconquest of Acre in 1291.

Lately historians have also recognized the presence of the crusading phenomenon in other theaters of war, as in the so-called Albigensian Crusade in southern France (1208–29) or the Baltic Crusades beginning in the thirteenth century. Similarly attention has been directed at the "Later Crusades," which might or might not be directed at Muslims, well into the early modern period (1500 and beyond). But even in these works the traditional perspective informs their exploration of crusading phenomena in these other times and settings. They are viewed as adjuncts to, though not part and parcel of, the traditional "Clermont-to-Acre" narrative. In short, the traditional story of the Crusades has been an elaboration of one narrative based almost solely upon data from European sources.

Even in many modern and more sophisticated surveys of Islamic history that feature the Crusades, we can see the impact of the traditional perspective at work, resulting in a situation whereby the Crusades are cast as an interruption in a larger narrative beginning with the rise of Islam in the seventh century, in which, at the close of the eleventh, Europeans suddenly thrust themselves, like rude houseguests, on an unsuspecting Levant, and then leave at the end of the thirteenth without a trace.

The Crusades, however, can and should be understood in the context of the Islamic world, treated as an active part of the dynamic relationship between medieval Islamic states and societies from Spain to

Iran. They need to be understood not just as an exotic episode of an otherwise stay-at-home medieval history but as an integral part of the history of Islamic civilization itself. This calls for geographical and chronological limits that are different from those usually inscribed in the traditional perspective. To take one obvious example, the medieval Islamic sources (like the medieval Christian sources, for that matter) never refer to these events as "Crusades"; no such word exists in classical Arabic, and the Arabic term for the Crusades in use today (*al-hurub al-salibiyya*, "the crusader wars") is a modern neologism. Nor do the Arabic sources see these events as commencing with Pope Urban II's speech in 1095 and ending with the expulsion of the last Crusaders from the city of Acre in 1291, as in the traditional narrative. To them, the invasion of the Levant associated with the First Crusade was simply one outburst of European aggression that began decades earlier, in the eleventh century, in Spain and Sicily. This surge would later extend to Turkey, Iraq, Syria-Palestine, Egypt, the Mediterranean islands, and even Arabia, and then direct its attention toward the Mediterranean and eastern Europe. It would not reach a satisfactory conclusion until the Ottoman conquests in the Balkans at the close of the Middle Ages, and perhaps beyond. The many ways medieval Muslims dealt with this new outburst of aggression form, in short, the subject of this book.

That said, this book does not pretend to be a "total history" of the Crusades, since such an endeavor would require the expertise of a team of scholars.[8] Instead it is an attempt to relate the history of the Crusades as medieval Muslims understood them.[9] This is not a *Muslim* history of the Crusades or, still less, a *Muslim's* history of the Crusades. I am not a Muslim, and it would be arrogant to presume to speak for the ways Muslims today appreciate their histories. By an "Islamic History of the Crusades" I am referring to what is called "Islamic history," which designates, simply, the study of the past of people who lived in the Islamic world, that is, in areas in which the ruling elite and (usually) the majority of the populace were Muslims.

Starting a history of the Crusades before there were crusades and in places far from Clermont or Jerusalem may seem a bit disorienting at first—but disorientation can sometimes lead to new vistas. Like Saladin's statue in Damascus, it can take us by surprise and lead us to seek out other stories that lay behind our histories.

-1-

The Abode of Islam

ARUN IBN YAHYA may have been lost or just in the wrong place at the wrong time, but he might never have left the slightest trace on the historical record had he not been taken captive by the Greek navy off the coast of Palestine sometime in the late ninth century. Harun seems to have been a Muslim, though there is a case to be made for his having been an Eastern Christian. His fondness for numbers suggests a mercantile mind; perhaps he was a scientist or a spy, or merely a bureaucrat. What we do know is that after being taken prisoner by the Byzantine Greeks he lived to tell the tale. He also wrote the first firsthand description of Europe in Arabic.[1]

Unlike most such captives, upon his release Harun did not return immediately home, to what some Muslims referred to as the *dar al-islam*, the "Abode of Islam." Instead he chose (or was perhaps obliged) to bide his time in infidel climes, the *dar al-harb*, or "Abode of War." Harun's Byzantine captors had brought him with their other prisoners to Constantinople (modern Istanbul), the capital of the Byzantine Empire, the Greek Christian neighbor and traditional enemy of the dar al-islam. Once freed, he made careful, if occasionally starry-eyed observations of the enemy's city, its size and wealth and wondrous monuments, the pageantry of the emperor's palace and its ceremonies, and some of the religious customs. He then embarked on a sort of reverse Grand Tour, leaving Constantinople for a journey that took him west through the Balkans to Thessalonica, past "a village, called

Venice," and finally to Rome, which he described in terms mixing fact and legend, much as he did for Constantinople. For example, he alludes to St. Peter's as an enormous church, containing the tombs of both the apostles Peter and Paul. Harun then adds that the church includes a tall tower topped by a lead dome upon which sits a bronze image of a bird. During the time of the olive harvest, a wind will blow through the statue and produce a call, which causes all the birds in the vicinity to flock to the city, each one bearing an olive and thereby providing all the oil that the church needs until the next year. Harun seems not to have traveled past Rome, though he tells us that beyond Rome, over the Alps to the west, was the land of a Christian people known as the Franks, and that beyond the Franks lay the land of Britannia, which he describes (ignorant, no doubt, of the achievements of the Irish) as "the furthest of the Roman territories; beyond it there is no civilization."

But it is Harun's description of the curiosities of the twin capitals of Christendom—Constantinople and Rome—that caught the eyes of subsequent generations of Arab geographers. Harun's original description itself is lost; we know of it only thanks to quotations made by later geographers, fragments of a book no longer with us. Eventually Muslims would come to grips with Byzantium as both a rival and a neighbor. Rome and the lands of the West, on the other hand, continued to provide some mystery. Around 1070, only a generation before the First Crusade, Harun's description was quoted at length by a geographer from the region embracing modern Spain and Portugal, a region known to Muslims, and throughout this book, as al-Andalus. That this Andalusi geographer, al-Bakri, could still use Harun's old account as a source for Rome and its inhabitants two centuries after Harun's visit might suggest that information regarding the lands and peoples that gave birth to the Crusades was becoming fossilized, and there is some truth to this. Muslim knowledge of Europe and its peoples, as with other parts of the world, was in fact a mixed bag of fact and fantasy. It was, however, becoming more accurate as the eleventh century came to a close.[2]

By that date al-Bakri could supplement Harun's antique account with more up-to-date and altogether more reliable data, though we don't know how he came upon this information. "The city of Rome," al-Bakri tells us after Harun's long excerpt (perhaps as a sort of update), "is set on a plain surrounded by mountains off at some distance.... It is forty miles in circumference and twelve miles in diameter; a river named Tiber [Tibrus] runs through it." After furnishing more of these dry topographical details, he goes on to describe the city and its monuments:

> Their affairs in Rome are governed by the Pope [*al-baba*]. It is incumbent upon every Christian king, whenever he meets with the Pope, to prostrate himself on the ground in front of him. He continues to kiss the foot of the Pope and does not raise his head until the Pope commands him to rise.
>
> Ancient Rome used to be called Roma Vecchia [Ruma Bakiya], that is, "Old." The river used to hem in the city, so the bishop Johannes built another city on the other side of the river-valley, and that way the river came to run through the city.... In the interior of the city of Rome is the church of Saint Peter [*kanisat* Shanta Patar], which has a picture of Charlemagne [Qarulah] with gold on his beard and on all his trappings, standing amidst a stern-faced crowd, raised off the ground on a timber, like a crucifix.... All of this church's walls are of yellow Roman copper and its columns and pillars are from Jerusalem. It is exceedingly fine and beautiful.... Inside the church is a chapel built in the names of the Apostles Peter and Paul.

Despite confusion about some of the details, one can nevertheless discern here a reasonably accurate and recognizable depiction of Rome and St. Peter's, one al-Bakri seems to have gained from eyewitnesses, perhaps from a monk or pilgrim visiting al-Bakri's native Spain. A distorted but nevertheless recognizable portrait can likewise be seen in al-Bakri's anthropology of Latin Christianity as practiced in Rome. Given that his point of comparison is Islam and its religious laws and rituals, one cannot expect him to be very objective. He continues:

> The Christians only started holding Sunday special because they claim that the Messiah rose from his grave on Sunday night and ascended into heaven on the Sunday night after he met with the Apostles. They do not observe the practice of washing the dead or performing ablutions before prayer.... They do not receive the Eucharist until they have said, "This is your (meaning the Messiah's) body and blood, not wine and not bread...." Not one of them marries more than one woman, nor does he ever take one as a concubine. If she commits adultery, he can sell her off, and if he commits adultery, she can sell him—they do not have any proper divorce. Women inherit two shares, while men inherit one....
>
> With them, fasting is a matter of little consequence, with no need to practice it intensely. According to them, its origin can be traced to the

fast that the Messiah undertook it, as they claim, seeking to defend himself from Satan. But his fast was for forty complete days, including the nights, or so they say, yet they never even fast one complete day or one complete night.... Even if someone should avoid prayer and congregational worship his entire life, no one would speak ill of him or find in him any fault.

The book of the Christians—the one that forms the complete register of their jurisprudence...does not contain more than 557 items. Among these items, despite their small number, are some forged ones, which make no sense and are completely inexplicable, never having actually taken place in any past time or since. Their guidelines for ideal conduct are not derived from revelation or from the pronouncements of a prophet, but rather all of them come from their kings.

There are two points especially worth noting about this remarkable account. One is that, despite the errors, al-Bakri's grasp of Latin Christianity, its rituals, and law was fairly detailed. Of course, we might expect this from a Muslim who spent all of his life in Spain, with its many Christians living under Muslim rule and so close to the frontiers of Latin Christendom. The other point is what it tells us about al-Bakri's perception of the relationship between Christianity and Islam. For him, on nearly every score, Christianity falls short of Islam: whereas Muslims congregate on Fridays, Christians choose Sundays; whereas Muslims are fastidious about ritual purity, Christians could care less; for Muslims, marriage and divorce are simple, aboveboard contractual acts dominated by men, not the monogamous emotional free-for-all practiced by Christians; in Islamic law women (generally speaking) can inherit half the amount that men do, whereas (according to al-Bakri) in Christian practice, the very opposite occurs. Christian fasting is a joke compared with the rigors of the Ramadan fast or the optional fasting practiced by the Muslim devout, and their "law," such as it is, is not, as in Islam, a comprehensive guide to living the Divine Will but merely a collection of kingly decrees. One almost senses al-Bakri's pity.

Harun's and al-Bakri's observations on Rome and Latin Christianity are a good place to start an Islamic history of the Crusades because they contain the mix of accurate information, plain misinformation, and utter fantasy that was quite typical of medieval (not just Muslim) writings about other cultures. Moreover this mix contains many of the raw materials that later generations of Muslims would develop when they tried to understand the motives and character of the Latin Christians who invaded and settled in the Islamic world. Educated medieval

Muslims were in fact familiar enough with Europe and its peoples, and, if Muslim observers were not always accurate in their information about Europe, Latin Christians nevertheless did not startle them as wild-eyed troglodytes, as some popular accounts of the Crusades depict it. That said, the peoples of Europe did occupy a rather specifically marginal place in the way Muslims conceived of the world. But to appreciate this, it will help to examine some maps.

The World Turned Upside Down

So far as we can tell, al-Bakri did not include any maps of the world in his geography (though he did provide a fascinating diagram of Jerusalem). But many of his fellow geographers did, and they all tend to share the same general picture, since their image of the world largely derived from ancient Hellenistic cartography, in particular that of the ancient Alexandrian scientist Ptolemy. Perhaps the most famous medieval Islamic map of the world appears in manuscripts of the treatise of the twelfth-century Moroccan geographer al-Idrisi and so is usually attributed to him.[3] Idrisi composed this work well after the Crusades had begun. (Indeed it was produced in 1154 for Roger II, Christian king of Sicily.) Yet despite its date and its remarkably detailed accounts of western Europe and England (and even Ireland), its worldview as such is fairly conventional, and we can take it for the sake of convenience as a representative illustration of how Muslims before the Crusades would have understood the shape of the world and the place of their neighbors in it (Fig. 2).

Modern observers of Idrisi's map are almost always disoriented when they first look at it. It is clear enough that the light-colored areas represent land, the dark bits bodies of water, and the squiggly, branching lines rivers; that would make those small light-colored spots various islands, surely. The dark-colored bumpy blobs must be mountains, and the long, centipede-like chains of bumps must be (what else?) mountain chains. It is a perfectly accessible way of representing the world. But which world? To modern eyes, Idrisi's map looks positively extraterrestrial.

Until you turn the book upside down.

Idrisi's map should now make sense. Compass points are of course just products of convention. There is no reason, scientific or otherwise, why North must be at the top of a map. For most medieval Muslim cartographers, North was conventionally located at the bottom. Their

Map 1 Line drawing of Idrisi map, with modern place-names. © 2013 Elisabeth Alba.

world was literally, to modern eyes, turned upside-down, and Idrisi would have said the same about ours. As a point of reference, Map 1 shows the area covered by Idrisi, labeled according to modern conventions but oriented in medieval Islamic fashion. The center of Idrisi's South-on-top world map is not Jerusalem, as in many medieval Christian maps, but rather the Arabian Peninsula and the Muslim holy city of Mecca, which occupies the central part of the central clime (a "clime" is one of the latitudinal zones of the earth marked by parallel lines on the map), proof of the perfection with which God has graced the cradle of Islam. This world is dominated not by the Mediterranean and Europe but by the Indian Ocean and Africa, which looms in the South across most of the top half of the page, the Horn extending far off to the eastern (left-hand) horizon, the rest of the continent continuing boundlessly to cover the southern quarter, an undifferentiated blank of terra incognita. Of this continent, only the Mediterranean coast of North Africa is recognizable, from Egypt in the east to Morocco on the western edge of the world. The Nile River runs south to north, bracketed by two parenthetical mountain ranges, and leads to the continent's most prominent feature, the source of the Nile itself, flowing in many streams from the mythical Mountains of the Moon into three circular great lakes.

Compared with Africa, the Eurasian landmass, punctured by the Caspian Sea, is much more cluttered, with the topography of Iran, Central Asia, Iraq, the Levant, and Arabia rendered in rich detail. Anatolia, roughly modern Turkey, juts out in a rather doughy peninsula to the northwest, almost touching Europe. And Europe itself, small and miserable as it is, nevertheless receives the same level of detail as Asia. Whereas the Indian Ocean and its multitude of islands obviously stretched Idrisi's cartographic skills, the Mediterranean is rendered as accurately as anything on the map, with Crete, the islands, and Idrisi's sometime-home of Sicily clearly picked out. And running east to west one can discern without too much trouble the Balkan Peninsula, cloven-hoofed Italy, and al-Andalus with its many rivers.

These parts of Idrisi's maps—the ones with the details—represented the world of medieval Muslims, what some modern historians, adapting a Greek term, call the Islamic *oikumene*, the "inhabited world" embracing Central Asia, the Middle East, North Africa, and Europe. It was, on the whole, a far bigger world than the one medieval Europeans recognized. Naturally, for medieval Muslims, the oikumene was dominated by the Abode of Islam, by Islamdom, if you will, but non-Muslim areas had their space in the oikumene too. The oikumene was the great playing field of civilization, of urban culture and true religion, where the lessons of old and faded empires of antiquity could instruct their medieval inheritors and where contemporary statesmen faced off against their rivals. For medieval Muslims before the Crusades, the peoples who lived way down north in Christian Europe were distant and dubious participants in the game of civilization, though acknowledged participants nonetheless.

Islam and the Peoples of Christian Europe

As Idrisi's map suggests, medieval Muslim writers were relatively well-informed about Europe (compared, say, with China or sub-Saharan Africa), but the details of the peoples who lived there were deemed unimportant.[4]

The context of Muslim encounters with Christian Europeans did not favor either group learning much about the other. The earliest Muslim interactions with Europeans were military, as Muslim armies conquered most of Spain and Portugal and then ranged far across southern France in the early eighth century. Eventually, joined by pirates and free-lance raiders, these armies were able to establish footholds across the Pyrenees in France, as in the short-lived occupation of Narbonne (719–759) or, in the early tenth century, the rather more successful stronghold at Fraxinetum on the gulf of St.-Tropez, whence Muslims raided into the Alps. These were small military emplacements, inhabited by groups whose main goals were plunder and conquest, not ethnography or interfaith relations.

On the other hand, if anyone were to have inside knowledge of the Franks, merchants were the logical source. Indeed in the middle of the ninth century, the Persian-born geographer Ibn Khurradadhbih provided one of the earliest Muslim accounts of Europe, what he calls Urufa. His mercantile interests in the region are clear: he notes that it was this part of the world from which came various rare commodities, including Slavic, Greek, Frankish, and Lombard slaves, furs, perfumes, mastic, coral, and other exotics and raw materials, some of it carried by Jewish merchants who "travel from West to East and from East to West, by land and sea," as he put it. Over time early Muslims came to recognize various ethnic groups inhabiting the European continent, including, but not limited to, Galicians and Basques in al-Andalus and Slavs, Magyars, and Bulgars in the East. In the North dwelled Russians (the Rus) and the Vikings, who are characterized as terrifying pagan "fire-worshippers," or Majus. In the West could be found Lombards and above all the Franks, the "remotest of the enemies of al-Andalus," as one early Muslim historian described them. The name Franks (in Arabic, Ifranj or Firanj) was quickly adopted as a blanket term for all the Christian peoples of continental Europe and the British Isles, much in the same way that medieval Christian observers referred to Muslims of many different backgrounds simply as Saracens. By the time of the Crusades, these Franks had started to think of themselves as distinct peoples, as Germans, Normans, Provençals, and so on, and Muslim observers would eventually follow suit, noting the existence of the English (Inkitar), Germans (Alman), Venetians (Banadiqa), and so on.

Firanja, the land of the Franks, was just one small part of the Abode of War, but it had special features. As we have seen from the evidence of Islamic maps, one of these was remoteness. (One shouldn't make too much of how Muslim geographers placed Europe on the edge of their world since, after all, medieval European geographers placed Europe on the distant margins of their Jerusalem-centered maps too.) In the terminology of the more scientifically inclined Muslim geographers, the land of the Franks occupied parts of the fifth and sixth of the seven climes—far from the favored, temperate fourth clime of the Abode of Islam. Muslim scientists believed that climate was destiny and that it directly influenced character. As residents of the northern climes, the Franks were believed to hail from a region of nearly perpetual darkness and cold. The tenth-century Baghdadi man of letters Mas'udi described the inhabitants of these northern climes as those "for whom the sun is distant from the zenith, those who penetrate to the North, such as the Slavs, the Franks, and those nations that are their neighbors." It was a bleak part of the world: "The power of the sun is weak among them because of their distance from it; cold and damp prevail in their regions, and snow and ice follow one another in endless succession." God singled out the most moderate of climes for the civilized peoples of the abode of Islam. As for the Franks, Mas'udi continues, their climate meant that they tended toward brutishness, being generally dull-witted, sluggish, and corpulent. Appropriate to their icy homes, they were pale-skinned and fair-haired. Other Muslim writers echoed these conclusions, some ranking all the inhabitants of these regions as closer to beasts than to humans.

In such a climate Frankish religion lacked stability. Indeed Mas'udi asserts that religious fanaticism, as well as a propensity for heresy (and, oddly, the ability to keep secrets), were characteristic of all inhabitants of the western quadrant of the world, the Franks included. These were considered feminine traits, since the West was dominated by feminine planets and the Moon. In the East, where the Sun reigned, the people were noted for masculine traits like long life, memory, wise government, science, and, interestingly, vanity.[5] In short, as we saw in al-Bakri's account of Latin Christianity, the Franks were the victim of the classic strategy by which one people defines itself against another, attributing to them qualities that were the very antithesis of the qualities Muslims claimed for themselves. Their geographic location only confirmed the Franks as a people that flirted with barbarity, inoculated from the ignominy of true barbarism only by their revealed religion and, some said, their statecraft. But they were nevertheless a cold and benighted people, subcontinental and antipodean.

As such, the Franks represented a double threat to Muslim observers. Muslims were familiar with Christians from the beginning of Islamic history, but Christians of the Islamic world had agreed to be subjects of an Islamic ruler. In return Islamic law accorded them the status of *dhimmi*s, or "protected" (albeit second-class) minorities, and so they posed no great concern. Similarly Muslims also had a long history with non-Muslim warriors from the margins, such as the Berbers and the Turks, but these people had eventually seen the light, converted, and taken to Islamic civilization with gusto. Not so the stubborn inhabitants of darkest Firanja; as both Christians and outsiders, the Franks came so very close to true religion and true civilization, and yet they defied them both with a stiff-necked resolve that puzzled and frustrated their Muslim observers.

Nonetheless, in this mix of half-truth and speculation, early Muslims also had some fairly accurate information on the Franks. Some early Muslim observers at least noted that they were hardy warriors, foes of the Slavs as well as the Muslims, an impression supported, no doubt, by stories from the battlefields of al-Andalus and France. Even Mas'udi could reproduce a fairly accurate list of Frankish kings that he derived from a Frankish source. He also noted that the capital of their vast lands was a city called Paris. (He later says it is Rome.) He claimed that the Franks all spoke the same language and obeyed one king. A Persian-born contemporary of his named al-Istakhri more accurately observed, "Their language varies even though their religion and kingdom are one, just as in the kingdom of Islam there are many tongues and one ruler." In the middle of the tenth century an Andalusi traveler called Ibrahim ibn Ya'qub traveled across Europe and left detailed accounts in Arabic of the lands he visited, in the Slavic East as well as the Frankish West.[6] In western Europe, he took note of, among other things, the verdant fields of Bordeaux, the tasty salmon of Rouen, the peat bogs around Utrecht, the venerable monastery of Fulda, pagan feasting at Schleswig, trading practices in Augsburg, and a little local history he picked up in southern Italy. Ibrahim even made time for Ireland, although his account of Irish whaling, while detailed, won't have changed the minds of his peers about the place.

Ibrahim admits to being appalled by the general filthiness of the Franks he met, since, "ignoring all propriety, they do not bathe except once or twice a year, with cold water. They never wash their clothes, which they put on once for good, until they fall into tatters." He was surprised that they shaved off their beards, which then simply grew back each time "in a rough and scraggly manner." "It was once asked of one of them concerning this. He said, 'Hair is just superfluous. If you people remove it from your private parts, why should we be expected to leave it on our faces?'" Yet, in all, he seems to have been impressed by his sojourn among these colorful natives, and in particular with their "vast kingdom." Despite the cold weather and harsh climate, the region was "rich in grains, fruits, and other crops, and in water-courses, plants, flocks, trees, honey, and game of all kinds." There were silver mines and swords sharper than those that could be found in India. They obeyed "a strong and valorous king supported by a considerable army." So brave were the soldiers, he warned, that they "would never prefer flight to death."

Amid all the stereotypes there were materials here with which Muslims might have created a portrait of the Franks different from the climatic one sketched earlier. That they did not, and that they spent the next five centuries generally embellishing the theme of Frankish barbarity just as Latins dwelt upon the barbarity of the "pagan Saracens," is one of the least tangible but no less disastrous consequences of the wars of the cross.

The Islamic Oikumene

From the perspective of the medieval Islamic world, then, the lands of the Franks occupied a place not unlike that occupied by the Middle East today in the minds of many in the West. To medieval Muslim eyes, western Europe was superficially an impoverished, one might even say "developing" region on the margins of the world. It was inhabited by a fanatical, war-like people, adherents of a backward creed. Its economy offered little besides cheap markets and raw materials. It presented some wondrous architecture and outré customs to contemplate, but little else. The Islamic world, by contrast, seemed the very model of civilization: it was wealthy, ordered, enlightened, imperial, and protected by a merciful God.

The comparison is somewhat unfair, on the simple grounds that the Islamic world circa 1050 was a far larger place than Latin Christendom (Map 2). Even were one to adopt a generous definition of Latin Christendom, say, from Austria to Ireland, excluding Scandinavia and frontier lands disputed with the Byzantine and Islamic worlds, the area amounts to some 1.7 million square kilometers. This is but a fraction of even a conservative definition of the dar al-Islam, stretching from al-Andalus to Iran and excluding frontier lands in Central Asia, South Asia, the Caucasus, and Africa: a vast swath of the earth's surface across three continents embracing some 12 million square kilometers. Even accounting for the thinly populated and remote zones of Saharan

Map 2 The Mediterranean World, ca. 1050 CE. © 2013 Elisabeth Alba.

North Africa and the Arabian Peninsula, it is still clear that the Islamic world and Latin Christendom could in no way be considered equals.

The most literal marker of civilization was the city, and unlike western Europe the lands of Islam had scads of them, almost wherever the land could support permanent human settlement. As many of the travel accounts discussed earlier suggest, Muslims on the eve of the Crusades had to acknowledge a few large cities like Rome and smaller towns like Rouen, Mainz, Prague, and Cracow. To these were added slightly mythical places like Paris and a few pestilential hamlets like Venice.

However, the fledgling city life of medieval Europe was nothing compared with the medieval Middle East, which was one of the most urbanized regions on the globe, a region not just of cities but of networks of cities. The Middle East was, as the archaeological cliché has it, the "cradle of civilization," where the first complex urban systems in human history were established. Since the fourth millennium BCE, the urban culture of the ancient Near East had had ample opportunity to go forth and multiply, and the result, by the time of the Crusades in the second millennium CE, was that the medieval Middle East was not merely an heir to ancient cities like Jerusalem, Aleppo, or Damascus but also the setting for urban expansion and creative new foundations, such as relative newcomers like the metropolis of Baghdad (founded 762) and

Cairo (founded 969). To these should be added Islamic cities outside the Middle East, such as Tunis in North Africa and Córdoba, the center of al-Andalus.

Moreover the countryside of medieval Islamdom was peppered with a vast hierarchy of interdependent settlements of different sizes and functions. By the year 1050 these cities had organized themselves into a number of regional networks. Persian, Hellenistic, Roman, and other urban patterns had been transformed after the great Islamic conquests of the seventh century and, augmented with entirely newly built cities, carried the imprint of Islamic urban ideals. Sharing the same Roman heritage, many cities of the medieval Islamic world had something in common with the look, layout, and function of those of Latin Christendom. But, shaped by different climates, centuries of Islamic history, and the requirements of Islamic law and institutions, they more often presented a different face to those of the Latin West. Throughout most of North Africa and the Middle East, for example, houses were made of mud-brick. Stone was usually reserved for Islamic civilization's distinctive architecture of power: mosques, palaces, fortifications, and marketplaces. Wood was rarer still.

Islamic cities also tended to be bigger. A lot bigger. Specific medieval population figures are mostly guesswork, but it can at least be said that by around the year 1050 the principal cities in the Islamic world held populations in the hundreds of thousands, whereas in Latin Christendom populations were measured in the tens of thousands. Baghdad, at its peak in the late ninth century, may have held 800,000; new as it was, Cairo and its suburbs probably boasted about half that. Córdoba could claim at least 100,000, probably more.[7] In the Christian world, as Harun ibn Yahya could have verified, only Constantinople, the capital of the Greek Orthodox empire of Byzantium, approached the scale of the great Islamic cities, at perhaps half a million. In the Latin West, where urbanization was, after all, only beginning to pick up from the decline of the urban life associated with the late Roman Empire, the major cities never got bigger than middle-ranking Islamic equivalents. In 1050 even mighty metropolises like Rome, Milan, and Cologne could probably boast populations of only around thirty thousand to forty thousand. In 1100 Paris and London were home to perhaps twenty thousand each. Islamic Jerusalem, to Muslims a sleepy, albeit sacred provincial town of about twenty thousand to thirty thousand, would have seemed suitably grand to the Franks who arrived there in 1099.

The cities and towns of the Islamic world varied according to their function: as market centers, sacred sites, transportation nodes, garrisons, administrative precincts, or some combination thereof. Power, however you might define it, was rooted in the cities. Nomadic conquerors have shaped the history of Islamic civilization at crucial moments, but they have done so by largely abandoning their desert and mountain homes and capturing and settling in cities. The lord's rural manor, that mainstay of the medieval West, was thus a comparative rarity in the Islamic world. The cities attracted all manner of people, and far-flung networks of trade, learning, and pilgrimage meant that any prosperous city could become a microcosm of the broader oikumene.

The medieval Islamic world was thus a more diverse place than western Europe. Its cities were crowded with Muslims, Jews, and Christians of various kinds—free men and women, but some slaves as well; merchants, pilgrims, beggars, and soldiers. They might be Arabs, Persians, Turks, Kurds, Greeks, Slavs, Africans, or even Irish, hailing from across the Islamic world and beyond, their variety perhaps the clearest testament to Islamic civilization's imperial, cultural, and economic success.

Thanks in part to its greater scale of urban life, the Islamic world was also a wealthier place. In both western Europe and the Islamic world, societies were founded upon agrarian economies, in which land and the revenues (and food) it generated constituted the central pivot around which life ultimately revolved. The medieval Middle East had the advantage of vast, extensively irrigated, and intensively farmed alluvial plains, such as those of Mesopotamia or the Nile valley. Although western Europe and the Middle East were bound together by commercial networks crossing land and sea, the balance of trade decidedly favored the Islamic world. With exchange based upon a relatively stable and consistent gold currency, the dinar, the merchants of the Middle East dominated a transregional luxury trade that handled, among other things, spices, medicaments, and cloth from the East and fur, timber, and—above all—slaves from the North and West. Moreover all commerce is, like all politics, ultimately local. In the Islamic world as in the Latin West, local exchange kept the economies in the cities' rural hinterlands humming, and so the rural populations were never total strangers to city life. Rural-to-urban commerce consisted primarily of food, including cereals (wheat especially but also barley and millet), sugarcane, cooking oils, fruits, nuts, and vegetables, and certain essential raw materials such as cotton, wool, fuel, and dyes. Unlike the local markets of Latin Christendom, the economy of the Islamic world reserved significant space for nomadic populations: Bedouin and Berbers, from an early date; later, in the East, Kurds, Turks, and Turcomans.

In addition to such traditional nomadic products as livestock (for food and labor), hides, and milk products, these populations also offered services, including "protection" to villages far from the more secure urban zones and caravans, and crucial military manpower to the states and statelets that constituted the political map of the Islamic oikumene.

The Circle of Equity

The political map of the Islamic world by around the year 1050 was fragmented and multifarious. Not only did different rulers govern different parts of the dar-al-islam (as one would expect of such a vast realm), but the varieties of rulers in evidence had different functions. Nevertheless there existed at least an ideal of political unity, a common sense of purpose in Muslim rulership. This ideal is perhaps most concisely summed up in a concept known as the "circle of equity" or "circle of justice," since it represented the cycle of interdependence that kept a kingdom afloat and was often depicted in circular form (Fig. 3). Although the concept hails from the pre-Islamic Near East, we find it cited throughout Islamic history, before, during, and after the period of the Crusades, in Arabic, Persian, and Turkish, from one end of Islamdom to another. A succinct version is this early maxim, from a medieval Arabic text allegedly quoting an ancient Persian one:

> There is no ruler without an army;
> and there is no army without revenues;
> and there are no revenues without cultivation;
> and there is no cultivation without equity and good governance.[8]

Should any part of the cycle become defective, the whole clockwork of state will come grinding to a halt. Everyone has a specific place in this cycle and a job to do to keep it healthy. For the ruler, that meant maintaining equity and good governance. The language of the maxim implies moral goodness in governance, which itself implies that good rulers would be guided by Islamic law and its interpreters, the *ulema*, or religious scholars.

In the year 1050 one of the oldest institutions of rulership was the office of caliph (*khalifa*). Following the death of the Prophet Muhammad in 632, the caliph was universally acknowledged as the sole ruler of the Muslim community, a successor to the Prophet though not a prophet himself. In practice, though, many Muslims contested the claims of certain individuals or lineages. The most notable such case was that of the followers of the Prophet's cousin 'Ali, who felt that only he and his descendants were the legitimate successors to the Prophet and thus venerated them as their religious leaders, or imams; this group, as partisans of 'Ali (*shi'at 'Ali*), have come to be known as Shi'ites. Over time Shi'ites themselves would witness the creation of dissenting lines of imams, such as the Isma'ili movement of the tenth century.

When the Prophet Muhammad died, his closest followers met to choose from among their ranks someone who might best lead the fledging Muslim community in accordance with the Prophet's lived example (*sunna*, whence Sunni Muslims). The first four of the caliphs were chosen in this manner and have come to be known (by Sunnis) as the "Rightly Guided" or Rashidun caliphs. They stand for many Muslims, then as now, as the leaders of the Muslim community during its Golden Age, before the political and theological crises that divided the unity of the Muslim world and before Sunnis and Shi'ites started down the road that would lead to their irrevocable separation as sects distinct in theology, law, and practice, as they are today. However, after 661, the fifth caliph, Mu'awiya, deviated from the practice of his Rashidun predecessors and had his own son named as his successor, founding Islam's first dynasty, the Umayyads. The Umayyads oversaw the expansion of the caliphate to its greatest extent and made Syria and especially Damascus their favored center, until they were ousted from power in 750. Another dynasty, the 'Abbasids, overthrew the Umayyads and made Baghdad (with some interruptions) their capital, claiming more direct descent from the Prophet's family than the Umayyads could and thus claiming to be better representatives of God's plan as contained in Muslim scripture (the Qur'an) and the sunna of His Messenger, the Prophet. It was the 'Abbasid dynasty of Baghdad, protectors of Islam's frontiers, kin of God's Prophet, and upholders (as they saw it) of true Sunni Islam, who retained the title of caliph in the year 1050.

Frankish observers, in the beginning at least, didn't do very well with all this information and had a habit of likening the caliph to the pope; some Muslims made the same comparison.[9] In fact the two offices are rather different. Though the figure of the caliph mixed political and religious authority in ways resembling the powers of the pope, caliphs were not clerics and did not, at least not for some time, provide any priestly function or interfere with proper Muslim practice or dogma. Caliphs did not in practice preach jihads, as popes did with their Crusades, though the theory was that they should at least authorize them. They tended instead retroactively to sanction jihads preached by the religious classes (the ulema) as the Prophet's representatives. That said, back in the glory days of the caliphate, they might, like a few of the more activist popes, be obligated to lead armies themselves. Nor did caliphs bother other rulers in their domains about how they invested their own clerics, or scold them about their marriage practices, or excommunicate rivals or thinkers. Indeed by the year 1050 the caliphs didn't do much at all, having long since shed any real authority beyond the symbolic delegation of administrative and military functions to other people. The caliphs nevertheless remained a potent emblem of the unity and might of Islam for their subjects.

On the other hand, caliphs did share one thing with popes: rivals for their title. In the centuries since the first caliph took power, the Rashidun, Umayyad, and ʿAbbasid caliphs all had to contend with claimants to their throne at one time or another. In two cases rival dynasties of caliphs succeeded in founding their own lines, ruling over their own caliphates—anticaliphs, if you like. Thus in the year 1000 there were in fact two men in addition to the ʿAbbasid caliph in Baghdad claiming the title of caliph for themselves. The ʿAbbasids, it turns out, had not been as assiduous as they might have been back in 750, when they attempted to wipe out their Umayyad rivals. One member of the Umayyad clan managed to escape his ʿAbbasid enemies and after some adventures arrived in the frontier province of al-Andalus, where he and his descendants ruled autonomously, with relatively little interference from Baghdad. In the tenth century these Umayyads of al-Andalus decided to make it official and adopted the title of caliph for themselves, ruling over their own subjects from their capital of Córdoba, never forgetting that their forebears had once ruled as caliphs in Syria.

But by then the ʿAbbasids were not the only caliphs on the minds of the caliphs of al-Andalus. Much closer to Córdoba than Baghdad, another line of caliphs had emerged in North Africa, troubling to Umayyads and ʿAbbasids alike. These were the Fatimid caliphs, the leaders of a Shiʿite movement that, allied with substantial Berber manpower, gained control of the ʿAbbasid province of Ifriqiya (roughly modern Tunisia). Eventually the Fatimids set their sights on the plum ʿAbbasid province of Egypt, where, after a quick conquest, they founded their capital of Cairo. By the year 1000 the Fatimid caliphs of Egypt had expanded their domains to include Sicily, western Arabia, Yemen, and much of Syria and Palestine. A few decades later the line of Umayyad caliphs in Córdoba was extinguished, their domains split into a mosaic of smaller, contentious principalities whose rulers are collectively known in English as the "party kings" (*muluk al-tawaʾif*), not so much for their feasting as for their seemingly endless faction-alism. Thus, on the eve of the first renewed Frankish assaults on Islamdom, al-Andalus, heretofore the Franks' traditional target, was broken into warring kingdoms, its caliphal might an increasingly dis-tant memory. The Near East, meanwhile, was split between the Shi'ite Fatimid dynasty of Cairo and their long-lived rival, the Sunni 'Abbasid dynasty of Baghdad.

The circle of equity claimed there could be no ruler without an army, and rulers within the dar al-islam had many options to choose from. While subject to important regional differences based upon cli-mate, recruitment, and custom, armies across the Islamic world shared many of the same structural features. In general, Islamic armies of the year 1050 varied greatly in size from polity to polity and had a much greater ratio of infantry to cavalry than would be the case a century later. Islamic infantrymen fought with bows and swords, but it was the spear, the mortal enemy of cavalry, that dominated their arsenal. While heavy cavalry was not unknown in the Islamic world, lightly armored cavalry, especially mounted archers, was favored. Such troops were usually recruited from two distinct social groups: slave troops and no-madic auxiliaries.

The use of troops of slave origin (*ghilman* [sing. *ghulam*] or *mamluk*) has long roots in Islamic military history. In general such troops entered the Islamic world as non-Muslim captured prisoners of war and then were sold to Muslims. Once converted, captive men with the appro-priate skills and potential were manumitted and employed as soldiers, commanders, and even governors. Being foreigners and newly con-verted to Islam, mamluks had, in theory, no local ties or regional claims other than loyalty to their commander. As men of slave origin, they were dependants of their commander or ruler, their former owner and now patron, whom they served as their private lord. While the Islamic world was not the sole medieval realm to make use of such troops, only in the Islamic world, with its sprawling, active frontiers, was it possible to make use of this practice on a large scale. Mamluk troops were usu-ally recruited from the Central Asian frontiers. The Turks of the region were especially esteemed for their skill as mounted archers. But when Turks could not be had, mamluks could be recruited from other ethnic groups, such as Africans or Slavs, who figured prominently in the ranks of the armies of Fatimid Egypt.

As for nomadic auxiliaries, these were drawn from Bedouin tribes or (in North Africa and al-Andalus) Berber tribes with whom various rulers had made alliances. Such troops were generally not a component of a standing army. Being more autonomous and less reliable forces, they were obliged to provide service when their tribal leaders called upon them. Given their particular set of skills, nomadic troops were also highly valued as light cavalry. In regions where pasture was scarce, as in Fatimid Egypt, such nomadic troops had a much smaller role than they did in states abutting nomadic zones, as in Syria. Finally, naval contingents were small across the Islamic world. Here the exception, again, is Fatimid Egypt, which, as long as timber supplies held out, could boast with Byzantium one of the most powerful fleets of the day.

One of the central problems facing any ruler was how to pay for these troops beyond the usual perquisite of plunder. By the year 1050, as if in keeping with the "circle of equity," revenues flowed almost straight from the cultivators to the pockets of the army, or at least its leaders. These revenues came almost entirely through an institution known as the *iqta'*, though different regimes used the iqta' with varying degrees of frequency. The iqta' is often translated as "fief" by modern authors, but it is in principle rather different from the fiefs of medieval Europe. Unlike the medieval fief, the holder of an iqta' was never the lord of the land but rather an absentee lord who lived in the city and spent his revenues there. The iqta' was not a domain but a temporary assignment of the rights to extract revenues from a given parcel of land. These might be small fields, whole villages, or, in rare cases, entire provinces. The revenues so extracted formed the salary of the iqta'-holder, who was required to provide military service and to support his own men. For this reason territorial expansion was crucial to any Muslim state—especially newly forming ones—in this period, as it alone guaranteed the holders the resources to pay the troops. To survive they must expand. Moreover receiving an iqta' did not involve a binding oath of fealty but was instead a reward for loyalty and could be taken away by the ruler at any time. As such, the iqta' was, in theory, a tool of strong central government, not the seed for provincial autonomy soon to be grabbed by rural barons. In practice, however, it had become a way for weakened rulers who were unable to pay their troops or collect taxes to kill two birds with one stone. As may be obvious, the iqta' system could also become a mandate for shortsighted holders to squeeze what revenues they could from the cultivators who sustained them without pausing on the notions of justice and equity that were supposed to underpin the system.

Keeping such thoughts of justice alive to everyone was the job of the religious classes, known generically as the ulema (*'ulama'*). Although the ulema are often likened to clerics in modern coverage of the Islamic world, in fact they are very different from the Christian clergy and men of religion in the medieval West. Indeed the Muslim ulema have much more in common with rabbis in their religious and social functions than with Christian clergy. Unlike priests, members of the ulema have no sacerdotal function; they convey no sacraments and preside over no sacred mysteries. Granted, their role is crucial in most of life's rites of passage, like weddings and funerals, but their role is that of interpreters and executors of law, not grantors of God's blessing. The medieval ulema were not organized by a formal hierarchy or Church but rather by an informal, self-regulating network of masters and students. The ulema are first and foremost scholars, and scholars of Islamic law above all else. They are specialists in sacred texts, interpreting them for non-specialists and applying their teachings to the real world. Their province and currency is thus religious knowledge, or *'ilm*. 'Ilm in turn can be gained only through years of study with masters of the various fields of religious instruction. These fields include the two principal sources of Islamic legal thought, the Qur'an and the traditions (*hadith*) of the Prophet and the early community, but also jurisprudence, legal theory, theology, and allied disciplines like grammar, biography, and history.

In the year 1050 it was the ulema who were the guardians of the *shari'a*, the "path" of Islamic law, and its guidelines for all Muslims on how to live a life that is most pleasing to a just, equitable, and merciful God. They performed this function in myriad ways: by debating one another as jurists they expanded and refined the community's knowledge of God's will; by teaching children they steeped the young in the shari'a's fundamental lessons (and skills such as reading and writing); by serving as preachers they reminded Muslims of their duties in accordance with law and evoked Islam's core values; by serving as judges (*qadis*) they executed justice and administered it for the state; and by serving as *muftis* they produced their personal legal decisions (*fatwas*) on any issue on behalf of the community at large. It was, in short, the ulema who put the equity in the circle of equity and so were sources of authority and inspiration to cultivators, commanders, and caliphs alike.

Holy Wars

Much has been made of the religious motivations of the Muslim soldiers who fought against the Franks who invaded their territory, and specific focus has been placed on the concept of jihad, the armed struggle "in the path of God." As we shall see in the chapters that follow, jihad was but one of the reactions that Muslims had toward the Franks. But given its prevalence in the medieval Islamic sources—and in modern commentary—understanding this concept and its history in the years leading up to the era of the Crusades is important.[10]

That the Franks and the Muslims both embraced a concept of holy war has often been remarked, but there is no evidence for any connection between the concept of jihad in Islam and the concept of crusade that developed later in Latin Christendom. Because of their common roots in a universal monotheism whose God is a jealous god, there is perhaps a certain family resemblance. But these concepts developed independently of one another and have important differences. It is true that crusades and jihads must both be launched by acknowledged authorities—popes and caliphs or imams, respectively. But as we have seen, caliphs are no popes, and most caliphs simply acquiesced to jihads preached by others. Both forms of holy war promise martyrdom and eternal salvation to those who fall in them. However, crusades also offered a host of institutional incentives, such as Church protection of family and property, that jihad never did. Crusading was a centralized principle, an act of loyalty to the Church and its leader, the pope. Jihads were, in practice at least, much less centralized and might, in the right hands, become "privatized" conquests that could become the basis for regimes to rival that of the caliph.[11] Crusading was a penitential act, which, like jihad, attracted the faithful inclined to acts of conspicuous self-abnegation. As such, crusades were votive and thus temporary, based upon a vow that might be fulfilled by death or absolution. Jihad, by contrast, was a perpetual obligation of the faithful. Finally, crusades were directed at the "liberation" of lands considered rightfully Christian, whereas the goal of jihad was the conversion of infidels to Islam. Crudely put, crusading was about rescuing sacred land; jihad was about rescuing souls.

The Islamic concept of jihad also shares with the Christian concept of crusade the distinction of being taken as evidence for the putatively "inherent" or "essential" violent nature of the civilization that produced it. Yet neither Islam nor Latin Christianity is inherently violent, and both were and are far too internally diversified as systems of thought to be essentialized in this way. Islamic law, including the concept of jihad, developed in a medieval, indeed imperial context in which warrior-elites dominated and in which warfare and the conquest of non-Muslim lands were common features. Accordingly the classical concept of jihad that was formulated (with slight differences) by the various schools of Islamic law was a way to control violence and warfare, establish the conditions for starting it and ending it, limit lawlessness while it was being carried out, define its targets, reduce the damage it brought to noncombatants, and spell out what did and did not make it meritorious. The merits of jihad were substantial and thus a weighty inducement for the pious to fight the enemies of God.

As a concept developed and debated by jurists among the ulema, jihad rested in the first place upon the two fundamental sources of Islamic law: the Qur'an and the example or sunna of the Prophet and his Companions, the sunna being accessed by the Traditions, or hadith. In the Qur'an, the hadith, and the writings of jurists, jihad was a principle with many meanings, all of them linked to a core meaning of "struggle," often qualified as "struggle in the path of God," *fi sabil Allah*. These included, of course, waging war against infidels, but also inner struggle against sin. This latter variety of jihad, sometimes called the "Greater Jihad," is often overemphasized by contemporary apologists uncomfortable with the prominent place of jihad in medieval Islamic sources, but it does have clear origins in the Qur'an and hadith and is every bit as authentic as the militant "Lesser Jihad." Nevertheless it is also perfectly clear that when medieval Muslims discussed jihad, they were almost always discussing it in the sense of armed struggle against infidels.

Jihad was missionary in intent, pitting the Abode of Islam against the Abode of War and demanding the conversion of non-Muslims (or the return to obedience of rebels). In the case of Jews and Christians not willing to convert (the vast majority of cases encountered in this book), they were given the option to surrender as subjects of an Islamic state, receiving the legal status of "protected peoples," or *dhimmis*. Dhimmis in medieval Islamic societies were generally left to practice their religion in peace and to be subject to most laws of their own courts, in return for the payment of an extra tax (called the *jizya*); under especially hard-line rulers (or those who wanted to appear hard-line), dhimmis might be subject to further social humiliations too, such as being forbidden to bear arms or being obliged to wear certain garments that distinguished them from Muslims. Such instances, however, were rare: it was the jizya that mattered most, and it was the jizya that most dhimmis understood as guaranteeing that they would be left alone—tolerated but subordinate guests in a triumphal, Islamic society.

Jihad is thus not militarism, to be contrasted with pacifism, but rather war with a pious intent, to be contrasted with the vast taxonomies of war that are secular. In theory, only the ruler, the caliph or imam or his representative, could declare a jihad, and depending upon circumstances, it might be defensive in nature or offensive—preemptive, to use a modern term. Most jurists thought of jihad as a *fard 'ala al-kifaya*, a perpetual religious obligation incumbent upon the Muslim community rather than on all individuals. The exercise of jihad by some sufficient number of Muslims at any given time relieved other Muslims of the duty. But in special circumstances it might be elevated to a *fard 'ala al-'ayn*, an obligation incumbent upon every able-bodied individual, like pilgrimage or prayer. Jurists were divided about whether one could pay others to fight as substitutes on one's behalf. The individuals engaged in jihad are called *mujahidun* (the label in common parlance today, *mujahideen*, is the same word) and are assumed by the jurists to always be men; women were almost never discussed as participants. A certain aura of machismo surrounded jihad, and this was consonant with the values of the patriarchal world of medieval Islam. Those who die in battle during jihad are accorded the status of martyr (*shahid*) and are assured of special treatment in the afterlife. Their sins are forgiven (though not their worldly debts), and they are saved the long wait for Resurrection that others must endure. They instead are immediately sent to be eternally alive with God and, like all the righteous, to be granted the delights of Paradise.

The rewards of jihad were not limited to a ticket to Paradise for the fallen. There were spiritual and social rewards that the living too might collect, having returned from their battlefields. For jihad was also closely entwined with notions of generosity and reciprocity. Muslim veterans were to be rewarded not merely with victory and the spoils of war but with all the honors due to men willing to "sell their lives" in the path of God, right wrongs, punish oath-breakers, and fight oppression on behalf of those who might not fight for themselves. "All of this was the fruit of his jihad in this world," explained a medieval Muslim historian commenting on the lavish reception in Baghdad of one veteran of Syria's Frankish wars, adding, "although the reward of the next world is greater."[12]

Jihad thereby dovetailed with one of the central moral impulses of Islam: the drive to "command the good and forbid the wrong." By this ideal all Muslims were encouraged to become activists, though not jihadis. The many compromises of daily life put the faithful on the slippery slope away from righteousness, and so devoted Muslims were encouraged to undertake minor acts of moral interference to counter this backsliding, such as haranguing fellow Muslims in the marketplace for unfair business practices. On this scale jihad was the very pinnacle of altruistic "commanding and forbidding." And it wasn't just fighting that attracted men to the jihad. One common feature of Islamic holy war was the presence of men who were members of the ulema, untrained in military matters but who went to the Abode of War to do their part. While there they might jump in the saddle and fight, but they might also be legal advisers to those on jihad or just preachers, mystics, or scholars meeting other scholars. To modern ears this melding of the scholarly and the martial worlds sounds almost contradictory. Yet the scholar-warrior was a valued and fairly ordinary figure.

Engaging in jihad also evoked the divinely guided warfare of the Prophet and his Companions and the derring-do of Arab warriors from early Islam's epic battles. "Among men there are those who go to battle just as the Companions of the Prophet (may God be pleased with them) used to go to battle: to obtain entrance to Paradise, and not to pursue some selfish desire or to gain a reputation," wrote one Arab observer of the Crusades, reflecting on the motives of two Muslim scholars who gained martyrdom at Damascus against the Second Crusade. The same observer also celebrated the true-grit exploits of early tough-guys like the Companion Malik al-Ashtar ("the Droopy-Eyed"), who, having been dealt a gruesome blow that cracked his skull, quickly bound his head, returned to his foe, and struck him, "splitting him in two down to his saddle."[13] To medieval Muslims, jihad could be embraced not only as righteous but also as manly, self-denying, and heroic, a reenactment of the deeds of Islam's Greatest Generation. For this reason Muslim armies engaged in jihad continued to attract warriors who had never been commanded to appear but who arrived of their own free will, as volunteers (*mutatawwi'a*), sometimes from places far removed from the active front. To the many Muslims who engaged in jihad against the Franks, they were making a gift of themselves to the Muslim community, to the weak they defended, and even to the stubborn infidels to whom they generously offered one last chance to be embraced by God's mercy.

Their foes, of course, did not see it this way. Nor, it should be stressed, did every Muslim warrior. In the pervasive discussion about jihad, medieval and modern, it is easy to forget that not all Muslims automatically conducted warfare against the Franks in terms of jihad, nor was warfare (jihad or not) their only response to Frankish aggression. Indeed the very observer who commended the jihad sensibilities of the two martyred scholars quoted earlier spent much of his life fighting the Franks—and never once referred to his own struggles with them as jihad (though he did so to others'). As we shall see, there was as much pragmatism as jihad on the Frankish-Muslim frontiers, as much accommodation, grudging tolerance, alliance making, and even downright friendship as holy war. Pragmatism was not something that our sources—most written by members of the ulema—liked to preserve, however, except to condemn it. Jihad may well have been the dominant force shaping Muslim relations with the Franks, but it was never the only one. Above all, it is important to remember that jihad was not some default mode for Muslim relations with infidels but rather was invoked for specific reasons in specific contexts. In the age of the Crusades, Frankish invasion necessitated jihad only when combined with other factors, as when religious leaders preached it as part of a program of spiritual renewal, enfeebled rulers encouraged it to mobilize the military energies of their subjects, or upwardly mobile politicians employed it to rally support for the formation of new states with unbeatable Islamic credentials.

Holy Lands

Even when a campaign had not been sanctioned as a jihad, there were some parts of the Abode of Islam where the landscape itself was so sacred that even garden-variety warfare was freighted with religious significance, and fighting there might lend a special urgency to jihad. At the broadest level, it is important to note that fortress-complexes called *ribats* housing the faithful who were drawn to the frontiers ringed the edges of the Islamic world, particularly along the Mediterranean coast, forming a kind of spiritual cordon sanitaire against the Christian powers of the Mediterranean's northern shores. In these ribats, on the very edge of Islamdom, fellowships of the pious might together engage in jihads Lesser and Greater. Al-Andalus, long the traditional target of Frankish attacks, was often celebrated as a land free of heresy, a uniquely orthodox zone, and depicted as a land of ribats set apart for the prosecution of jihad, a land given up to holy war, as was also the case in the frontier zones of Sicily and northern Syria.

But, as it was for Christianity and Judaism, Palestine was undeniably sacred land, the Holy Land (*al-ard al-muqaddasa*) vouchsafed for God's people as mentioned in the Qur'an itself (5: 21), and the seat of the city of Jerusalem, the holiest Muslim city outside of Islam's cradle in western Arabia. Jerusalem, also known as al-Quds or al-Bayt al-Muqaddis (the Sacred House), was redolent with associations with prophets and religious figures whom God had sent in various ages, such as Abraham, David, and Jesus the Messiah, accompanied by his mother, Mary. For

Muslims, it was and remains a city unlike others; before they focused on Mecca in the earliest days of the community, it was the first place to which the first Muslims directed their prayers and the site of the Prophet's miraculous night journey and ascension through the heavens, where he met many of God's earlier prophets and interceded with Him to lighten the burden of worship for His people. These events in the Prophet's life were subsequently commemorated in the stunning monuments of the Dome of the Rock and the al-Aqsa Mosque, both located on al-Haram al-Sharif, the ancient platform known also as the Temple Mount (Fig. 4). Jerusalem was, moreover, a city with a storied past. It was, for example, one of the few locales that the pious caliph 'Umar visited when the city surrendered to Muslim armies in 637, his visit commemorated in the Mosque of 'Umar that he founded not far from—and, it is said, in deference to—the Church of the Holy Sepulcher. Jerusalem also had an important "future history," for, as with Jews and Christians, Muslims expected the city to play a central role in the battles with Antichrist, the coming of the Messiah, and humanity's Final Judgment.

And yet Jerusalem and Palestine were only parts of the larger territory of geographical Syria (a region much larger than the modern country of Syria), known in Arabic as al-Sham, which was also claimed as sacred space, from Egypt in the west to the Euphrates in the east, and from the Taurus Mountains in the north to the Red Sea in the south. Like al-Andalus, certain traditions have it that Syria was to be treated as one immense ribat. "Whoever stays in one of its cities, he is in a ribat; whoever stays in one of its frontier-fortresses, he is on jihad." Its armies were styled the swords or arrows of a wrathful God; it was a region protected by the wings of angels; prayer there was held to be virtuous beyond prayer in other regions, for "God has divided goodness into ten parts; He put nine-tenths of it in Syria and the remainder in the rest of the world." During the End Times "true belief will be in Syria," where the righteous will assemble and from which all of humanity will be judged. During the fiercest of the battles of the Apocalypse, "the encampment of the Muslims will be in a land called the Ghuta [the oasis of Damascus] in which is a city called Damascus, the best dwelling-place for Muslims on that day." Moreover Syria was littered with the tombs of patriarchs, prophets, and holy men, and virtually every city could boast a holy site. Many of these sites became places of devotion, developing their own cults of visitation for Muslims and, perhaps not surprisingly, for Jews and Christians too. For medieval Muslims, then, Jerusalem was the most sacred city in Palestine, although Palestine in turn was the most sacred district in the much broader sacred land of Syria.[14]

By the year 1050 the dar al-islam was thus mighty and confident, the home of a vigorous civilization kept fluid by a diverse population and a robust economy. It was proud of its accomplishments, at ease with, albeit wary of, its neighbors and disdainful of the peoples on the fringes of the oikumene who merely sat warming their hands at the edge of the light. It was also a realm that embraced order, where God's faithful and their subjects dwelt in divinely protected domains, hemmed in by fortresses manned by the pious, ruled over by caliphs and kings who were expected to uphold divine justice, to strengthen Islam, and to send armies to defend the borders of its abode.

Then, in ways that neither Harun ibn Yahya, al-Bakri, nor any other visitor to the darkened climes of Ifranja could have predicted, the Abode of Islam and the Abode of War collided. The Franks were on the move.

– 2 –

The Frightened Sea

IBN AL-THUMNA LIKED to drink, but it got him into trouble. One of a number of Muslim commanders in eleventh-century Sicily who emerged as rulers of small principalities of their own, Ibn al-Thumna laid claim to the cities of Syracuse and Catania. The distant Fatimid masters of the island were increasingly unable to manage its affairs, providing a context in which men like Ibn al-Thumna thrived. As a measure of his growing political capital, he was allowed to marry the sister of his rival, Ibn al-Hawwas, the ruler of the central cities of Castrogiovanni and Agrigento and the most powerful of the petty commanders on Sicily.

Ibn al-Thumna's new wife, Maymuna, was no shrinking violet. One day, while Ibn al-Thumna was deep in his cups, he said something disagreeable to her, and she returned the abuse in equal measure. Enraged that his wife would talk back at him, Ibn al-Thumna devised a gruesome punishment. He arranged for her to be bled and then left her to die, employing the ancient medical technique with murderous intent. Fortunately Ibn al-Thumna's son had heard the row and summoned his father's physicians, who bound Maymuna's wounds and tended to her until her strength returned. The next morning a sober and contrite Ibn al-Thumna begged his wife's forgiveness, blaming his drunkenness for his actions. Maymuna, a veteran of Sicily's civil wars, made a show of forgiveness and later demurely asked permission to call upon her brother, the powerful commander Ibn al-Hawwas. Ibn al-Thumna readily granted her this permission and sent many gifts along with her, as was proper. Once arrived at her brother's court, Maymuna related the whole sordid tale to him, and then and there Ibn al-Hawwas swore an oath never to let his sister return to Ibn al-Thumna.

Ibn al-Thumna demanded his wife be returned, but, his entreaties rebuffed, he eventually gathered his troops and marched on his brother-in-law to reclaim her. The two armies fought back and forth across Sicily, until it looked as if Ibn al-Thumna's forces might finally fall. In May 1061 Ibn al-Thumna resorted to a time-honored emergency strategy, employing mercenaries to round out his badly reduced troops. The men he hired were Franks. To be specific, they were Normans recently arrived in Italy from northern France. Under the leadership of Robert, called Guiscard ("the Fox"), and his brother, Roger, and bearing the blessing and banner of the pope, these Norman warriors crossed over to the island and by 1091 had made all of Sicily their own, the first streams of what a Muslim poet living in the aftermath of the First Crusade later called "a flood, whose extent frightens even the torrent of the sea."[1]

It's a useful story, that. From the very earliest sources, medieval Muslim observers saw the crusades that were launched into Syria and Palestine not as some radically new phenomenon emerging from Christendom but simply as the latest episodes of a much longer history of Frankish assaults on the Abode of Islam. This history entered a new phase in the middle of the eleventh century with an unparalleled wave of successful, long-lasting Frankish invasions of Muslim territory, invasions that took place long before Pope Urban II dreamed up the more famous First Crusade of 1095–99. From this perspective the first of these new and worrisome Frankish invasions was the one that cost Islamdom Sicily and opened the floodgates for further Frankish conquests in al-Andalus, North Africa, and, eventually, the Near East. Sicily, then, needed a fall guy.

The chroniclers who reflected on these events needed someone to relieve the Muslim community of the collective onus of failure, and they focused blame on someone whose strategic and moral shortcomings could satisfactorily explain the loss of Sicily and everything else that followed. Ibn al-Thumna fit the bill perfectly. Rather too perfectly. True enough, he had taken on Robert Guiscard and his men to assist him in his struggles against Ibn al-Hawwas on Sicily. Yet the Normans had been involved in Sicilian affairs before then. And as instructive as the story of his marriage troubles might be, we really know nothing of Ibn al-Thumna's inner qualities, or those of his wife, for that matter. That the historians caricatured him as an arrogant tyrant, a wife beater, and a drunkard—qualities sure to be condemned by Muslim audiences—should further make us wonder how much we can really pin on this one man. For even if Ibn al-Thumna's actions might explain the loss of Sicily, they cannot explain the subsequent waves of Frankish conquest and settlement in the Abode of Islam during the rest of the eleventh century. For that, we have to look not at the man's marriage but at his context and the changes around him that reconfigured the entire Mediterranean in the decades after the year 1000. But that too is something for which the Arabic chroniclers reserve quite a lot of comment.

The Origins of Frankish Aggression

The very first reference to the Crusades by a Muslim author explicitly describes them as part and parcel of earlier Frankish activity elsewhere in the Mediterranean, beginning with Sicily. In the early years of the twelfth century, the Syrian preacher 'Ali ibn Tahir al-Sulami composed the *Book of Jihad* and preached from it in Damascus and environs, just as the dust of the First Crusade was settling and the Franks were consolidating their newly won conquests in Syria and Palestine. In his text al-Sulami urged the Muslims of the region to unite against these invaders, contrasting the early and glorious centuries of Islamic history with the dire situation of his own times: "After [the death of] the Prophet (God's blessings and peace be upon him), the four caliphs and all the Companions agreed that *jihad* was incumbent upon everyone. Not one of them neglected it during his caliphate, and those who were appointed as caliphs or who ruled their own dynasty afterwards followed them in that, one after another. The ruler would carry out an expedition every year personally, or else send someone out on his behalf. And so it remained until one of the caliphs neglected [this duty] because of his own weakness and impotence."[2] In this vision of the past, the jihad spirit of the golden age of the early caliphs was unimpeachable. Then something went wrong, and al-Sulami blames a certain caliph—it is impossible to know which one, exactly—for letting the duty of jihad fall by the wayside. Since many of the earliest 'Abbasid caliphs were famous jihad warriors, he can have only one of the later 'Abbasid caliphs in mind. One of this unnamed caliph's kinsmen still sat on the throne in Baghdad even as al-Sulami broadcast his accusations. His little history lesson, then, bore contemporary criticism. He was not the first preacher to compare the jihad spirit of earlier times with that of politicians of his own day and find the latter wanting. Nor would he be the last. He saw in it the sign of some larger act of divine will. The "abandonment of jihad" caused God to break apart Muslims in order "to hurl enmity and hate between them and so to tempt their enemies to snatch their lands from their grasp and thereby distress their hearts." The enemy had attacked Syria because it had received reports that "disagreements between its masters and the ignorance of its lords" had left it vulnerable. "And because of that their ambitions became stronger and extended to all they surveyed. They did not stop, striving steadily in jihad against the Muslims."

For al-Sulami, looking back from Damascus over the whole swath of Islamic history, the events of the First Crusade were a story not just about Syria and Palestine but about the entire Abode of Islam. These Frankish invasions were a trial sent by God, a punishment of Muslims everywhere for having let the duty of jihad lapse. Its most proximate cause was the weakness of and division within the Muslim community, a community that had become fragmented spiritually as well as politically. Division and in-fighting made the lands of Islam all too tempting to the Franks who dwelt on their northern limits, and so they pounced: first on Sicily, then on al-Andalus, and later on Syria and Palestine. This earliest of all Muslim observers of the crusaders understands perfectly what the most "heartfelt goal" of this Levantine wing of the Frankish invasions is: Jerusalem. He also knows holy war when he sees it, and he describes the Franks' campaigns against Islamdom not just as attacks but as jihad, pointedly making them—infidels all—avid prosecutors of the spiritual duty that his fellow Muslims had long ago decided to ignore.

Most of the medieval Muslim sources do not trouble themselves with understanding the motives of the Frankish crusaders, attributing their actions to their bellicosity and greed, which they were said to naturally possess.[3] Of those sources that do concern themselves with this question, most shared with al-Sulami a sense of the bigger picture and emphasized the broader Mediterranean context of Frankish expansion. This, for example, is the message of the mid-twelfth-century historian al-'Azimi, whose *History of Aleppo* at least implicitly connects the coming of the Franks to the Near East with their earlier conquests in Spain and North Africa (and Sicily).[4] And in his modestly titled *The Perfect Work of History*, the thirteenth-century chronicler Ibn al-Athir established a more or less definitive narrative of Islamic history that was in use throughout the later Middle Ages. He sees the Franks as having established what he calls a *dawla*, often translated as "state" or "power," but which adds to those meanings a nuance of divine planning; it suggests that the Franks had been blessed (for good or ill) by Fortune's favor to try their hand at kingship, such as the ʿAbbasids, Fatimids, and all the others had done. He sees this Frankish dawla as one that encompasses Spain, Sicily, North Africa, and Syria, and even refers his readers to the relevant sections of his work: after taking Toledo and other cities of al-Andalus, in 1091 they completed their conquest of Sicily, which first began in 1061, and after that "descended on the coasts of north Africa and seized some part, which was taken back from them. Later they took other parts, as you shall see. When it was the year 1096, they invaded Syria."[5]

Ibn al-Athir then relates an anecdote that seeks to explain the Franks' specific choice of Syria as their final goal, stressing Frankish geopolitics over other motives. In his account it is Roger, the Frankish (i.e., Norman) king of Sicily, who convinced a relative of his to invade Syria because his relative was originally bent on invading North Africa, which was too close to Sicily for Roger's comfort. When his counselors countered that fighting Muslims in North Africa might be good for Christianity, Roger expressed his disdain for the plan by raising a leg and farting. "By the truth of my religion," he said, "there is more use in *that* than in what you have to say!" Roger apparently then went on to explain that an invasion of North Africa, whether or not it succeeded, would be costly and would certainly alienate the Muslim ruler there, with whom he was on good terms. "The land of North Africa can wait for us. When we find the strength, we will take it," he concluded and urged his relative eastward to "wage jihad on the Muslims," to conquer Jerusalem and "free it from their hands."[6]

Despite the occasional nod to the Franks' Christian identity (as above), no Muslim source concerns itself in any detailed way with the religious motivations of the Franks. Notwithstanding current debate over the linkages between pilgrimage, papal reform, just war, and holy war among scholars of the European experience of the Crusades, these issues were of no concern to the Muslim sources. To them, the marriage of Christian devotional piety and military culture that culminated in Pope Urban II's notion of the crusade does not feature in their efforts to understand the origins of Frankish aggression. Nor does any Muslim source mention papal involvement or oversight of these campaigns. (Indeed, medieval Muslim references to the papacy in any context are very scarce.) The Franks had always been aggressive quasi-barbarians. The finer points of how they justified this aggression were thus of no interest. What marked the mid-eleventh-century wars with the Franks was not their ideology but the fact that they were more frequent, more menacing, and—for the first time that any Muslim observer could remember—successful. In Christendom the concept of holy war clearly shaped Frankish incentives over the course of the eleventh century, but in Islamdom this did not alter the fate that Muslims faced at the ends of Frankish swords in Sicily, Spain, and the Near East.

Some Muslim authors did mention other motives that might lie behind Frankish interest in the Near East, but these are in the minority.[7] Al-'Azimi, for example, makes the suggestion that it was a response to Muslims who had prevented Frankish pilgrims from reaching Jerusalem. This was precisely one motivation that Pope Urban II is said to have aired in his preaching of the First Crusade. It is certainly true that Christian pilgrims to Jerusalem would often have to endure many travails on their way to Palestine. The predations of nomads and bandits were a recurring problem, even well before the coming of Islam. Indeed the most famous case of pilgrim raiding is that of the so-called Great German Pilgrimage of 1064, in which just a few days' ride from Jerusalem bandits attacked and robbed a massive group of pilgrims; many were killed or captured. Had it not been for the swift action of the Muslim authorities, the Germans would have been wiped out. The Fatimid governor in Palestine arrived and dispersed the bandits, and the pilgrims were led to al-Ramla, "where," in the words of the German annalist who recorded the event, "at the invitation of the governor and the townspeople, they rested for two weeks" and then visited the Holy City.[8] There is the distinct possibility that al-'Azimi, writing well after the success of the First Crusade, was just recycling what was in fact old Frankish lore by his day. Whatever the case, if there was one dominant Muslim line of reasoning for the origins of the Crusades, it is that Frankish jihad against the Muslims began in the 1060s, that it was fought on many fronts across the Mediterranean, and that blame for its success should be placed squarely at the door of a divided Muslim community.

The Sunni-Shi'i Cold War

When the preacher al-Sulami bemoaned the divisions within the Muslim community of his age, he was certainly thinking of factional in-fighting, such as that of Ibn al-Thumna and his rival warlords on Sicily, not to mention their analogues in Spain and in his own homeland of Syria. But he also spoke of divergent opinions and viewpoints, in short, of creeds. For ardent Sunni Muslims like al-Sulami, the most damaging disagreement in Islam was that which divided Sunnis from Shi'is. That Sunni Muslims and Shi'i Muslims do not always get along remains commonly accepted today, but such conflict was not necessarily the norm. Sectarian identities in Islam—despite a few exceptional phases—have never been as hotly politicized as they are today. In the medieval Islamic context, Sunnis and Shi'is certainly came to blows, but for the most part they learned to manage differences without recourse to armed conflict. This is largely because in the medieval Near East there were no nation-states or parliamentary politics to seize on sectarian identities as a cover for their own agendas. Moreover Shi'is were vastly outnumbered and essentially powerless, a minority in a mostly Sunni world.

The fundamental issue dividing Sunnis and Shi'is was religious authority following the death of the Prophet Muhammad in 632. In a world without prophets, who now spoke for Islam? Each sect defined itself based upon how it answered that question, which touches upon interpretations of history as well as theology. Not until the ninth century did distinct historical, theological, legal, and devotional approaches coalesce into what we can with some confidence call Sunni and Shi'i Islam. For the majority of Muslims—those who came to be recognized as Sunnis—the true heirs of the Prophet's authority were the caliphs, whose legitimacy was proven by the fact that they were chosen by the leading Companions of the Prophet and recognized by the consensus of the Muslim community. Whatever their individual failings might be, over time the caliphs continued to serve as symbols of unity. But their authority as sources of guidance on matters of faith and religious practice was eventually ceded to the ulema, who were held to provide the most direct access to the exemplary practice (sunna) of the Prophet and recognized as humankind's best hope to follow God's will. For the vast majority of Muslims, then, the sunna of God's Prophet and the consensus of His believers (and especially the ulema) were the twin supports of their religious identity. The 'Abbasid caliph in Baghdad symbolized both of these.

Sunni derives from this consensus-based concern for upholding the sunna of the Prophet. Nonetheless Shi'is had their own sunna as well.[9] For Shi'is, the true heirs of the Prophet were not the ulema, still less the caliphs recognized by the Sunni mainstream, but rather kinsmen of the Prophet, specifically the descendants of the Prophet's cousin and son-in-law, 'Ali ibn Abi Talib. For them, 'Ali and his kin (whence the adjective 'Alid) had been designated by the Prophet himself as his successors to serve as their imams, the leaders of the Shi'i community.[10] For Shi'is, the sunna of the Prophet *and* that of their imams provided the guidance they needed to live righteous lives. The Shi'i imam was an essential feature of a godly society: God provided each generation with an 'Alid imam, who received spiritual designation from his predecessor. Unlike the caliphs of Sunni theory, the 'Alid imam was held to be infallible, and so he retained the role of decisive interpreter of religious law that, in Sunni Islam, passed instead to the ulema and the consensus of the community. For Shi'is, a community without an imam was rudderless.

Not surprisingly, it was around the figure of the imam that dissent within the Shi'i community concentrated. A crucial figure was the eleventh imam, Hasan al-'Askari, who died in 873 in the Iraqi city of Samarra while under house arrest by the 'Abbasid authorities. The question naturally arose as to whether he had designated an heir in his short lifetime. (He was only twenty-nine.) It was eventually decided that yes, he had a son and designated heir as the twelfth imam, named Muhammad. But this Muhammad's location was kept secret to protect him from his enemies. Over time Shi'i scholars developed this idea of a hidden imam into one of cosmological occultation: a spiritual leader who had not simply gone into hiding but absented himself from this plane, and who would return at the end of time as a messiah-like figure known as the Mahdi. The Mahdi would usher in a period of justice and equity when God's will for His followers would be finally accomplished and all the righteous would be embraced in a community of the faithful. While the Shi'i faithful awaited the return of the hidden imam, the Shi'i ulema labored hard to account for his absence theologically and to grant the scholars the authority to interpret his will as they waited for his return. Hence most Shi'is, who belong to this Imami or "Twelver" sect, still wait today.

There were earlier arguments of equal consequence about the imam. In 765 the sixth imam died. While the Shi'i mainstream recognized his son Musa as the seventh of their twelve imams, a minority branched off from the mainstream and recognized another son, Isma'il, as his rightful successor, and are therefore known as Isma'ili Shi'ites. Isma'il, it turns out, had predeceased his father, so many Isma'ilis argued that he had not died but had gone into occultation, whence he guided his followers. Others argued that his son Muhammad had been named heir and would return as the Mahdi. As we shall see, the details and accuracy of these claims are not important. The murkiness surrounding them is.

For all that Shi'ism was viewed as a rival and heretical approach to Islam by the Sunni majority, from the ninth century onward there was little in the way of outright confrontation between the two sects, thanks in large part to the moderating influences of some of the imams, who made no attempt to rebel against 'Abbasid authority and argued instead that, while the history of the Shi'i community was indeed that of an oppressed community, this in no way compromised the validity and authority of the imam to his followers. It also helped that Shi'i law allowed the faithful to dissimulate and hide their religious beliefs if maintaining them openly proved to be a threat. Major Shi'i communities flourished in Iraq, especially in Baghdad and Kufa, and smaller communities could be found in Iran and Syria. High-ranking Shi'is mingled with their Sunni peers at the 'Abbasid court in Baghdad, and some even served as viziers and administrators. In some cases, dynasties emerged that openly promoted Shi'ism side by side in the fraternity of Sunni statelets that emerged as the 'Abbasid caliphate fragmented. These included the Hamdanids of northern Syria and Iraq, who prided themselves as champions of the jihad against Islam's Byzantine enemies, and, more spectacularly, the Buyids of Iraq and western Iran, who kept the 'Abbasid caliph a virtual prisoner in his own regime during the tenth and early eleventh century. Indeed this period has been singled out by some historians as "the Shi'i century" given the sudden appearance of Shi'i regimes all over the map.[11]

Such a situation could threaten entrenched interests and lead to violence; the sectarian street fighting that contemporaries reported in eleventh-century Baghdad, for example, provides ample evidence of this. But all in all, Sunnis and Shi'is adopted a kind of grudging acceptance of or hostile acquiescence to one another and to the simple reality that neither sect was likely to give in on its claims to preeminence. In effect this was a sectarian "cold war" in which representatives of both sects rarely clashed in open combat, but in which rivalries were fought in the open through learned polemic and public spectacles (such as Shi'i cursing of the first Sunni caliphs and Sunni desecration of Shi'i shrines) and covertly through the use of clandestine agents and missionaries. All this while Sunnis and Shi'is continued to trade, work, and live with one another. However, this Sunni-Shi'i cold war did not, and perhaps could not, last. It became white hot toward the middle of the eleventh century, long after Shi'ism found not just a dynasty, but also an empire.

Although based in Egypt and the mighty capital of Cairo since the middle of the tenth century, the Fatimid caliphate was more than an Egyptian state. The Fatimids began their rise to power as a movement of the Isma'ili branch of Shi'ism. By the late ninth century Isma'ili missionaries had begun successfully spreading their teachings from Syria and the east and attracting followers in North Africa, particularly among the Kutama Berbers there. Considered heretics by Sunnis and other Shi'is alike, Isma'ilis had learned to be wary of the quietism favored by the "Twelver" Shi'i elite of Iraq. By the early tenth century, motivated by messianic expectation (with their leader taking the title of al-Mahdi), held together by deft administrators and leaders, and backed up by a Berber military, the movement took a decisive step. They confronted and easily defeated their most proximate rivals: the local representatives of 'Abbasid authority in the province of Ifriqiya, roughly modern Tunisia. There the Fatimids set up their first sedentary state, initially—and perhaps fittingly, given their Berber connections—in their capital outside Qayrawan, close to the desert, and then in their leader al-Mahdi's new capital city on the coast, which he named al-Mahdiya after himself.

Many Isma'ilis refused to accept that this auspiciously named yet otherwise unknown al-Mahdi could adopt the title of caliph (which pointed to open conflict with the Sunni caliph and his defenders), still less the title of imam (which flew in the face of the succession disputes about Isma'il, even as it exploited the murkiness surrounding them). But the Fatimid caliphs who succeeded al-Mahdi could live with the confusion, for soon the Fatimids captured Egypt, and the Fatimid caliphs, whatever their Isma'ili coreligionists might think, boasted an empire that stretched from North Africa to Egypt and beyond, and included Sicily, western Arabia, Yemen, and much of Palestine and Syria. Fatimid imperial and missionary ambitions reached their pinnacle in 1059, when al-Basasiri, an amir in the employ of the 'Abbasids in Iraq but recently in open revolt against his masters, threw in his lot with the Fatimids. Through a combination of skill and luck, al-Basasiri and his troops were able to take and, for a few months, hold Baghdad later that year. And so the Fatimid caliph's name replaced that of the 'Abbasid caliph in the pulpits of Baghdad: a realization, however brief, of long-held Fatimid ambitions and a very public salvo in a now very hot sectarian war.

As if fulfilling a century of Fatimid propaganda, this far-flung empire building coincided with a noteworthy period of economic prosperity. Egypt was a famously lucrative province, a breadbasket for any empire that controlled it, and an important source of textiles and not inconsiderable mineral wealth. Commerce was the real beneficiary of the Fatimid empire. This was aided by the interruption and collapse of rival commercial routes connecting East Africa and India to trade routes up the Persian Gulf. Beginning in the decades after 1000, this Persian Gulf commerce began rerouting itself farther west into the Red Sea and thus solidly within the control of Fatimid Egypt. Egypt (and above all Cairo) became a sort of commercial prism, in which the wealth and commodities of the Mediterranean and the Indian Ocean economies mingled, were consumed, and were passed on. As it happens, the awakening market economy of western Europe—Ifranja itself—was one of the areas on the margins now being drawn into the Fatimid-dominated Mediterranean commercial world, spurring increased seaborne traffic and substantial ties between Egypt and Italy and (less directly) Europe beyond the Alps. Moreover commerce continued with the old Fatimid lands in Tunisia, which has been called the commercial hub of the Mediterranean, connecting Egypt and its merchants to North Africa, al-Andalus, and Sicily.[12]

Imperial confidence, economic prosperity, and faith in the inherent justice of Islamic law all combined under the Fatimid caliphs of Cairo to create a setting that was especially accommodating to non-Muslims and even subject Sunnis. During the Fatimid period the population of Egypt, especially in the countryside, was mostly Coptic Christian. Jews were found in most of the cities, with Cairo being the center of Egypt's large and vibrant Jewish community. Of the Muslim population (concentrated mostly in the cities), the vast majority were Sunni. In other words, the Fatimids were a small ruling minority who made few doctrinal inroads into their non-Isma'ili subjects. Indeed, the mighty "city" of Cairo founded by the Fatimids is more accurately thought of as a palace compound, in which the Fatimid caliphs, the army, and the Isma'ili elite were housed, splendidly isolated from the populace of the surrounding residential districts. Most of the inhabitants of the city were in fact Sunnis who cleaved to the settlement at Fustat, the adjacent, older capital of Egypt that had been founded during the Arab Conquests and which was integrated into the capital as the neighborhood that is today called "Old Cairo." The regime itself staffed its administration with Christians and Jews as well as Muslims, a process that, while it does not seem to have encouraged conversion to Isma'ilism, certainly accelerated the spread of the Arabic language and the creation of a Fatimid meritocracy. In Fatimid Egypt you didn't have to be Isma'ili to make it big.

Nonetheless there was fragility to the Fatimid dynasty's imperial achievements. Even as this Shi'i caliphate seemed poised to overwhelm the Sunni world, its power was beginning to ebb, and what imperial reach it had was revealed to be largely symbolic. Western Arabia, for example, was not a securely held Fatimid possession. Rather, local rulers in the holy cities of Mecca and Medina, who were used to almost complete freedom, simply agreed to recognize the authority of Cairo instead of Baghdad in return for ample subsidies. Matters were not much better in Tunisia and the Maghrib, where, once the caliphs had moved to Cairo, the Fatimids had installed their own dynasty of governors, a Berber dynasty known as the Zirids, who ruled with wide autonomy. Once the Fatimids had abandoned Tunisia, the Zirids were hard-pressed to stop the periodic anti-Isma'ili pogroms that wracked their tenure in North Africa. With the imams in distant Cairo and the small Isma'ili community in Tunisia facing extinction, it was only a matter of time before the Zirids gave up and threw in their lot with the 'Abbasids in Baghdad. Indeed they did so repeatedly over the eleventh century, apparently hoping to play 'Abbasids and Fatimids off one another to their own advantage. This only succeeded in annoying their old masters. The Arabic sources seize upon this episode to explain the devastating influx of the Banu Hilal, nomadic Arab tribesmen from Egypt who overwhelmed much of the central Maghrib in the eleventh century, leaving the Zirids in control of only a handful of towns. For these writers, the Banu Hilal were a plague sent from Egypt by a vengeful Fatimid ruler bent on punishing the faithlessness of their Zirid proxies. Whatever the cause of these predations, Fatimid authority wavered in the Zirid lands of North Africa and, by the 1060s, was lost.[13]

Sicily, always closely connected to North African affairs, was another area of Fatimid concern. Although there had been Muslim raids on Sicily from an early period, the island was not fully conquered until the middle of the ninth century by the 'Abbasid governors of Tunisia. Muslim control of Sicily was thus late and hard-fought. When the Fatimids conquered Tunisia in the early tenth century, Sicily was a virtual dependency of the province, and so the Fatimids claimed the island as part of the bargain. As with the 'Abbasid representatives who ruled it before them, the Fatimids were eager to make use of the island's role in the geography of jihad, conducting raids against Christian shipping and occasionally occupying small parts of the Italian coast. When the

Fatimid imams moved to Egypt, they left behind in Sicily, as they had done in North Africa, a vassal to serve as their representative, choosing a trusted amir whose descendants, the Kalbids, ruled the island dutifully but quite independently. Just as Zirid North Africa split as the Fatimid dynasty turned to Egypt and the east, so too did Kalbid Sicily. Local rulers often found themselves at odds with each other and with the Kalbid amirs, the last of whom was expelled by the populace of Palermo in 1052–53. Thereafter the island fragmented into rival city-states of commanders, all very much in the mold of the bibulous Ibn al-Thumna and his brother-in-law, Ibn al-Hawwas, whose tale began this chapter. In this setting, direct Fatimid control of Sicily was out of the question.

The weakness of Fatimid authority in the provinces coincided with debilitating problems in the center. The almost total collapse of the caliphate did not come until the middle of the century, but there were signs of trouble even earlier. The most famous of the examples of Fatimid decline in the eleventh century is associated with the reign and, indeed, the person of the early tenth-century caliph al-Hakim. Al-Hakim's behavior as caliph can most charitably be characterized as impulsive. His reign was marked—more so than was normal even in Fatimid Cairo—by bloody purges and clandestine plots that greatly weakened the machinery of state. Al-Hakim himself generated fear and insecurity in his subjects, issuing radical decrees only to suddenly repeal them. At one point, for example, he ordered all women to be confined to their home, going so far (according to hostile sources) as closing the shops of cobblers who made women's sandals. At other times he instituted new dietary laws or altered long-established Shi'ite rituals. Among other odd decrees, and despite a noted Fatimid tradition to the contrary, al-Hakim instituted repressive measures against non-Muslims (and Sunnis). One such act, in 1009, was directed against Christian pilgrims in Fatimid Egypt and Palestine, when he ordered the Church of the Holy Sepulcher in Jerusalem—believed by Christians to contain the very tomb of Christ—to be leveled. The church remained in ruins until it was rebuilt with Byzantine help many decades later. The reaction in Western Christendom to the destruction of the Holy Sepulcher was relatively muted, though one piece of evidence, if it is not a forgery, suggests that Pope Sergius IV had appealed to the Italian city-states to organize an expedition of armed pilgrims "to sail to Syria to avenge the Redeemer and His tomb."[14] If the appeal was actually ever made, it was clearly an important precedent.

In 1021 al-Hakim disappeared during an outing in the hills outside Cairo. His sister probably had him murdered as part of a palace coup, but the mysterious circumstances only added to his mystique. Some contemporaries, the Druze, took the imam's eccentric behavior and mysterious disappearance as an indication of his divine status. More recently scholars have looked to Neoplatonic philosophy or messianic beliefs to explain his actions. Perhaps he was simply mad.[15]

Mad God-caliphs were only the beginning for the Fatimids. The 1060s issued in a period of political chaos so draining that the chroniclers refer to this period as the "Great Calamity" (*al-shidda al-'uzma*). In addition to the failing situation in the provinces, which assured a reduced tax yield, a series of low Nile floods produced nearly uninterrupted famines for almost two decades, forcing the caliph into the humiliating position of having to beg for surplus grain from the Byzantine emperor. The constrained fiscal situation made the Fatimid armies, with their salaries already in arrears, restive and fractious. Soon rival factions of Turkish and black slave troops—which had already replaced the Berber troops who brought the Fatimids to power—were openly fighting in pitched battles in the streets of Cairo. The caliph al-Mustansir was ultimately forced to sell off some of the contents of the royal treasuries just to raise the funds to restore order, but to no avail. Desperate for any help, in 1073 the caliph called on Badr al-Jamali, the ruthless governor of Acre, and appointed him his vizier. Badr and his private army of Armenian troops forced a semblance of law and order in the capital but in the process inaugurated a period of increased militarization of the Fatimid state that lasted until the dynasty's demise in 1171.

Terror Mundi

This abbreviated survey of Fatimid decline has been necessary to show how, despite being one of the Islamic world's great superpowers, the Fatimids could not be expected to be on hand when their distant provinces, especially in the west, were threatened. It is thus the collapse of Fatimid provincial authority that provided the immediate context for Ibn al-Thumna's gambit on Sicily and the gradual but alarming Norman conquest of the island by 1091. For perhaps obvious reasons, the Islamic sources are tight-lipped about how Sicily was lost, but Christian sources, such as Geoffrey Malaterra and Amatus of Montecassino, fill in the details.[16]

To early medieval Muslims, Sicily was best known as a frontier province, a jihad zone abutting the Abode of War. Its location and many fine ports also made it a trading hub, and its rough inland terrain boasted abundant mineral products, timber, and, thanks to many natural sources of irrigation, fruit, grain, and other crops. Although the island would become famous as a place of Muslim, indeed interconfessional learning, much of the most famous cultural heights achieved by Sicilian Muslims in literature, science, and the arts occurred later in the Middle Ages under Frankish aegis. That said, early Islamic Sicily did produce its share—perhaps more than its share—of poets and intellectuals. And, attracted perhaps by the merits of jihad, many members of the ulema class also made Sicily their home, transforming the island into a destination for the study of (Sunni) Islamic law and the religious sciences. Then again, there is a well-known account of the island in the late tenth century by the geographer Ibn Hawqal, himself the product of the frontier lands of Syria and Anatolia, who claimed to be scandalized by the ignorance of Sicily's ulema and their lax attitude toward what he felt was their duty of jihad. By the 1050s jihad was not much on the minds of Sicily's Muslim leaders.[17]

By then the island was split between several competing warlords and local bosses, of whom Ibn al-Thumna was only the best known. Having risen to prominence in obscure circumstances in Syracuse in the 1050s, he seized power in Catania, killing the local ruler there and marrying his widow. He also seems to have thought himself the successor of the Kalbid amirs as ruler of the island in its entirety, arrogating the Fatimid title al-Qadir for himself. If his mistreatment of his wife did indeed contribute to his falling out with Ibn al-Hawwas, who was the other leading commander in Sicily, then Ibn al-Thumna's boundless ambitions cannot have helped matters. As the upstart, it was Ibn al-Thumna's responsibility to prove his case, and so it was that he came to blows with Ibn al-Hawwas and, his fortunes failing, made his fateful appeal for military aid from the Normans of southern Italy, offering, according to the Muslim sources, to hand control of the entire island over to them.

In 1061, when Ibn al-Thumna crossed over to Mileto (the Christian sources say it was Reggio) on the Italian peninsula to meet with the Norman warlord Roger, both men were well aware of each other's situation. Much of the populace of Sicily, especially in the northeast, were Greek Christians with close connections to the Greek communities of southern Italy that were currently under Norman sway. Similarly the small Muslim community known to exist in Reggio surely had some contact with their coreligionists back on the island. Both of these communities would have served as important vectors of intelligence for the Normans and the Sicilian Muslims. But there were other, more direct channels. On the one hand, Sicilian pirates had been raiding Calabria and Apulia for years and would have been thoroughly aware of the arrival and establishment of Norman power in these regions. On the other hand, Sicily had been on the Normans' "to conquer" list for some time now.

By the 1050s the Normans of southern Italy were no longer the Vikings they were when they arrived to settle in Normandy during the ninth and tenth centuries. Since the early eleventh century, Norman lords and their war bands had been serving as mercenaries and auxiliaries in the armies of southern Italy, a regular, even disciplined feature of the military culture of the region, alternately serving and vexing the Byzantines, the papacy, and the many smaller local authorities who held power throughout Italy's "boot." By the middle of the century they had turned the tables and had conquered lands and begun ruling them independently, becoming a force to be reckoned with. The rise of Norman influence in Italy was marked most clearly in 1059. In August of that year Pope Nicholas II accepted as his vassal the Norman leader Robert Guiscard, whom he also recognized as lord of the lands he had conquered, granting his conquests to him, through a nice little fiction, as fiefs of the Holy See. Although Nicholas had sought the support of the Normans for his own ends, his actions were of great consequence for the Islamic world. For though Robert's oath of fealty contained many promises to protect the papacy from its enemies at home, it also contained a direct claim on Islamdom. The text of his oath recognizes Guiscard as "Robert, by the grace of God and St. Peter Duke of Apulia and Calabria," but also "and in future, with the help of both, of Sicily," a territory he had yet to conquer. As a sign of Robert's new role as papal protector and vassal, Nicholas gave him the papal banner to carry in battle.[18]

Thus it was, in autumn of 1060, that Roger, Robert Guiscard's brother and his count of Calabria, dutifully crossed the choppy two miles or so from Reggio and landed with some sixty knights near Messina, Sicily's main Italy-facing port. A group of Muslim soldiers from the city sallied out to meet the invaders, and the result seems to have been a draw: Roger and his knights forced the Messinans to flee back to the city, but so small a force could hardly accomplish anything more than reconnaissance. So they sailed back to Reggio as quickly as they had come. During the winter that followed, Roger joined his brother in Apulia, and Robert was able to inform his vassals there that he was planning an expedition to Sicily for the summer of 1061. The conquest of Sicily was thus cooked up and reconnoitered even before the conquest of southern Italy was complete and before Ibn al-Thumna ever became involved with the Normans. The Muslim chroniclers, it seems, need not have bothered with a fall guy after all, as Ibn al-Thumna did not bring on the Norman conquest of Sicily so much as contribute to a conquest already under way.

In March 1061 a larger, but still modest, Norman force of 150 knights followed up on the reconnaissance of the previous autumn, landing on the northern coast and raiding the lands and livestock around Rometta, "in a happy and playful spirit," Amatus tells us.[19] As before, the Muslim forces at Messina marched out to confront them, bearing torches to light their way during the night. But this time their defeat was clear-cut, and many Muslim casualties were reported, despite what one presumes to have been their larger numbers. Bad weather stalled any attempt to cross the treacherous straits back to Italy, and the Normans were forced to camp on the beach, where the remaining Muslim troops rained arrows down upon them. Roger, however, had seen the enemy coming and had sent a detachment of troops to outflank them and cut off their path back to Messina. Thus, when the remaining Messinan troops withdrew—Malaterra improbably calls it a "retreat"—they were ambushed. Few survivors of the Messina guard made it back alive. Bereft of troops to defend them, the Muslims of Messina armed whatever citizens they could, women included, to defend the city walls "as if they were fighting for their very lives" when Roger's siege finally started the next morning.[20] Roger must have seen the folly in his actions. Trapped by bad weather, his small force already reduced, besieging a resilient foe whose supporters elsewhere on the island might be wakened to their threat any moment, he did the sensible thing. As soon as the weather permitted it, he lifted the siege and crossed back to Reggio.

Roger was prescient: his raiding at and around Messina had finally raised the ire of the authorities. This was Ibn al-Hawwas, the effective ruler of Sicily now that Ibn al-Thumna had turned coat, and who himself must have understood how vital it was to hold Messina were he to prevent further Frankish incursions from across the straits. From Palermo, the capital and principal northern Sicilian port, he therefore sent a fleet that even included a few large warships to patrol the straits and keep Messina safe. Yet though the Normans' ships were small, they had more of them, and this allowed Roger, in May 1061, to detach his boats from the fleet of his brother Robert and cross undetected under cover of night. Robert remained in Calabria with the main fleet, for all the world (and to all Sicilian observers) acting as if his invasion had not yet begun. Thus, when Roger suddenly turned up at the walls of Messina with a force twice the size of his previous visit, the already weakened city was easily taken. Some of the Messinans tried to escape to the fleet from Palermo. Not everyone made it; in one case, we are told, a Muslim nobleman killed his young sister rather than let her be defiled by the Franks.[21]

With Messina in Frankish hands, the Muslims' one friendly port in the northeast was lost. Their supplies limited and the haven of Messina's port closed to them, the Muslim fleet, and what refugees from Messina were able, withdrew to Palermo. Robert Guiscard, his path cleared, crossed over with his main force and joined his brother to complete what he no doubt assumed would be the rapid conquest of Sicily. The Muslims of Sicily ensured that it would take thirty years.

The Course of the Conquest

The first phase of the Muslim defense of Sicily lasted until the summer of 1071, culminating in the Norman siege of the capital, Palermo. This was a fitful period of startled surrenders and organized skirmishes that aimed to nip Norman successes in the bud (Map 3). It did not begin well: after a delegation of Sicilian Muslims arrived in Tunisia seeking help, the Zirid amir there sent a fleet to provide troops to aid in the island's defense. The fleet foundered in a storm off the coast of Tunisia and was lost, weakening the military reach of the amir in Tunisia and delaying any rescue from that quarter. With Messina lost and freshly garrisoned with Frankish troops, the Muslims of Sicily had first to confront the invaders as they followed the northern coast toward Rometta. There the citizens were aware of recent events at Messina, and so a group of local notables rode out to surrender the city, swearing to the terms of surrender on the Qur'an.

Their rear now secure, the Normans headed south along the western slopes of the great dozing volcano of Mt. Etna, pausing briefly to besiege the small town of Centuripe. The Muslim inhabitants put up a stout resistance, dragging catapults to the walls to pummel the Norman armies. In the meantime rumors had spread that Ibn al-Hawwas had sent an army to intercept them, so Robert Guiscard and his brother lifted the siege before more damage could be done and proceeded

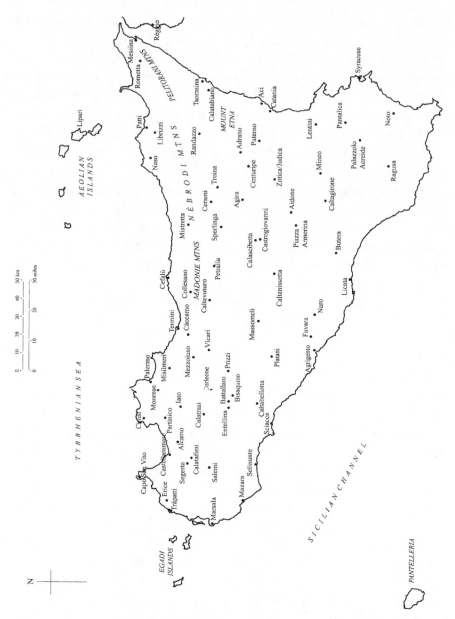

Map 3 Medieval Sicily. From Alex Metcalfe, *The Muslims of Medieval Italy* (Edinburgh: Edinburgh University Press, 2009), fig. 2.

southward, pausing in the plain outside Catania, the capital of their ally, Ibn al-Thumna. They had hoped to meet Ibn al-Hawwas in battle there, a place of their own choosing, with a nearby refuge to which they could flee and plenty of space in which to maneuver. But Ibn al-Hawwas bided his time.

Ibn al-Thumna sent out spies, who reported that Ibn al-Hawwas was still amassing his troops, and so the Normans headed west, apparently spoiling for a fight. By this time Ibn al-Hawwas had assembled a large army of local troops and "Africans," which must mean troops, possibly Berbers, sent from the Zirids in Tunisia. The enemies met to the east of Castrogiovanni on the River Dittaino. The African and Sicilian components of Ibn al-Hawwas's hastily assembled army seem not to have been well-coordinated. Despite their apparently greater numbers, the Muslim troops fled back to Castrogiovanni at the first sign that the Normans were gaining. The Normans pursued, but putting Castrogiovanni to siege now was out of the question. They returned to Messina. From there, both Robert and Roger returned to the mainland to see to pressing business on other fronts there, and Ibn al-Thumna retired to Catania, whence he continued his raids in the southeast.

At the end of 1061 Roger returned with a small force, plundering all the way to Agrigento. The fortress of Troina, a predominantly Christian town, surrendered to him, and he celebrated Christmas there before returning to the mainland to get married. In early 1062 he returned and, with the assistance of Ibn al-Thumna, captured Petralia, which, with Troina, became important forward bases for the inevitable push to the west. He returned again to Italy and left Ibn al-Thumna in charge of all the lands they had conquered in Sicily.

It was then, however, that the Normans suffered a serious blow at Entella. The town was a former possession of Ibn al-Thumna's, and the garrison was still commanded by one of his men, who requested to meet with his former lord privately to settle the terms of surrender. When Ibn al-Thumna arrived at the meeting, the men waiting for him attacked, and their leader ran the old turncoat through with his spear.

With Roger and Robert on the mainland, the small groups of Normans left to garrison Troina and Petralia now found themselves surrounded in hostile territory without a single ally on the island. They abandoned their positions and scurried back to the safety of Messina to await their orders. Local support was eroding in other areas too. When Roger returned with troops in the autumn of 1062, the Greek population at Troina refused to billet them. While he was out campaigning, the citizens rose up in revolt. Joined by Muslims from surrounding towns, they trapped the garrison and Roger's new bride. Ultimately they were thwarted when Roger returned to rescue them. Roger rounded up the Greek ringleaders and had them publicly executed.

While the Normans were momentarily distracted, the Muslims of Sicily received some support. By late 1062 there was apparently no one central power left in Sicily to coordinate its defense, and Ibn al-Hawwas seems to have kept to himself. Into this vacuum stepped the Zirids of North Africa, whose new amir, Tamim, sent his two sons, Ayyub and 'Ali, with a large fleet to spearhead the rescue of the island. Ayyub landed in Palermo and established himself there, while 'Ali was based at Agrigento, presumably to assist Ibn al-Hawwas against Norman attempts on Castrogiovanni. In June 1063 the Zirid army and its Sicilian allies met the Norman forces at Cerami, a few miles west of Troina. Only one—highly biased—Christian account of this battle survives, but it appears to have been a disaster for the Zirid armies, who, as they had at Dittaino years earlier, began to flee after a small Norman victory, precipitating a massive rout. Many Muslims fell on the battlefield; many more died in the pell-mell pursuit of the routed. The Normans also plundered the Muslim camp and, remembering who it was who ultimately commanded them, sent four captured camels to Rome as exotic tribute to the new pope, Alexander II. At Cerami the possibility of a Muslim revanche had not exactly been squashed, but it was surely scattered. Taking advantage of the lull on the island, Roger returned to Italy to assist his brother and to plan his advance on his next Sicilian target: Palermo.

Almost immediately after its capture by Muslims in the ninth century, the port of Palermo had been the capital of Muslim Sicily, where its various governors had always resided. When the Normans invaded Sicily, it was still the largest and most prominent city on the island. Surrounded by orchards and gardens, the city was really an agglomeration of several districts, including the old city, called al-Qasr (today's Cassaro), behind its own city walls and a newer palatine complex called al-Khalisa (today's Kalsa district), which the Fatimids had founded next to the old city, rather as they had done at Cairo. A stout curtain wall encircled them all. Palermo also boasted a busy harbor, which, as we have seen, could be used to deploy Muslim ships where needed. Such a city could be taken only by a joint assault, by land and sea, and the Normans needed time to gather the men, ships, and breathing space to do so.

By 1066, while Roger and Robert's kinsmen in Normandy were busy invading an entirely different splintered island kingdom, the Normans in Sicily had reoccupied and fortified the town of Petralia. In 1068 the Palermitan Muslims launched an assault on a Norman raiding party at Misilmeri, about five miles from the capital. It was a bloody defeat for the Muslims, made all the more demoralizing when, Malaterra tells us, Robert sent carrier pigeons back to Palermo bearing scraps of cloth dipped in Muslim blood. Sicilian patience was wearing thin. The Zirids, despite their uneven showing at Cerami, were still supporting Muslim efforts to stymie the Normans, but their largely Berber troops were very unpopular with the Sicilians. Ibn al-Hawwas resented their interference in his domains and even rose in revolt against them at Agrigento; he was killed in the fighting. In Palermo riots broke out against the Berbers, and so in 1069 the Zirid commander Ayyub gathered his men and returned to North Africa, leaving Palermo and Sicily to its fate.

Two years later, it came. The siege lasted five months, with Roger surrounding the city by land and Robert arriving with a small fleet to blockade the port. Although the Muslims appear to have made several quick sorties, the siege held firm, and soon hunger set in. By early January 1072 Palermo was ready to fall. Roger launched an attack from the landward side, and as the Muslim troops rushed to defend the walls Robert and a small band of knights scaled the walls that faced the sea, killing as they came. The populace fled to their last refuge: the inner walled old city. Of the last authorities in Islamic Palermo, thanks to a few Jewish documents, we know of at least one leader by name, a certain Muslim merchant called Ibn al-Baʿbaʿ. He may well have been involved in the discussions among the besieged about their fate. Their path seemed clear. When dawn broke the next day, the Palermitans sent a delegation of notables with the prisoners they had taken and surrendered on terms to Robert, who promised them their lives and the freedom to practice their religion. Mazara, the island's principal African-facing port, surrendered shortly thereafter. Sicily was all but cut off from the rest of Islamdom.

A few days later Robert made his triumphal entrance into Palermo and thence to the main mosque, which was ritually cleansed and converted into a cathedral. Robert also had the gates of the city carted off to rebellious Troina and erected as a trophy. He then set about garrisoning his new prize and arranging with Roger the details of the division of the lands conquered up to now—roughly half of Sicily. These affairs set in order, the Fox then left Sicily for the mainland, never to return. He died in 1085 while fighting the Greeks and was buried in Venosa in Italy, where his epitaph proudly proclaimed him *terror mundi*, the Terror of the World.

Twilight in Sicily

Despite the demoralizing loss of Palermo, Norman domination was not a foregone conclusion when Roger took over the conquest of Sicily on his own. There were strong arguments in favor of continued Muslim control. Muslim armies still outnumbered the Normans, for whom manpower was a constant struggle. This was exacerbated by the fact that Roger was frequently called back to the mainland to assist his brother in his campaigns there, leaving the island in the hands of subordinates and stripped of seasoned fighters. Important Muslim towns in the center still held firm, none more so than Castrogiovanni. Two valuable ports, Syracuse in the southeast and Trapani in the northwest, still remained in Muslim hands. And the rugged terrain of all that was left to conquer in Sicily forced the Normans away from quick grabs of territory into long, wearying sieges of town, forts, and other strong points. Small wonder, then, that even with Palermo in Norman hands, the final conquest took another twenty years. Small wonder too that once Roger was on his own, the Muslims of Sicily struck back.

This was not a centrally organized plan to oust the Normans, but a gritty, no-holds-barred surge of resistance from Sicily's Muslims. It began on the eve of Robert's departure. A Muslim notable from Castrogiovanni named Ibrahim had entered into a pact with Serlo, Robert and Roger's nephew (and the rising star in Norman Sicily), and pretended to befriend the young man. Ibrahim then lured him to a prearranged location where a group of his men set upon him and killed him. His body, Malaterra tells us, was mutilated and his head publicly displayed in Castrogiovanni, where it was announced that, with the death of this man, "Sicily could henceforth rest more easily."[22] He also states that Ibrahim sent the heads of Serlo's men to "the king in Africa," that is, the Zirid amir in Tunisia, who was still involving himself in thwarting the Normans. In 1074 Zirid ships raided Calabria; in the following year they landed at Mazara and took back the city, putting the citadel within under siege. A week or so later Roger arrived with a relieving force that trapped the Zirid troops inside the city, with heavy casualties resulting.

There were still other ways to sting the Normans, however. Late in 1075 Ibn al-Ward, the amir of Syracuse, struck at Catania, where Roger had left his second-in-command and son-in-law, Hugh de Gercé. Ibn al-Ward used a favorite ruse, sending a small force to draw Hugh's troops from the city, stretching them out in pursuit until they found themselves in an ambush. Many Normans were killed, including Hugh. Ibn al-Ward returned in triumph to Syracuse with the spoils.

This coup was sufficiently startling that Roger rushed back to Sicily from the mainland, slashing and burning crops wherever he went (it was threshing season) and precipitating a general famine as a result. In 1077 his armies took the port of Trapani. In 1079 Taormina was threatened by sea and land, and Roger's fleet convinced a Zirid fleet that arrived to back down, meaning that Syracuse was the only major port left in Muslim hands. Muslim (and Norman) revolts kept Roger from capitalizing on these successes, but he returned to the field in 1085, in the wake of a treaty that sealed Sicily's fate: the Normans had made peace with the Zirids, ending any Muslim hope of external aid. Syracuse was the logical first target. It was taken in the autumn, after a four-month combined siege, during which Ibn al-Ward was killed in a naval skirmish with Roger's fleet. Next came Agrigento in 1087, and finally, the town where it all began, in a way, Castrogiovanni, whose lord surrendered the city when Roger captured his wife and children and held them hostage.

After the surrender of Castrogiovanni, one can almost feel the winding down of Norman energy in the chronicles themselves. By the spring of 1089 Roger was positioning siege engines around Butera in the southeast, the one Muslim zone left unconquered. But he was briefly distracted from his task by a visit to Sicily from the new pope, Urban II, the future architect of the First Crusade to Jerusalem. He was, in any case, back in time to see the city fall, and Butera's leaders, like many other captured Sicilian Muslims, were resettled in Calabria. Sicily's last holdout, the tiny town of Noto on the island's southeastern tip, surrendered of its own accord in 1090. The town's notables crossed all the way to Calabria to submit to Roger and spare him the trouble of a siege. He sent his son back with them to sort out all the details. The final years of the Sicilian conquest also saw desultory Frankish naval campaigns in the islands nearby. In 1087 a joint Pisan and Genoese fleet, buoyed, perhaps, by papal goodwill, sacked and burned the Zirid capital of al-Mahdiya on the Tunisian coast (which recovered soon enough), as well as the island of Pantelleria. In 1090 Roger himself oversaw the surrender of the Muslim island of Malta, an afterthought with its own consequences for the history of the later Crusades.

The fall of Sicily in 1090 marked the permanent end of Muslim rule over the island. It was the first Muslim province to be lost in its entirety to Frankish armies, and the new Norman county of Sicily was the first of the "Frankish states" to be gouged out of Islamdom. It was certainly the most strategically important Muslim zone ever to be absorbed into Christendom. From Sicily Latin ships could and did engage in further menace on the shores of North Africa and Spain, the islands of the Mediterranean, the Byzantine Empire, and the coasts of Syria and Palestine. Even now, on the basis of the brute mathematics of the situation, its loss is difficult to explain. The Normans were both distracted (by campaigns in Italy) and outnumbered: the sources suggest no more than a thousand knights and equal numbers of infantry in the field at any one time. And while it is not clear how badly the Normans were outnumbered, it does seem likely that Muslim forces were rather larger and better armed.

On the other hand, the Normans had at least two advantages. The first was that they began their conquest from the northeast of the island, where the Greek Christian population was most heavily concentrated. Despite prevailing tensions between Greeks and Latins throughout the Mediterranean, the Greeks of Sicily seemed—with some important exceptions—to welcome the Normans, making these lands easier for them to hold. Indeed as the conquests progressed, the Normans could also draw upon the subject population, Christian and Muslim, as a source of manpower for their troops.

The second advantage was that the Normans had Ibn al-Thumna on their side, and eastern Sicily was his turf. He ably served as a guide and ally against the earliest Muslim counterattacks by Ibn al-Hawwas and the Zirids. Other factors could also be adduced. Despite the tenacity of home-grown Sicilian resistance (acknowledged by all the sources), the ill discipline and poor soldiering of the Zirid troops from North Africa was something of an embarrassment. Sicilian resentment toward Zird attempts to "assist" them cannot have helped their cause either. And for all the distraction it posed, close connections to Italy did at least mean that the Normans had the weight of their kin and allies always behind them, while Sicily's Muslims slowly found themselves ever more cut off from the broader support of Islamdom. Most of Sicily's Muslims remained on the island under Norman rule, but many fled throughout the thirty years of fighting. Sicilian refugees are attested throughout the Muslim Mediterranean, in North Africa, Egypt, Syria, and even Spain, where many found a new situation tragically similar to the one they had thought they had escaped. There too the tide had turned.

The Thirst for al-Andalus

Long before things fell apart in Sicily and other Fatimid lands, caliphal unity had also disintegrated in al-Andalus, the domain of the Fatimids' old rivals, the Umayyad caliphs of Córdoba. By the end of the first decade of the eleventh century, civil war was in full swing in al-Andalus. The details of the various campaigns, coups, and countercoups that dominated Umayyad politics until 1031 need not detain us. Suffice it to say that, where once a single Umayyad caliph in Córdoba had fairly dominated political life and exerted regular pressure on the petty Christian kingdoms of the north, now the Umayyads of Córdoba were but one—and often the least—of many rival foci of power around which swirled overanxious courtiers, ambitious generals, and factions from the Berber army, all jockeying for a piece of the action. In 1031 Hisham III, the last Umayyad to call himself caliph, was expelled from Córdoba; he died in exile a few years later, and with him died his dynasty's future.[23]

In the absence of the political unity provided by the Umayyad caliphs of Córdoba, there emerged a number of smaller successor states, usually centered, as in Ibn al-Thumna's Sicily, on one or two cities and their lands. In Arabic the ruling household of such a regional kingdom is called a *ta'ifa*, a "faction" or "party," whence these rulers are sometimes called "party kings" or, in Europeanized form, "taifa kings." The history of the taifa kingdoms of al-Andalus immediately after 1031 is bewilderingly complex, since many such states were ephemeral and their borders shifting. A detailed history of all the taifas in their variety is not central to our concern here.[24] Out of all the early confusion, there emerged a handful of larger, stable, and mutually suspicious Muslim kingdoms. In the south these were Seville and Granada; Badajoz in the west; Valencia in the east, not to mention the Balearic Islands off the coast; Zaragoza in the northeast abutted the Christian kingdoms in the foothills of the Pyrenees; Toledo stood in the center of them all (Map 4).

Such a fragmented political situation in al-Andalus, with all its attendant conflicts, was surely bad for the life expectancy of Andalusi kings. But, as in Renaissance Italy, it was very good for high culture. The taifa kingdoms attracted a steady stream of poets, musicians, craftsmen, philosophers, theologians, and men of science, as rival rulers competed for the luster that such cultural production added to their courts. The Cordoban theologian, jurist, philosopher, and man of letters Ibn Hazm is probably the best-known representative of the high culture of the taifa kingdoms. Famously sharp-tongued, a die-hard (if nostalgic) Umayyad loyalist, and a man of prodigious learning, he is said to have composed some four hundred works, of which a few dozen survive, among them his most famous, the *Ring of the Dove*, a vivid and intricate treatise on the art of love written during the last days of Umayyad al-Andalus.[25]

Another example of the sort of itinerant polymaths who flourished in this setting—and the dismissive attitude of the cultural elite to the

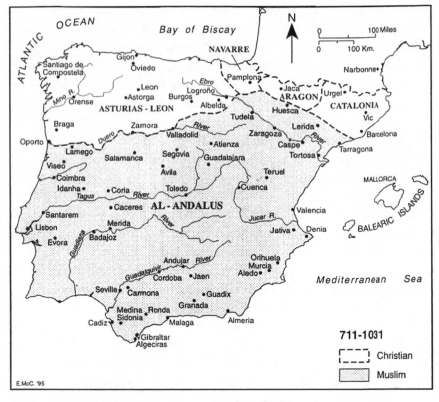

Map showing al-Andalus with the following labels:

ATLANTIC OCEAN
Bay of Biscay
N
0 100 Miles
0 100 Km.
NAVARRE
Narbonne
Santiago de Compostela
Gijon
Oviedo
Pamplona
Jaca
Urgel
ARAGON
CATALONIA
Leon
Logroño
Astorga
Burgos
Ebro
Albelda
Huesca
Vic
ASTURIAS - LEON
Braga
Zamora
River
Tudela
Lerida
Barcelona
Oporto
Valladolid
Zaragoza
River
Lamego
Atienza
Caspe
Tarragona
Salamanca
Segovia
Guadalajara
Tortosa
Viseo
Avila
Coimbra
Teruel
MALLORCA
Idanha
Coria
Toledo
Cuenca
Tagus
River
Caceres
AL - ANDALUS
Valencia
BALEARIC ISLANDS
Santarem
Merida
River
Jucar R.
Lisbon
Jativa
Denia
Badajoz
Evora
Guadiana
Andujar
River
Orihuela
Guadalquivir
Murcia
Cordoba
Jaen
Aledo
Mediterranean Sea
Seville
Carmona
Guadix
Medina Sidonia
Ronda
Granada
Cadiz
Malaga
Almeria
Gibraltar
Algeciras

711-1031
Christian
Muslim

E.McC. '95

Map 4 Medieval al-Andalus. From O. R. Constable, ed., *Medieval Iberia: Readings from Muslim, Christian, and Jewish Sources*, 2nd ed. (Philadelphia: University of Pennsylvania Press, 2012), 32, map 1.

threats that loomed—is provided by Saʻid al-Andalusi.[26] Born in Almería in 1029 to a prominent family, he was a philologist, historian, natural philosopher, and Muslim judge (*qadi*). His father later became a high-ranking official in Córdoba, where Saʻid received the beginnings of his education. As a teenager he toured al-Andalus in pursuit of learning and eventually settled in Toledo at the jaded age of seventeen. At Toledo the local ruler had made his court a destination for intellectuals, including jurists, religious scholars, mathematicians, astronomers, geometers, physicians, and litterateurs. While there Saʻid composed works in a number of fields, including astronomy, history, and comparative religion.

Shortly before his death, in 1070, he wrote a svelte treatise with the modest aim of surveying and categorizing the entirety of all human knowledge (a fairly common genre in Arabic literature, in fact; Ibn Hazm too found time to churn one out). Called the *Book of the Categories of Nations*, it provides an overview of the intellectual world that people like Saʿid inhabited, its debt to antiquity, and the broad range of the pursuits of his contemporaries. It even includes, for the sake of completeness, a chapter devoted to those nations that have *no* interest in learning. Given the climatic interpretation of culture that was in vogue, it is no surprise to find him consigning most European and African peoples to darkness and ignorance due to their distance from the temperate climes. Yet the unlettered Berbers and Spanish Christians ("Galicians," as he calls them) pose a problem, given their closeness to the civilized clime of al-Andalus. For Saʿid, these are nations for which, despite their location, God has gone the extra yard and has especially inflicted with "despotism, ignorance, enmity, and violence."

What Saʿid could not have known is that these very two groups—Spanish Christians and Berbers—would transform Toledo and all the rest of his beloved al-Andalus in the decades after his death. Just as the fractured political scene in al-Andalus allowed ambitious poets and scholars to play off the rivalries of competing royal patrons to their own benefit, so too did it provide a crucial opening for the taifa states' Christian enemies and a new relationship between the Muslim South and the Christian North, a relationship that would bear terrible fruit for al-Andalus. For over the course of the eleventh century, it became common practice for taifa rulers to secure military assistance from Christian kings in return for tribute paid in ever more ruinous amounts of cash or land or plunder, including slaves drawn from the Muslim subjects of their rivals. It was, as one modern historian put it, "no more and no less than a protection racket."[27] With easy Muslim gold underwriting Christian expansion onto Muslim lands worked by Muslim slaves, the Christian kings of the North and their dependents found themselves hooked. They competed with one another for the tributes of the richest kingdoms and recklessly squeezed their charges with threats and punitive raids. Perceptive Muslim contemporaries were outraged at the trend, among them Ibn Hazm, who lambasted his rulers, calling them tyrants: "By God, I swear that if the tyrants were to learn that they would attain their ends more easily by adopting the religion of the Cross, they would certainly hasten to profess it! Indeed, we see that they ask the Christians for help and allow them to take away Muslim men, women and children as captives to their lands. Frequently they protect them in their attacks against the most inviolable land, and ally with them in order to gain security."[28] But the outrage fell, for the moment, on deaf ears. Tributary relationships were codependent relationships, allowing Muslim rulers to hold at bay their rivals in the dog-eat-dog world of taifa politics yet dragging the Christian kingdoms of the North ever deeper into the concerns of al-Andalus and fueling their interest in the ripe and weakened taifa states. According to another Muslim contemporary, it was at this time that "the Christians' thirst for al-Andalus became quite evident."[29]

Of the kings of the North, Fernando I of León-Castile was one of the thirstiest. In 1043, for example, he helped to restore to power al-Ma'mun, the Muslim ruler of Toledo, who had been ousted by a rival, in return for annual tribute. When the tribute was not forthcoming, Fernando accordingly raided the countryside of the kingdom and put two of its towns under siege. Eventually the payments resumed. While he was at it (ca. 1060), he captured castles in the neighboring state of Zaragoza and forced tribute from them. Badajoz and Seville were obliged to be generous too. Fernando especially picked on Badajoz, seizing little towns like Lamego (in 1057), Viseu (in 1058), Coimbra (in 1064), and Coria (1065). He died in 1066 on campaign against the Muslim king of Valencia.

Just as the cultural efflorescence of the taifa period produced men like Ibn Hazm and Sa'id al-Andalusi, the political fluidity of the period had its representative figures too. Foremost among these is Rodrigo Díaz de Vivar, better known as El Cid. Born into a line of Castilian minor officials, Rodrigo served his king, Sancho II, and his somewhat suspect successor, Alfonso VI, as an official, a diplomat, and a highly successful general. However, he fell out of favor with his new lord and, after 1080, was forced into exile. His skills were valuable, so he sought service from a logical quarter: the Muslim king of Zaragoza, whom he served (along with his successor) for five years, capturing the count of Barcelona at one point and defeating the king of Aragon. In the 1090s we find him again in the field—astride a horse from Seville and wielding a blade from Córdoba, if the epics are to be believed—this time fighting on behalf of his once-estranged lord, Alfonso VI, but ultimately carving out his own independent principality, a personal taifa kingdom, around the city of Valencia, where he died in 1099.

A similar freelancing career path can be discerned in the community of Christians living under Muslim rule. From this other side of the confessional divide in al-Andalus came Sisnando Davídiz, a less-storied contemporary of El Cid. Sisnando was born near Coimbra but was captured in Córdoba by the Muslim king of Seville, who employed him as an administrator and diplomat. He later left Seville and entered the service of Fernando I of León and played an active role in the king's many campaigns against the Muslims of the southwest. Unlike

El Cid, he served Fernando I's son, Alfonso VI, quite dutifully, participating in campaigns against Granada and his former home of Seville,
and was richly rewarded by his lord from his newly conquered lands.
He died in 1091, after nearly two decades as the semi-independent
ruler of Coimbra.[30]

The fact that El Cid's and Sisnando's meandering paths would
eventually cross in the palace of Alfonso VI is not an accident. Of all of
Fernando I's sons and heirs, Alfonso was the leading figure. He eventually came to rule the entirety of his father's realm, including the expec-
tations of tribute attached to it, and continued his father's relentless
pressure on the taifa kingdoms. As a result his realm was a suitable
destination for culturally fluent warriors like these two. Alfonso's successes and those of his peers were attractive to other sorts too, and in
their campaigns against their Muslim neighbors Spanish ruling elites
found themselves inadvertently assisted by Frankish warriors and
churchmen who, drawn by news of the wealth and pious virtue to be
won in Spain, now streamed across the Pyrenees, bringing with them
radical new ideas about the power of the Church and the benefits of
Christian holy war.

Nay, We Do Still More

In the three decades during which Robert Guiscard and his brother
Roger slowly but decisively conquered and settled Muslim Sicily,
Spanish lords and their knights began a piecemeal conquest of much
of al-Andalus.[31] That they were able to do so owes much to the
game-changing presence of Frankish (some of them Norman) clergy
and warriors, newly arrived in Spain to take advantage of the boom
times that these successes were creating. This was not an entirely new
development. The Frankish inhabitants of the lands north of the
Pyrenees had made their presence felt in Spain in numerous ways over
the course of the eleventh century—through pilgrimages to Santiago
de Compostela, through ties of marriage between the ruling houses of
northern Spain and those of France, and through the mobility of
Frankish monks, who were making their particular presence felt in
Spain at this time. Their growing influence in Spain surely encouraged
Spanish monks to study in French monasteries and French monks to
settle in Spain.

These trends came to a head in 1064, the catalyst being the ambitions of Ramiro I, "king" of Aragon, at the time a tiny kingdom locked

in the valleys of the Pyrenees and hemmed in by the Muslim kingdom of Zaragoza. Ramiro had a bigger image of himself than his little kingdom would allow. He had succeeded in marrying the daughter of a French count and even marrying off two of his daughters to sons of the powerful counts of Toulouse and Provence. He also had quixotic aspirations concerning Zaragoza and its Muslim king, al-Muqtadir of the Hudid dynasty. Despite his neighbor's reputed power, Ramiro managed to capture a few Zaragozan castles in the 1050s, and then, in 1063, he attacked the city of Graus. Al-Muqtadir needed to show he could defend himself. He thus contacted King Fernando I of León-Castile, who was regularly receiving tribute from him, and urged him to hold up his end of the bargain. Fernando could hardly allow Ramiro to threaten his golden goose in this way, so he sent an army—including his general, El Cid—to assist the troops of al-Muqtadir to relieve the siege of Graus. They defeated Ramiro's small army and killed him.

A few months after Ramiro's death, Frankish troops under Count Thibaut of Châlon joined men from Aquitaine as well as Catalans and Normans and crossed the Pyrenees in order to assist Ramiro's son and heir in Aragon, Sancho Ramírez. They demanded that al-Muqatadir of Zaragoza face punishment. The coalition chose as their target the Zaragozan city of Barbastro, halfway between Huesca and Lleida. Their adventure was eased somewhat by Pope Alexander II, who in 1063 issued a papal bull promising (it seems) a commutation of penance for those knights who went to fight in Spain. Thus knights who once might have had to atone for their sins by retiring to a monastery, undertaking an arduous pilgrimage, or other penitential devotions, could now absolve themselves by fighting Muslims in the ripe lands of al-Andalus. This may be only proof of papal appreciation for Christian efforts in Spain, but the fact that a Muslim chronicler describes one of the leaders at Barbastro as the "commander of the cavalry of Rome" suggests a deeper papal sanction to the campaign.[32]

Unable to take the city immediately by force, the Christians besieged it for a month or so. Al-Muqtadir's family, locked in a power struggle of their own, simply left the citizens and the local garrison to deal with the siege. With the city's water supply blocked off, the inhabitants eventually surrendered, as was traditional, on condition that their lives and property be spared in return for large amounts of cash and slaves.

But the citizens of Barbastro had misunderstood their enemies. This was no tribute-squeezing mission like the old days. This was Christian holy war. And now, at Barbastro, all heaven had broken loose. The

Christians happily accepted the cash and slaves, granting the terms of the surrender. But then they immediately broke them, massacring the citizenry, carrying others off into slavery, and plundering the city at liberty. Explaining the unusual bloodiness, Ibn Hayyan, a contemporary of these events, wrote that the Christian king (presumably Sancho) grew fearful of the large numbers of conquered Muslims before him and the implications of these hostile crowds should Muslim troops in the area come to their aid. "He therefore decided on exterminating them all, if he could, and ordered a general slaughter, which lasted until upwards of six thousand Muslims fell by the swords of the Christians." Eventually he called a halt and allowed those who remained to flee. In the mad rush to get to the gates of the city, many were trampled. Some of the citizens hid themselves until an amnesty was called, allowing everyone to return to their homes. But after they left their hiding places, the amnesty was revoked, and thus many of the civilians were seized as captives and enslaved. Some of the Muslim slaves taken at Barbastro were hauled away to France when the troops withdrew; some were sent as far away, it seems, as Constantinople. Of the rape, plunder, and similar excesses on the part of the Christians, Ibn Hayyan spares his readers, claiming, "There is no pen eloquent enough to describe them."[33]

The brutality of the siege and its aftermath deeply shocked contemporaries in Spain. Ibn Hayyan provides an exemplary anecdote that, while undoubtedly fictional, provides some insight into how Muslims understood the roots of this new Frankish brutality and the psychology of barbarian revenge. A Jewish merchant is sent into Barbastro after the siege to negotiate the ransom of a prominent citizen's daughter. The girl had been taken captive by one of the Christian lords who now occupied her father's house and who had made her one of his serving girls. The setting suggests she has also been forced into concubinage. When the merchant arrives at the man's home, the Christian makes a great show of demonstrating to him his wealth from the plunder of the city, making the point that there is nothing the merchant can offer him that will tempt him to part with his captive. Indeed the Christian pointedly refuses to yield her to him even for a suitable ransom, for, he gloats, he intends "to keep her in my service, as the people of her nation were wont to do with our women, whenever they fell into their hands, at the time when they were all-powerful in this country. Now that the scales are turned, and that we have the superiority over them, we do as they did; nay, we do still more."

For all its violence and outrage, the conquest of Barbastro—a little town, after all—had little impact in the short term. In its immediate wake, al-Muqtadir of Zaragoza oversaw a jihad appeal that stirred volunteers from the frontier kingdoms and even moved his rivals to send aid. This allowed him to quickly reconquer the town a few months later, once many of the foreign fighters had gone home. He limited himself to the conventional brutality attendant upon reconquest, slaughtering the garrison and enslaving the captives that came his way. In this way, Ibn Hayyan unblinkingly tells us, the city "was purified of the filth of idolatry and cleansed of the stains of infidelity and polytheism."

The Fraying at Toledo

In the long term the Barbastro campaign was significant for two reasons. The first was that it led the papacy to become more involved in Spanish affairs than ever before and to bring the Christian North more firmly into the Latin mainstream of the Franks. The second was that it sent thousands of plunder-laden Franks back home with tales of the treasure and pious heroism to be won in Spain, which would encourage further conquests at the expense of Muslim al-Andalus. More immediately Barbastro whet local Spanish appetites, spurring a change in priorities among the Christian kings of the North, from seeking tribute to seeking outright conquest. It is in this transition from tribute seeking to conquest that al-Qadir, ruler of the taifa of Toledo, and King Alfonso VI of León-Castile and Galicia, nicknamed El Bravo ("the Valiant") and self-styled "Emperor of All Spain," fatefully met.[34]

The city of Toledo, once the capital of the pre-Islamic Visigothic kingdom, was a major taifa kingdom now and in full flourish, thanks to a sequence of strong rulers from the Dhu al-Nun family, most recently the prince al-Ma'mun. Al-Ma'mun patronized many scholars and made Toledo a home for them, among them the aforementioned Sa'id al-Andalusi. At its height the kingdom of Toledo had conquered the neighboring taifa of Valencia and absorbed it, and also briefly controlled the old Umayyad capital of Córdoba. But by 1075 Toledo's glories were fading. Al-Ma'mun died and was succeeded by his weak and embattled grandson, al-Qadir, who promptly lost Córdoba and, by purging from his court certain popular figures among his grandfather's men, alienated the local notables and his subjects in Toledo, who revolted. The court and the city sank into anarchy. Valencia fell from al-Qadir's grip as the governor there declared his independence. Besieged by enemies at home and surrounded by hostile taifas abroad, al-Qadir fled to Cuenca in 1079. In his wake the Toledans invited the ruler of Badajoz to take his place. Al-Qadir then appealed to Alfonso VI for assistance.

Alfonso had long been involved in tribute-harvesting in the Muslim South, raiding as far south as Tarifa near the Straits of Gibraltar, making clear that he could range throughout the peninsula with impunity. And Toledo had long seen Alfonso as a grudging ally. In 1072, for example, al-Ma'mun offered Alfonso refuge (or perhaps house arrest) at Toledo when he was briefly exiled from his own kingdom during a power struggle with his brother. According to one source, this visit gave Alfonso ample time to study Toledo's defenses. Following a familiar pattern, it was with the aid of Castilian troops that al-Ma'mun was able to capture Córdoba in 1075. In this context Alfonso was only too happy to answer al-Qadir's appeal for help and to return this desperate and dependent ruler to his throne. In the end, though, al-Qadir, adopting a realist stance for once, realized the futility of his designs and signed a treaty with Alfonso to cede control of Toledo to him, provided he would place him in control of Valencia as compensation. The deal was done—on paper. In Toledo, however, there were other thoughts on the matter, and the city resisted its new master. Alfonso was obliged to besiege the city in the autumn of 1084, a long, uncomfortable, but well-supplied siege, thanks to the supplies sent to him by his other tributary taifas in the south. Finally, in May 1085, Toledo surrendered, its lord a Christian king now triumphant in the palace where he had once sought refuge, its main mosque soon (albeit against Alfonso's will) to be converted into a cathedral.

Despite the relatively peaceful surrender of the city and the generous terms granted to its citizens, the fall of Toledo sent shockwaves throughout the Muslim world. This was no frontier port like Palermo in Sicily, but a major kingdom located in the very heart of al-Andalus and the greatest city that the Christians had yet conquered from the Muslims anywhere. Strategically speaking, it meant that al-Andalus was effectively doomed unless Alfonso's conquests could be rolled back. Christian control of Toledo meant that Christian settlement could expand south to the Tagus River valley and that Christian troops could raid unimpeded almost anywhere in the remaining Muslim territories, which clung to its eastern and southern borders.

The very structure of al-Andalus, welded together over the centuries since the first Muslim conquests, was disintegrating. A poet of the day captured the sense of urgency and gloom: "People of Andalus! Urge onward your mounts, for you may stay there only by mistake.

Clothing frays from the edges, but I see the garment of the peninsula coming apart at its center."[35] Such a turn of events demanded a response from the remaining taifa kingdoms. As we shall see in the next chapter, the response of the Muslim kings of al-Andalus came, and came quickly, borne by Moroccan ships.

The Franks Look East

Sicily and al-Andalus were just the beginning. In 1096, just a few years after the conquest of Sicily and the fall of Toledo, Frankish armies, with the assistance of Byzantine Greeks, arrived on the shores of Anatolia, what is now modern Turkey, the first steps at the Frankish invasion of the Islamic Near East. Yet in crossing from the mighty Byzantine capital of Constantinople to the Asian side of the Bosporos Straits, these Franks were entering a stateless zone, the Near East's Wild West, not, as is sometimes supposed, a courtly center of Turkish Islam.

The Franks who invaded Anatolia thus encountered a frontier society utterly unlike any they had encountered in Sicily or al-Andalus, with their distinct city-states and opulent taifa kingdoms. Anatolia was home to Islam's most ancient and most famed frontier with the Christian world, which, to most Muslims, was embodied not by the petty rulers of western Europe but by the "east Roman" or Byzantine Empire of the Greeks. During the seventh century, as most of Byzantium's holdings in the Near East and North Africa were conquered by Muslim armies, Anatolia became a refuge and heartland for the empire; even Muslims recognized Anatolia as the Roman territory par excellence, referring to it consistently as Bilad al-Rum ("the Land of the Romans"), or simply Rum. Yet as time wore on, this refuge became a buffer zone caught between the imperial designs of the caliphate and the empire, back and forth over the centuries since the rise of Islam. To conquer, finally conquer Byzantium became a deeply held desideratum for many of Islamdom's jihad-focused warrior and religious elites.[36]

Over the second quarter of the eleventh century, however, Turcoman tribesmen had migrated into Iran, Iraq, and eastern Anatolia as part of a larger migration of Turkish-speaking peoples from Central Asia. The most notable group among them was the family of chieftains from the Oghuz Turkish people known as the Saljuqs. The Oghuz Turks had had long exposure to Islamic civilization as members of the armies of numerous Muslim principalities in eastern Iran. By the time they entered Iraq, the Oghuz (the Saljuq family included) were relatively firm adherents of the faith, and they were also, in theory, Sunni Muslims. This gave the Saljuqs a special interest in the plight of the 'Abbasid caliphs, whom they felt were under threat from a Shi'i dynasty, the Buyids, who dominated Iraq at the time. By 1055 the Saljuqs had swept across Iran and ousted the Buyids from Baghdad. In return for these services to the caliphate and to Sunni Islam, the caliph confirmed the Saljuq chieftain as sultan, a title that conferred upon him the control of all the affairs of state, particularly its military matters. In effect the 'Abbasid caliphs had merely changed jailers, and the Saljuq sultans (conventionally known as the "Great Saljuqs" to distinguish them from other branches) and their Turkish troops settled comfortably into the positions created for them, as effective rulers of the Islamic world from Iraq to Central Asia.

Other bands of Turcoman nomads who accompanied the Saljuqs into Iraq had preceded them into northern Iraq, Armenia, and eastern Anatolia—the lands of Rum—where, taking immediately to the role of *ghazi*, or frontier fighter, that had been constructed by generations of Muslim warriors, they began living off the land, raiding settlements, rustling livestock, grazing their own herds, and occasionally serving as mercenaries in the service of the Byzantine Empire. These were not exactly Saljuq-sanctioned activities, and the sultans, who depended upon Turcoman muscle, occasionally felt the need to bring these nomads to heel. In Anatolia these ambient activities were punctuated by occasional large-scale campaigns, increasing pressure upon the Byzantine Empire throughout the century.[37] In 1071 the most celebrated Turkish victory occurred near Manzikert in Armenia. Among the many humiliations was the fact that the Byzantine emperor himself, Romanos IV Diogenes, had been captured and held for ransom, though the new sultan, Alp Arslan, soon released him. And still the pressure continued: for the Turcomans, Anatolia was a raiding zone of pasture and plunder, a region not yet to be annexed.

The Greeks could hardy argue. The Byzantine Empire, which had become so identified with the lands of Anatolia, was now simply unable to administer them. Since the catastrophe at Manzikert, the empire had been crippled and its military capabilities shaken. Romanos IV's absence from Constantinople during his captivity had precipitated a series of coups, beginning with the accession of Prince Michael VII and ending with Emperor Alexios Komnenos. Alexios began his career as a very able general, famed for crushing uprisings in the Balkans and in Anatolia. Yet in 1081, even as Alexios was gathering an army to see to the threat posed by none other than that terror of the world, Robert Guiscard and his fellow Normans, a palace faction conspired to elevate him to the throne of Byzantium, the founder of a new dynasty, the Komnenids. In the meantime almost all of Anatolia had been lost.

Yet the Great Saljuq sultans could hardly claim the spoils either, and much of Anatolia remained a no-man's land. All of the early sultans had shown a keen interest in the region, and none more so than Alp Arslan and his son Malikshah. Both endeavored to command—often with Byzantine cooperation—the Turcoman tribes now living there. But this interest was short-lived, and none of these sultans was able to build upon the success of Manzikert. Anatolia was, after all, merely one frontier of their expanding empire, which stretched east to Iran and now included a busy and promising front in northern Syria, where Malikshah's brother, Tutush, was taking the lead after other Turcoman troubles there (as we will see in chapter 3). Moreover, after the death of the sultan Malikshah in 1092, the sultanate was itself rent by civil war, in which for three years Malikshah's son Barkyaruq defended his throne against all challengers. In this context the reach of the Great Saljuqs of Iran could hardly be expected to extend to Anatolia.

Already at home in Anatolia's frontier society, the Turcoman tribes there now thrived in this power vacuum. There were but two confederations who offered anything like a structure to organize their energies. The first of these was led by a renegade branch of the Saljuq family, which saw the tribes of Anatolia as their own key to achieve power. One of these Saljuq rulers (known, due to their Anatolian base, as the "Saljuqs of Rum") was Qilij Arslan, who had been a prisoner of his kinsmen in Iran. In 1092 he was released from confinement and fled back to Anatolia and his capital at Nicaea (Iznik). The Saljuqs of Rum made their power felt throughout central and southern Anatolia as far east as Iconium (Konya), but no farther.

To the northeast, beginning in the 1070s, another, more obscure confederation dominated the peninsula's northern roads, including the lands of Sivas, Tokat, and Amasya. These Turcomans were led by a man who bore the Persian title of *danishmend* ("wise man"), and so his polity may have its origins, as so many did on the frontier, in some kind of religious or spiritual movement among the tribesmen pursuing jihad. Between the Saljuqs of Rum and the Danishmendids, the interstices of Anatolia went unclaimed, and from them the Turcomans maintained relentless pressure on the Byzantine Empire.[38]

It was this "Turkish threat" in the east, combined with a "Norman threat" in the west and total instability in Constantinople that induced many of the Byzantine emperors after the disaster of Manzikert to seek military and political assistance from Frankish rulers, including the pope. And indeed Frankish contingents did come to the aid of the emperor to fight the Turks in Anatolia in the decades before the First Crusade. The most spectacular case of Frankish engagement with the Turks before the invasion of 1096 is certainly that of Roussel de Bailleul, a Norman adventurer who had fought in Sicily at the battle of Cerami with Roger but who later found employ as a mercenary under the Byzantine emperor Romanos IV. Although accused of treachery at Manzikert, Roussel was nevertheless kept on in imperial service and sent with a large force of Franks to fight Turks in the region of Galatia, which he did, in 1073. He then promptly set himself up as prince of his own Frankish principality, thinking, no doubt, of his kinsmen, who were doing much the same in Italy. Michael VII appealed to the Saljuqs to help oust him, but Roussel escaped and holed up in Amasya. There, in 1074, Alexios, still a general at the time, caught up with him and took him prisoner. In 1077, however, he was released after paying out a large ransom and was sent to lead troops against a rebel Byzantine general in Anatolia, with whom he characteristically allied himself, joining the rebellion. The emperor requested Saljuq aid against Roussel yet again, and they captured him at Nicomedia. He was sent to Constantinople, where he was executed. No doubt the body was carefully checked, just to be sure.

It was thus with some trepidation that in the summer of 1096 Alexios, now emperor, expected a group of Franks that was headed toward Constantinople as a result of a request he had sent in March 1095 to Pope Urban II at the Council of Piacenza. He was doubtless hoping for more than the usual body of Frankish mercenaries such as had passed through Constantinople before. (Roussel's statelet at Galatia, for example, had been built with some three thousand men; other bands were much smaller.) But what arrived was, to put it mildly, beyond what he could have imagined: a host of Latin Christians many tens of thousands strong, warriors and noncombatants, men and women, rich and poor, fired up by tireless preaching at the papal and popular levels, bound by oaths of devotion and fealty, all come on an armed pilgrimage to the aid of their Christian brothers in the east and to liberate Jerusalem from the hands of "the pagans" and, if wealth was unlikely to be gained, then perhaps a little glory. Later generations would call this movement the First Crusade.

Once he recovered from his astonishment, Alexios urged this first wave of Franks to abide a while in Constantinople, for he learned there were even larger and more organized armies of other Frankish lords still in the west. But the disorder caused by the new arrivals encamped near the capital was proving to be a liability. Alexios thus shipped them across the straits to an outpost at Kibotos (Frankish Civetot), where, supplied from the capital, they could await their compatriots. The Franks, having come more than a thousand miles to cut their way to Jerusalem, were thus left to bide their time at the tip of Anatolia. Nicaea, the capital of Qilij Arslan, sat a mere twenty-five miles to the west.

It fell to the leaders of the Franks to negotiate the issue of supplies in the capital; during one such absence, the idle soldiers left hanging around in Kibotos took matters into their own hands, sending groups foraging into the countryside, farther and farther to the east. A dangerous game of chicken soon commenced, with different regional contingents from among the Franks competing to see just how close they could safely forage in the shadow of Nicaea. The Germans won, but in doing so they lost big. A few miles from Nicaea, at Xerigordon, they captured a castle, sparing the Greeks there but putting everyone else to the sword. This immediately attracted the attention of Qilij Arslan, who sent Turkish troops from Nicaea to surround the place. Finding their initial siege uneventful, they set the castle afire and picked off the Germans as they fled; a few others they took as slaves, and then they returned to Nicaea.

About a week later, in October 1096, Qilij Arslan sent out a smaller scouting force to investigate the situation at Kibotos. They encountered more foragers, whom they killed. Having gained what intelligence he needed, Qilij Arslan then assembled a larger force and marched on Kibotos, apparently in person, to put an end to this Frankish nuisance. On the way they unexpectedly encountered the rest of the Frankish troops, who in the meantime had themselves decided to march on Nicaea to avenge the German debacle at Xerigordon and "to provoke...the rest of the Turks to war."[39] On a wide plain suited to their style of battle, the Turkish archers decimated the Frankish knights and pursued the rest, who fled all the way back to Kibotos, which the Turks plundered, taking many captives among the noncombatants whom the Frankish troops had left behind. The few Franks who survived fled to an abandoned fortress on the coast. The Turks were unable to take it before Byzantine ships arrived to rescue its occupants and ferry them back to Constantinople.

The sight of Byzantine ships ferrying the Franks back to Constantinople was surely proof to the Turks that the invaders had powerful friends, though it is unlikely Qilij Arslan needed the proof. He would have been well apprised of Byzantine connections to these Franks thanks to his fairly regular diplomatic contacts with Constantinople. Later sources note the formal, if troubled allegiance of the Franks to Alexios. Indeed a chronicler from Aleppo, al-'Azimi, even goes so far as to claim that, prior to their arrival, Alexios had "written to the Muslims to let them know about the coming of the Franks," though he does not specify which Muslims were so warned.[40] The sultan (for so the Saljuqs of Rum were now calling themselves) thus chose poorly when, instead of being on hand to annihilate what was surely a foreseeable new invasion of Franks, he left the area altogether to stake his claim to Malatya (Melitene), a town far to the east that he disputed with the Danishmendids. Beginning in April 1097, the Franks came, in greater numbers, with greater leaders and greater allies, and by June they were encamped before the walls of Nicaea. There were, according to modern estimates, seventy-five thousand of them, a prodigiously large force of combatants and noncombatants, not counting the Byzantine troops assembled nearby. Within a few days they had routed Qilij Arslan's army, captured his capital, and ceded it to the control of the Byzantine Empire.[41]

Thanks in large part to the absence of a settled Muslim court in Anatolia, there are no dynastic chronicles that relate the exploits of Qilij Arslan (or anyone else) against the Franks or that detail the progress of the Franks across Anatolia in the way that some Latin sources do. As Anatolia was, strictly speaking, a mostly Christian zone anyway, this leg of the Frankish invasion of the Near East attracted scant interest among Muslim historians, until the Franks entered the more solidly Muslim and sedentary zone of Syria. But the sources make clear that, after the loss of Nicaea, the Saljuqs of Rum were now on the defensive. Qilij Arslan withdrew with his troops to the east. At about this time news of this latest Frankish invasion of the lands of Islam began to have an effect far away in Damascus. "In this year [1097]," the Damascene chronicler Ibn al-Qalanisi tells us, "there began to arrive a succession of reports that the armies of the Franks had appeared from the direction of the sea of Constantinople with forces not to be reckoned for multitude." "As these reports followed one upon the other," he continued, "and spread from mouth to mouth far and wide, the people grew anxious and disturbed in mind."[42] Qilij Arslan, now pressing fast as he moved to the east, on the territory of his rivals, the Danishmendids, was able to convince the Turcoman tribes to settle their differences and appealed to the duty of jihad. Even his rival, the Danishmend, came to his aid.[43] The combined Turkish forces set about a massive scorched-earth campaign to thwart the progress of the Franks any farther to the east, burning fortresses, blocking up water sources, and ambushing them at seemingly every path they took. A great many died.

Yet the Franks seemed unstoppable. In July, at Dorylaeum, an abandoned Byzantine legionary camp several days' march east of Nicaea, Qilij Arslan pounced on the Franks, who had split up into two contingents to speed travel. The first Frankish contingent was able to hold firm for the better part of a day, until the rest of them arrived. The Turks were overwhelmed by these unexpected reinforcements: "When [Qilij Arslan] had thus killed a great number, they turned their forces against him, defeated him, and scattered his army, killing many and taking many captive.... The Turcomans, having lost most of their horses, took to flight. The king of the Romans bought a great many of those whom [the Franks] had enslaved, and had them transported to Constantinople."[44] The result was, for Qilij Arslan, a "shameful calamity to the cause of Islam, [and so] the anxiety of the people became acute and their fear and alarm increased."

At this point Qilij Arslan seems to have decided that letting the Franks pass through as quickly as possible would be the best thing for his lands, and he seems to have let them be. The Franks continued to the southeast, "capturing whatever they encountered...in the frontier-forts and mountain-passes."[45] The Christian sources confirm that at Eregli (Heraclea), in the southeastern part of Anatolia, the Franks split into two groups. The smaller group proceeded south through the pass known as the Cilician Gates into the fertile, open country of Cilicia, along modern Turkey's southern coast and abutting northern Syria. There they easily dislodged the Turkish garrison at Tarsus and Mamistra; the other, the main force, went north into Cappadocia to Kayseri (Caesarea) and thence through the Anti-Taurus Mountains to Mar'ash. Along the way, in both regions, isolated Turkish garrisons put up little resistance, and the Franks cultivated new ties with the local Armenian Christian population and, in some cases, installed governors on behalf of Alexios.

In Cilicia one of the leaders of the Franks, Baldwin of Boulogne, was approached by an Armenian warlord and ex-convict who urged him to seek his fortune by helping to capture Turkish-controlled towns farther to the east. Baldwin needed little persuasion. As the rest of the Franks headed south into Syria en route to their goal of Jerusalem, Baldwin gathered a company of a hundred or so knights and struck off into the borderlands of Anatolia and northern Syria, capturing the towns of Tell Bashir and Rawandan by the end of 1097. As the crusaders in Cappadocia had also noted, the simple terror that preceded the coming of the Franks seems to have been sufficient to convince many Turkish garrisons to surrender or abandon their holdings.[46] Baldwin's presence was certainly a boon for the Armenian warlords in the region. His progress caught the attention of T'oros, the Armenian ruler of the city of Edessa (Urfa), across the Euphrates. The Muslim sources do not describe how Edessa (or al-Ruha, as it was known in Arabic) fell to Baldwin, but the Armenian and Latin chroniclers are fairly clear. Held in suspicion by his subjects because of his close ties to Byzantium (whose Church considered Armenians to be heretics), and nearly surrounded by Turkish foes, T'oros hoped Baldwin might come east and "liberate" him too. And so he did, in early 1098. By March, however, the populace had turned against Baldwin's hated patron and killed him, elevating Baldwin to ruler of Edessa. In that capacity he simply purchased the fortress of nearby Sumaysat (Samosata) from its Turkish lord, making him his vassal, and established a Frankish garrison at Saruj at the invitation of its Turkish lord, Balak. In the process he created what has become known as the county of Edessa and the first of the more or less Frankish states created in the Islamic Near East.[47]

By this point panic was spreading through the Levant. It was as if the once unassailable and resolute borders of the Abode of Islam had collapsed all at once. By 1098 Sicily had been lost and what was left of al-Andalus was under siege. Frankish ships sailed the central and western Mediterranean with impunity. And now, despite their attempts, the Saljuqs of Rum and the Danishmendids, with their wild but fearsome Turcoman troops, had failed to prevent the Franks from crossing Anatolia. The collapse of the Rum frontier allowed Byzantium to extend east into Anatolia and gave Baldwin the opening to create a solid base in Edessa that threatened northern Mesopotamia and—who knew?—perhaps ultimately Iraq and Baghdad itself, the very heart of Islamdom. In the meantime the vast majority of the Franks had assembled before the walls of Antioch, at Syria's very doorstep. The fate of Ibn al-Thumna and his rivals on Sicily and of the fragmented taifa kingdoms of al-Andalus should have been warning enough that the prognosis for Syrian's divided elites was not good.

- 3 -

Prey for the Sword

THE FACT IS, for most Syrians at the time of the first Frankish conquests, Syria had already been invaded. In fact it had been invaded twice, by the same army: that of the Great Saljuqs. Saljuq control of Syria should have made a Frankish invasion unthinkable, but the manner of their arrival and governance actually helped the Franks more than it hindered them. Had the political events of the decades leading up to the Frankish invasion taken a different course, it is unlikely that the Franks would have ever made it to Jerusalem. As it was, however, by the time the Franks had cut their way across Anatolia and arrived in northern Syria, the political situation in Saljuq lands there had become so poisonous that a concerted response to the Franks was impossible. Seen from Syria, then, the road to Jerusalem in 1099 begins in Aleppo in 1064.

In that year rival claimants to the throne of a minor Arab dynasty known as the Mirdasids were each making their latest moves to seize power in the prize northern city of Aleppo, each with the tacit backing of the Fatimid dynasty of Egypt. The amir 'Atiyya, the incumbent, could not match his rival, his nephew Mahmud, in battle on his own. Yet he was rich, and he could at least seek some external assistance. So, to supplement his small army of Bedouin tribesmen, he made the decision to call in the aid of some other nomadic auxiliaries. These men were new to the Near East, but their reputation for military skill and ferocity preceded them: the Turks.

As it happened, ʿAtiyyaʾs call for Turkish assistance would have consequences for Syria analogous to Ibn al-Thumnaʾs overtures to the Normans of southern Italy or the Byzantine emperor Alexios I's call for Frankish assistance from the pope in 1095. All of these gestures opened the door to the migration of new peoples to the region, and all of their hosts got more from their guests than they had bargained for. By the time ʿAtiyya of Aleppo hired this contingent of Turcoman freelancers, the Saljuqs and the outlying satellites of Turcoman tribes who accompanied them had already, as we have seen, penetrated far into the frontier zone of Anatolia and tangled with the Byzantines. However, none had yet crossed into Syria or the settled lands of the Levant. ʿAtiyyaʾs cry for help changed this, opening up Syria and Palestine to a new political and military force. In the end they didn't even help ʿAtiyya, who, having dealt treacherously with his Turcoman saviors, soon found himself ousted by them and replaced. Now Mahmud, his hated nephew, ruled in Aleppo, and his new Turcoman allies roamed throughout much of northern Syria (Map 5).

The flood of Turcoman nomads and Saljuq troops that would follow upon these first advances would also upset the delicate balance of power between the Fatimids, the Byzantines, and smaller local amirates throughout Syria. For with the political situation in Aleppo so unstable and the Shiʿi Fatimids in the south never far from the action, it was inevitable that the Great Saljuqs themselves, based in Iran, would eventually come to Syria on the heels of the Turcoman tribes who preceded them. Still, the arrival of the Saljuqs in Syria was different from that of the Turcoman nomads who came before. This was not migration; it was conquest. And the sultans and the men who worked for them were not seeking pasturage or employment, like the men ʿAtiyya had hired, but provinces to add to their already considerable domains.

The threat of this massive—and ardently Sunni—new threat from the east did not go unnoticed among the Shiʿi elite of Fatimid Egypt and Syria. Yet bizarrely, according to one story, it was from Fatimid Cairo that the first invitation to the Saljuqs to enter Syria came.[1] A cunning amir and adventurer named Nasir al-Dawla, himself a relic of an old Bedouin dynasty, took note of the opportunity that the situation in Aleppo offered and the resulting indecision of the Fatimid court. He sent a messenger to the new Saljuq sultan, Alp Arslan, urging him to invade Egypt and overthrow the Shiʿi Fatimids. Much to everyone's alarm in Aleppo, Alp Arslan accepted the invitation. On January 19, 1071, the Saljuq army crossed the Euphrates, headed for Cairo by way of Aleppo and the rest of Syria. It was a crossing pregnant with meaning.

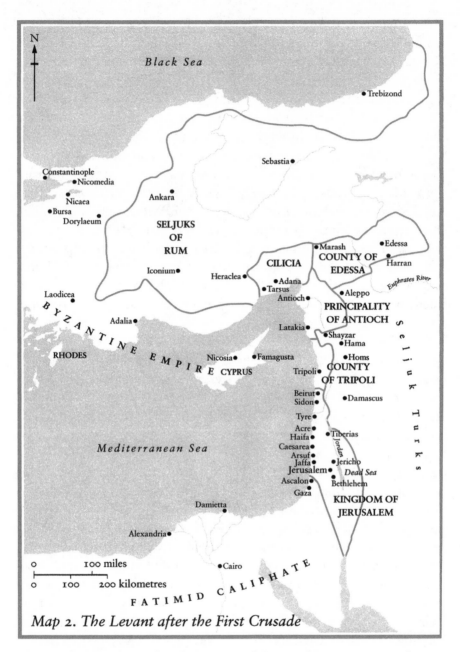

N

Black Sea

Trebizond

Constantinople
Nicomedia

Sebastia

Ankara

Nicaea
Bursa
Dorylaeum

**SELJUKS
OF
RUM**

Iconium

Marash ● Edessa

**COUNTY OF
EDESSA**
Harran

CILICIA

Heraclea ● Adana
Tarsus
Antioch ● Aleppo

Euphrates River

Laodicea

B Y Z A N T I N E

Adalia

Latakia

**PRINCIPALITY
OF ANTIOCH**

Shayzar
Hama

S e l j u k

RHODES

Nicosia ● Famagusta

E M P I R E   CYPRUS

Homs

Tripoli ● **COUNTY
OF TRIPOLI**

Beirut
Sidon ● Damascus

Tyre

Acre
Haifa ● Tiberias
Caesarea
Arsuf
Jaffa ● Jericho
Jerusalem ● *Dead Sea*
Ascalon ● Bethlehem
Gaza

T u r k s

Mediterranean Sea

Jordan

**KINGDOM OF
JERUSALEM**

Damietta

Alexandria

o   100 miles

o   100   200 kilometres

Cairo

F A T I M I D   C A L I P H A T E

Map 2. The Levant after the First Crusade

Map 5 The Near East after the coming of the Franks. From Usama ibn Munqidh, *The Book of Contemplation: Islam and the Crusades* (Harmondsworth, UK: Penguin Classics, 2008), map 2.

The messenger from Cairo accompanied the sultan and took the opportunity to place it in historical context.[2] After Alp Arslan crossed the Euphrates, "he encamped in some of the meadows along the river. He saw it to be pleasing and marveled at it. And so [the messenger] said to him: 'My lord! Give praise to God the Exalted for the grace he has given to you!' [Alp Arslan] replied: 'And what is this grace?' [The messenger] said: 'This river has never before been crossed by a Turk except those who were slaves. But you today have crossed it as a king.'" Later historians noted that the coming of the Saljuqs to northern Syria had ended the "reign [dawla] of the Arabs" and had initiated a new "reign of the Turks."

As for Mahmud in Aleppo, he did the most sensible thing when faced with the reality of the Saljuq threat: he changed sides. In 1070, with great public opposition in the city, Mahmud rejected the suzerainty of his Fatimid patrons and acknowledged instead the authority of the Saljuq sultan Alp Arslan and his overlord, the Sunni 'Abbasid caliph of Baghdad. Aleppo submitted to the sultan on May 5.[3] As it happened, the sultan never did make it to Egypt as he had intended. A few days after subduing Aleppo, he received word that the Byzantine emperor Romanos IV was leading an army in the field, marching east across Anatolia. The sultan assembled his men and headed north to Manzikert, where, as we have seen, he was obliged to entertain Romanos for some days.

The Saljuq Enterprise

After Manzikert the triumphant Alp Arslan returned to the East to march on an enemy in Central Asia. In 1072, during a quarrel in his camp, one of the prisoners who had been brought before him managed to kill him. Eventually Aleppo once again slid into civil war, and in 1078 a new Saljuq sultan, Malikshah, was obliged to send his brother Tutush with an army to reassert control in Syria. This time the Saljuqs brought more than just armies, instilling by their attitudes toward power and their approach to empire a distinctive new look to Syrian politics and society, as we shall see. Indeed Syria was only a small part of the bigger Saljuq picture. The long and sometimes tumultuous migration of the Oghuz Turks and the Saljuq clan across much of the Islamic world was the most important engine of change in Islamdom since the career of the Prophet Muhammad himself. Well before they were recognized as sultans in Baghdad, the Saljuqs had interacted with a variety of Muslim states and societies in Central Asia and Iran, and this shaped how they came to rule the territories they conquered. Everywhere they ruled, including the distant and disputed frontier province of Syria, the Saljuqs left their stamp, a recognizable assemblage of institutions and practices that mixed long-established 'Abbasid precedent with Saljuq innovation and provided models for virtually every Muslim state in the region that succeeded them.[4]

The Saljuq enterprise was essentially a family business. Although one member of the family was (usually) recognized as the paramount sultan, he was obliged to look after his kinsmen by ceding them control over their own territories, what modern historians usually term "appanages." The sultanate was therefore not a centralized empire of constituent provinces, as in classical Rome, but rather a heavily decentralized collection of private appanages controlled by various members of the family, from whom, like siblings at the dinner table, a given sultan could hope for only intermittent cooperation. These other ruling Saljuqs were usually given the title *malik*, "king," though modern historians tend to call them "princes." Moreover the office of sultan itself was considered family property, and so when a given sultan died or was overthrown, his brothers were within their customary rights to contest the appointed heir if a case could be made.

Such cases, it should be understood, were made with armies, led by commanders, called *amir*s. And, as the thirteenth-century Syrian chronicler Ibn al-Athir noted, himself fed up with the warring amirs of his own day, it is not at all certain that the Saljuq commanders of these earlier times minded the tendency of sultans and their kin to stay busy plotting against one another. "The sultanate," he tells us, "had become a prize for ambitious men and an office without authority, the rulers being the dominated after having been the dominators. This was something the great amirs preferred and were in favor of, so that their own sway, insubordination, and arrogance might continue."[5]

Despite superficial appearances, the Saljuq army was not one vast host of nomadic and intractable Turcoman horsemen (although they did predominate) but also contained some infantry and various auxiliaries: local nomadic groups, jihad volunteers, urban militias, and so on. A successful prince or commander—malik or amir—thus had to be more than a good strategist on the battlefield; he also had to be a good manager, able to juggle the various components of his army to maximum effectiveness. To further counteract the often discipline-averse Turcomans, the Saljuqs made a practice of recruiting personal military households, the *'askar*, or standing army, usually composed of free-born horsemen but more commonly of mamluk troops of slave origin. Like other Islamic states before them, the Saljuqs rewarded their military men with assignments of tax revenues tied to land (iqtaʿs). But the Saljuqs broadened the use of iqtaʿs and extended it throughout the sultanate, at all levels; the Saljuq family appanages were, in effect, massive examples of this practice, and equally massive sources of wealth and patronage. A Saljuq prince's household thus became by nature a hothouse of intrigues for competition for fat iqtaʿs and for advancement among the Saljuq warrior-elites.

The most successful amirs to emerge from this were acknowledged with elevated titles and lucrative responsibilities. Foremost among these was the office of *atabeg*, a Turkish title whose meaning, "Father-Lord," conveys something of the nature of the position, a combination in loco parentis of tutor, regent, and commander. An atabeg was ostensibly assigned to oversee the education and political training of a Saljuq prince, who might, after all, be one day ruling as sultan. However, an atabeg with ambition could, in the right context, easily overshadow his ward and seize power himself. And there were very few atabegs without ambition. Decentralized power, competitive amirs, ambitious atabegs, and liberal assignment of iqtaʿs: this was a volatile mix. So long as ties of recruitment, kinship, and patronage overlapped sufficiently, the system worked. But very occasionally, in crucial moments, it crashed.

The Saljuqs also reshaped the religious classes as much as they did the military, taking careful steps to ally themselves with key members of the ulema. Their distinctive approach to patronizing the Sunni ulema is usually depicted as part of a concerted "Sunni Revival," but that is something of an overstatement.[6] For one thing, it is often not at all clear from our sources who was really patronizing whom: the Saljuqs manipulating scholars' careers to highlight their own Islamic credentials, or the scholars playing needy elites off of one another to better feather their nests. Whatever the case, the active involvement of the sultans and other Saljuq elites in institutions of religious learning did contribute to a renewed commitment and active expression of Sunni Islam.

A symbol of this renewed commitment was the college of Islamic law, or *madrasa*, where Sunni law and theology were studied and elaborated by scholars and their students, and whose professorships and other posts provided a source of intense competition among the Sunni ulema. For Saljuq elites, endowing a new madrasa was seen as an act of selfless piety, and this certainly redounded to the Sunni credentials of the regime. But just as assignments of plum titles and iqtaʿs were used in the military sphere, new religious endowments like madrasas were also a tool for rewarding religious elites who complied with Saljuq religious attitudes and punishing those who did not. The result was a proliferation of such religious institutions over the centuries, their distinctive architecture becoming a standard feature of any city, and the works of law, theology, and mysticism composed and studied in them classics to this day, such as the idiosyncratic encyclopedia of Sunni thought known as the *Revival of the Religious Sciences*, by the twelfth-century master al-Ghazali, the leading Sunni theologian of his day.[7] Through tools such as these, the Saljuq sultans and their successor regimes slowly and inexorably made their mark, even in the vexing terrain of Syria.

The Legacy of Tutush

In Saljuq Syria, troubles with Bedouin and Turcomans were not just a problem confined to the north. In southern Syria, the zone of heaviest Fatimid influence, various Bedouin clans had been harassing town and country in Palestine and threatening Fatimid operations there. In response, and in keeping with what had by now become a leitmotiv of the eleventh century, the Fatimids hired barbarian outsiders to solve their Bedouin problem. In this case, in 1071 they appealed to a contingent of Turcoman troops led by a warlord named Atsiz, who, having immigrated into the Byzantine frontier zones of Anatolia, found them too crowded with rivals, and so considered the more distant Fatimid opportunities to be all the richer. Atsiz and his men were sorely disappointed, however, since by this late age Fatimid opulence was no longer what it had been. When the Fatimids were unable to pay him for the services he rendered for them in Palestine, he responded by occupying Jerusalem and much of southern Syria, not without some destruction at the hands of his unpaid and ill-disciplined fellow tribesmen. After various Fatimid-engineered attempts to dislodge him, Atsiz decamped to Damascus, which he had conquered in 1075. From there he led further raids into Palestine, returning to sack Jerusalem after its populace rebelled against him in 1078. He also menaced northern Syria and even Egypt.[8]

It was left to the Saljuqs and Tutush, the Saljuq commander in Syria, to confront Atsiz. Tutush, it should be understood, had been granted Syria *in its entirety* as an appanage by his brother the sultan, and he did not take kindly to some enterprising underling engaging with the

Fatimids and claiming lands that were not his. Perhaps Atsiz hoped he could cut a deal with Tutush. It's hard to say. At any rate the interview did not go well: after a brief meeting, Tutush had Atsiz killed and, his patience with indirect rule running thin, he installed his own man in Damascus. Nonetheless it took until July 1086, after a flurry of changes in amirs (and indeed of whole dynasties), for the city of Aleppo to surrender for the last time. Now almost all of Syria, miserable after two decades of civil war, imperial competition, and nomadic predation, found itself firmly under Saljuq control.

Just as the first Saljuq conquests had ended with the historic crossing by the sultan Alp Arslan to Syria—whose meadows had so pleased him and whose populace so riled him—so this second round was sealed, definitively, by the arrival of the sultan Malikshah before the walls of Aleppo in 1086. He stayed on in Aleppo for a few days, hunting wild game, and then proceeded to the mighty city of Antioch, which had recently been conquered from the Byzantine Greeks. There he visited the city's port of St. Simeon and prostrated himself in prayer, giving thanks to God that he should rule a kingdom that stretched from the eastern seas to the Mediterranean. In the major northern cities, Malikshah appointed new Saljuq governors and secured the region for the caliph in Baghdad, for Sunni Islam, and for the Great Saljuq sultans.[9]

This was the high-water mark for Saljuq power in Syria. After the death of Malikshah in 1092, the sultanate descended everywhere into civil war, and one of the major players was the dead sultan's brother, Tutush, who unsuccessfully tried to make his own bid for the Saljuq throne from Malikshah's son and heir, Barkiyaruq. When Tutush died in battle against Barkiyaruq in Iran in 1095, some of Tutush's armies melted back to Iraq and Syria as loyal servants of the new sultan. Nonetheless the sultans were never able to gain firm control of Syria. Indeed on the eve of the Frankish invasion of Syria, it was Tutush's legacy, not the sultan's, that lived on in Syria, where his sons Ridwan and Duqaq were made princes of Aleppo and Damascus, respectively. In Damascus, Duqaq was assisted by one of Tutush's inner circle, an old officer named Tughtakin, who was appointed atabeg. In Aleppo, Prince Ridwan too technically had an atabeg, but he was less of an influence—indeed he was often a foe.

The death of Malikshah after two decades of steady rule was only one crisis on the eve of the Frankish invasions. Within two years the Islamic Near East lost not just a firmly established Saljuq sultan but nearly all its political leadership, both Fatimid and Saljuq, clear across the map. Malikshah's death in 1092 had been preceded by the murder of Nizam al-Mulk, Malikshah's vizier and chief administrator, who had effectively held real authority over the sultanate. After Malikshah, other key members of his household died, in particular those who might have been expected to provide some sense of stability even as claimants to the succession struggled with one another. The year 1094 was equally grim, what one later Egyptian chronicler termed "the year of the death of caliphs and commanders."[10] That cheery sobriquet was well-earned, since in that year the 'Abbasid caliph al-Muqtadi himself died in Baghdad, the same year in which his Shi'i rival, the Fatimid caliph al-Mustansir, died after a remarkable fifty-eight years on the throne. The same year also saw the death of Badr al-Jamali, the mighty Fatimid military vizier who had done so much to restore order to Egypt and its provinces. It was as if the entire chessboard had been swept of all its pieces.[11]

Fortunately for Egypt, Badr al-Jamali had arranged for his capable son al-Afdal to succeed him in his office, and so, at this level of the administration at least, there was little trouble in Egypt. But crisis came to Egypt soon enough, thanks to al-Afdal's inexpert handling of the Fatimid succession. His actions would have important consequences for the history of the Near East under Frankish occupation, and beyond. When the Fatimid caliph al-Mustansir died, al-Afdal proclaimed the caliph's youngest son as his successor (which also meant he was the new Isma'ili imam), with the regnal title al-Musta'li. In doing so al-Afdal willfully overlooked the claims of the dead caliph's older son, Nizar. Many in the Fatimid capital and the broader Isma'ili community cried foul, but none so loudly as the overlooked Nizar, who fled to Alexandria and rebelled against this new upstart caliph/imam. Numerous dissenters in the far-flung Isma'ili community flocked to his cause.

Given the significance of the caliph/imam in Isma'ili Shi'ism, this dispute was not a mere succession squabble but genuine schism. When al-Afdal squashed the uprising in Alexandria and had Nizar murdered, Nizar's followers steadfastly continued in their refusal to recognize al-Musta'li and formed their own, new branch of Isma'ili Shi'ism. This new sect had its greatest success in Iran and Syria. Though led by a talented spiritual and political guide named Hasan-i Sabbah, the sect is known properly as the Nizaris, after their imam. To their enemies, Sunni and Shi'i, they were labeled either "Batinis," heretics whose leaders guarded access to the sect's secret, esoteric (*batin*) lore, or "Hashishiyun," ignorant rustics deluded into error due to a penchant for mind-addling hashish. This last bit of slander caught the eye of the Franks and has stayed on in the West, where Nizaris are still referred to even in otherwise respectable circles under the obnoxious label of "The Order of Assassins."[12] In medieval Syria these "Assassins" would, among other things, form a potent source of opposition to the Frankish and Muslim authorities alike.

Back in the crumbling empire of the Great Saljuqs, trouble did not end with the sultan Barkiyaruq's victory over Tutush in the civil war of 1095. Once on the throne, the young sultan was still beset by rivals and internal distractions, until his death in 1105. In Syria the failed gambit of Tutush during the civil war had had a deleterious impact upon the ties of service and loyalty that bound the various Saljuq amirs to one another. One of the reasons for Tutush's failure—and death in battle— was the fact that he failed to secure the loyalty of the amirs whom Malikshah had appointed with him as governors in Syria and Iraq. Having first made a show of supporting Tutush in the succession, these amirs balked and instead withdrew their support when it came to actually marching on his rival, the son of Malikshah. Tutush was therefore left abandoned and forced to march on his own subordinates in Syria before heading to Iran, distracted and embittered. Of the men who deserted Tutush's cause, however, there was one glaring exception: the amir Yaghi-Siyan, lord of Antioch, who, despite the fact that he had been a mamluk of Malikshah's, had become a favorite of Tutush, to the point that Yaghi-Siyan's daughter was married off to Tutush's son, Prince Ridwan of Aleppo. Indeed some sources claim that Tutush's excessive favoritism of Yaghi-Siyan was among the factors that pushed his other, jealous amirs to abandon his cause for that of his rival Barkiyaruq.[13] And yet, despite his patron's downfall, Yaghi-Siyan survived, even as his former comrades were executed or bided time in prison as rebels.

When a more or less general amnesty was proclaimed in 1095, many commanders, from both sides, returned to their posts, but bearing grudges. One of these was a certain Karbuqa, a loyalist of the sultan Barkiyaruq who had been captured and imprisoned by Tutush. After his release, Barkiyaruq reappointed him to Mosul, where he ruled with almost complete independence. There he now found himself a neighbor of none other than that oldest of old loyalists of Tutush, the man who had imprisoned him: Yaghi-Siyan of Antioch. The Frankish invasion would throw these two mutually spiteful men together with disastrous consequences.

These tensions among the governing cohort only exacerbated what had become a full-blown family dispute between the sons of Tutush,

Ridwan of Aleppo and his brother Duqaq in Damascus, as each hoped to gain preeminence in their father's old Syrian domains. This rivalry led to a curious episode in Ridwan's reign, perhaps the most egregious example of the sorts of temptations that encouraged political divisions within Syria. In an effort to bolster what dwindling support he possessed, Ridwan—the son of the very Saljuq commander who had been sent to wrest Syria from the Fatimids—received a messenger from the Fatimid caliph al-Musta'li, inviting him to give his oath of loyalty. For motives that remain mysterious, Ridwan accepted the invitation and made the traditional public gesture of loyalty during Friday prayers: "the invocation was offered for the Egyptians in all the pulpits of Syria that were in [Ridwan's] hands," the preacher calling out the names of the Fatimid caliph, followed by his vizier, followed by that of Ridwan himself. But, as one source put it, "it didn't last more than four Fridays." Ridwan quickly reversed his policy, and the names of the 'Abbasid caliph and the sultan Barkiyaruq were invoked once more. Ridwan's name, of course, continued to be invoked from Aleppo's pulpits.[14] That a Saljuq prince like Ridwan could almost whimsically grant his allegiance to a Fatimid overlord and just as simply withdraw it is just one indication of the shifting political sands confronting any Muslim ruler on the eve of the Frankish invasion.

Their Scattered Multitudes

Such bad blood and internal fractiousness informed how the Saljuq amirs of Syria first responded to the Frankish threat. In the summer of 1097 Ridwan, Yaghi-Siyan, and a group of other prominent commanders, including Karbuqa of Mosul and Sukman, lord of the region of Diyar Bakr in southeastern Anatolia, all marched into central Syria against a common rival. When they stopped at Shayzar on the Orontes River, however, reports arrived about a host of Franks heading toward Antioch. "And so Yaghi-Siyan said, 'We should return to Antioch and first engage the Franks.' But Sukman said, 'First, we should head for Diyar Bakr and seize it from the people ruling there and firm up our power; I can then establish my people over it, and then we can return to [Syria].'"[15] So they argued among themselves.

Angered to have his little campaign frustrated, Ridwan returned to Aleppo while Yaghi-Siyan went back to Antioch, and the others returned to their posts. At this point news arrived that the Franks were making progress across Anatolia: Qilij Arslan and the Danishmendids had failed to stop the Frankish advance.

Antioch was known to be the Franks' next stop. An ancient center of Christianity, Antioch had had great strategic as well as cultural value to the Byzantine Greeks, dominating as it did the passes into northern Syria and embracing one of the few fords of the Orontes River. Over the past centuries it had repeatedly changed hands between Arab, Byzantine, and Turkish conquerors. It was logical that Alexios, the Byzantine emperor, would try to use the Franks to retake it, and the Franks themselves, exhausted and low on supplies, had every reason to want it for themselves. If for no other reasons than these, the loss of Antioch to the Franks would be a terrible blow to Saljuq power in the north.

Yaghi-Siyan leaped into action. He sent one of his sons with a body of troops to Damascus to rouse Prince Duqaq. He sent another to Karbuqa in Mosul and to other commanders in the east to raise troops among the Turcomans. He also sent messengers to "all the amirs of the Muslims."[16] As it happens, we now know that the arrival of the Franks at Antioch in 1097 immediately inspired at least one scholarly discussion in Damascus of the theoretical limits of jihad, a debate that hinged significantly on whether the duty should be met locally or whether Muslims in neighboring regions were also expected to pitch in. It was the latter position that won out, which bode well for Yaghi-Siyan's efforts. Not surprisingly the army that he raised also included a body of men who volunteered expressly to engage in jihad. Once constituted, this large Muslim army marched to the vicinity of Antioch to engage the Franks.[17] The Fatimids, for their part, thinking perhaps of their relations with Byzantium and even the possibility of Frankish success, sent envoys to negotiate a separate peace treaty with the Franks, thus relieving them of a threat from Egypt for the time being.[18]

Fatimid scheming aside, Yaghi-Siyan must have been grateful for the support he received from his Saljuq colleagues.[19] In advance of their arrival at Antioch, the Franks had planned their siege well and had taken pains to claim adequate foraging lands and secure supply lines to last them during what was expected to be, given Antioch's indomitable fortifications and inaccessible citadel, a long and grueling siege. The Franks continued their policy, first worked out in Cilicia, of securing the loyalty of neighboring castles and their lands, in some cases seizing them outright or allowing native Christians to seize them on their behalf,—"all of this," one chronicler later wrote acidly, "due to Yaghi-Siyan's ugly conduct and oppressive grip over his lands."[20] But were Frankish contacts with the West to be maintained, they needed to secure a port. Antioch was an inland city, rolling astride the Orontes

River. It was serviced by a very fine port, that of St. Simeon, nine miles west of the city. To take it, ships would be required, and the Franks seem to have planned accordingly, for a fleet from England arrived and captured the port as well as the coastal town of Latakia.[21]

By late summer the Franks were foraging perilously close to Aleppo, "plundering and killing whomever they came across." Attempts by Prince Ridwan of Aleppo and Duqaq of Damascus to thwart then came to naught. Ridwan and Yaghi-Siyan's son even joined forces to try to rescue Antioch, but, thinking better of it, fell back to Harim, a strategic fortress located halfway between Antioch and Aleppo. There a contingent of Franks caught up with them, and they fled to safety in Aleppo. Though they could not have known it at the time, these early Muslim failures around Aleppo only emboldened the Franks and their local allies to advance more aggressively throughout the north.

Having witnessed this Muslim failure firsthand, the Armenian Christians in Harim apparently seized control of the fortress, just as other Armenian groups had been ousting their Turkish garrisons and seizing control across northern Syria. Elsewhere the Muslim authorities still managed to retain some control. At Tall Mannas, a town then in Armenian hands near Shayzar, Bedouin troops attacked "because they had heard that [the people there] had sent messages to the Franks, exhorting them to come to Syria." Duqaq arrived and bought some of the captured Armenians as slaves and then took the rest to be ransomed back in Damascus. In another case, a Turkish contingent managed to gain the upper hand and sent the rebels scurrying for refuge in the ruins scattered throughout the countryside. Troops from Aleppo soon arrived to hunt them down and take them back to Aleppo, where they were summarily executed, a sentence rarely inflicted upon prisoners who might, as at Tall Mannas, be more profitably ransomed or sold—a testament to the new religious tensions that were already creeping into the region.[22]

At Antioch, Yaghi-Siyan and a large garrison held the city, from which he had expelled the able-bodied Christian men in the interests of security. Though the Franks at first viewed these natives with some suspicion, the Christian Antiochenes endured the siege of their city encamped with the Franks; Yaghi-Siyan had vowed to ensure the safety of their families during their absence. In the meantime Duqaq of Damascus, Karbuqa of Mosul, and other local lords and all their troops had emerged again and encamped at Marj Dabiq, a wide plain some twenty-five miles north of Aleppo, planning their next move.

It was at this moment that one of the guards posted on one of Antioch's many towers offered a proposal to one of the Frankish leaders.

The guard, named (it seems) Firuz, was an armorer in the service of Yaghi-Siyan and, though Muslim, is pointedly described as being of Armenian Christian origin. He offered a plan to Bohemond of Taranto, an ambitious and ruthless knight seasoned in many battles and, perhaps unsurprisingly at this point, a Norman. In return for safe conduct and other unspecified demands, Firuz offered to hand the city over to the Franks. Bohemond agreed but kept this new development to himself. Then, according to one chronicler, he arranged a general meeting of all the Frankish leaders, including his nephew, Tancred of Lecce, from southern Italy; the nobleman Godfrey of Bouillon, from southern Belgium; Godfrey's brother "the Count"—that is, Baldwin of Boulogne—who was in fact at his base in Edessa during the siege of Antioch; another Baldwin, Baldwin of Le Bourcq; and "Sanjil," that is, Raymond of St.-Gilles, also known as Raymond of Toulouse, a hoary but wealthy Provençal lord and veteran of the Frankish invasions of al-Andalus. These men met with Bohemond and argued over property rights in Antioch, should the city fall to them. With Firuz's secret offer at the forefront of his mind, Bohemond humbly suggested to his colleagues that Antioch should belong to whoever conquered it first.[23]

At the appointed time and place on June 4, 1098, Firuz let down ropes over the walls under cover of night, allowing a small group of Bohemond's men to hoist themselves up and into the city proper. What followed was described as total chaos: "The number of men, women, and children killed, taken prisoner, and enslaved from its population is beyond computation. About three thousand men fled to the citadel and fortified themselves in it, and some few escaped for whom God had decreed escape."[24]

Adding to the chaos was a blunder of colossal proportions. Yaghi-Siyan's men might easily have stood a chance against the few hundred or so Normans who stole into the city that night. But Firuz's tower stood in the general direction of Mt. Silpius, which looms over the city and was also home to its citadel. When Yaghi-Siyan was wakened, he heard to his horror the alarm sounding from that direction. He assumed the Franks had finally taken not one small tower but the citadel itself, a sign that the city was as good as lost. He panicked and fled with a small bodyguard, heading south—significantly *not* in the direction of the Muslim army encamped north of Aleppo. His fate was ignominious: his men deserted him, and he is variously said to have fallen from his horse and died from his wounds or else died from thirst. A wandering Armenian peasant, we are told, came across the body and brought its head back to show the Franks.[25]

When they learned that the Franks had taken Antioch, the main Muslim coalition army, led by Karbuqa of Mosul, set out from Marj Dabiq to relieve the city, pausing at the fortress of Artah. From there a contingent was sent on to the Iron Bridge, a strategic crossing of the Orontes and the main entry point to the area of Antioch. A small Frankish force guarded the ford there, and the Muslim troops wiped them out and continued on to the northeastern suburbs of the city. Here they learned that all was not lost, that the Muslims still held the citadel high in Mt. Silpius, and so they sent word back to Karbuqa and the main Muslim army. With this news, Karbuqa advanced and over-whelmed Mt. Silpius and the mountainous highlands on the eastern edge of the city, scattering the Franks who had encamped on that side and gaining control of the citadel and its environs. Karbuqa appointed a new commander in charge of the citadel from among his own men. To prevent the further progress of the Muslim troops into the city proper, the Franks erected a wall, sealing off the citadel from the lower town. It also sealed the Franks in a city that had been depleted of supplies by their own long siege. Hunger soon set in: "The powerful fed on their horses, while the wretched poor ate carrion and the leaves of trees."[26]

One source claims that the trapped and starving Franks, trying to negotiate a surrender to leave the city, were met with Karbuqa's arrogant retort, "My sword alone will eject you."[27] The leadership of the Muslim armies had started to lose perspective. While the sources are nearly unanimous in singling out Karbuqa as a headstrong and over-bearing commander, there is evidence of deeper rifts too. Once the citadel at Antioch had been secured, Ridwan of Aleppo—who remained safely behind his own walls—sent messages to Karbuqa, making insinuations against his brother Duqaq, which led many of the Turcomans with him to desert. Other leaders likewise found themselves stationed alongside bitter rivals, and a major fight broke out between the Bedouin troops and the Turks, causing many of the Bedouin to abandon the whole enterprise.

After some discussion about how to capitalize on their victory, the leaders of the Muslim armies agreed to descend and encamp on the plains to the west and thereby tighten the noose around Antioch. Disagreements also emerged over strategy. Some of the Muslim commanders urged Karbuqa to attack the Franks as they emerged in small raiding and foraging parties and in the process slowly wear down the enemy. But Karbuqa and others knew they had the advantage. They ignored these smaller fry and waited in the hope that the Franks would soon emerge en masse. Indeed Karbuqa expressly forbade his men to engage these smaller groups of Franks, at one point physically intervening in person—a terrible blow to the honor of tribesmen spoiling for a fight and the reward of plunder.[28] It would not be forgotten.

In the meantime a minor miracle occurred, according to Frankish sources. One of the members of the camp began having visions of St. Andrew, who told him that the Holy Lance, which Christian tradition held had been used to pierce the side of Christ while he was crucified, was to be found buried in Antioch's cathedral of St. Peter and would provide them with victory. A lance was indeed discovered, and the miraculous discovery of the relic is said to have galvanized the Franks at their darkest hour. The one Muslim source that mentions this episode is understandably less convinced and depicts it all as a cunning ruse to rally the troops.[29]

In fact the Franks too were biding their time. On June 28, 1098, they emerged, "a massive host," for the final confrontation. The Turcoman troops, who by now made up the majority of the men still remaining to fight, immediately set upon them, but, finding the fighting taking its toll and their loyalty to Karbuqa stretched thin, they routed: "They broke the ranks of the Muslims and scattered their multitudes."[30] At first the Franks assumed this was a trick—feigned flight was a classic Turkish strategy for luring the enemy into an ambush—and so they stayed put, allowing the Turcomans to flee safely instead of hunting them down. Karbuqa was now left virtually alone, with only a small core from the original coalition to serve him. According to sources, he burned down his tents in despair and fled toward Aleppo.

Some Muslims abided before Antioch. Alone on the wide plains facing the city's many-towered walls stood a large, untrained but steadfast corps of volunteers come to exercise their duty of jihad, "vehement in their desire to strike a blow for the Faith and for the protection of the Muslims."[31] They "stood firm and fought zealously, seeking martyrdom."[32] The Franks cut them down by the thousands and plundered the Muslim camp. The survivors who straggled away from Antioch were then seized by Armenians who had taken over many of the local fortresses that guarded the roads and passes. The same fate awaited the Muslim garrison in the citadel, which surrendered on terms and was released, along with many of the Muslim prisoners who had been taken. They made their way toward Aleppo but were attacked en route; only a few managed to make it to safety.

The loss of Antioch provided the invasion's first and most stinging shock and painfully revealed just how ephemeral were personal loyalties among the Saljuq military elites. Some sources, as we have seen, would blame Yaghi-Siyan's poor statesmanship; others applauded his conduct. Still others focused on the personality of Karbuqa of Mosul, who, it is said, "angered the [other] amirs and lorded it over them, imagining that they would stay with him despite that. However, infuriated by this, they secretly planned to betray him...and they determined to give him up when the armies clashed." The same chronicler tells us that, upon seeing the Franks arrayed before Antioch, "the Muslims turned their backs in flight, firstly because of the contempt and scorn with which Karbuqa had treated them and secondly because he had prevented them from killing the Franks [earlier, when they sallied forth in small bands]."[33]

Whatever the ultimate cause, the fragile unity achieved by Yaghi-Siyan's initial call for jihad at Antioch soon fell apart when tested by battle, and the various defeated contingents that had made up the Muslim defense of Antioch quickly returned to their separate domains. Significantly it was in this year that the 'Abbasid caliph in Baghdad sent an envoy to the Saljuq sultan "to seek aid against the Franks, stressing the importance of the matter and the need to deal with it before it became more serious."[34] The idea of a massive centralized jihad campaign to drive the Franks back would not disappear in the years after 1098, but centralized reactions to this new threat were slow and infrequent. This meant local amirs were free to adopt their own, different and fluctuating attitudes toward the Franks. It was all very nice to bemoan the abstract threat to Islamdom that the Frankish invasion might pose to sultans and caliphs, but there was the immediate future to think of: Edessa, under Baldwin and his heirs, and Antioch, under Bohemond and his heirs, had been lost. At least Jerusalem, the ultimate goal of the Frankish pilgrims' progress, still lay many miles to the south.

No One Came to Their Rescue

This decentralized response also has an effect upon this narrative, as no Muslim chronicler saw fit to leave any detailed account of the Frankish progress from Antioch to Jerusalem. For this phase we must rely primarily upon Frankish accounts. The first Frankish steps toward Jerusalem took the form of desultory raids into territory once controlled by the Banu Munqidh, lords of the town of Shayzar on the Orontes. In July 1098 the Frankish count Raymond and a small detachment of his men captured the fortress town of Tall Mannas and a nearby unidentified fortress, where the population was forced to embrace Christianity or be killed. Raymond also made a tentative assault on Maʿarrat al-Nuʿman (also known simply as Maʿarra), but the city was protected by troops from Aleppo, Damascus, and probably Shayzar as well. The Muslim army killed many of the Franks and brought their heads back to display at Maʿarra.[35] Later in the year the Muslim commander at the small fortified town of Aʿzaz rebelled against his master, Ridwan, who promptly put the place under siege. The rebel commander then solicited aid from the Franks in Antioch, and they dutifully arrived with a large army that dispersed Ridwan's troops and plundered its train as they fled back to Aleppo. Ridwan eventually caught up with the rebel commander and retook Aʿzaz. The rebel was carted off to Aleppo, where he stewed for a while in Aleppo's dungeons before being executed.[36]

The more decisive Frankish move toward the south came in late September 1098, when Raymond captured the town of al-Bara, southeast of Antioch. This was the first serious effort of the Franks to gain control of the fertile plains southeast of Antioch, an area whose former prosperity is evident even today in the ghostly limestone and basalt ruins of the "Dead Cities," little farming towns dating from late Roman times. It is said that at al-Bara water was scarce and so the town quickly agreed to the terms of surrender and safe conduct. Despite the treaty, Raymond "attacked the populace, chased after the men and women, made off with their property, capturing some, killing others."[37] The Crusaders then returned to Antioch, where, after a fruitless debate about where next to proceed, Raymond and Robert of Flanders "and the Armenians under their authority, as well as local Christians" made another attempt upon Maʿarra, this time with success.[38]

Once arrived, in December 1098, the Franks began chopping down the trees in the area—always the first sign that a siege was purposed. Seeing this, the alarmed populace sought out the aid of Prince Ridwan and his atabeg, "but no one came to their rescue."[39] Using the wood they had just cut down, the Franks assembled a siege tower, which they pushed against the walls of the town. As the Franks climbed up, they were met with the town's militias on the top of the walls and at its feet. It was a clumsy affair, the Franks apparently scrambling about in the open air attempting to undermine the walls, the Muslim defenders hurling everything they could find down upon them: stones, darts, fire, lime, even hives of bees. The fighting lasted throughout the day, until in the end morale flagged and group after group of defenders fled their posts. The Franks took the wall and entered the city.[40]

Just to the south the Banu Munqidh of Shayzar viewed this progress with mounting horror. If the conquests of Edessa and Antioch were not persuasive enough, the reports that emerged of Frankish behavior in al-Bara and Maʿarra were enough to convince the Banu Munqidh at Shayzar to take practical steps. At al-Bara, according to Frankish eye-witnesses, the Franks "killed all the Saracens, males and females, noble and lesser folk, whom they could find there," and "slaughtered thousands, returned thousands more to be sold into slavery at Antioch, and freed those cowardly ones who surrendered."[41] They "killed the citizens to a man, and confiscated everything."[42] At Maʿarra the populace that remained after the battle hid in underground caverns, probably cellars and cisterns; once the town was looted, they were smoked out of their hiding places and either killed or taken captive.[43] Some citizens were promised safe conduct if they remained, but, as at al-Bara, the treaty meant nothing: these Muslims, "men, women, and children," were later robbed, killed, and sold into slavery.[44] Still other townsmen died after the Franks tortured them to reveal where their wealth was hidden.[45] Worse yet, some of the miserable and starving Franks "were so famished that they cut the flesh of the dead into bits, cooked, and ate it."[46]

Even before the slaughter, the Franks had divvied up the real estate in the town among themselves even as the Muslim proprietors watched. One chronicle mentions that "they raised up crosses throughout the town"; this too is probably connected to the dividing up of the spoils.[47] For Muslim and Frankish observers alike, the incidents at Maʿarra were dutifully recounted as a litany of horror. Indeed for one later Muslim chronicler, the place became the yardstick for atrocity: in his one laconic reference to the conquest of Jerusalem later, in July 1099, he passes quickly over the usual gory details with a simple phrase: "They did there like what they had done at Maʿarra."[48]

Despite the attention that the Franks devoted to the distribution of property at Maʿarra, arguments over the progress of their campaign weighed against staying put. Jerusalem, more than three hundred miles away, still beckoned. In January 1099, in an effort to dissuade Raymond from resting on his laurels at Maʿarra and to prevent enemies from reusing it as a base, the Franks pulled down the city's walls and burned the houses and mosques within to the ground. Nearby Kafartab fell soon thereafter, and Raymond was joined by Franks from Antioch.[49] Shayzar was their next destination.

The lord of Shayzar, named Sultan (his name is not to be confused with the Saljuq royal title), was a fierce but cunning old survivor of many trials. Sultan and the rest of his clan, the Banu Munqidh, would have been well-apprised of the Frankish forces headed toward them, for waves of refugees fled before the Franks as word of their ferocity circulated throughout the countryside. Some of the refugees fled to Damascus, some to Aleppo. Others sought safety closer to home at Shayzar, where the castle walls could afford some protection from the invaders.[50] This advance information on the Franks was crucial, and when Raymond and the other Franks captured Ma'arra, Sultan made a decisive step. Rather than fight this apparently unstoppable menace, which had ravaged the surrounding countryside and captured heavily fortified towns and cities, Sultan sought to reach an agreement with the Franks before they even got within sight of Shayzar. He played upon their greatest weakness: supplies.[51] The Frankish chronicler and churchman Raymond d'Aguilers was part of Raymond's entourage, and he writes, "News of the resumption of the crusade caused nearby rulers to send Arab nobles to Raymond with prayers and many offerings and promises of future submission as well as free and salable goods."[52] Peter Tudebode, a contemporary from Poitou in France, also notes the importance of Sultan's supplies in this arrangement: after sending word that he would be willing to give Raymond "as much revenue as the count demanded," the lord of Shayzar also pledged to "make pilgrims secure and free of fear as far as his jurisdiction permitted."[53] Finally, he "offered to furnish a market in horses and food. As a result the pilgrims moved out and pitched their tents along the Orontes near Shayzar."

Sultan also provided the Franks with guides, who led them west across the Orontes and safely through his own territory. Between Shayzar and Masyaf, the guides led the Franks to a valley to which numerous head of livestock had been driven and where other provisions were stored. Whether the guides had inadvertently led the Franks to Sultan's private hoard of supplies, as one source maintains, or this was Sultan's way of using the Franks to raid a rival neighbor's lands is unclear.[54] Sultan, was, in any case, no fool, and, once relieved of the immediate menace posed by the Franks, he moved to avert the worst, sending a messenger ahead to pass the Franks unseen, in the hope of warning the Muslims of the coastal regions to prepare. Unfortunately the Franks captured the messenger, and Sultan, badly embarrassed, was obliged to encourage his fellow Muslims to extend them every hospitality.[55] The Franks moved on and thus no longer posed a concern for

Shayzar. In a few months' time these Franks, some of them mounted on horses that had been raised on the green fodder of Shayzar, would found a Latin kingdom based on Jerusalem.[56]

Other Muslim cities followed Shayzar's lead. The amir of the city of Homs, still stinging from his involvement in the defeat at Antioch, arranged for safe passage and supplies for the Franks on similar terms. The amir of Hama did likewise. At Rafaniya the Franks pillaged the gardens and orchards surrounding the river town without resistance. They then followed the foothills of the Jabal Ansariya, entering the "Homs gap" pass to the coast. On the eastern edge of this pass there now stands the most famous of all Crusader fortresses in the Near East, Crac des Chevaliers (Fig. 5), an imposing castle used as a base in the twelfth and thirteenth centuries by the crusader Order of the Knights of St. John, the Hospitallers. When the Franks passed by it in early 1099, however, it was a much more modest Muslim fort called Hisn al-Akrad, designed to protect the caravans that plied the road through the pass. Despite the large size of the Frankish army, the Muslim garrison there dutifully attacked, only to be repelled. When Raymond's men surrounded the fort, the garrison gathered what they could and fled into the night. Except for a few bandits harassing the Frankish stragglers, this was the only serious obstacle the Franks met on their progress to the coast.

By the middle of February 1099 the Franks were besieging 'Arqa, near the coast, after having secured the Syrian ports of Tartus (Tortosa) and Marqab. The siege of 'Arqa was protracted, lasting three months and accomplishing little at 'Arqa itself. In the interval another Fatimid delegation arrived from Egypt. The stunning Frankish successes at Antioch had realized Fatimid fears, and, with the Franks appearing ready to proceed deeper and deeper into Fatimid domains, they were now ready to negotiate a settlement. By now the Fatimids were in a stronger position than they had been a year earlier at Antioch, for one simple reason: they had Jerusalem, which they had captured from the Saljuqs a few months earlier. It was on Jerusalem that the negotiations foundered. To forestall an outright invasion of Palestine and the Frankish approach to Egypt, the Fatimids offered instead to allow groups of unarmed Franks to visit the city and so fulfill their vows as pilgrims. But the Franks would not give up their intent to take the city outright. The Fatimid envoys withdrew to Egypt, and the Fatimid army prepared for the worst.

Yet the Franks were still stymied as the siege at 'Arqa continued. The siege's commander, Raymond of Toulouse, was a veteran of the

Frankish invasion of al-Andalus, and he was surely aware of what such a protracted siege could produce: tribute. Indeed, just as in al-Andalus of the taifa kings, the Muslim lord of Tripoli sent envoys to Raymond and the Franks at ʿArqa with vast amounts of coins and gifts to buy them off—hardly an inducement to move on, if more such wealth could be extracted. In the end the rest of the Frankish army arrived to reunite with Raymond, and the drive to reach Jerusalem was too strong. ʿArqa and nearby Tripoli would have to wait for Raymond's attentions at a later date. The Franks lifted the siege and proceeded down the coastal road into Palestine, "and the people fled in panic from their abodes before them."[57] At Arsuf, on the coast, they cut inland toward al-Ramla, which they captured, while Bohemond's rough nephew Tancred, his hour come round at last, slouched toward Bethlehem to take it as his own. The next day, June 7, the Franks encamped before their heartfelt goal: Jerusalem.[58]

The Cross in the Prayer Niche

Jerusalem was itself just recently the site of another siege, being one of the many cities that furiously changed hands with the coming of the Turks to Syria. As we have seen, the Turcoman adventurer Atsiz had occupied the city in the 1070s, and he subjected it to a brutal reprisal when the Fatimids attempted to oust him. When the Saljuq prince Tutush finally did remove Atsiz in 1079, he replaced him with an amir loyal to him, named Ilghazi. Ilghazi belonged to the Artuqids, a family that would later found their own state in northern Iraq and eastern Anatolia, and his brother was among the generals present in the Muslim coalition army at Antioch.

After the fall of Antioch, the Fatimids soon took advantage of the Saljuqs' disarray and reasserted their control over the Holy City. The Fatimid army was led by the mighty vizier al-Afdal. After arriving at Jerusalem "they set up forty and more trebuchets against the town and demolished parts of its wall. The inhabitants fought back and the fighting and the siege lasted somewhat over forty days."[59] By September 1098 the city had had enough, and Jerusalem surrendered to the Fatimids.[60] The Saljuq representatives were treated well and allowed to leave to continue their careers in Saljuq service.

Thus, on June 7, 1099, when the Franks finally sighted their goal, Jerusalem had recently been through three changes of hands, two of them destructive, and had been under the control of its Fatimid masters for less than a year. Nevertheless its garrison, commanded by the governor Iftikhar al-Dawla, was in a good situation. The Jerusalem besieged by the Franks was a modest city, of about twenty thousand to thirty thousand people, a mixture of Christians, Muslims, and Jews, some resident, others from the substantial itinerant population of tourists and pilgrims. In 1047 the traveler Naser-i Khusraw, a Persian Shi'ite, passed through Jerusalem on his way to Egypt and noted the large number of Muslim pilgrims who flocked to the city and that "from the Byzantine realm and other places too come Christians and Jews to visit the churches and synagogues there."[61] As Naser also noted, the city boasted bustling bazaars; a plethora of shrines and sites holy to Christians, Jews, and Muslims; a fine hospital; and stout defensive walls that followed roughly the same course as that of the Ottoman-era walls ringing Jerusalem's Old City today. The city had its own water sources, though the countryside was dependent upon wells. The Fatimid garrison defending the city was, for such a small place, generous in size, perhaps one thousand strong. The Fatimid governor made the necessary preparations for the city's defense as news of the Frankish approach arrived, expelling local Christians and blocking the wells in the surrounding countryside.[62]

For their part, the Franks had managed to replenish their supplies en route, but their advance from 'Arqa to Jerusalem had been fast, even headlong, as they passed one Muslim town after another without securing it, leaving them dangerously exposed. As the Franks began their first attack on the city, the news arrived that al-Afdal of Egypt was again on the march, "on his way from Egypt with a mighty army to engage in jihad against them, and to destroy them, and to succour and protect the city against them."[63] The Franks thus focused their energies in earnest, hoping to take the city before al-Afdal's relieving forces arrived.

According to one source, this was effected by a simple ruse: as dusk set in, the Franks pretended to withdraw from their siege, encouraging the Muslim defenders to do likewise. At this the Franks launched into a renewed assault, gained the wall, and stormed the city.[64] A later source, the thirteenth-century chronicler Ibn al-Athir, accords more closely with the Frankish accounts, though even he avoids most of the details to be found in those extended accounts of the conquest. Like the Frankish sources, Ibn al-Athir depicts the siege as one carried out on two fronts. In the south, near Mt. Zion, the garrison concentrated most of its energies, successfully fending off the Franks there and burning Raymond of Toulouse's siege tower to the ground. In the north, however, near St. Stephen's Gate, the Franks had assembled another tower. With the garrison distracted in the south, the Franks managed to force an entry, and although men were called over to repel them, it was too late to stem the tide.[65] The end result was the same in both Frankish and Muslim accounts: the Fatimid garrison holed themselves up in the Tower or Oratory of David, the city's ancient citadel that juts from the center of the western walls. There they held out for three days, at which time they agreed to a truce with the Franks, who let them depart along with some civilians for the city of Ascalon on the southern route toward Egypt.

Others were far less fortunate. As the jubilant and exhausted Franks first poured into the city, "the inhabitants became prey for the sword."[66] Some Jews of the city assembled in their synagogue, but this was burned down around them.[67] Many more were taken as captives, along with other members of the general populace.[68] Another contingent of Franks, led by Tancred, captured the Haram al-Sharif, as the Temple Mount is known in Arabic, by arranging a treaty of safe conduct with the Muslims who had gathered there.[69] As the site of the al-Aqsa Mosque (which the Franks identified as the Temple of Solomon) and the magnificent Muslim shrine of the Dome of the Rock, among other shrines, the Haram was and is the spiritual center of Islamic Jerusalem, where scholars, mystics, and the ordinary faithful flocked. Perched high above the city, it was a natural refuge for the pious—and therefore a natural target for the fanatical. Altogether ignoring the agreement of safe conduct, the Franks are said to have killed (improbably) thousands in the al-Aqsa Mosque, "a large number being imams, ulema, righteous men and ascetics, Muslims who had left their native lands and come to live a holy life in this august spot."[70]

From the Dome of the Rock they carried off the silver and gold candelabra, like Titus and the legions of Rome desecrating the Temple. "The plunder they took," one source simply states, "was beyond counting."[71] But death and destruction were only the quotidian tragedies at Jerusalem. The enslavement of Muslim women and children by infidels, the breaking of oaths, the desecration of holy sites, the transformation of mosques into churches or worse, the pillaging of Jerusalem's sacred precinct: these were acts of cosmic defilement not easily cleansed. "What is right is null and void and what is forbidden is made licit," lamented a later poet, invoking images of ritual impurity. "The cross has been set up in the prayer-niche / Pig's blood would be suitable for it now."[72]

The conquest of Jerusalem horrified Muslims of the Near East as much as it exhilarated the Franks. But, for all the emotive accounts surrounding its loss, it was above all a local, Levantine calamity, requiring piecemeal, local responses.[73] As Jerusalem was so recently a Fatimid city, its loss was foremost a blow to Fatimid imperial authority. As a result the Fatimid army under al-Afdal took a direct approach "when he heard what had befallen the people of Jerusalem" and advanced, finally, into Palestine. Al-Afdal was temporarily delayed, however, as he waited for other contingents of the planned relieving force, including ships from the ports of the Syrian coast, to arrive at his camp at Ascalon, Egypt's traditional bridgehead into Palestine. He sent a messenger to the Franks "condemning their actions and threatening them," and the Franks returned the gesture. The Frankish envoy did not come alone: hot on his trail was a large Frankish army exultant from its victory at Jerusalem. "The Egyptians had no intelligence of their coming," says one source, "or that they had made any move. They were not ready for combat. The cry went up, 'To horse' and they donned their armour but the Franks were too quick for them and put them to flight. Having inflicted losses on them, the Franks took the property, weapons and whatever else was in their camp as plunder."[74] While al-Afdal fell back to the safety of Ascalon, other soldiers tried to hide among the trees in the area, but the Franks smoked them out and killed them as they ran, for "the swords of the Franks were given mastery over the Muslims."[75] Among the dead that day was Jalal al-Mulk ibn 'Ammar, brother to the lord of Tripoli, who had bought off Raymond of Toulouse at 'Arqa to protect his independence, only to die fighting in service to a Fatimid lord he resented. Al-Afdal, peering over the walls of Ascalon, could see his cause was hopeless; he and his personal retinue retreated to Cairo. Ascalon was abandoned to its citizens, who suffered a Frankish siege until they negotiated a truce for an extortionate amount and arranged, with the help of agents of the Fatimid caliph, the ransoming of some of the prisoners still in Frankish hands.[76]

Precisely as al-Afdal was attempting to relieve Jerusalem, a delegation of refugee Syrians arrived in Baghdad, led by a Muslim judge, Abu Saʿd al-Harawi. The Syrians had come seeking the ear of the caliph, who was the leader of the Sunni Muslim community, after all, to see if he could somehow muster an adequate response to the Frankish invasion of the Near East; the caliph had, it was known, urged the Saljuq sultan to do so before. To convince the assembled officials, al-Harawi offered a cri de coeur on the plight of Syria's Muslims, "a narrative which brought tears to the eye and pained the heart." It was Ramadan (July–August 1099), the Muslim sacred month of fasting and celebration, and the delegation went on to harangue the congregation at the mosque on the Friday after their arrival with tales of what befell Jerusalem, "the killing of men, the enslavement of women and children and the plundering of property that had fallen upon the Muslims in that revered, sacred place."[77] So vivid was their account and so plain their suffering that they were excused, as Islamic law warrants, from the added exertion of the Ramadan fast.

In response the caliph formed his own delegation of leading religious scholars from different schools of religious law, to go east to persuade the sultan Barkiyaruq, the only man who could muster the necessary army, to counter the Franks. At Hulwan, on the main road from Baghdad into Iran, the delegation caught news of the murder of the sultan's powerful adviser (who happened to be a Shi'i); they knew then that civil war was in the offing yet again for the fractured Saljuq ruling house. They returned to Baghdad "without achieving any aim or any goal. The rulers," our chronicler succinctly concludes, "were all at odds with one another…and so the Franks conquered the lands."[78] It was an assessment that could have been applied to Sicily or al-Andalus, which Jerusalem and the lands of the Levant now joined as lands lost to Frankish predations. For nearly a century after 1099, Jerusalem remained in Frankish hands as the principal city of their far-flung holdings in the Levant, which they called "the Lands across the Sea," or Outremer, a prize not so much the product of divine will or Crusader fervor as of Fatimid vacillation and the disunity of a distracted Saljuq elite.

– 4 –

Against the Enemies of God

T A HAIRPIN bend in the Orontes River in Syria, perched high
atop an almost insurmountable outcropping of the native bed-
rock, sits Shayzar Castle. The castle looms over the river, which
nearly surrounds it on three sides, and guards the town of Shayzar
below and its strategic river crossing. If Syria in the eleventh century
was a frontier zone between the Muslim world and the Latin states of
the Franks, then Shayzar was a frontier within a frontier, wedged between sometimes hostile Muslim kingdoms at Aleppo and Hama and
abutting the Frankish states at Antioch and Tripoli (Map 5). In this
setting, Shayzar's lords, the venerable and aristocratic Arab clan called
the Banu Munqidh, quickly learned the new rules of survival in postinvasion Syria: know when to fight and when to bribe, and be ready to
make uncomfortable alliances. And the Banu Munqidh were very
skilled survivors. Had an earthquake not leveled the castle in 1157,
taking most of the family with it, there's no telling how long they would
have lasted.

We know a great deal about the inner workings of the household of
the Banu Munqidh—its wars, its hunting parties, its servants' squab-
bles and family intrigues—largely thanks to one of their sons, Usama
ibn Munqidh, who wrote a collection of autobiographical reminis-
cences about his long and adventure-filled life called *The Book of
Contemplation*. In it Usama shows that he had learned Shayzar's lessons
very well, for he lived to the rather astonishing age of ninety-three and

had served nearly every major Muslim prince in the region, spending considerable time among the Franks as well. Usama's long life is ample evidence that in the postinvasion Near East, it helped if, like Usama, you had marketable skills as a warrior, poet, or diplomat. And it didn't hurt if you were also a cold-blooded schemer of the highest order. Usama's newly divided and fragmented world was one where only those with enough might or enough cunning could be expected to last. In such a setting, expelling the Franks could never be a priority.[1]

Initial Reactions

By 1100 the Franks had penetrated deep into the borderlands of the Saljuq and Fatimid realms and were intent on staying. As if building upon the precedent of the Norman county of Sicily, founded during the conquests there in 1071, the invasion of the Near East resulted in not one but three new and distinct Frankish states; a fourth would soon follow. Foremost among these three was the kingdom of Jerusalem. With the Holy City as its center, the kingdom always held preeminence among its peers, even if its kings did not always exude much charisma. Eventually stretching along the Palestinian coast from Ashdod in the south to Beirut in the north, the kingdom would also incorporate territory conquered east of the Jordan River, including the area now known as the Golan Heights, the far shores of Lake Tiberias in the north, and, in the south, the two vital castles at Karak and Shawbak on the road to the Red Sea. This alignment placed the kingdom in a tight spot, squeezed between Fatimid Egypt and Saljuq Damascus.

Yet Jerusalem had protection from the other Frankish states, which formed a sort of shield far to the north, preventing Muslim armies from unhindered invasions of the region from that quarter and allowing the Franks to launch their own raids into Anatolia, Syria, and even Iraq. The county of Edessa, straddling the rough country on either bank of the upper Euphrates, was the first Frankish state to be created in the region. It included important fortresses and strong points like Saruj and Tall Bashir and was sure to be the first target for any Muslim army emanating from Iraq or the East. The principality of Antioch, which dominated the fertile Orontes valley from Apamea in the south to the Amanus Mountains in the north, was a constant thorn in the side of the lords of Aleppo, Damascus, and Shayzar. On its eastern reaches, a line of fortified towns, running from A'zaz and Atharib in the north to Artah and Harim in the south, provided a bulwark against Aleppo, and these towns seemed to be constantly taking the heat intended for Antioch. Antioch had other worries too. Emperor Alexios I, for one, had originally hoped to use the Franks to reclaim this ancient city from the Saljuqs. When the Franks refused to turn it over to him, the Byzantines looked upon Frankish Antioch less as a fellow Christian ally and more as valuable property that had been unjustly seized.

The final shape of the Frankish states was due not simply to Frankish conquests but also to the responses of Muslims who reconquered territory, stymied advances, and negotiated treaties with these new regional powers. Of the major Muslim states in the region, there were five principal zones from which emanated these initial Muslim responses. Their number and variety alone illustrate the complexity of the setting. They include Fatimid Egypt, which quickly saw its attempts to regain the coastal district collapse; Damascus, held by the Saljuq prince Duqaq and his virtuoso atabeg, Tughtakin; Aleppo, held by the Saljuq prince Ridwan, Duqaq's brother and bitter rival; the various commanders of the Upper Mesopotamian zones of Diyar Bakr and al-Jazira, of whom the Artuqid clan was the most prominent; and finally the Saljuq sultan himself, who, in the decades after 1099, repeatedly sent formal, massive, and centrally organized jihad campaigns of tens of thousands of men against the Franks, albeit with little positive effect. For the most part, the sultan chose as his representative in these campaigns the lord of Mosul in northern Iraq. Other Muslim warlords, such as the lords of Shayzar and the Danish-mendids of Anatolia, played a much smaller and intermittent role.

In this early period, in all these zones, success mixed with failure. In the north there were some immediate Muslim successes against the Franks. In August 1100, for example, Turkish troops under the Danishmend defeated and captured at Malatya the ruthless Norman Bohemond, now lord of Antioch, one of the most successful leaders of the whole Frankish invasion.[2] He remained a guest in the dungeons of the Danishmend for the next four years. Muslim observers viewed these events with great relief, but for the Franks it was a setback that, combined with the death in July 1100 of Godfrey, the Frankish lord of Jerusalem, could not have come at a worse time. For it was just then that the Franks in Europe staged another invasion through Anatolia.

In 1101 the old Provençal veteran Raymond of St. Gilles happened to be in Constantinople; as he was one of the more prestigious secular lords associated with the First Crusade, he was chosen to lead a large group of this new wave of Franks across Anatolia. Other sections of the Frankish army took different paths under different leaders, the glow of the victories of 1099 still fresh in their minds. However, 1101 was not

1099, and the Saljuqs of Rum and the Danishmendids were by now prepared and, more important, in alliance together and with Ridwan of Aleppo. By the summer the entire invading force, comparable, Frankish sources claim, to the First Crusade that set out in 1096, was wiped out, and very few of the Franks survived to make it to Syria.[3] For decades hence the land route through Anatolia would be effectively denied to any more Frankish armies. The alliance between Qilij Arslan and the Danishmend did not last long, however, and by 1103 the two were at loggerheads. Bohemond saw his opportunity: in return for a certain ransom, he convinced the Danishmend to release him, sweetening the deal with a promise to aid him in battle against Qilij Arslan.

With Bohemond restored to Antioch, and Edessa enjoying comparative security, in 1104 the two Frankish states launched a joint attack on Edessa's neighbor, the city of Harran, which had recently undergone a quick succession of rulers. At this alarming development, Jikirmish, the new Saljuq lord of Mosul, assembled a large army to assist Harran, to "prosecute the jihad against the Franks, the enemies of God." The Franks were confident enough that they would take Harran eventually, and so they broke off their siege to engage these troops arriving from Mosul. They met at a minor tributary of the Euphrates, the Balikh, where the two Frankish divisions, caught separated from one another, were decimated. As they attempted to flee across the river, Baldwin and Joscelin were captured, leaving Edessa leaderless. The Antiochene troops, under Bohemond and Tancred, dispersed, though Tancred remained briefly to hold Edessa. Jikirmish easily occupied Harran. The Muslim troops then reassembled at Edessa and put it under siege, though they were obliged to withdraw. Despite this failure at Edessa, Jikirmish and his Turcoman troops had demonstrated Muslim strength and badly defeated a combined Frankish force. The victory at the Balikh resonated among contemporaries as a "great and unexampled victory for the Muslims," one that had broken the Frankish offensive. "The people joyfully noised abroad the good news of the victory over them, and became assured of their destruction and the turning of fortune against them."[4]

Misfortunes on the Coast

Elsewhere the record was mixed. Egypt, for example, was the biggest loser in the wake of the first Frankish invasions. Having already lost what tenuous hold they had on Sicily, the generals and diplomats of

Cairo had worked hard to contain the ambitions of the Franks as they progressed down the Syrian coast, but to no avail. The failure of al-Afdal at Ascalon in 1099 forced an entirely new policy, one that became an obsession on the part of the Fatimids, namely, maintaining a foothold on the coast from which to drive out the Franks. In July 1101 an Egyptian army amassed again at Ascalon. In September it advanced into Frankish territory. After a fitful skirmish the Muslims managed to rally and push the Franks back toward Jaffa.[5]

In spring of 1102 the Egyptians returned to Ascalon. Baldwin of Jerusalem launched a campaign against the town, but the Egyptians were victorious and inflicted serious casualties.[6] In 1103 the Fatimids invoked the duty of jihad and arranged with Tughtakin of Damascus for a joint campaign against the kingdom of Jerusalem. However, though the Egyptian fleet arrived to resupply some of the besieged cities on the coast, not all of the troops did, and so the campaign dissolved.[7] In 1105 they made another attempt, and a massive Egyptian army some ten thousand strong once again headed toward Ascalon. The commander invited Tughtakin to join him in the jihad against the Franks. Tughtakin wavered slightly but eventually joined the Egyptians at Ascalon. At the end of August, between Ascalon and Jaffa, the Franks, aided by renegade Muslim allies from Damascus, met the combined Muslim forces in battle. The Franks prevailed, killing the governor of Ascalon and scattering the Muslim troops to their various home bases. Ascalon itself, however, remained unconquered.[8]

As long as Ascalon in the south remained Fatimid, the hopes of Muslims elsewhere in Syria to reclaim control of the coast centered on Tripoli, one of the few large ports still in Muslim hands. But the Muslims were not the only ones focused on Tripoli, for Raymond of St. Gilles was also bent on taking the city. Outmaneuvered from winning his own principality at Antioch and then again at Jerusalem, and nonplussed by the failure of the Crusade of 1101, Raymond badly needed his own domain in the Near East, for reasons of pride if nothing else. The region around Tripoli was the one area of the Levantine coast still unconquered, and Raymond had been, we may recall, the first of the Frankish lords to attack it, during his prolonged siege of 'Arqa. Tripoli's lord, Fakhr al-Mulk ibn 'Ammar, had been quick to arrange a truce with Raymond then as the Franks passed on to Jerusalem. Now the area was back in Raymond's sights. Moreover Duqaq of Damascus, or rather his energetic atabeg Tughtakin, was also interested in Tripoli, and Damascus had already shown that its influence reached to the coast. In June 1101 the Muslim lord of nearby Jabala could not cope with the relentless Frankish assaults on his lands and so offered to hand the city over to Tughtakin if the latter could guarantee his safe passage to Baghdad. They reached an agreement, and so Tughtakin sent his own son Buri to act as the city's lord—a Damascene foothold on the coast.[9] But Buri so mistreated the populace of Jabala, "contrary to the approved custom of justice and fair-dealing," that they secretly wrote to Fakhr al-Mulk of Tripoli to come to their aid. His troops arrived and fought alongside the populace against Buri's troops. Buri himself was captured, treated honorably in Tripoli, and then sent packing back to Damascus, carrying a letter with Fakhr al-Mulk's apologies. Tughtakin seems to have understood.[10]

In 1102, however, Raymond returned to the region, besieging Tartus before moving on to Tripoli and styling himself "count of Tripoli" before the city had even fallen. The Persian traveler Nasir-i Khusraw had passed through Tripoli on his way to Jerusalem some sixty years before and noted its defenses. It was, as he describes it, a compact town around its ancient harbor, surrounded on three sides by the sea and defended from the landward side by a stout wall and fosse. The surrounding countryside was thick with fields and orchards of lemons, date palms, and oranges, and the port was busy enough that the tolls levied there alone kept its ruler, who also had his own merchant fleet, quite rich.[11] That Tripoli today has something of a schizophrenic layout in two separate and distinct parts is thanks in some way to the nature of Raymond's siege. Confronted with Tripoli's unique situation around the harbor, he ordered a castle built on a hill outside the city during the siege, named Mons Peregrinus, "Pilgrim's Mount." The little town that grew up around Raymond's fort (which, with many subsequent alterations, still stands) thrived, while the Tripoli that Fakhr al-Mulk knew was reduced to its harbor.[12]

Once the siege began in earnest, Fakhr al-Mulk requested aid not from the Fatimids, who were the nominal overlords of his principality, but from Tughtakin of Damascus. Tughtakin responded by sending a body of troops along with the garrison from Homs. They made straight for Tartus, hoping to draw away Raymond's siege of Tripoli. But when the armies finally met, the Franks were victorious, and the Muslim troops retired back to their home cities, suffering considerable losses in the process.[13] Raymond returned and maintained the siege. Fakhr al-Mulk resorted to sending out raiders by ship to attack Frankish lands and burn the fields in the hopes of reducing Raymond's supplies.[14] In one skirmish Fakhr al-Mulk sallied out and burned a part of the Frankish camp below Raymond's castle, and Raymond was injured.

His health failing, Raymond agreed to a truce with Fakhr al-Mulk, who retained the city. In February 1105 Raymond died and was buried in Jerusalem, never having entered the city he claimed to rule.[15]

The siege, however, continued. Tripoli's situation was so dire that, in 1108, Fakhr al-Mulk set out for Damascus and thence to Baghdad to make a personal plea for help from the Saljuq sultan. In both cities he was lavishly received and honored, and the sultan seems to have been impressed, immediately arranging for assistance: "The sultan commanded a number of the great amirs to go with him to give him assistance and reinforcement in repelling those who had besieged his city, to inflict condign punishment upon them, and drive them off."[16] This force, however, never made it to Syria, as it was ordered first to stop at Mosul, where it became involved in a local political imbroglio and was dispersed. Fakhr al-Mulk grew increasingly impatient as the sultan's guest and returned to Damascus, where he learned that, in his absence from Tripoli, some of the populace had appealed to the Fatimids. The Fatimids happily sent a fleet to resupply and take the besieged city, rounding up Fakhr al-Mulk's men and property in the process. Now an exile from the city he had sought to save, Fakhr al-Mulk requested some troops from his host, Tughtakin, and set up shop in nearby Jabala, from where he could watch his former city suffer through the still-steady Frankish siege.[17]

In March 1109 Raymond of St. Gilles's son, Bertrand, arrived from Europe to claim his father's estate as nominal count of Tripoli and to direct the siege. He immediately fell into conflict with Raymond's cousin, the count of Cerdagne, who had taken over the Frankish siege in the interim. Baldwin of Jerusalem was obliged to settle the dispute between them, but it happened that the count of Cerdagne died soon thereafter (allegedly during a brawl), and Bertrand was given a free hand to subdue the remaining unconquered towns of the surrounding region.

Finally, Tripoli fell on July 12, 1109, after a promised Fatimid relief fleet was delayed by bad winds. Tripoli finally received its count, becoming the fourth and final "Frankish state" in the Near East. Fakhr al-Mulk's city was given over to plunder—the Muslim sources universally mourn the loss of its famous book collections—and the men were held captive while the women and children were taken as slaves. The governor and his men, however, were granted safe passage to Damascus, and the Franks took up residence. Bertrand of Tripoli's new neighbor, Tancred of Antioch, also took the opportunity to besiege Jabala, where Fakhr al-Mulk was still clinging to power, and he soon took the city.

Fakhr al-Mulk, though assured he would retain the town as Tancred's vassal, preferred not to live under infidel rule and so emigrated briefly to Shayzar, where he passed up the lord's invitation to remain as his guest, and then joined the service of Tughtakin in Damascus. Tughtakin granted him lands and honors. A few days after the fall of Tripoli the Fatimid fleet finally and unhelpfully arrived, and before returning distributed some supplies to the Muslim cities that still remained under threat from Frankish attack: Beirut, Sidon, and Tyre.[18]

Tyre was indeed the focus of the Frankish drive to mop up the coastal region in general; at this they were assisted by a fleet sent by the Genoese, who always had an interest in the affairs of port cities. The Franks seemed to be everywhere at once. In 1100 they captured Jaffa, Haifa, Arsuf, and Caesarea.[19] In 1101 Baldwin of Jerusalem besieged Beirut, though he was forced to withdraw.[20] In 1104, when Raymond was still alive and besieging Tripoli, he enlisted the aid of the Genoese in blockading the port, but without much success. They moved on and captured and sacked the port of Jubayl, ancient Byblos.[21] In May 1104 the same Genoese ships assisted Baldwin in his siege and conquest of Acre, whose commander fled and returned to Egypt.[22] In 1108 Baldwin and the Genoese also menaced Sidon, but a Fatimid fleet and a Damascene army arrived to convince them to withdraw.[23] In the same year the Franks finally took 'Arqa, despite an attempt by Tughtakin to regarrison the town before the Franks arrived.[24] In May 1110 Beirut fell to a combined Frankish force. The Muslims of the city refused an easy surrender; a bitter battle for control of the city took place, "and never before or after did the Franks see a more hard-fought battle than this." The Fatimids did their best to relieve the city: a fleet arrived and attempted to deliver supplies, but they could not dislodge the tenacious and ever-present Genoese, who had blockaded the port. A small contingent, arriving from Egypt by land, was ambushed in Transjordan and never made it.[25]

In the autumn of 1110 King Sigurd of Norway, the first crowned head of Europe to visit the region, joined Baldwin of Jerusalem on a kingly siege of Sidon, from which he had already exacted tribute, blockading it by land and sea. "When those in Sidon saw what was afoot," one chronicler notes, "their hearts sank, and they feared a repetition of a disaster like that at Beirut." A group of the town's leading citizens sent a delegation to the Franks to negotiate a surrender and guarantee of safety for the populace; all those who wished it were allowed to leave for Damascus. However, Baldwin rather ignobly forgot these terms and exacted a heavy tribute once again from the populace and confiscated their property.[26]

Baldwin then set out to attempt Ascalon, Egypt's vital bridgehead, long sought by the Franks. The governor there was known to be on friendly terms with him, and so the Fatimids sent an army to replace him with someone more reliable. The governor, however, rebelled when he learned of this and expelled his garrison of Berber troops, replacing them with a group of his own Armenian slave troops. The Berbers refused to comply and joined in a general uprising with the local populace. The governor was eventually captured and killed. The local postmaster, who was thus also the local spymaster, seems to have taken control of the city and maintained the peace until the Fatimids could install a proper replacement.[27] Ascalon therefore remained (barely) in Muslim hands.

With most of the coastal region—Tripoli, Beirut, Sidon, Acre— conquered, the Franks concentrated the bulk of their energies once again on the bustling port of Tyre. The siege started in February 1112, but the locals held firm. One quick-thinking Arab sailor jury-rigged a winch on the city wall, and it proved successful for dumping noxious liquids onto the Franks. He also devised tools with which to deflect their battering rams. However, the Tyrians, who were nominally under Fatimid control, could not keep this up forever, and so they offered the city to Tughtakin of Damascus if he would come to their aid. Tughtakin and a host of volunteers from the countryside set out and harassed the Franks at Tyre and tried to divert them by raiding and capturing smaller forts in Frankish territory, even blockading Sidon. Finally, under this pressure, the Franks lifted their siege and withdrew to Acre. The Tyrians plundered their camp and eventually handed control of the city to Tughtakin. Yet, in a surprising gesture of goodwill, Tughtakin wrote to the Fatimids that he would hold the city only until they came to claim it.[28] For the moment Tyre remained in Muslim control.

Tughtakin and Ridwan

Damascus was unable to devote its full energies to defending the coastal zone; one reason for this was that the atabeg Tughtakin was heavily invested in conducting jihad against the Franks elsewhere throughout Syria and, moreover, had his own internal affairs to juggle. In 1104 Duqaq, the Saljuq prince of Damascus, had died; as Duqaq's atabeg, Tughtakin now found himself facing an uncertain future. With the blessing of Duqaq's widow, however, it was agreed that Tughtakin would remain as atabeg to Duqaq's young heir, auspiciously named

Tutush II. However, Tughtakin had first to find a way to deal with young Tutush II's brother and rival, Bektash, who, resentful at his brother's rise and scheming for revenge, resisted the whole arrangement. Tughtakin first tried placing Bektash under house arrest in Baalbek in Lebanon, then tried conciliating him and welcoming him to Damascus. But Bektash was soon expelled and returned to Baalbek to take up banditry with a group of his rowdier companions, marauding into the fertile Hawran south of Damascus and making overtures to Baldwin of Jerusalem, appealing for his aid in a bid to retake Damascus. Nothing came of this particular scheme, and Bektash retired to an estate on the Euphrates and never bothered Damascus again. But in the meantime the young prince Tutush II died, without an heir, in late 1104. Without any Saljuqs at hand, Tughtakin ruled Damascus on his own, an atabeg without a prince.[29]

To maintain this unusual position, Tughtakin made certain that his relations with the Saljuq sultan were always quite correct, and he worked tirelessly to be seen as the most active leader of jihad against the Franks. As we shall see, he did so by participating in coalition campaigns officially authorized by the sultan. But he also repeatedly took to the field on his own steam. In April 1105, for example, he recaptured Rafaniya from the Franks, razed the fortress that the Franks had built there, and put its garrison to death.[30] When the Franks retook Rafaniya, Tughtakin returned in 1115, having given orders to his officers "to make preparations and hold themselves in readiness to…acquire the merit of jihad and to deal with a matter of importance." His troops took large amounts of plunder and captives, and "the Muslims returned to Damascus, victorious, rejoicing, and laden with plunder, without having lost a single man." They also brought some of the heads of the slain enemy, which were paraded in morbid spectacle through the city.[31] In the autumn the Franks had completed a new fortress near his southern borders, so he marched on it and razed the fortress there too. This zone, stretching between Muslim Damascus and Frankish Tiberias, was Syria's breadbasket and contained some of the most fertile land under tillage. He returned to the area many times during his career to fend off any Frankish presence that threatened it, as in 1108, when he sent a diversionary force into Palestine while he besieged Tiberias itself. In the battle that resulted, Gervase, the Frankish lord, a veteran of the First Crusade, was captured along with his men and put to death; Baldwin of Jerusalem had refused their ransom. Some of the prisoners were sent as tribute to the sultan.[32]

In exchange for all these exertions, in 1116 Tughtakin received the recognition of his position that he craved, in the form of a diploma of investiture granted in Baghdad from the sultan, confirming him as amir and *isfahsalar* of Syria, roughly Syria's commander in chief. The language of the diploma goes on, echoing the priorities of the "circle of equity," to urge him to maintain his troops and make war on the infidels, administer his taxes wisely, prosecute criminals, and establish justice for his subjects, Muslim and non-Muslim.[33]

However, for all his campaigning, Tughtakin was a pragmatist; he knew that driving the Franks into the sea was not possible, and he made skillful use of truces and treaties with his Frankish foes to better handle the challenges that came his way, as in 1108, when he agreed to a four-year truce with Baldwin of Jerusalem that one chronicler said was "for the Muslims a blessing from God Almighty."[34] Much of this treaty work concerned agricultural areas over which Damascus and its Frankish neighbors made claims. In 1109, for example, on the heels of a stinging defeat, Tughtakin signed a treaty with Baldwin that divided up the harvests produced in the disputed lands that straddled their two kingdoms.[35]

Soon his other Frankish neighbors wanted in, and so in the same year, 1109, he signed a treaty with Bertrand of Tripoli, who agreed to desist from raiding Muslim lands in return for the rather inaccessible Lebanese mountain villages of Munaytira and 'Akkar, annual tribute from a few others, and, most important, one-third of the produce of the verdant Beqaa valley. (Bertrand soon broke the treaty.)[36] A year later Baldwin too wanted his share of the Beqaa, and a new agreement was drawn up.[37] A victory against Baldwin in 1111 resulted in a similar arrangement in other lands abutting Tughtakin's southern borders.[38] Controlling access to basic necessities in this way gave Tughtakin as much of a tool to use against the Franks as did his army.

Tughtakin emerged as the leader of the local response to the Frankish invasions. Other Saljuq rulers and commanders were also coming to terms with this new foreign element. Ridwan of Aleppo had been a bitter rival of his brother Duqaq of Damascus while he lived, and even after Duqaq died his suspicion of Tughtakin's intentions kept him aloof of most campaigns against the Franks south of his kingdom. Ridwan's main concern was the continued survival of his own kingdom, which, the threat of Damascus aside, was virtually a stone's throw from the Frankish principality of Antioch, lay within easy striking distance of Edessa, and was the first stop in Syria for any Saljuq commander from the east seeking a kingdom of his own. The sources make clear the anxiety that his subjects felt at their precarious position on the front lines, something that their brethren in Damascus rarely experienced. His anxieties aside, in 1102–3 Ridwan had had some striking successes against the Franks, effectively clearing them out of his domains and threatening even Antioch itself.[39] And in April 1105 he offered a large contingent (including the local urban militia, or *ahdath*) in a jihad campaign to help relieve the Frankish siege of Tripoli. En route, however, the troops encountered Tancred of Antioch's armies at Artah, and Ridwan's cavalry was routed, leaving the infantry to be butchered; Artah itself was taken. The remnants fled back to the city, with Tancred hot on their heels. The citizens of Aleppo then saw their worst fear realized: a Frankish siege of their beloved city. Many of the populace fled, only to be killed or captured by Tancred's men. And so "the people of Syria, after enjoying security and peace, were brought into a state of distress and anxiety." After imposing a truce and exacting tribute from Ridwan, Tancred withdrew. Ridwan's appetite for assisting his neighbors seems to have faded thereafter.[40]

The truce that Ridwan made with Tancred in 1105 seems to have been beneficial to both parties and, in the end, bore strange fruit, and stranger bedfellows. To the east of Ridwan's kingdom, in northern Iraq, the landscape had changed since Jikirmish's much-trumpeted victory against the Franks on the Balikh. By 1106 the sultan had grown suspicious of Jikirmish's ambitions at Mosul and replaced him with a commander from Iran named Jawuli, who was "ordered by the sultan to march against the Franks to take their territory from them." As part of this arrangement, Jawuli confiscated all of Jikirmish's property, including his very valuable prisoner, Baldwin of Le Bourcq, the count of Edessa, who was still in captivity after being taken at the Balikh years earlier. (His cousin Joscelin had already managed to ransom himself.) Jawuli cashed in this windfall, releasing Baldwin after extracting promises of payment from him.

However, after taking Mosul, Jawuli in his turn seems to have become overreaching, coming into conflict with most of the local and regional powers. The prickly Ridwan of Aleppo saw in Jawuli a threat to his own independence and so opened negotiations with his neighbor, Tancred of Antioch, to suggest a pact against him. The two—Muslim and Frank—agreed to join forces in a preemptive strike before Jawuli could follow the sultan's orders to invade Syria. In response Jawuli called upon Baldwin of Le Bourcq and waived the remainder of his ransom payments in return for Edessa's help.

And so it was that, in September 1108, in the first of many of those ironic political tangles common to this period, the plains near Tall

Bashir saw the strange spectacle of the Frankish lord of Antioch marching alongside Muslim troops from the lord of Aleppo, arrayed in battle against the sultan's representative, the Muslim lord of Mosul, who marched with his own Frankish allies from Edessa. It looked as if Jawuli might defeat his rivals, but news arrived that spelled his doom: the sultan had replaced him at Mosul. At this Jawuli's men melted away, back to their homes, abandoning their commander with a few men from his personal guard and a contingent of jihad volunteers. Jawuli fled the scene, and the army of Antioch and Aleppo plundered his baggage train and returned to their respective homes in Syria, victorious. Jawuli eventually returned, defeated and humbled, to the sultan; he carried his burial shroud with him as an indication that he was ready to pay the price for his failure. The sultan, however, forgave him and relocated him to his old province in Iran, where he died in his service.[41] As for Ridwan, his pact with Tancred did not mean any love was lost between them, and he continued to suffer Frankish raids into his territory and, in particular, on the border fortress of Atharib.[42]

Much of Ridwan's career was also spent managing what we might call his "Shi'ite problem." His subject population in northern Syria included a sizable Shi'ite community, mainstream Isma'ilis, and Nizari "Assassins." Although there is no indication that he had any personal affinity for Isma'ili Shi'ism (as many sources hostile to him claimed), he saw the need to curry the favor of his Shi'ite subjects, if only as a political expedient. This was the same Ridwan, after all, who had suddenly declared allegiance to the Fatimid caliphs of Egypt, only to return to the 'Abbasid fold a few weeks later, after popular protest. He was equally compliant toward the Nizaris, allowing them to establish a *dar al-da'wa*, or "missionary center," for the teaching and propagation of their sect. Although Nizaris were a distinct minority within Syria's Isma'ili community, their ranks would grow in Syria. Ridwan's policies ensured that Aleppo emerged as a center for their earliest activities in the region.[43]

Nizari power really lay quite far away, in the mountain fortress of Alamut in northern Iran, where the sect's chief missionary, Hasan-i Sabbah, had taken advantage of the fragmentation of Saljuq power to establish a Nizari statelet, much as the Franks had done in Syria. But there are clear indications that Nizaris from Iran were now conducting affairs in Syria too, spreading their teachings and eliminating their enemies. In 1103 Ridwan's old atabeg and enemy, the lord of Homs, was stabbed to death in the mosque by three Persians disguised as ascetics. They are universally identified in the sources as "Batinis," that is, Nizaris. That Ridwan benefited directly from this act did not go unnoticed.

The Nizaris of Syria would spend the next decades following the successful model of their Iranian coreligionists, acquiring castles that stood in territory that was already home to Isma'ili populations (and hence easier to convert) yet were also remote enough to discourage their enemies. This effectively limited their activities to the lands around the Lebanon, Anti-Lebanon, and Jabal Ansariya ranges. In 1106, for example, Nizaris from Aleppo managed to enter the service of the Isma'ili lord of Apamea—bearing Frankish plunder to establish their credentials, according to one source—and then murdered him while he slept and took over the town. The lord's sons, however, managed to escape and enlisted the aid of Tancred of Antioch, who eventually captured the town for himself. Sentiment against the Nizaris was growing in Aleppo, and after Ridwan's death in 1113 the local prefect launched what amounted to a pogrom, rounding up suspected Nizaris and killing or imprisoning them. Many others fled to Frankish and Muslim lands throughout Syria. Over the next century the Nizaris would be dispersed throughout Syria but rarely subdued.[44]

The Sultan Responds

The death of the embattled sultan Barkiyaruq in 1105 meant that his successor, Muhammad, ruled as the undisputed ruler of a sultanate stretching from Iran to the Mediterranean. Within this vast empire Syria was merely a distant troubled frontier, but still the sultan was moved on occasion to organize official, elaborate jihad campaigns to the region. In 1109, after the fall of Tripoli, the sultan wrote to all his amirs that he was assembling an army to make war on the Franks and specifically ordered Tughtakin of Damascus (who had already requested aid many times) to hold his position until the main army could arrive from the east. When the promised army failed to arrive because of unspecified delays, Tughtakin prepared an official delegation to Baghdad to remind the sultan, sending Fakhr al-Mulk, the former lord of Tripoli, in 1110 "to make complaint of what had befallen the Muslims within their realms, of the seizure of cities, the slaying of men and the enslavement of women and children, and of their covetous ambition to reach out and conquer...Iraq."[45]

These were powerful images indeed, reminiscent of the impassioned pleas the judge Abu Sa'd al-Harawi had made in similar circumstances following the fall of Jerusalem. The sultan was moved enough to mount a campaign. As requested, a coalition army led by Mawdud of Mosul, aided by the Muslim governor of Armenia and the omnipresent Il-Ghazi and his Turcomans, set up camp before Edessa—the first of the Frankish states—in early May "and surrounded it on all sides like a girdle, preventing all ingress and egress." In view of the likely fall of Edessa, the leaders of the other Frankish states settled their many differences, and Antioch, Jerusalem, and Tripoli all sent men to come to the aid of Edessa. Tughtakin of Damascus (accompanied by a portentous comet in the eastern sky) likewise marched out to join his Muslim allies and intercept the Franks. The Frankish coalition soon thought better of crossing over to what they assessed to be their certain doom, and, despite attempts to lure them, they dispersed back to Syria. Muslim troops plundered their baggage train, but little else was accomplished. Tughtakin was forced to abandon his allies by rushing back to Damascus lest the fleeing Franks wreak havoc in his own lands. Eventually the remaining Muslims, who were encamped before Edessa, gave up as they themselves seemed to be running out of supplies faster than were the Franks and Armenians trapped inside the city.[46]

And so, just a few months later, yet another delegation arrived before the sultan, this one from Aleppo. It included men handpicked to persuade a sultan who himself was desperately seeking religious legitimacy: theologians, sufis, and even a descendant of the Prophet Muhammad. To bring the argument home, the delegation also included merchants, whose livelihood had been imperiled by recent Frankish successes. They appeared in the sultan's mosque, where their actions reveal a palpable tension and impatience toward the regime: "They drove the preacher from the pulpit and broke it in pieces, clamouring and weeping for the misfortunes that had befallen Islam at the hands of the Franks, the slaughter of men, and enslavement of women and children." It was an ugly scene. The delegation's arrival in Baghdad coincided with the arrival of the caliph's new bride, who also happened to be the sultan's daughter. The pomp and splendor of her entourage, the "jewelry, moneys, utensils...gorgeous raiment, attendants, guards, slave-girls, and followers" were cast in revolting contrast to the plight of the Muslims described by the Syrians. The caliph was incensed that his bride's homecoming should be marred by riots, and he ordered the culprits to be rounded up. But the caliph was not to have satisfaction. The sultan quietly squelched the investigation and instead commanded his amirs to prepare for jihad.[47]

In late July 1111 they moved on Tall Bashir, near Edessa. Mawdud was assisted by a group of volunteers and prominent commanders, including the Kurdish amir Ahmadil and the Turcoman Sukman of Armenia. They were also joined by Bursuq, lord of Hamadhan in Iran, handpicked by the sultan himself. The siege went well, and the Muslims succeeded in breaching the walls of Tall Bashir, forcing its lord, Joscelin, to sue for peace. He offered the Muslims substantial tribute if they would withdraw, but this was a jihad campaign, so most of the commanders were against being bought off once again by the Franks. Not so for the Kurdish Ahmadil, however, who happily accepted the offer over the heads of his peers. When the army left Tall Bashir for Aleppo, hoping Ridwan would pitch in supplies and men to assist, they found the gates locked—Ridwan had his own problems—and so the troops "ravaged its territories and created worse devastation than the Franks had done."[48]

The sultan's campaign was now revealed as the sad sham that it was. A large part of the Muslim army was under Ahmadil's command, and they followed his lead. The mighty Bursuq of Hamadhan had been able to round up only a fraction of his own troops and was himself so stricken with gout that he had to be carried around on a litter; it is reported that he was so ill that he could neither move nor speak. Sukman contracted an illness so grave that he had to return to Armenia; he died before he could even leave Syria. Ahmadil could think of nothing else to do but seize Sukman's lands now that he was dead. At this juncture Tughtakin of Damascus arrived at Aleppo, bearing a letter from the lord of Shayzar, who was concerned about a fortress the Franks were building near his lands, and so Tughtakin urged the army to proceed deeper into Syria. This was not the campaign these commanders had signed on for, however, and so they dispersed.

Only Mawdud and his men remained to assist Tughtakin, and the two forces encamped on the Orontes before relocating to Shayzar itself.[49] From there the armies of Mosul, Damascus, and Shayzar confronted those of Antioch, Jerusalem, and Tripoli. Usama ibn Munqidh, the nephew of Shayzar's lord and an eyewitness to these events, was quite proud of his family's role, though he did condescend to note that Mawdud too "had some excellent men with him." It was a well-executed contest, the Muslims constantly harrying the Franks as they moved from camp to camp in search of water, pinning them with arrows and constant feints. Eventually, in a lull in the fighting as the Muslims retired for Friday prayers, the Franks beat a retreat northward to Apamea, while Mawdud and Tughtakin—now fast friends—withdrew to Damascus, "and all the people were rejoiced at the discomfiture of the Franks."[50] But as the victory had little lasting effect, it was cold comfort.

In May 1113 Mawdud went to Damascus again to assist Tughtakin in a punitive campaign against the Franks of Tiberias. The Franks attempted to assuage Tughtakin by ceding him lands and offering a truce. He would have none of it, however, and in late June the Muslim armies made their way into northern Palestine. By chance the Franks and Muslims had taken a similar course and wound up camping on either side of the same bridge. This was in hilly territory, and a Muslim foraging party almost literally stumbled upon the Frankish camp, raising the alarm. Battle was immediately joined, both sides locked in furious hand-to-hand combat, Tughtakin taking up position on the bridge to prevent a Frankish crossing. The Muslims overwhelmed the Frankish camp, taking many prisoners; many more were killed. Baldwin, the king of Jerusalem himself, was captured and stripped of his weapons, but, ever the survivor, he managed to escape. The remaining Franks, under Tancred and Bertrand of Tripoli, sought refuge in a hill fort near Tiberias. The Muslims determined a siege would be impracticable and so withdrew, "knowing that the signs and evidences of their victory were manifest, the enemy humbled, broken, defeated and dispirited, and that the squadrons of Islam had penetrated to the environs of Jerusalem and Jaffa." They made a last attempt to lure the Franks into battle. But the Franks were staying put, and eventually Tughtakin and Mawdud withdrew.[51]

Mawdud had earlier sent a letter proclaiming this victory to the sultan, accompanied by Frankish prisoners and various other treasures and trophies, and so he thought it best to await further orders as a guest of his friend Tughtakin in Damascus. It was there, while walking into the beautiful Umayyad mosque in the heart of the city, that a man got up from the crowd of worshipers and approached as if to implore God's blessings on the victorious Mawdud. Instead the man grabbed Mawdud's belt for purchase and stabbed him twice in the groin. As Mawdud was surrounded by his bodyguard, the assassin was dead before a third blow could be struck. Mawdud was rushed to a physician, but he died within hours. No follow-up to his minor victory at Tiberias, therefore, ever came.[52] The next time the sultan ordered a campaign to Syria was in 1115, under Mawdud's successor at Mosul, the amir Aq-Sunqur. This campaign was directed at Edessa, and after two months it failed.[53]

No matter how assiduously the sultan tried, it seemed as if all his centralized campaigns against the Franks were ineffectual. Yet still he sent them. Later in 1115 he ordered yet another army into Syria, but it was not so much a jihad campaign against the Franks (though it was officially that) as a retaliatory strike against Tughtakin, who, with his kinsman Il-Ghazi, the former lord of Mardin, had since risen in what the sultan regarded as open rebellion. Il-Ghazi had lost his position in Mosul, and so Tughtakin was now sheltering him in Damascus. As for the otherwise steadfastly loyal Tughtakin, his many successes in Syria had long produced jealousies among the warrior elite of the sultanate, and on more than one occasion rumors had been circulated against him in the sultan's court. Mawdud's assassination while under his protection certainly raised eyebrows, and, when rumors were combined with the fact of his protection of Il-Ghazi, the sultan smelled a plot. When Tughtakin learned that the sultan had sent an army against him, his local options limited, he made an alliance with his enemy Roger of Salerno, the new lord of Antioch. Roger was a successful raider closer to his home turf, so much so that the Muslim lords in his vicinity had come to view him as a devilish thorn in their side. Perhaps this is what suggested him to Tughtakin as an ally against the sultan. Whatever the case, the sultan's army, under Bursuq, the lord of Hamadhan—now apparently cured of his gout—was delayed at Aleppo, where Tughtakin and Il-Ghazi were holing up. Finding the delay there fruitless, Bursuq proceeded deeper into Syria, to menace the lands belonging to Tughtakin and his amirs. It was a brilliant move. The rebellion quickly disintegrated as the various Syrian amirs rushed to defend their holdings. The Franks observed all this carefully and opted to remain aloof, betting, they claimed, that Bursuq's massive army would disband once winter came. When it didn't, they themselves disbanded, and Tughtakin's and Il-Ghazi's men did likewise.

Bursuq, meanwhile, remained in the field near Shayzar, capturing Frankish-held Kafartab and Ma'arra before setting out in formation for Aleppo. It was then that the Franks struck, intercepting the Muslim baggage and mounts near Danith while they were separated from the main army, massacring the camp followers and plundering the mounts and supplies. (Some sources suggest this was the result of Muslim treachery.) As the Muslim troops caught up, the Franks killed them as they arrived. Bursuq's army was scattered. In retaliation some of the Muslims guarding the prisoners from Kafartab put them to death; others were simply released. It was a terrible defeat for the sultan and a personal one for Bursuq, who is said to have died full of remorse and planning another campaign to repay the Franks. Bursuq's reprisal never came, however, and the Saljuq sultans never again sent an army to fight the Franks in Syria. Henceforth jihad against the Franks would be a local affair, conducted solely by the region's amirs, atabegs, and military men.[54]

Of the many smaller campaigns led by individual amirs in Syria and Iraq, the most significant took place in 1119 and resulted in a devastating Frankish defeat on the plain of Sarmada west of Aleppo. The site of the battle is known by various names in the Arabic sources, but the Franks called it *ager sanguinis*, the "Field of Blood."[55] In 1118 Roger of Salerno, the lord of Antioch, captured A'zaz, a strategic town, whose loss opened up Aleppo to attack from the north, which Roger demonstrated by raiding the hinterland of the city. At this Il-Ghazi, now lord of Aleppo, agreed with his old friend Tughtakin of Damascus to take matters into their own hands and prepared to march on Antioch. Il-Ghazi first retaliated by raiding the lands of Edessa, exacting promises from the Franks there not to interfere, and then marched into Syria without even stopping in Aleppo. With him was a large army of Turcomans and Bedouin, many thousands strong, some of whom raided Muslim lands to the south. Il-Ghazi paused to besiege Atharib, which he took, and awaited the arrival of Tughtakin's army from Damascus. Roger meanwhile encamped with a much smaller force of some seven hundred knights and perhaps three thousand foot soldiers. He chose a steep hillock on the eastern edge of the plain outside the town of Sarmada, a flat bottom of a bowl-shaped depression with steep sides that admitted only a few roads for access. While Roger waited for the armies of Jerusalem and Tripoli to arrive, this unique position seemed to offer all the security his army needed.

He was wrong. Il-Ghazi, with his large army of nomads, knew he had to act quickly before his troops dispersed, so, without waiting for Tughtakin, he marched on Roger. During the night of June 27 Il-Ghazi's men mounted the high ground surrounding Roger's camp. When dawn broke, the qadi of Aleppo, who had accompanied the army, gave a rousing speech before the troops. As dawn became a windy, dusty morning, they let their arrows fall. A Frankish eyewitness provides a vivid account of Roger's attempt to maintain his battle formation against the Muslim troops encircling him on the plain, but the Turcomans had the upper hand. The battle was remembered as a decisive one. Al-'Azimi, a contemporary chronicler, was moved to compose an ode on the occasion, inserting a few lines of it into his otherwise terse and dry chronicle. His contemporary, Ibn al-Qalanisi, could not restrain his Schadenfreude: "God Most High, to whom be the praise, granted victory to the party of Islam against the impious mob, and not one hour of the day...had passed ere the Franks were on the ground, one prostrate mass...so that no one man of them escaped to tell the tale, and their leader Roger was found stretched out among the dead."[56] It was also remembered as a miracle, one in which the *abdal*, green-shrouded heavenly warriors associated with Syria, provided a helping hand to God's people, a literary riposte to the Franks' ghostly armies and miraculous Lance at Antioch.[57]

The Muslim (and Frankish) sources make much of the fact that Il-Ghazi, allegedly immobilized by drink, failed to capitalize on these victories when he might well have taken Antioch. But realist military goals, not the wines of Syria, seem to have been what really guided Il-Ghazi, who turned from Antioch itself and captured the smaller but strategic towns of al-Atharib and Zardana, valuable listening posts between Antioch and Aleppo. A final confrontation at Danith, closer still to Antioch, ended ingloriously, as Il-Ghazi and Tughtakin and their troops fled the field, and the Franks under Baldwin of Jerusalem and Pons of Tripoli withdrew. In keeping with the blurriness of loyalty and motive prevailing during these early years, both sides claimed victory.

- 5 -

Tasting Our Might

ABU BAKR AL-TURTUSHI was an eleventh-century Muslim jurist
from the town of Tortosa on the Andalusi coast. Like many
scholars of his day, he was compelled to embark upon his *talab
al-'ilm*, or search for knowledge, by traveling throughout Islamdom to
meet and study with the best scholars in every region. He studied with
eminent jurists in Baghdad, then wandered a bit in Syria, living an austere and contemplative life. He passed some time in Jerusalem shortly
before it was taken by the Franks in the hopes of meeting the real
scholar of the age, Abu Hamid al-Ghazali, the powerhouse Sunni theologian who, as we've seen, had written his encyclopedic *Revival of the
Religious Sciences* under Saljuq auspices. Al-Ghazali had embarked on
some Syrian wanderings of his own, but the two never did cross paths
there.

Eventually, probably as a refugee from the Frankish invasion of
Syria, Turtushi made his way to Egypt in the middle decades of Fatimid
rule. As an activist Sunni jurist in Egypt of the Shi'i Fatimids, he probably felt he had to tread somewhat carefully, but it happened that the
fearsome vizier al-Afdal was himself a Sunni, and so Turtushi found
some favor with him and his successor. He practiced law in Alexandria,
often welcoming students traveling from his native al-Andalus. He also
spent time composing works in Sunni theology and apocalyptic and
prophetic tradition. He became best known as a political thinker, composing a well-received treatise, *The Lamp of Kings*, for the Fatimid

vizier who replaced al-Afdal, in the hope his fortunes might rise. The work is a fascinating collection of political lore supporting the ideals of the Circle of Equity centuries before the biting pragmatism of Machiavelli, with examples taken from Islamic history, pre-Islamic empires, and even al-Andalus. It doesn't seem that Turtushi's little mirror for princes had much effect on the Fatimids, however. In 1122, when he completed his work, the caliphate was sliding into some of its darkest days, barely capable of managing its palace, let alone taking on an agile Frankish enemy. This was the context in which Turtushi's airy evocations of the timeless blessings of justice seem almost surreal. But eventually Turtushi's dreams of a ruler inspired by justice, and one who could put infidels in their place, would be realized in both the Near East and the Maghrib, through means he could never have imagined.[1]

Zangi Comes to Aleppo

During the immediate aftermath of the first Frankish invasion of the Near East, the responses of the Muslim authorities to this new presence were fragmented and largely ineffectual. As we have seen, even the Saljuq sultan, try as he might, could not surmount the intrigues and self-interest of his own elites in order to effectively organize them in campaigns against the Franks. Military responses to the Franks were left largely in the hands of local lords like Tughtakin of Damascus, who, though they had much more consistent luck in the field than the sultan's armies, were also deeply involved in the web of alliances and counteralliances that characterized Saljuq Syria. Within a decade upon arriving in the area in 1099, the Franks had inserted themselves into the political landscape, becoming recognized if resented players of the game of Syrian politics, much as their coreligionists and kinsmen had done in al-Andalus. Pushing them out of this game would be even harder than before. To do so, what was required was a political leadership that married Syrian military savvy with an authority that transcended the petty factionalism of the province. Some atabegs and amirs like Tughtakin and Il-Ghazi had come close to achieving this, but with the legacy of the first Saljuq sultans having less and less meaning for a new generation of beleaguered Syrians, it was time for a change of vision from outside Syria. It was thus fittingly at Aleppo, where Iraqi politics have almost always entered Syrian affairs, that these changes came.

Aleppo had been through a world of trouble since the Saljuqs first took the place. The death of Prince Ridwan in 1113 permanently severed what tenuous connection there had been between Syria and the Saljuq ruling family. His two sons did not rule for long: one was assassinated and the other was a minor ruling in the shadow of the regent Lu'lu', who was himself assassinated in 1117. With Tughtakin solidly in control of Damascus, this meant that of the former Saljuq domains in Syria, Aleppo was, in effect, the only one up for grabs. Indeed the five-year reign of the Artuqid amir Il-Ghazi, the great victor at the Field of Blood, was just one relatively stable moment in an otherwise troubled post-Saljuq period in Aleppo. Il-Ghazi himself, though firmly in alliance with Tughtakin of Damascus, ultimately squandered what luster he had won at the Field of Blood as the Franks made serious inroads on Muslim gains in northern Syria and even in the Artuqid heartlands of Upper Mesopotamia.[2]

After Il-Ghazi's death in 1122, his on-again, off-again Artuqid successors in Aleppo badly mismanaged the city, even if they did have their share of successes in the field,[3] some of them spectacular. His nephew and successor Balak, for example, managed to capture not just Joscelin, the count of Edessa (in 1122), but Baldwin himself (in 1123), who was at the time king of Jerusalem and regent of Antioch. Joscelin managed to return to Frankish territory, but King Baldwin and many other Frankish knights and nobles remained imprisoned for more than a year, when Timurtash, Balak's successor, agreed to release him in return for a vast sum and to make certain political concessions, such as surrendering the contested town of A'zaz. Baldwin promptly broke the terms of his release (he claimed his patriarch had forbidden any oaths made with Muslims) and, reunited with Joscelin, began to organize a new assault on Aleppo.

In all this back-and-forth in and around Aleppo, those who truly fared the worst were the city's populace. As no amir had shown much loyalty to the city since the death of Ridwan, the populace returned the sentiment. As a result, whenever the people of Aleppo found themselves in desperate straits, they were ready to yield their city to whatever Muslim amir could promise them safety. Thus in October 1124, when Baldwin and Joscelin, assisted by Muslim Bedouin allies from Iraq, surrounded Aleppo in a long and bitter siege, a delegation went to Mosul, whose ruler was Aqsunqur al-Bursuqi, a mamluk and chief officer of the Saljuq sultan who had spent his earlier career in Iraq bringing the Bedouin of the region to heel. He agreed to see to Aleppo's needs and dispersed the forces besieging the city. He thereupon took over control of the city, settled various disputes flaring between rival parties, reorganized its defenses, and pursued the Franks in northern

Syria, linking, for the first time, Aleppo's fate with the manpower of Mosul and Upper Mesopotamia. A crushing defeat at A'zaz in 1125 obliged him to divide some of his lands with the Franks, but his subsequent campaigns against them were largely successful, regaining territory lost to the Franks and fending off Frankish feints toward his city. When he returned to Mosul in 1126, leaving his son behind as his deputy, Aleppo could breathe a sigh of relief knowing that, in Aqsunqur and son, stable government had returned.

It was not to be: shortly after his arrival in Mosul, Aqsunqur was cut down in the congregational mosque by a group of men dressed as ascetics—Nizari assassins, it was claimed—who may well have been wary of the threat that a capable lord like Aqsunqur would pose to their communities, which, after all, had a long history in Aleppo and northern Syria. Aleppo was once again in play for the region's warlords, so in 1128 the populace once again turned to Mosul for help, and to its new atabeg, 'Imad al-Din Zangi.[4]

Zangi was in many ways a transitional figure, and it was in him that Syria first found the combination of military success and ideological certainty it needed to make a lasting impact against the Franks.[5] As a Turcoman amir and atabeg of Mosul, he was a familiar type in the Saljuq military, a rough-and-ready warrior cut from the same cloth as many of his predecessors, such as Il-Ghazi and Aqsunqur. They were, after all, products of the same milieu. And though his personal ambitions and energetic campaigning against the Franks were features of earlier Saljuq amirs like Tughtakin, his willingness to use jihad as a basis for carving out his own independent domain set him apart from his colleagues and linked him to the phenomenon of the jihad-savvy statesmen of later times, such as Saladin. Though largely associated with Syria, Zangi spent most of his early career in the service of the sultan in Iraq. His father, a former governor of Aleppo, had died when Zangi was still a child, and he was adopted by the governor of Mosul and remained in service to subsequent governors there, making a name for himself. In 1122 the Saljuq sultan Mahmud named him *shihna*, a sort of chief prefect, of the southern Iraqi towns of Wasit and Basra and, in 1127, shihna of Baghdad itself, drawing him into the often strained relationship between the sultan and the caliph. Later that year the sultan made him governor of Mosul and entrusted him with the guardianship of two of his minor sons as atabeg.

At Mosul, Zangi could let his ambitions run more freely, and he often clashed with his major local Muslim rivals in Upper Mesopotamia, the Artuqid dynasty. He whittled away at their lands, subduing the

Turcoman tribesmen who inhabited them. These tribes then supplemented his own army of mamluks in his larger, more flamboyant campaigns in Syria. There Zangi's first forays were notably free of any conflict with the Franks; given that he arranged a truce with Joscelin upon arriving in Mosul, this was presumably a deliberate policy, allowing him to focus his energies on his Muslim rivals. In 1128, as we have seen, Zangi, armed with a diploma from the sultan investing him with control over "the West," answered the call of the populace of Aleppo and took control of the city and its territories out of the hands of the Artuqids. He also established a garrison, and, to show that his relationship with the Saljuqs was unimpeachable, he married a local Saljuq princess, one of Ridwan's daughters. As soon as the sultan recognized his new Syrian possessions, however, Zangi promptly decamped to his base in Mosul, not returning to Syria for another two years, when he again attacked his Muslim rivals there, besieging Homs, to no avail, but capturing the city of Hama on the Orontes. He also led a lightning campaign in the spring of 1130 into the territory of Antioch, capturing the border town of al-Atharib from the Franks in the process.

These campaigns left their mark. Al-Atharib had been a thorn in Aleppo's side for some time now, being the main launching point for Frankish raids on the city. The Franks there had even imposed a tribute on Aleppo that the citizenry must have found especially odious. When the Franks learned that Zangi had set his sights on them, "they realized that this was a battle which would determine their future," according to Ibn al-Athir. "They mobilised all and left none of their potential strength unexploited." Zangi consulted with his companions about how to handle this imposing enemy force. When his advisers suggested it would be folly to face the Franks on their own turf, Zangi reacted defiantly, vowing to confront them come what may. At al-Atharib, Ibn al-Athir attributes to Zangi a sort of Turcoman's St. Crispin's Day speech, in which Zangi rallies his men against the enemy, saying, "Let us make them so taste of our might that the fear of it remains in their hearts." Few details are given of the ensuing battle, save that the Franks were routed and the Muslims emerged victorious. Zangi urged his men to show no mercy. Fifty years later Ibn al-Athir was told that the bones of the dead from that day still littered the land. From his victory at al-Atharib Zangi proceeded to its twin, the border fortress of Harim, and agreed to a truce with the Franks.[6]

Zangi was an Iraqi ruler first and foremost, so when news came of threats from his Artuqid neighbors to his base in Mosul, he returned to Iraq. There, dragged into wars with these local rivals, a Saljuq succession struggle, and the politics of a dangerously independent-minded new caliph, Zangi was bemired and had to hold off from moving on his primary Syrian goal: Damascus itself.[7] But Zangi would return soon enough to Syria, striking the greatest blow yet to the odds of Frankish survival.

Tughtakin's Damascus

Compared with the tumult in Aleppo, political life in Damascus after the Saljuqs was fairly staid, though not without its disturbances. The Nizari "Assassins," for example, became a new force in the region at precisely this time. As we have seen, the Nizari community of Aleppo, whose Shi'i beliefs and firmly guarded secrecy Sunnis found so threatening, had been almost completely expelled from that city after the death of their protector Ridwan. And so their leaders turned to Damascus and its vicinity as their new base of operations, a development that the Sunni populace of the area did not wholly welcome. The new Nizari leader, Bahram, is said by a terrified Damascene chronicler to have lived "in extreme concealment and secrecy, and continually disguised himself, so that he moved from city to city and castle to castle without anyone being aware of his identity."[8] It was probably he who directed the murder of Aqsunqur in Mosul in 1126. In the same year Bahram arrived in Damascus before its ruler, Tughtakin, who showed the Nizaris a certain amount of favor, granting Bahram the contested frontier town of Banyas and allowing them to establish their headquarters in Damascus. Though some observers thought that an evil adviser had twisted Tughtakin's mind to make such concessions, in fact he may simply have been biding his time. As it happened, the Nizaris were able to make only short-term gains out of this arrangement. Much as in Aleppo, where the death of their protector Ridwan led to their expulsion, in Damascus the death of Tughtakin in 1128 led to a citywide pogrom against what was seen as the evil influence of the Nizaris and their backers in the city. Muslim sources say that thousands, even tens of thousands of Nizaris were killed—an impossibly large number. We can at least be certain that the local branch of the movement was decimated. The Nizaris fled the area altogether, abandoning Banyas to the Franks (Zangi later captured it) and soon finding refuge back again in the north in a new network of castles and strongholds in the Jabal Ansariya, among them Qadmus and, most famously, Masyaf, the most imposing of the Nizari castles in Syria.[9]

The Franks too occasionally menaced Damascus, but, thanks in large part to Tughtakin's leadership, never was the city in such straits as Aleppo was, even as the Franks regained their composure after the Field of Blood, their greatest loss yet. In 1124 they finally conquered Tyre—it had taken nearly twenty-five years—and were in almost complete control of the Mediterranean coast; the captive King Baldwin of Jerusalem was released shortly thereafter. The Franks were now at liberty to apply pressure where it was needed inland, including, as we have seen, Aleppo (in 1124) and A'zaz (in 1125). Although they threatened Damascus on a few occasions, as they did in 1125 and 1126, they never imperiled it. In the larger attack of 1126, for example, Baldwin met Tughtakin in battle at Marj al-Suffar, a historic battlefield south of Damascus. Although the Franks clearly defeated the Muslims, who were assisted in this instance by armed urban militias and even by the Nizaris, Baldwin could not follow up on his gains, since the routing Damascene troops found the courage to stop and, in their turn, charge on the Franks and cause them to flee the scene. Bereft of his men, Baldwin chose to simply retire to Jerusalem, leaving Tughtakin free to withdraw homeward.[10]

However, these raids seem to have whetted Baldwin's appetite, and in 1127 he began preparing for a larger campaign against Damascus, sending embassies to Europe to raise a new army of volunteers to defend Frankish interests in Syria.[11] It is possible that local conditions at least partly dictated Baldwin's plan and its timing, since Tughtakin was known to be in failing health. Yet oddly, when, in February 1128, after a long career of service on the front lines against the Franks, the old atabeg finally died, Baldwin seems not to have taken advantage and instead watched and waited.[12] In the interval Damascus passed under the rule of Tughtakin's son, Buri, after whom his short-lived dynasty, the Burids, is named. By coincidence, the year that Tughtakin died was also the year that Zangi took Aleppo, and so Burid Damascus now had to worry about its new Muslim neighbor in Aleppo as much as it had to fear the Franks. In November 1129 the Franks were the first to move. Bolstered by fresh troops from Europe under the rich and vigorous Count Fulk of Anjou and contingents from all of the Frankish states, the Franks fielded a massive army of perhaps fifty thousand men. They were assisted by a group that combined knightly training and monastic piety in a relatively new military order, the Knights Templar, so called because their headquarters were in the al-Aqsa Mosque in Jerusalem, which the Franks (and indeed Muslim tradition) had associated with the Temple of Solomon. With such a force at their disposal, the Franks were confident of their victory. According to Usama ibn Munqidh, who was a contemporary to these events, the Franks had even begun dividing up real estate in Damascus in preparation for what they assumed would be its final capture.

They were premature. Having encamped a few miles south of Damascus, the Franks led an expedition into the countryside to forage for supplies for their over-large army—a dangerous division of forces that the Muslim armies promptly exploited by sending one contingent to ambush the foragers as they returned while others raided Frankish lands in the north that were now left unprotected. So totally devastated was the foraging party, the Arabic sources tell us, that the Franks who were still in camp beat a hasty retreat upon hearing of their ambush. (A violent autumn storm may also have shaped their opinion.) The Franks paused only to burn their encampment, and the sources all indicate that the Muslims took large numbers of horses and other animals as plunder. "The host of infidels dispersed to their castles in the most abject state of abasement,"[13] we are told, and Usama later crowed in recollection that "the Franks left Damascus on a most miserable and contemptuous journey."

Zangi and Syria

With the Franks in disarray, one would think that a Syrian commander would take the opportunity to press the Muslim advantage against them. Zangi, still preoccupied in Iraq, was surely the ablest of the region's commanders. He eventually would reenter the fray in Syria, but, like the Franks before him, he too would fail before Damascus. He would have to leave his mark some other way.

By the time the Franks had met their ignominious defeat at Damascus, Zangi had settled his affairs in Mosul and had done with the distraction of Iraqi politics. The situation in Damascus cried out for his attention. In 1132 Buri, the lord of Damascus, was attacked by Nizaris and died from his wounds. Now real power in the city, whatever the fortunes of its princes, was held by a Turkish commander named Unur, who had few friends in Damascus. And so, in 1135, Zangi returned to Syria. By the winter he had the city under siege and was demanding its surrender. Unur, however, responded with sufficient defiance, and the caliph himself wrote to Zangi to demand peace. And so Zangi lifted his siege for the moment, to turn his attention to Aleppo and to gaining firm mastery of its approaches. By the end of the year the city of Homs alone remained unbowed, but Zangi was obliged to return to Mosul before he could force the issue.

In his absence, Zangi's lieutenants maintained (without success) the pressure on Homs and Damascus and, in the spring of 1136, invaded the territories of Frankish Antioch. With fresh reinforcements of Turcoman tribesmen flooding into Syria's frontier, Zangi's men penetrated as far as the coast, looting Latakia and leaving the Franks there in shock that their foe could strike so quickly and so deeply into their territory. In the following year an army from Damascus, aided by the Syrian Christians of Mount Lebanon, invaded the county of Tripoli and captured its count, Pons, who was put to death. In retaliation, Pons's heir, Raymond II, ravaged the villages of Mount Lebanon.[14]

In the spring of 1137 Zangi returned to Homs, emboldened by a treaty with Damascus. But the city remained defiant. When Zangi learned that the Muslim governor of the city had requested military assistance from the Franks, he changed tactics and moved instead to invest the nearby Frankish fortress of Ba'rin. Raymond II of Tripoli and Fulk of Anjou, who had by now recovered nicely from his defeat at Damascus to become king of Jerusalem, joined forces and marched to relieve the fortress. Zangi was only too delighted. He at once lifted the siege and pounced on the Franks, and many were killed in the fighting. Raymond II himself was captured. At this Fulk abandoned the relief attempt and joined the Franks in relative safety behind the fortress's walls. Zangi took up the siege again, even as, unbeknownst to the besieged, a massive Frankish army from Jerusalem, Antioch, and Edessa assembled to come to Fulk's aid. Zangi didn't stand a chance. Instead he kept news of the arriving Frankish relief force secret and craftily offered terms, accepting the surrender of Ba'rin for the safe conduct of Fulk and his men, and the Franks happily agreed. As the Franks marched off, they encountered the coalition relieving force and learned to their infinite chagrin that they need not have surrendered anything.[15]

But Zangi's startling conquests in Syria, combined with fractious internal disputes in Frankish Antioch, awakened a sleeping giant: the Byzantine Empire. Antioch and much of northern Syria, as we have seen, were lands that had once belonged to Byzantium, and the Franks were long delinquent in handing them back after taking them during the First Crusade. It was time to remind them of their obligations to Byzantium. After reconquering cities held by the Franks and their Armenian allies in Cilicia, the Byzantine emperor John II arrived before Antioch in August 1137 and put it to siege. The Franks rushed to Antioch after their defeat at Ba'rin but quickly agreed to a peace, consenting to retain Antioch, but as a fief from John II, and to cooperate with the emperor in campaigns against Zangi's recent conquests, the Muslim-held towns and fortresses in northern Syria.

In April 1138 this odd Greco-Frankish army began its siege of Aleppo, which, reinforced by one of Zangi's lieutenants, withstood the assault. The Christian armies then moved south into the Jabal al-Summaq and the Orontes valley and set up a ring of mangonels around Shayzar to convince its lord to surrender. While the Banu Munqidh and their castle's stout defenses kept the Christian army occupied at Shayzar, Zangi wore down their troops by menacing the surrounding countryside and, through clever propaganda, seeding doubts among the allied Franks and Greeks about the real intentions of each group toward the other. Meanwhile Zangi sent a judge from his entourage on a mission to Baghdad to harangue the populace and sway the sultan into sending troops for an official jihad campaign. Instead Syria was saved from another quarter: the Danishmendids began nipping at the Byzantine supply lines in Anatolia. As a result, joint operations at Shayzar became half-hearted at best, and when the lord of Shayzar offered to buy his way out of the siege, the emperor was happy for the excuse to withdraw.[16]

Zangi could now return to mopping up in northern Syria, retaking Kafartab and Atharib, for example, and devastating 'Arqa, the fortress near Tripoli that had so stymied the armies of the First Crusade. Damascus remained in his sights. Through some hard-nosed negotiations with Mahmud of Damascus, Zangi concluded a significant marriage alliance: he married Mahmud's rather daunting mother (and finally received the city of Homs as her dowry), and Mahmud was granted the hand of one of Zangi's daughters. The disparity in status demonstrated by this exchange of mates made clear to everyone who was the real power in Syria now. When Mahmud of Damascus was assassinated in 1139, Zangi and his new wife inserted themselves directly into the succession dispute, siding with an exiled brother of Mahmud's as a pretext for attacking Damascus. The rival claimant was the lord of Baalbek, and Zangi overstepped even his customary cruelty when he captured the town, breaking his oath of safe conduct and flaying and crucifying the garrison. As in all his conquests, Zangi appointed one of his commanders to serve as the town's new governor. In this case he chose a rising warrior from one of the fierce Kurdish contingents in his army named Ayyub ibn Shadhi, who, though he would never have imagined it himself, would one day become the eponym of a mighty Muslim dynasty, the Ayyubids.

Zangi now turned to Damascus and set up a blockade. Unur responded by reopening negotiations with the Franks, offering Fulk of Jerusalem the contested town of Banyas—should they capture it from Zangi—and annual tribute in return for his aid in ousting Zangi from Damascus. Given the choice between a Damascus ruled by a penned-in Unur or a rampant Zangi, Fulk readily agreed to the treaty. Though Zangi dutifully put Damascus to siege and launched a few raids against the Franks, he realized his own energies would be wasted against such an alliance. Banyas fell to the Franks. Damascus would have to wait. In June 1140 he returned to Mosul, still unsatisfied.[17]

Edessa and the Fall of Zangi

By 1143 Zangi had set his house in order in Mosul, defeating local rivals and concluding a noninterference treaty with the Saljuq sultan. Aleppo remained quiescent and loyal to their new lord. Unur of Damascus continued to enjoy the fruits of his treaty with Jerusalem, periodically sending the suave Usama ibn Munqidh to the court of King Fulk to keep relations smooth. Zangi could now turn his attention once again to his own agenda. Perhaps by now he had learned that a march into southern Syria—the domain of Unur, King Fulk, and all their allies—would be fruitless. So instead he looked closer to home and embarked on his greatest achievement: the conquest of the Frankish-held city of Edessa.

Neither as great nor as meaningful as Jerusalem or Damascus, Edessa would nevertheless be a prize that would amply confound the Franks and redound to Zangi's glory among his peers. A city that was home to a large and ancient Christian population of perhaps forty thousand, it was also relatively easy picking; it was the poorest of the Latin states and, being an outlier far on the northern tier, it was separated from the other Latin states and worn down from decades of raids from the Muslim statelets that surrounded it. Muslim sources, written in hindsight, like to depict the conquest of Edessa as forever foremost in Zangi's mind, all part of his plan. Zangi actually benefited from a sudden confluence of events. From Mosul his greatest concerns were not the Franks of Edessa, led by Joscelin II, but his local Muslim rivals, the Artuqids of Upper Mesopotamia. In the summer of 1144 his principal foe, the Artuqid lord of Hisn Kayfa on the Euphrates, died, and his son and successor negotiated a rather worrisome treaty with Joscelin. This was a union of enemies, Frankish and Muslim, that Zangi could not have welcomed. However, Joscelin, it seems, had left Edessa in the hands of a small garrison of Armenian mercenaries and took up residence at the more rustic fortress town of Tall Bashir, his county's "second city." Moreover Joscelin had openly broken with Raymond II of Antioch, and so Zangi could be assured that if assistance did indeed come to Edessa, it would not come from mighty Antioch but much farther afield. Edessa was an ancient, populous, and well-fortified city, but, as a later Frankish chronicler quipped, "walls, towers, and ramparts avail but little if there are none to man them."[18]

Zangi pounced.[19] He wrote to the various Turcoman tribes of the region and urged their participation in his campaign, casting it as jihad against the Franks. It was, by all accounts, a vast army that surrounded the city, ringing it with archers and siege equipment. "Even the birds could scarce approach it," said one historian in a flight of hyperbole, "in fear of their lives from the unerring shafts...of the believers."[20] But it was Zangi's corps of sappers, some from as far as Khurasan, that brought victory, tunneling under the city walls and undermining their foundations. When a breach was finally created, on December 24, 1144, the Muslim troops poured in, taking heavy casualties in the process. Once inside, the realization of what they had accomplished against the Franks sank in. It was time for payback. "The troops set to pillaging, slaying, capturing, ravishing and looting, and their hands were filled with such quantities of money, furnishing, animals, booty and captives as rejoiced their spirits and gladdened their hearts."[21] Zangi intervened and gave orders to cease the looting and killing, promising to establish the rule of law in the city and even lightening the tax burden of the citizens. Ever the practical warlord, once the city and its citadel were secured he directed his troops' energies to rebuilding the fortifications that had been damaged, lest his prize fall from his hands again.

With Count Joscelin and the Franks of the county of Edessa in total disarray, Zangi pressed on, capturing Saruj and all Frankish lands east of the Euphrates save al-Bira. Tall Bashir, to the west, remained Joscelin's main base, an Edessan court in exile. Zangi's conquests sent shockwaves throughout the region, energizing Muslims and, as we shall see, virtually demanding a response from the Franks. It was bruited about that Zangi was now considering his final push toward Damascus, and much was made of the siege equipment that he was amassing. His ultimate intentions, however, are unclear; in September 1146, while besieging an Arab rival at Qal'at Ja'bar on the Euphrates, he was murdered while he lay sleeping.

It was an appropriately dramatic and sudden end to a violent career: risen from the ranks of the Saljuq Turcoman warrior-class, Zangi had literally hacked his way to the top, slowly and ruthlessly, fending off his foes, among whom were numbered even caliphs and sultans. Yet his last campaign was merely the siege of a minor castle that cannot have been more than an irritant. Fresh from his glorious victory at Edessa, he was at the height of his powers, lauded as "the adornment of Islam, the victorious prince, the helper of the believers," and yet he was clumsily murdered, gasping in his bed in a darkened tent on the banks of the Euphrates, with confidantes close enough at hand that they found him prostrate, still alive despite his wounds, sputtering to name his killer. The sources are split on the identity of the assassin. Some believe it was a group of his mamluks; others that it was a lone servant of Frankish origin. Either works as a fitting coda to the chronicles of the day, providing a moral to the story of a man who used jihad against the Franks as a cover for his ambitions against his Muslim rivals.[22]

Zangi does not seem to have made any plans for his succession. Like those of the Saljuq sultans themselves, Zangi's domains were ruled as family appanages. His two eldest sons, Sayf al-Din Ghazi and Nur al-Din Mahmud, were the most suitable heirs, and his other sons found positions within the regimes of one of their two brothers. As Zangi's domains had been based around two urban centers, Mosul and Aleppo, his inner circle too underwent its own mitosis, with one group of officers returning to support Sayf al-Din in Mosul and Upper Mesopotamia, and another group, led by Zangi's old Kurdish confidante, Shirkuh, rallying around Nur al-Din in Aleppo and Syria. Because of his activities fighting the Franks, Nur al-Din inevitably becomes the focus of histories of the Crusades. However, this distorts the picture somewhat. Nur al-Din ruled as a partner of his elder brother, who ruled from Zangi's old capital of Mosul and received his appointment from the sultan himself. It was Sayf al-Din, not Nur al-Din, who was the true heir to Zangi. Eventually Nur al-Din would have to address the relationship between Aleppo and Mosul. For the moment, however, relations between the two brothers remained subdued but not openly hostile. A few months into his reign, for example, Nur al-Din formally recognized his brother in Mosul as his overlord and was charged to continue Zangi's jihad against the Franks in Syria.

In this, and in other aspects of his career, Nur al-Din must have felt the weight of his father's accomplishments bearing on him.[23] It would have been hard for him to mark his regime with his own stamp. Merely the second of two Zangid princes, Nur al-Din had inherited a domain conquered by his father, an inner circle of advisers and commanders cultivated by him, and an army raised by him. He also inherited his father's problems. The first of these was the recently conquered city of Edessa, where a group of Armenians staged a rebellion upon Zangi's death and were joined by the Frankish count Joscelin, who hoped to take this opportunity to regain his former capital. Joscelin managed to recapture Edessa itself, but the citadel remained firmly in Muslim hands.

By making forced marches from Aleppo, Nur al-Din arrived at Edessa in a few days. Joscelin was no fool and could see he was outnumbered; he sensibly abandoned Edessa and withdrew to Tall Bashir. When Nur al-Din entered Edessa to reclaim it, he punished the citizens for their disloyalty. Whereas his father had made a point of restraining his men from their customary rights of plunder at Edessa, Nur al-Din gave them a free hand. The city was sacked and many of its inhabitants killed or taken captive. "This was the occasion," Ibn al-Athir notes, "when the city was plundered and became devoid of inhabitants. Only a small number remained there. Many people think that it was plundered when [Zangi] conquered it but this is not so."[24]

The second of Nur al-Din's problems inherited from his father was Damascus. As we have seen, through shows of brute force, cajoling, and quiet diplomacy, Zangi had striven against the commander Unur and the Burids of Damascus to make the city his own, but without success. It was thus up to Nur al-Din to pick up where Zangi left off, using the same mix of strategies. Furthermore he had even more pressing motives of his own. For unlike his father, Nur al-Din could not draw upon the resources and supplies of Upper Mesopotamia, which was his brother's domain, and so control of the agricultural lands around Damascus was vital to feeding, paying, and supplying his men. The Franks of the kingdom of Jerusalem had much the same interest in the region, and for the same reasons, and so in the spring of 1147 they invaded the Hawran, whence a local Muslim governor had invited them to assist him in his own attempt to break away from Damascus. Seeing an opportunity to exert influence in Damascus, Nur al-Din agreed to an alliance with Unur, and the two compelled the Franks to withdraw.

The Carcass of Unbelief

But most of all the Franks had Damascus on their minds. The treaty of 1140 that Unur had worked out with the Franks of Jerusalem meant that the city was, for the moment, a familiar and acceptable neighbor for the Frankish states. But the new rapprochement between Aleppo and Damascus, seen most clearly in the joint operations of Unur and Nur al-Din in the Hawran, and sealed with a marriage alliance in 1147, was a development with alarming implications, raising the specter of a united Muslim front from Damascus to Aleppo.[25] At best, any Frankish observer could see, Damascus would remain in Unur's hands and become a staging ground for occasional joint operations against Frankish territories. At worst, the city stood in danger of outright annexation from Aleppo and becoming Nur al-Din's new forward base in the very heart of Outremer. And so, for the Franks, quite apart from the promise of new agricultural lands, treaty or no treaty, the city needed to be taken off the table while the taking was good. But how?

It was at precisely this juncture that the Franks received the help that they thought would settle the matter. In the wake of Zangi's conquest of Edessa in 1144, the Franks had initiated a massive appeal in Europe to raise an army to regain the city, a campaign that later generations would label the Second Crusade.[26] Although, as we have seen, there had been many new campaigns against Islamdom directed from Europe, this was by far the largest since the First Crusade and was the first to be led by European kings, Louis VII of France and Conrad III of Germany. It was also the first to involve invasions on multiple fronts—in the pagan Baltic and, simultaneously, in Muslim al-Andalus and the Near East. In capturing Edessa, Zangi could not have conceived of the threat that the Franks brought to the rest of Islamdom in response. That said, Frankish activities in al-Andalus at this time appear to have been opportunistic; from the beginning the Franks were primarily focused on marching to the east and, with the help of Byzantium, to continue through Anatolia and reclaim Edessa.

As had happened so often in the past, the Saljuqs of Rum and the Danishmendids did their level best to snuff out the whole invasion once the Germans, followed by the French, crossed into Anatolia from Constantinople. Anatolia was now rather different from the lawless no-man's land it must have seemed during the first Frankish invasion more than a generation earlier. On the one hand, Byzantium held western Anatolia in a much firmer grip and had much steadier relations with its Turkish neighbors; on the other, the Saljuqs of Rum under their sultan, Mas'ud, had begun transforming their ragtag confederation of Turcoman tribes and frontier warriors into an urban-based Islamic sultanate much like the states neighboring it. Mas'ud's power base was situated around his new capital at Konya, one of medieval Islamdom's leading centers of Islamic civilization. However, the borders of both states were porous, and Turcomans ranged freely across Saljuq and Byzantine territory.

News of the calling of the crusade and its march eastward reached the Islamic world quickly. The scale of the preparations clearly left an impact on the Damascene Ibn al-Qalanisi, who was a contemporary to these events. "They were said to be making for the land of Islam," he wrote, "having issued a summons throughout their lands and strongholds to set out on expedition thither and hasten towards it and to leave their own territories and cities empty and bereft of protectors and defenders. They brought with them amounts of their money, treasuries, and weapons, beyond reckoning."[27] Of course, none of this had gone unnoticed, and "the governors of the neighboring lands and of the Islamic territories in their proximity"—presumably the Rum Saljuq sultan Mas'ud or his sub-alterns—at once took action to deter any progress of the Franks through his domains, ordering local governors to prepare their defenses, muster troops, and fortify mountain passes. A recent treaty between Mas'ud and the Byzantines may well have been part of these preparations too.[28]

In October 1147 Turcomans in Byzantine territory were the first to encounter the German troops under Conrad, who had crossed the Bosporos in advance of the French troops under Louis. Conrad had divided his army into two divisions, one proceeding along the Aegean coast in the south, the other proceeding, like the First Crusade, to Dorylaeum. Both German divisions made easy targets for the Turks. A Turcoman ambush appears to have nearly wiped out the southern detachment near Alaşehir, while a constant barrage of attacks along the road in the north eroded Conrad's morale and manpower and forced him to retreat back to Nicaea. "Death and slaughter commingled with the Franks until a vast number of them perished," and hunger and disease haunted them in their retreat.[29] At Nicaea, Conrad was joined by Louis and the French army, who did their best to resupply and assist the Germans, and both groups marched together and reached Ephesus by December. By now, however, Mas'ud had made his intentions clear. Having recently patched up an alliance with his neighbor (and father-in-law) the Danishmend, Mas'ud organized a joint campaign against the Franks and the combined Turkish forces assembled together near Konya.

Conrad gave up. Already ailing from wounds received during the retreat from Dorylaeum, he shipped back to Constantinople in January 1148 to be treated by the emperor's physicians. The bulk of his army probably returned overland. As Louis and the French pressed on to Antalya, Turkish troops nearly ended their progress as they crossed

Mt. Cadmus. But by March Louis and a core group of his army were shipped to Antioch. By early April 1148 Conrad and the few surviving veteran contingents of his army, now rested and resupplied by a winter in Constantinople, arrived by sea at Acre. Still, the state of the invading forces caused Muslims in the Levant to breathe a collective sigh of relief: "Fresh reports of their losses and of the destruction of their numbers were constantly arriving…with the result that men were restored to some degree of tranquility of mind and began to gain some confidence in the failure of their enterprise, and their former distress and fear were alleviated in spite of the repeated reports of the activities of the Franks."[30]

For the Muslims of Syria, those "activities" became worrisome soon enough. In light of Nur al-Din's final conquest of Edessa and the general disarray of the newly arrived Frankish armies, the idea that the Franks could recapture Edessa was no longer a consideration. That said, the recent arrivals, even in their present condition, were just the thing to alleviate Jerusalem's old concerns about Damascus, and so this city became the new goal of the campaign.[31] When news of this new Frankish threat reached Unur in Damascus, he "set about making ready equipment and preparing to engage them and to counter their malice," securing the approaches to the city, repairing fortifications, and blocking the wells in the countryside.[32]

And so it was that in July 1148 an army led by three kings—Louis of France, Conrad of Germany, and the young Baldwin III of Jerusalem—arrived before the walls of Damascus. They made quick work of the scattered resistance as they approached from the southwest, traversing the Ghuta oasis that surrounds Damascus, a landscape cluttered with orchards and fields and mud-brick enclosure walls and, in places, cut by multiple canals.[33] Unur's troops, including local volunteers and urban militias, stymied the Frankish advance as they tried to cross the Barada River near al-Rabwa, a hillock along the river due west of the city. As this spot was popularly identified as the place mentioned in the Qur'an to which Mary and Jesus fled from the Massacre of the Innocents (23: 50), it was also redolent with Christian and Islamic associations. Muslim archers had the Franks temporarily pinned down. Eventually, however, Conrad and his men managed to smash their way through to the northern side of the Barada, and the Franks overwhelmed the Muslims there by sheer numbers. The Franks made camp there, quite close to the city walls, and began cutting down trees and destroying orchards to build fortifications. The fighting continued the next day and did not go well for the Muslims; among the dead particular note was made of the elderly shaykh al-Findalawi and his companion al-Halhuli, who had seen this as an opportunity to gain the merits of jihad.

Behind the city walls, however, the atabeg Unur remained firm, as he had an ace up his sleeve: he had called in reinforcements, which were pouring in from the Lebanon Mountains. What's more, his erstwhile Zangid allies, Nur al-Din and his brother Sayf al-Din, had marched to his aid and were encamped at Homs, a few days away. It was undoubtedly this new reality that pushed the Franks to reconsider their position, as they would be trapped between the city and a Zangid army arriving from the north. Relocating their forces to the south of the city was briefly mooted, but that area could not offer the abundant water and pasturage required for a siege that their current position could. And so, just four days after arriving, the Franks faced facts, lifted their siege, and retreated to Frankish territory.

The threat of a combined resistance from both the Zangids and Unur was instrumental in the Frankish failure before the walls of Damascus, and the two effectively campaigned together in the months afterward. A major blow was struck in the territory of Frankish Tripoli, whose lord Raymond II—who had opted out of the attack on Damascus—requested the urgent aid of Nur al-Din and Unur in ousting his rival and cousin, Bertram, who had constructed a fort nearby. In September, with help from Sayf al-Din of Mosul, they quickly seized the fort, captured Bertram, his men, and his household, and dismantled the fort, lest it trouble Raymond again. At the Battle of Inab in June 1149, the two armies confronted a reckless raid by Raymond of Poitiers, prince of Antioch, resulting in a very public victory for Nur al-Din (and death in battle for Raymond). In the aftermath Nur al-Din was able to threaten even Antioch enough to force a truce from it and to recapture Apamea for good. These campaigns seemed to so successfully dismember the various Frankish states that one poet was moved to a rhetorical question about the results, employing a pun on Nur al-Din's name, Mahmud: "How should we not celebrate our praiseworthy [*mahmud*] life, when the sultan himself is praiseworthy / And the sword of Islam is only turned aside when the carcass of Unbelief lies cut in pieces?"[34]

Unur was the linchpin in this relationship, and when he died in August 1149 (followed shortly by Sayf al-Din of Mosul), so too did the cooperation of Damascus and Aleppo that Nur al-Din enjoyed and that the Franks had so feared. Abaq, Unur's weak-willed successor in Damascus, was much less inclined to see Nur al-Din as an ally and instead threw in his lot with Jerusalem. Nur al-Din took this opportunity to try to intervene in Damascene affairs to his benefit, arriving in the city's southern reaches and declaring his intent to protect the inhabitants from their ruler's new Frankish "friends." However, although Nur al-Din's presence was said to delight the populace of Damascus and cause the very rains to return to the drought-parched lands of Syria, nothing immediately came of his grandstanding. Abaq was certainly unmoved, and Nur al-Din himself was called away to Aleppo by exciting news: his Turcoman troops had finally captured Joscelin, the exiled lord of Edessa, and imprisoned him in Aleppo. There was now nothing to impede the final reconquest of the lands remaining in the county of Edessa. The sultan of the Saljuqs of Rum led the charge, with Nur al-Din assisting. By the autumn of 1150 Tall Bashir had been recaptured and all the territory once controlled by the Franks of Edessa retaken. The first of the Latin states to be created was thus the first to be expunged once and for all. The borders of the abode of Islam were in this way shifted farther westward, from the Euphrates in Iraq to the Orontes in Syria. Nur al-Din followed up on this success by raiding along the Syrian coast, capturing the port of Tartus in 1152 and thereby driving a wedge between the formerly contiguous Frankish principalities of Tripoli and Antioch.[35]

Nur al-Din and Damascus

With Aleppo's northern and western fronts in good shape, Nur al-Din could now return his attention to Damascus, so long the goal of his father. In 1150, before leaving for Aleppo, he had managed to squeeze a token victory out of Abaq, who agreed to recognize him formally and symbolically as his overlord, even though Damascus retained its independence from Aleppo and even its special alliance with the Franks of Jerusalem. But now Nur al-Din moved to turn on the pressure, blockading the city and sending food prices skyrocketing. The populace began to wonder if loyalty to their prince and his infidel allies was really worth it. Abaq could see where this was headed; he locked himself in the citadel with his entourage and called upon his allies in Jerusalem for help in restoring order. But before the Franks could come to Abaq's aid, Nur al-Din entered the city virtually unopposed, quieted the mob, and restored order, distributing badly needed supplies. He negotiated a final surrender with Abaq, who accepted the governorship of Homs in return for leaving Damascus for good. Nur al-Din then gathered together all the leading figures in the city and announced with much pomp new tax cuts and measures of clemency. It was a new dawn for Damascus. And every inch of it was theater.[36]

Public posturing like this was an important tool for any medieval Muslim ruler, and Nur al-Din, far more than his predecessors, became very adept at the art. But one must not confuse image with reality. For example, part of Nur al-Din's appeal to the populace of Syria was his reputation as a fighter of jihad, and his chroniclers (medieval and modern) have long championed him as such. In decrees and monumental inscriptions, he was very careful to make use of the epithet *mujahid*, "jihad warrior," among other such titles. But the truth is that Nur al-Din's embrace of jihad against the Franks was just one small aspect of a broader image of the pious and just ruler consonant with the ideals of the Circle of Equity, much as theorists like the wide-eyed Turtushi had dreamed of in Fatimid Egypt—and this image is one that he strove to project primarily to maintain and extend his rule over other Muslims.

Thus, although his inscriptions do proclaim him as a mujahid, they almost never do so without also claiming him as a *zahid*, an ascetic; many also stress his dutiful relationship to the caliph in Baghdad. Although he met the Franks many times in battle, perhaps even in person, he just as frequently resorted to treaties and paying tribute to ensure peace on the frontiers of his consolidating domains. Although he definitively conquered lands previously in the hands of the Franks, these acquisitions pale in contrast to the lands in Syria and Mesopotamia (to say nothing of Egypt) that he wrested from the control of Muslim rivals. And although he poured his own treasure into raising and supplying armies, he also endowed dozens of religious institutions, including madrasas for the study of Islamic law and meetinghouses for the ascetics and mystics he so admired, more than Syria had ever seen before.[37]

In effect what was happening under Nur al-Din was the final melding of, on the one hand, a frontier-forged military worldview familiar to Turcoman warriors with, on the other, the goals of kingship and religious reform familiar to the Sunni urban masses and ulema of Syria. This can be seen in Nur al-Din's first capital, Aleppo, where he forbade the Shi'ite formula for the call to prayer then in use in the city's main mosque and where he renovated or established many madrasas and ribats, underwrote the careers of a new generation of Sunni ulema, "and made justice and equity come to prominence there."[38] But it is especially clear in Damascus, the city so associated with his career. It is surely significant that after taking the city in 1154, his titles begin to stress his role not as a warrior but as *al-Malik al-'Adil*, "The Just King," a model of statesmanship much more in line with long-held political ideals of Islamic urban society. Al-Turtushi would probably have been thrilled—but he had died decades earlier.

In Damascus Nur al-Din found a valuable ally in the Sunni scholarly establishment. Chief among them was 'Ali ibn 'Asakir, the most prominent Syrian scholar of his day. Ibn 'Asakir was born in 1105, just a few years after the First Crusade, to a family of noted scholars, the Banu 'Asakir, who held many of the most prestigious positions in the city as judges, jurists, and teachers for not just a few decades but for close to *three centuries*. At the age of six he began attending teaching sessions with his father, and, as a young man, he embarked (twice) on his own *talab al-'ilm*, the journey in search of knowledge from masters in foreign lands, traveling to study in Baghdad, Mecca, Medina, and the various centers of learning in the East, such as Herat and Isfahan. In later life he tallied up the authorities with whom he had studied, and they totaled some 1,700 men (and about eighty women). Such prodigious learning gave him a reputation as a master of the hadith, the traditions of the Prophet and early community that underpin the system of Islamic law and belief.

When Nur al-Din met him after taking Damascus in 1154, Ibn 'Asakir was at the height of his scholarly career. Both men must have seen in the other a natural ally. For Nur al-Din, Ibn 'Asakir provided an entrée into the legitimating world of Syria's ulema, a stamp of approval that the sultan, in his new guise as a "just king," would have craved. For Ibn 'Asakir, Nur al-Din provided a receptive ear for his intellectual agenda, one that was very consonant with Nur al-Din's own, namely, restoring Sunni Islam throughout Syria through jihad against the Franks and against Shi'ite heretics, coupled with a broader reform of Islamic law and theology. Nur al-Din became an avid patron of Ibn 'Asakir, and the scholar did not disappoint his sultan, composing many works throughout his life, including a book of hadith devoted to jihad, a book on the religious merits associated with Ascalon, theological treatises, and, his most important work, the massive *History of Damascus*, which is in fact not a history at all but rather an immense, eighty-volume biographical dictionary of prominent personages, scholars, and religious figures who are said to have lived or even visited Damascus, from the time of Adam himself to Ibn 'Asakir's day. By sheer bulk alone it stands as an irrefutable argument for the centrality of Syria in the history of the Sunni Muslim community.[39]

Naturally Nur al-Din received his own biographical entry in this work, and it makes interesting reading for what it reveals about the scope of the so-called counter-Crusade under Nur al-Din. Ibn ʿAsakir is careful to mention Nur al-Din's victories against the Franks before and after he took Damascus, but this praise sits alongside a much more elaborate encomium for his efforts against Shiʿites and in social programs in the city that brought, among other things, madrasas, meetinghouses, and mosques, relief for widows and the poor, aid and religious instruction for Muslim orphans, posts for the ulema, a hospital for the mentally ill and one for the blind, an endowment for copyists of the Qurʾan and other books, tax breaks and other help for pilgrims, and bridges, halting stops, and road repairs where needed. Ibn ʿAsakir also notes that his patron showered favors on the Holy Cities of Mecca and Medina, and in 1161 went himself on a very public pilgrimage there. In every Muslim city he conquered, we are told, he left a similar imprint of just and pious rule. In all these activities jihad was but one plank in a much broader platform.[40]

Although the ʿAbbasid caliph is said to have invested Nur al-Din with authority over Egypt and the as-yet-unconquered Frankish lands in Syria, the years after 1154 saw both victories and defeats for Nur al-Din and resulted in a form of stasis in the north. Skirmishing with the armies of Antioch around Harim, for example, resulted in a treaty, by which this crucial border fort remained in Frankish hands, though the agricultural produce of the region was divided between the two sides.[41] Certainly 1157 was a tense year. There appeared to be a storm brewing when the Franks of Jerusalem violated their earlier treaty with Damascus by raiding the fertile lands and livestock of the Hawran. These actions demanded retribution, and public sentiment for jihad ran high. It must have seemed like a gift to Nur al-Din, who made ready for "an immediate attack upon the accursed enemies of God and the raiding of those infidel antagonists who were opposed to him, the sowers of disorder in the lands and the breakers of their solemn oaths to maintain friendly and peaceful relations." With an eye toward his subjects, Nur al-Din took the opportunity to indulge in an unprecedented public spectacle: "He commanded that the citadel and royal residence should be decorated by adorning their walls with weapons of war, such as cuirasses, breast-plates, shields, swords, spears, Frankish bucklers, lances, banners, flags, kettledrums, trumpets, and various kinds of instruments of [martial] music. Troops, citizens, and strangers all pressed to view this sight and expressed their admiration of the spectacle, which lasted for seven days."[42]

Nur al-Din raised a large army and attacked Banyas, which the Franks had recently regarrisoned. But although he took many Frankish prisoners during an ambush at Jacob's Ford, near Lake Tiberias, Banyas itself remained in Frankish hands. A massive earthquake in 1157 also intervened, destroying cities and fortresses on both sides, and this will have shifted Nur al-Din's priorities in the short term. He returned to the area in the following year, but both sides gained no ground and Nur al-Din withdrew, bringing with him a few prisoners to parade in his capital.[43]

Nur al-Din himself became gravely ill and arranged for the succession to fall to his younger brother. There were brief outbursts of sectarian violence in Aleppo as many thought Nur al-Din was near death, but he suddenly recovered. Yet for all the drama, little came of these events. When the Franks and Byzantines (under Emperor Manuel) entered into a treaty, they campaigned together in Cilicia and northern Syria, even, in 1159, menacing Aleppo. But Nur al-Din, in ill health once again, easily negotiated away even this threat, happily agreeing to assist Manuel against the interfering Saljuqs of Rum and to release thousands of prisoners taken during Second Crusade. Eventually the Saljuq ruler was obliged to sign separate treaties with both Manuel and Nur al-Din. It was as if all the major players in the north—Muslims, Franks, and Byzantines—had settled into the roles assigned to them. But in the south, Nur al-Din was to realize, the field was still wide open.[44]

A Muslim Revanche in al-Andalus: Camels and Swine

Long before Saljuq and Zangid rulers in the Levant had found the wherewithal to definitively respond to the presence of Frankish invaders and settlers in their lands, the independent rulers of al-Andalus, Muslim Spain, had found one seemingly inspired solution to their own Frankish problem. As we have seen, the Frankish invasion of the Near East was precipitated when the Byzantines resorted to a time-honored imperial strategy of using one group of barbarians (the Franks) to fight another (the Turks). In al-Andalus the various kings ensconced in their various taifas adopted much the same ploy, invoking the aid of Berber warriors from North Africa to help them fight back the Franks who were invading their lands in al-Andalus. The hardy Berber warriors of North Africa seemed just the thing to counter the threat of the Franks, who had wrested control of much of northern al-Andalus, including now even Toledo in the heart of the peninsula. These Berber armies belonged to a newly constituted Islamic reform movement based in Morocco, who called themselves al-Murabitun, "those who fight together." The name is an allusion to the Qur'an (3: 200), which enjoins believers to "persevere in fighting together and fear God that you may triumph," a succinct description of this movement's militant and pietistic stance. In English they are generally known as the Almoravids.[45]

The Almoravids were not merely bearers of a new Islamic religious movement. When Toledo fell to Alfonso VI in 1085, the Almoravids were the major Muslim political power in the Maghrib, with a capital of sorts at Marrakesh, which they founded, and Berber tribes and territory subject to them from the Straits of Gibraltar to the Sahara. Their territory included the small towns and cities of the mountainous north as well as the desert of the south. The original raison d'être of the Almoravids was to correct what they saw as injustices and improper conduct (in particular illegal taxes) among their Muslim coreligionists in Morocco and to lead them back to proper observance of the sunna— by force if necessary. And it usually was. But Morocco was a poor region compared, say, with al-Andalus. No one was more aware of this than the Almoravid ruler, Ibn Tashfin, who had been responsible for shepherding the Almoravids in their transition from a loose Islamic reform movement to a more settled conquest state. In 1085 Ibn Tashfin's successes in consolidating Almoravid control over Morocco meant that, in his domains at least, a certain kind of peace finally prevailed. But something still had to be done about the armies.

Thus whereas Ibn Tashfin needed something to occupy the energies of his armies, the taifa kings of al-Andalus badly needed armies to come to their aid against the Franks. It was a marriage made in heaven. And so in 1086 the taifa lord of Seville arranged a meeting with his neighbors, the lord of Granada to the east and the lord of Badajoz to the west. They discussed how they might best deal with the threat of unclean Christians like Alfonso VI on their doorstep, and whether inviting so volatile a power as the Almoravids was really the best solution for al-Andalus. Would they be courting disaster, merely substituting one barbarian overlord for another? In the end the group of three decided to send a delegation across the Straits to propose an alliance with Ibn Tashfin. The Berbers were rough and fanatical, but at least they were Muslims. When confronted with his options, al-Muʿtamid, the lord of Seville, is said to have quipped, "Better to pasture camels than to herd swine."[46]

In July 1086, then, Ibn Tashfin sent an advance force to occupy Muslim Algeciras; soon thereafter the main force arrived, much to the joy of the

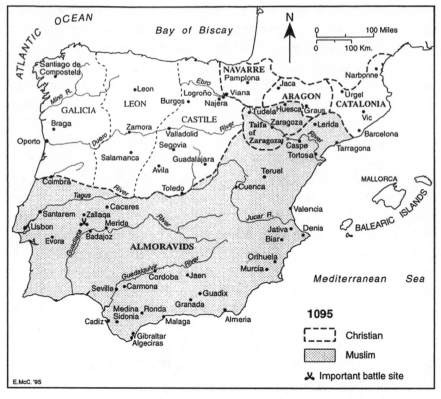

Map 6 Al-Andalus under the Almoravids. From O. R. Constable, ed., *Medieval Iberia: Readings from Muslim, Christian, and Jewish Sources*, 2nd ed. (Philadelphia: University of Pennsylvania Press, 2012), 156, map 2.

populace, who viewed them and Ibn Tashfin as their saviors against the Frankish threat (Map 6). The Almoravid army then marched on to Seville, and from there to Badajoz. On hearing of this alarming new challenge, Alfonso VI lifted his siege of Zaragoza in the northeast and marched toward Badajoz to confront the Muslim armies. On October 23 they met at Zallaqa (Sagrajas), not far from Badajoz, where Alfonso was overwhelmed by the Berber armies. Soundly defeated, he and his Christian army were forced to retreat to the safety of Toledo. It was just what the lords of al-Andalus had hoped for. Indeed the lord of Seville urged the Almoravids to pursue their enemies while they were in flight, but Ibn Tashfin was reluctant to range too far from home and the threats that might arise there, so he crossed back to Morocco, leaving a contingent of troops to assist in the further defense of his new Andalusi allies.

It was not enough. Ibn Tashfin was obliged to return several times to al-Andalus to confront the Franks. But only in 1090 did he do so definitively, and on his own terms. This time his first target was not Alfonso VI but the taifa kings, whom he had already begun deposing, one by one. If this wasn't worrisome enough, the Andalusi ulema were now accusing the remaining taifa rulers of all manner of backsliding and sinfulness—music, if the metaphor is appropriate, to the Almoravids' reformist ears. In 1090 Ibn Tashfin forced the surrender of Muslim Granada and Malaga and exiled their rulers. Over the next decade or so the remaining taifa kingdoms were absorbed into the Almoravids' Moroccan empire. In 1094 Badajoz and the west fell. Valencia, which changed hands between Muslim rulers and the Christian El Cid, was the last to fall, in 1102. Only the kingdom of Zaragoza in the far northeast remained independent, and it wisely signed a treaty with their new Moroccan neighbors. But in 1110 it too eventually fell to the Almoravids. As for al-Mu'tamid of Seville, who had been personally responsible for bringing the Almoravids to al-Andalus in the first place, he too was forced to surrender his city and was exiled to Morocco, where he no doubt spent the rest of his life musing over the merits of pasturing camels.[47]

It must have been an especially bitter exile, since the Almoravids had, after all, done very little against the Frankish threat. The frontier between the Christian kingdoms of the north and Muslim al-Andalus in the south remained essentially the same as it had been before the Almoravids invaded. In 1112 Almoravid raids ranged around Huesca, but this would be the last time Muslim armies would ever see the Pyrenees. The Christian kings remained unsubdued. Toledo abided, unconquered, only the newest addition to the kingdom of León-Castile. And from the kingdom of Aragon, King Alfonso el Batallador ("The Battler") even whittled away at Almoravid lands, taking Zaragoza in 1118 and Tudela in 1119.

The Almoravids did provide a veneer of Muslim unity where once were only fractious taifa kingdoms, however, and Andalusi cities no longer paid the odious *parias* to Christian overlords. Ibn Tashfin's actions against the taifa rulers were backed by a legal ruling, or fatwa, by none other than our old friend al-Turtushi in Egypt, who may well have seen him as Muslim Spain's only hope for just governance. Still more impressively Ibn Tashfin found approval from the epitome of the Sunni Revival, al-Ghazali, off in distant Iran. Al-Andalus now technically fell under the aegis of the 'Abbasid caliphs. But Almoravid al-Andalus was emphatically merely one frontier province of a Moroccan empire increasingly preoccupied with problems in Africa.[48]

The source of Almoravid troubles in Morocco was an Islamic reform movement that was, in the abstract at least, very similar to the one that gave birth to the Almoravids themselves. This new movement was led by a charismatic preacher and holy man named Ibn Tumart, who had himself once studied law with al-Turtushi in Alexandria, or so Ibn Tumart claimed. His followers claimed to stress God's encompassing Oneness better than did the Almoravids who ruled them, whom they saw as backsliders and hypocrites whose watered-down Islam, they claimed, flirted with polytheism. As such they referred to themselves as those who (par excellence) affirm Divine Unity, in Arabic al-Muwahhidun. In English they are known as the Almohads. Their similar name and Moroccan origins make them seem like close cousins to the Almoravids, whom they toppled, but the Almoravids and Almohads should never be confused. True, like the Almoravids, the Almohads encouraged an austere approach to Islamic practice among the Muslims of Morocco—and the Berbers of the High Atlas in particular. One might think this would make the Almoravids and the Almohads natural allies. But by this time the old Almoravid movement had lost much of its rigorist color, and the failure of its policies in al-Andalus was causing it to lose supporters on both sides of the Straits of Gibraltar. Both of these factors opened up the Almoravids and their servants to charges of having gone soft and having strayed from the straight path.[49]

From the point of view of the Almoravids, the new Almohad movement was a dire threat, an uprising that drained their resources in Morocco precisely when they should have been directing them toward jihad against the Franks in al-Andalus. In 1121 the Almohad followers of Ibn Tumart proclaimed him the Mahdi, that divinely guided figure who would lead all true Muslims to righteousness in preparation for the Final Judgment. This was a worrisome development, as such a movement would have the potential to attract many followers, and it stood as a direct challenge to the religious authority of the Almoravids and the ulema who interpreted Islam on their behalf. What followed was nearly a decade of warfare in Morocco, as the Almoravids tried to suppress Ibn Tumart's Almohad movement and the Almohads made bolder and bolder claims against Almoravid rule. This conflict culminated in 1130, when the Almohads led a futile attack on Marrakesh, the Almoravid capital. During the assault, many of Ibn Tumart's staunchest allies were killed and the Almohad movement was left in tatters. Ibn Tumart himself died later that year. It seemed as though the Almoravids would continue unchallenged in Morocco and al-Andalus.

But, almost miraculously, from this nadir the Almohads managed to climb back to challenge the Almoravids once again and leave their mark on al-Andalus and the Frankish threat there. Ibn Tumart's heir was a vigorous early follower of his named 'Abd al-Mu'min, who presented himself as Ibn Tumart's successor or caliph—the allusion to the golden age of the Prophet Muhammad and the caliphs who succeeded him was undoubtedly intentional. After a decade of back-and-forth, by the 1140s the Almohads had rebuilt their hierarchy and recruited new armies. They began capturing lands outside their mountain heartlands and moved onto the plains, taking major cities like Fez and, finally, in 1147, Marrakesh itself, which now became the capital of the Almohads. Much of Morocco and all of al-Andalus had still to be mopped up, but the old Almoravid regime had little hope for survival.

Across the Straits, in al-Andalus, there was certainly no love lost between the last Almoravids and their subjects there, where their hold was crumbling under the twin strains of relentless Frankish conquests—even, in 1146, of Córdoba itself—and rebellious local notables. In cities across the peninsula, military men, ulema, and even sufi masters were taking advantage of Almoravid weakness to make bids for their own independence—if they were not really running the show already. To better defend themselves against Christian aggression and their Muslim rivals, these reinvented taifa rulers saw in the new Almohad movement just the sort of ally they needed. The parallels with the coming of the Almoravids decades earlier are striking. The crucial invitation was sent (it seems) by one Ibn Qasi, a sufi master and former ruler of Silves, from which a Muslim rival had expelled him. Ibn Qasi pleaded with the Almohad caliph 'Abd al-Mu'min to come to his aid and that of al-Andalus. In the spring of 1147 an Almohad force crossed the Straits and secured Tarifa and Algeciras as a bridgehead. They then kept their promise to Ibn Qasi by subjugating his lands in the Algarve before moving on to Seville, which became their capital.[50]

Crusaders and Almohads

The arrival in 1147 of the Almohads, a militant reform movement with humble roots in Morocco, briefly shifted the focus of Frankish-Muslim conflict to western al-Andalus. There what was left of Almoravid authority was now collapsing under the weight of Almohad intervention. This made these western lands an ideal arena for Christian rulers to pick up the already hectic pace of their advances on Muslim territory.

Indeed one of the first such advances, the siege of Muslim-held Lisbon by Duke (later King) Afonso Henriques of Portugal, was undertaken with the aid of Frankish auxiliaries on their way to Syria as part of the Second Crusade, a serendipity so miraculous that it could only have been planned from the first to take advantage of the situation. The Almohads had stumbled into a conflict that was stoked by the full fury of Christendom, from England to Outremer. Now both the Almohads and the Christian armies found themselves engaged in the same pursuit: bringing to heel the Muslim cities of al-Andalus as loyalty to the old Almoravid regime evaporated around them.[51]

Afonso began by raiding the region around Lisbon as he waited for the Crusader fleet to arrive from England, capturing the nearby town of Santarém, and then encamping on the hills overlooking the city. In late June the Crusader fleet finally landed at the mouth of the Tagus River in Lisbon to coordinate with Afonso. Almost immediately a detachment of Muslim troops was sent out to intercept the first groups of invaders. However, the Crusaders were able to beat them back to the suburbs of the city; in their zeal some of the Christian warriors had to be prevented from pursuing them all the way into Lisbon. Soon the rest of the Crusader army disembarked, assembling, as if to confirm the Frankish reputation for filthiness, in one of the city's extramural cemeteries. After the traditional Christian call to surrender was rejected, the siege began on July 1, and the Muslims prepared their city for an endurance test.[52]

The Franks had surrounded the city to the east and west, attempting to fight and burn their way through the suburbs to the walls of Lisbon. The Muslims were able to repulse them for a short time, but even in their smaller numbers the Crusaders slowly advanced, and the Muslims retired behind their walls. By chance it happened that a large store of Lisbon's grain was housed near the spot where the Franks were pressing the city on the west, and they made off with these vital supplies. Muslim troops periodically sallied out in attempts to fend off the besiegers, but the Franks held tight. Some of the besieged resorted to vulgar psychological attacks, mocking the Franks for their transparent motives, insulting their religion and its icons, and inviting them to speculate about what their wives back home might be up to.

By the middle of summer it was clear both sides were in for a long siege. With the help of a Pisan engineer hired expressly for the task, the Franks began building siege engines to give them the edge they needed against Lisbon's stout walls. The Muslims made short work of their creations, burning them to the ground again and again almost as soon as they were set up. Bad omens were seen in the Frankish camp; spirits were flagging. But it was a shortage of Muslim supplies, not Christian enthusiasm, that turned the tide. Simply put, the Muslims of Lisbon were starving. The supplies that the Franks had discovered and stolen gave them a far more significant edge than any piece of siege machinery. To save themselves, some of the Muslims, it is reported, converted to Christianity and threw themselves on the Crusaders' mercy, but they were generally not welcomed, and a few had their hands cut off and were sent back to Lisbon. With the Franks blockading them by land and sea, the Muslims badly needed a lifeline to the outside world. They managed to send a plea for assistance to a Muslim ally, the lord of Evora, nearly a hundred miles to the east. However, the lord of Evora had recently made a truce with Afonso Henriques and so could not involve himself in the affair. Lisbon had been abandoned to its fate.[53]

By autumn that fate was sealed. After some fits and starts, the Franks successfully undermined a section of the east wall of the lower city and, on October 20, managed to place a siege tower at a poorly defended spot on the walls and capture one of the city's towers. Muslim defenders swarmed out of the city to oust them, but a few Franks managed to hold on long enough for more troops to claim another point on the wall. The Muslims saw that they could not keep this up forever. On October 22 negotiations for the surrender of the city began and were soon over.

On the following day Afonso and his allies entered the starved and brutalized city of Lisbon. Its inhabitants were ordered to deposit their valuables in a central location in the citadel; anyone found to be hiding any possessions was to be killed. The Muslims of Lisbon had apparently been using the mosque as a makeshift hospital (or perhaps it already functioned as such, as was sometimes the case), as the conquerors found it filled with hundreds of the dead and dying. Despite attempts by the Frankish leadership to maintain order, the transfer of power in Lisbon devolved into a sacking. Property was confiscated willy-nilly before it could be collected; the Muslim governor, who was to retain his property as part of the surrender terms, was attacked and robbed; the native Christian bishop, perhaps mistaken for a Muslim grandee, had his throat cut. Eventually order was restored, and the plunder was distributed among the conquerors. Many if not most of the Muslim inhabitants packed up and fled the city, and some neighboring towns were taken by Afonso's forces. On November 1 the Frankish clergy purified the mosque and elected one of their own as the first Latin bishop of Lisbon, who took his seat in the building that, over the years that followed, would be transformed into the Sé de Lisboa, Lisbon's still standing cathedral.

But Lisbon was only part of the picture. In the eastern lands of al-Andalus, Christian rulers also took advantage of the collapse of Almoravid authority. In late August 1147 the residents of Almería, a wealthy port located deep in southern al-Andalus, were alarmed to learn that a small fleet of Genoese ships was headed toward their port. Alarmed, but not surprised: Christians, including the Genoese, had long seen the city as a den of piracy and had tried repeatedly to capture it, to no avail. And so, when the Genoese galleys disgorged their men, the Muslim garrison poured out of the city and overwhelmed them, sending them scurrying back to their ships. But then, at a prearranged signal, the remainder, indeed the bulk of the Genoese fleet, assisted by a Catalan contingent from Barcelona, rounded the Cabo de Gata and forced its way into the heart of the port. The Muslim defenders, having already played their hand and still engaged with the Genoese, could do nothing as these new arrivals disembarked and joined in the combat. The Muslims scattered back to the safety of their walls; some who tried to flee by sea were intercepted by the Genoese. A change in the wind obliged the fleet to depart, but the residents of Almería knew that more was to come.

In the morning the residents woke to the unmistakable clamor of a siege. Now the Genoese and Catalans had been joined by their principal ally, King—indeed the self-styled "Emperor"—Alfonso VII of León-Castile, grandson of the conqueror of Toledo, who brought with him artillery and siege engines. As at Lisbon, the Muslims worked hard to destroy or repel these engines, but eventually the Christians managed to close in on the city and reduce a section of wall and seize a few of its towers. With their city about to fall, the Muslim leadership tried one last ploy: they sent a messenger to the king and offered him a substantial payment if he would lift the siege and abandon the Genoese to defeat. On hearing of this, the Genoese responded by forcing an immediate assault. In the quiet of the next morning, October 17, the Christians stole into the city through the gap in the wall and, if the Frankish sources are to be believed, indulged in a massacre not seen in al-Andalus since the taking of Barbastro. Immense plunder, in treasure and in slaves, was taken, most of it carted back to Genoa. As it happened, Almería did not long remain in Alfonso's hands, as the Almohads retook it in 1157, just as they retook Córdoba in 1148. But that a Christian king and his allies could strike so deeply into al-Andalus at such a prize demonstrated clearly the fragility of Muslim political co-hesion there. The lesson would be repeated again and again.

After wintering in Barcelona the Genoese prepared for their next target, much closer to home: Tortosa. Alfonso VII did not join them but remained in the south.[54] The Genoese and Catalans were joined by other Frankish allies, including some Crusaders who had been in-volved in the conquest of Lisbon, lingering before heading east to Syria. As at Almería, previous failed attempts on the city undoubtedly familiarized the Franks with Tortosa's defenses. The lower city fell almost immediately, and the defenders took refuge in the city's re-doubtable citadel. Its massive fosse gave any besieging army pause, and even as the Crusaders began to fill it up and place their siege engines, the Tortosans simply rained missiles down on them. Some of the Christians began to desert. But the siege pressed on, and eventually the Muslims, sensing their doom, sent a message suggesting one of the oddest surrender proposals in the history of siege-craft, made odder still as the Crusaders agreed to it. They proposed to surrender the city after a forty-day ceasefire; however, if, during those forty days, Tortosa's Muslim allies from Valencia (they were quite specific) came to their rescue, then the deal was off and the Crusaders would have to fight their allies to win the city again.

It says something of the disunity of Muslim al-Andalus that the Crusaders clearly calculated that the damage that might be done to themselves by prolonging the siege was a greater risk than any Muslim aid coming from Valencia. Perhaps the Christians knew something the Tortosans did not. At the time Valencia was in the hands of a colorful Muslim adventurer known to the Christians as El Rey Lobo, "The Wolf-King." This man was one of those flexible, border-crossing sur-vivors in the mold of El Cid that seem so common in al-Andalus at this time. Christian subsidies largely kept him afloat as the Almohads pressed on his lands; he preferred not to intervene at Tortosa. And so, forty days later, in December 1148, the Muslims capitulated as agreed. By the following November the count of Barcelona had captured the city of Lérida and some surrounding fortresses to consolidate his hold-ings in the northeast. "In those parts," Ibn al-Athir mourns, "there was nothing the Muslims held that was not seized by the Franks because of the internal dissensions of the Muslims, and all has remained in their hands until now."[55]

By the middle of the twelfth century Christian assaults on al-Andalus finally began to stall, a result as much of inter-Christian conflict as of Muslim resilience. For the next century, from 1150 or so, the River

Tagus would serve as the effective boundary between Muslim al-Andalus and the Christian North. But the fall of Lisbon, Tortosa, and other towns to "international" Christian armies, some of them avowed participants of the Second Crusade, is vivid evidence of the degree to which the Christian kings of the Iberian Peninsula were now integrated into Christendom's mainstream. Minor Christian kings like Afonso Henriques of Portugal now found themselves backed by all the ideological and material resources Europe could offer, whereas even the Almohads staked their claims in what was left of al-Andalus utterly isolated from the support of the broader *dar al-islam* and facing dissent in their own lands. In February 1148 the Crusaders who had been at Lisbon finally took ship to cross the Mediterranean to Syria. That expedition resulted in a terrible Frankish defeat before Damascus, but it must nevertheless have confirmed to many Muslims—if confirmation was necessary—that the Franks truly had put nearly the entire Abode of Islam, from Spain to Syria, under siege.

Sicily in Africa

Adding to this sense of a global Frankish assault on Islam was the fact that the Norman conquerors of Muslim Sicily now, and perhaps inevitably, had their sights set on the North African mainland.[56] Having taken final control of Muslim Sicily by 1091, Count Roger I ruled the island until his death in 1101. His son, Roger II, became count in 1105, and from 1130 he ruled independently as king of Sicily (succeeded in 1154 by his son William I). Under its Norman kings, Sicily experienced what is frequently lauded as its golden age. During this time most of Sicily's Muslims worked the land as peasant cultivators, though some also came to hold important positions in the Norman administration. The royal court at Palermo also patronized Muslim poets, scholars, artists, and scientists who contributed to an explicitly cosmopolitan court culture that drew upon elements from Sicily's Greek-, Arabic-, and Latin-speaking populace, which had made the island famous since the Middle Ages for its alleged multicultural horizons and for the Norman kings' apparently "tolerant" approach to the various religious communities in their realm. But, as in other areas of alleged medieval tolerance, such as al-Andalus, these displays were often little more than political theater; the realities faced by religious minorities, and the Muslims in particular, were rather different. In the case of Sicily, the Normans' cosmopolitan ambitions reflected the fact that the kingdom was no isolated island realm but was connected in myriad ways to the broader currents of Mediterranean politics and culture. And as the twelfth century dragged on, politics and culture were not at all favorable to a vulnerable Muslim subject population, either on the island or in other areas of interest to the Normans.

It was Roger II, the king who had commissioned the Arab geographer al-Idrisi to produce his famous upside-down map of the world, who first brought Norman rule to North Africa. His motivations appear to be mostly driven by commercial concerns. Roger's first African conquest was the island of Jerba, just off the southern coast of Tunisia. But in fact he had been ensnared in Muslim affairs in North Africa since 1117, when the local governor of Gabès appealed to him for aid in a dispute with his lord, the amir of Mahdiya. Mahdiya served as the capital of the Zirid dynasty, which had been so ineffectual in assisting in the defense of Muslim Sicily. Long since recovered from its sacking by Franks a generation earlier, Mahdiya was also an important port linking the Mediterranean (including Sicily) to African trade routes, and significantly the dispute between Gabès and Mahdiya specifically involved commercial fleets. For their part, the Zirids were incensed that the upstart Roger would involve himself in these matters, and so they and their allies began raiding Sicily and Calabria, while Sicilian pirates returned the favor in the Maltese islands and on the North African coast. Throughout the 1120s the central Mediterranean was a hive of pirate activity, and this, frankly, was bad for business (Map 7).

Jerba, for example, Roger's first lasting conquest, had a reputation as a pirate's den, suggesting that the new king of Sicily was bent on restoring order to this commercial zone not by negotiating with the Zirids but through outright conquest. A contributing factor was that this was a time of terrible famine in North Africa, and Sicily's role as a grain exporter (and refugee importer) further enhanced its dominance over the Muslim rulers of the coast.[57] Indeed by 1142 Mahdiya was effectively a Sicilian protectorate, kept afloat by Sicilian grain and cash; its conquest was practically a formality. In 1146 Roger took Tripoli in Libya, prompting many local lords, including the governor of Gabès, to accept him as their overlord. To the Zirids in Mahdiya, food subsidies were one thing, but it was insufferable that one of their own governors would throw off their allegiance and became an outright underling of a Christian lord. In an earlier incident the Zirids had arrested an envoy from Gabès for even negotiating with the Normans, parading him around town in humiliation with a crier proclaiming, "This is the reward of anyone who strives to make the Franks masters of Muslim lands." For the lord of Gabès

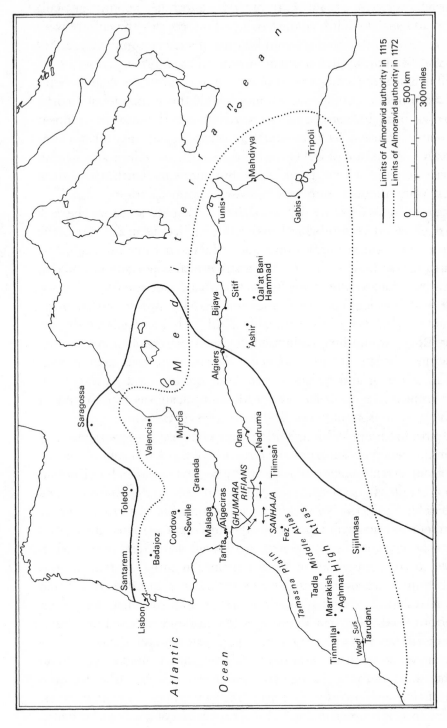

Map 7 Medieval North Africa. From Jamil M. Abun-Nasr, *A History of the Maghrib in the Islamic Period* (Cambridge: Cambridge University Press, 1987), 78, map 3.

himself to become a Norman vassal was inexcusable. The Zirids raided Gabès, carried off the governor, and had him brutally tortured, cutting off his penis and stuffing it in his mouth before killing him.[58]

To the Zirids this was a strictly internal affair, and so they hoped Roger would not involve himself. They were reassured when a Norman fleet spotted off the coast reported in to say that they were headed to raid the shores of Greece (for the Normans were still at war with Byzantium too). But it was all a ruse. Roger could hardly stand by while one of his vassals was publicly murdered, and this became the perfect excuse to bring direct rule to Mahdiya. On June 22 the Norman fleet arrived, and the Zirid amir, the last of his dynasty, fled with his family to Morocco. The city was looted but spared the destruction that had dogged it in the past at Frankish hands. A few days later, Sousse fell, followed by Sfax and various smaller places. By 1148, according to Ibn al-Athir, "the Franks now held from Tripoli [in Libya] close to Tunis and the Maghrib almost up to Qayrawan."[59]

The Muslims of these cities seem to have acquiesced to their new situation. True, in the longer term some sources strongly suggest that the loss of life, deportation, and physical destruction accompanying Roger's conquests were not just literary tropes and that the Norman conquests here may well have set these cities on a downward spiral. But the short-term benefits in the form of economic support from Palermo were undeniable. Norman rule, once established, was also relatively light-handed, though Roger seems to have encouraged Muslim and Christian settlers from Sicily to relocate to Africa, and the pope even announced an "archbishop of Africa" as a result. But for most, their situation remained largely unchanged, as the Normans retained most of the local elites in their positions of power. Roger II especially made a concerted effort to keep up regular supplies of grain to his new vassal states and thus retain their loyalty; hunger was his main African ally.

It was no way to win hearts and minds. Within a few years after Roger's death in 1154, the Norman moment in Africa had passed. However much Norman rule buoyed individual regimes, for many Muslims, being ruled by infidels riled and disgusted them. Given the choice, the population of the cities of the North African coast preferred a Muslim regime, even an austere one like the Almohads. And the Almohads, despite their second front against the Franks in al-Andalus, were only too happy to oblige. It helped that Almohad troops were hardly even necessary to the process of reconquest. For they were aided by the fact that Roger II's successor, William I, faced revolts of his own on Sicily and in North Africa, as local notables ousted their Norman overlords on their own and threw in with the Almohads, even before the caliph's troops arrived. And to make matters simpler, William's fleets seemed to be everywhere *except* North Africa: raiding Egypt one year, Greece the next, and sacking Ibiza in the Balearics. Sfax rose up in 1156, and Tripoli fell to the Almohads in 1158, and the caliph's armies swept easily over the former Norman territories.[60] Tunis surrendered in July 1159, and the non-Muslim populace there was—quite illegally—forced to choose between conversion or death. Only at Mahdiya, the old Zirid capital, was there resistance. There, over the summer and autumn of 1159, the caliph 'Abd al-Mu'min wrapped the city in a siege, its defenders described as "the scions of Frankish princes and their leading knights."[61]

A tale told by Ibn al-Athir about the siege sheds some light on how Muslims in the Near East viewed the predicament of the Muslims of North Africa and on the cyclical nature of history. Among the men at Mahdiya that 'Abd al-Mu'min brought with him from Morocco was the former Muslim lord of the city, who, as we have seen, had fled to the Almohads when the Normans ousted him more than ten years earlier. Impatient at the length of the siege, the caliph is said to have asked his guest about his city, "Why did you give up such a fortress?" "Because," the exile replied, "of too few trusty men, lack of provisions, and the decree of Fate." In response the caliph halted the siege and instead gathered two immense mounds of wheat and barley in full view of the besieged. In thus addressing his guest's concern about provisions, he also addressed the other concerns, for the implication was that the caliph was one in whom to place one's trust now and that the will of Fate had never been clearer. Sfax, Tripoli, Gabès, and other cities fell to the Almohads as the siege continued, but in January 1160 Mahdiya was finally taken and returned to Muslim rule.

Yet though the Norman occupation of Islamic North Africa was short-lived, it proved that Norman Sicily was as much a threat to Muslim states in the central Mediterranean as were the Spanish Franks in the west or the Crusader states in the Near East. That this rush of Christian expansion in al-Andalus and North Africa took place just as Nur al-Din was consolidating his hold on Syria must have made the Zangids and the men who served them seem like Islamdom's only hope.

Egypt and the Zangids

When Nur al-Din returned from his pilgrimage to Mecca in 1162, he found that Frankish interest in Egypt, vague and intermittent heretofore, was resolving into something more serious. Since the First

Crusade the Fatimids of Egypt had retained a crucial bridgehead in Palestine at the coastal city of Ascalon, which, even as the Franks captured the rest of the Syrian coast in the decades that followed, successfully thwarted any Frankish attempts to range into Sinai. The Fatimids relied upon Ascalon as a staging point for full-scale invasions against the Franks and for launching raids into the kingdom of Jerusalem's southern reaches. It was also an important naval base from which the Fatimids extended their reach all along the eastern Mediterranean coast, as we have seen during the unsuccessful defense of Tripoli and Tyre. Although an attack on Ascalon was briefly mooted in the context of the Second Crusade, the Franks in the region preferred instead a policy of containment, surrounding the city with fortresses and cutting it off from Egypt. In 1153 the Franks finally enjoyed the fruits of this strategy when Baldwin III captured Ascalon, isolated from any assistance, after a long siege. In response, in 1155 Egypt began paying tribute to the Franks of Jerusalem to keep them at bay. The opposite, of course, was the inevitable result.[62]

For any external observer, Egypt was ripe for the picking. As we have seen, the collapse of Fatimid authority in the eleventh century had been shored up thanks to the rise of a long line of military viziers, who served the Fatimid caliphs by securing the frontiers of the Fatimid state, suppressing military unrest, and centralizing administrative power. But by the middle of the twelfth century the viziers began to wonder if the caliphs were really necessary at all. The caliph al-Hafiz, who died in 1149, was the last Fatimid to rule as an adult; all his successors were mere children, and all of them puppets, surrounded by an entrenched and poisonous faction of palace dependents. With the caliph couched in splendid isolation, the position of vizier became the most coveted in Egypt and, among the palace elites and the army's highest-ranking amirs, the most contentious. In 1163, for example, a Fatimid provincial governor named Shawar marched on Cairo, ousted the vizier, and had himself raised in his place. But a few months later he too was ousted by an ambitious court official named Dirgham. While Dirgham consolidated his hold on Egypt, Shawar fled to Syria and sought the aid of Nur al-Din. In the meantime Dirgham pulled the trigger: he canceled Egypt's tribute to the Franks.

As it happened, King Baldwin III had died in the same year and was succeeded by a young and vigorous new king, Amalric (also Amaury), whose reign witnessed the high-water mark of Frankish power in the Near East. Amalric reacted to Dirgham's gesture by staging a full-scale invasion of Egypt: if Egypt would not pay tribute, then the Franks would take it themselves. In September the Franks got as far as Bilbays, a traditional stopping place in northeastern Egypt on the Cairo-Jerusalem road, but the Egyptians had resorted to the time-honored but desperate ploy of cutting the dikes that watered the Delta, flooding the surrounding fields. Amalric could go no farther, and so withdrew.

With the exiled Shawar begging his aid, Nur al-Din now made a fateful decision. The Fatimids had approached him many times before to forge an alliance, but each time he had rebuffed them; he had his own troubles conquering and ruling Syria, after all. But now the situation was changed. Intervening in Egypt was in fact a perfect solution to many of his problems. After suffering a humiliating defeat against the Franks at Crac de Chevaliers (Qal'at al Hisn), he needed a victory. The Fatimids were a Shi'i dynasty, and this could be his moment to strike a decisive blow for Sunni orthodoxy. Intervening in Egypt could thus bolster his image against heretics and infidels, conquer badly needed lands and wealth, assure his preeminence in the region, and make a final statement that would definitively overshadow the legacy of his father, "the martyr," Zangi. Moreover the crisis in Cairo and Amalric's aggressive attitude made it plain to all that Egypt was soon to fall. It had better fall to him, then.

The man he chose to lead the Zangid army into Egypt to restore Shawar to his post as vizier was the Kurdish amir Shirkuh, one of his most trusted men. The campaign was a quick success: Cairo was captured in April 1164, Dirgham was executed, and the vizier Shawar was restored to power. But Shawar was playing both sides. Egypt was bankrupt and in chaos; he couldn't possibly pay the tribute he had promised Nur al-Din for his assistance. And so he made a preemptive move, striking a bargain with (who else?) Amalric of Jerusalem, promising him renewed tribute if he would only provide him with his independence and dislodge Shirkuh and the Zangid army from Egypt. The two armies met near Bilbays, but both were stretched thin by campaigns in Syria and so, in October, they drew up an armistice and withdrew. Shirkuh returned in 1167 to force the issue again with Shawar, but the latter again appealed to his Frankish neighbors for help. This time both armies ranged freely around Cairo playing cat-and-mouse, but without result. In the end both sides withdrew from Egypt, although the Franks did wheedle more tribute out of Shawar and agreed to supply him with a resident Frankish adviser in Cairo and a small detachment of soldiers to help guard its fortifications.

But by the end of 1168 the Fatimid caliph himself was writing to Shirkuh and Nur al-Din for help, for Amalric had once again invaded and was now poised to become master of Egypt. Bilbays had fallen in November 1168 and its populace massacred. Even as the caliph wrote, the Franks were encamped outside Cairo, locked in negotiations with Shawar. At this unsettling news Nur al-Din ordered Shirkuh to assemble the army and march on Egypt. Amalric, to his credit, made a quick assessment of the situation and realized that his gambit had failed. Even as Shirkuh and the Zangid troops were arriving, the Franks were withdrawing to Palestine without so much as an insult hurled. Shirkuh was undoubtedly tired of conquering Egypt. One of his first acts was to arrest Shawar, whom he promptly executed at the Fatimid caliph's behest. Shirkuh was then himself named vizier of Egypt, but it was not to be: a few weeks later the old commander died of natural causes (or so we are told). His nephew, who had served briefly as governor of Alexandria and had become his right-hand man during these years of Egyptian adventures, succeeded him. His name was Salah al-Din Yusuf; he is better known in the West as Saladin. He would come to be the most famed Muslim opponent of the Franks and one of the chief Muslim statesmen of his day. Before that, however, he had to survive as the last vizier of Fatimid Egypt.[63]

To begin with, there was dissent immediately within the ranks of the Zangid army that had accompanied Shirkuh into Egypt. Some of his amirs, especially the Turcomans, objected to Saladin's swift seizure of Shirkuh's old post, which they saw as a Kurdish coup d'état, supported by Kurdish troops and jurists. Those who could not be persuaded simply left Saladin's service and returned to Nur al-Din. This meant that Saladin's forces, already dwarfed by the Fatimid army, were greatly reduced, and so it is not surprising that, in 1169, unrest among the Fatimid military nearly toppled him. Much of this unrest came from the Fatimid's black African corps, who resented how Saladin was seizing their iqta's to cultivate his own army. But Saladin prevailed, and, although groups of rebel veterans cropped up from time to time in Upper Egypt, the Fatimid army was crushed and quickly phased out by Saladin's Zangid contingents.

With the Fatimid army de-fanged, the next step was obvious. For all that Saladin was technically functioning as the vizier of the Fatimid caliph al-'Adid, no one forgot that he was Nur al-Din's man and thus an agent of the 'Abbasid caliph in Baghdad. The dismantling of the Fatimid caliphate came swiftly. He replaced key positions in the administrative hierarchy with his own men in the spring of 1171; by autumn al-ʿAdid was mortally ill; by September 13 he was dead. Egypt officially entered the Sunni fold on the following Friday, when, in the sermons in the mosques, al-ʿAdid's name was replaced with that of the ʿAbbasid caliph al-Mustadiʾ, the first caliph of Baghdad to be proclaimed in Egypt in more than two hundred years.

Nur al-Din reacted to these events with a mixture of delight and anxiety. On the one hand, he had united the Muslim Levant from Mesopotamia to Egypt under his sole regime and restored Sunni authority where it was lacking. This alone was the realization of a goal held by the ʿAbbasid caliphs and their sultans since the Saljuq Turks first appeared on the scene. Now the Frankish states in the area were surrounded by Nur al-Din's domains. Nur al-Din and Saladin took full advantage of the situation and enjoyed a few joint campaigns together, invading Transjordan twice, in 1171 and 1173, for example, and attacking the great Crusader castles of al-Shawbak and al-Karak there. But, on the other hand, Nur al-Din seemed unable to stop Egypt from slipping ever more firmly into the hands of Saladin and his kin. To limit the possible damage, he had already withdrawn most of his own troops from Egypt and confiscated Saladin's own iqtaʿs in Syria. But soon Saladin's brothers joined him, followed by the family patriarch, his father, Ayyub, a gesture that must have smarted in Damascus, for Ayyub had been one of Nur al-Din's most venerable and trusted allies. Thus reinforced by kinsmen and their troops, Saladin set to work quickly to expand Egypt's borders, sending his brother Turanshah at the head of an army into Nubia to squash pockets of resistance and, later in 1174, across the Red Sea into Yemen, where a line of Ayyubid princes came to rule rather independently of Egypt. Yet, despite this expansion, Saladin's revenue payments to Damascus were suspiciously small. Nur al-Din sent in his own tax men to examine the situation and began gathering troops just in case.

For this to come to pass was a disappointment, to be sure, as Nur al-Din had given Saladin nearly everything, elevating his family from among his father's obscure Kurdish henchmen, granting him a post in his regime, iqtaʿs with which to raise his own troops, the favor of ready access to his person, and the opportunity to be involved in Nur al-Din's greatest conquest. In May 1174, as Zangid and Ayyubid troops were being mustered for the inevitable, Nur al-Din gave Saladin one final gift: he died. His tomb—the final resting-place of the ascetic Turcoman prince who had united the Muslim Levant, conquered the mightiest Shiʿi state in premodern times, pushed the Franks back to the

Syrian coast, outmaneuvered almost all his foes, and strove to rule as a "just king"—can still be seen today inside the Nuriya madrasa that he had built in the Tailor's Market in Damascus, largely bypassed by most visitors to the city (Fig. 6). It is a short walk from the more famous modern bronze statue of the triumphant Saladin, his ambitious and ungrateful underling, darling of historians, dictators, and other makers of myths.

– 6 –

The Fallen Tent

With the death of Nur al-Din in 1174, the seesawing of Frankish and Muslim fortunes in the Near East came to a sudden halt. When, just two months after Nur al-Din's death, King Amalric of Jerusalem died following a decade of rule, both the Franks and the Zangids found themselves facing strangely parallel political crises, stymieing military operations and leaving them preoccupied with their own space. Both men had been energetic rulers, personally responsible for extending their influence and strengthening central power against contentious vassals in their respective domains. Amalric in particular had built upon the achievements of his predecessor, his childless brother, Baldwin III, establishing, for example, warm ties between Jerusalem and the Byzantine Empire and shepherding his kingdom into what would turn out to be its last phase of effective military power. Both men, it also happened, were succeeded by children; Baldwin IV acceded to the throne of Jerusalem at age thirteen (and suffering from leprosy), and the eleven-year-old al-Salih Isma'il succeeded Nur al-Din. For the moment, then, both kingdoms were in the hands of regents.

The Franks had the better deal, as Baldwin's regent was the very able Raymond, count of Tripoli and lord of Tiberias. Until 1176, when Baldwin came of age, Raymond managed the kingdom on a comparatively steady course, mitigating, for example, the more belligerent foreign policy demands of certain factions in the kingdom, notably the

Knights Templar, whose influence had grown since their foundation two generations earlier. Al-Salih, on the other hand, was overshadowed by the veteran commander Gumushtakin, a eunuch and old Zangid loyalist, who spirited the boy away to Aleppo, where he could be kept on a short leash but where he remained the target of vicious succession disputes. Thanks to the statesmanship of Raymond at this crucial juncture, the Franks enjoyed comparative stability and appeared to have gained the upper hand in the crisis. But the Muslims had one thing the Franks did not: Saladin.

The Trenchant Sword

In hindsight it might seem as if, by involving himself in the quagmire that was Zangid Syria, Saladin was simply preparing the way for his more famous successes against the Franks. However, it is doubtful that Saladin was thinking in those terms in 1174. He did test the Franks during these early years, as in 1177 at Mont Gisard, near Ramla, where Baldwin IV's troops routed and very nearly captured him. A series of encounters over the Franks' new fortress at the strategic crossing of Jacob's Ford, located on the Jordan River about a hundred miles north of Jerusalem, ultimately resulted in Muslim victory in 1179 and the fortress being taken and razed. For the most part Saladin let the Franks be; indeed in 1175 he apparently signed a treaty with Jerusalem and certainly did so in 1185, when he ratified a four-year truce with the kingdom. For Saladin, Frankish Outremer, the collection of rump states governed by some leper boy-king and his minders, simply did not present as great a threat or as important an obstacle to his ambition as did Zangid Syria. And now the very crisis that the Zangid house was facing gave Saladin precisely the entrée he needed.[1]

For the former subjects and followers of Nur al-Din, there were only three men with a realistic chance of taking the dead sultan's place. Saladin was one of these, though he had so far remained aloof. The other two were princes of the Zangid house. One was the child al-Salih Isma'il, Nur al-Din's son and legitimate heir, who was under the tight control of the amir Gumushtakin in Aleppo. The other was Ghazi II, Nur al-Din's nephew and ruler of Mosul. In Damascus, Nur al-Din's old capital, the sultan's former amirs were rebuffed by Ghazi II when they sought out his protection; so, after assessing the situation, they opened their city to Saladin.

In 1174 Saladin moved from his Egyptian domains to Damascus, scrupulously presenting himself not as a usurper but as the rightful atabeg to the young al-Salih Isma'il in Aleppo, whom he recognized formally as his lord. From Damascus Saladin spent the next twelve years putting all of Muslim Syria under his sway. Gumushtakin in Aleppo and Ghazi II in Mosul were united in their opposition to him. Saladin tried to capture Aleppo outright on several occasions, without success. However, he was able to defeat the combined armies of Aleppo and Mosul in the field, as at Hama (in 1175) and at Tall al-Sultan, outside Aleppo (in 1176). He was thereby able to impose terms on Aleppo, by which al-Salih Isma'il remained lord of the city, but Saladin was to take charge of his armies. The fall of Zangid power from Syria was formalized when the 'Abbasid caliph sent Saladin, not al-Salih Isma'il, a diploma granting him rights over his territories in Egypt and Yemen, as well as any lands he might conquer in the future. The new arrangement received its final polish when Saladin returned to Damascus and married Nur al-Din's widow. In 1181 al-Salih Isma'il of Aleppo died, and by 1183 the city and all of Muslim Syria was now Saladin's. By 1185 he even had Mosul and its recalcitrant amir surrounded (Ghazi II having died in the interim). But the campaign in northern Mesopotamia dragged on, and, as winter approached, Saladin and the core of his army settled in for a long bivouac.

It was during this overwintering that, while encamped outside the city of Harran, Saladin fell dangerously ill. The situation was thought so serious that news of his health was kept tightly guarded and the movements of his physicians closely watched. As he passed in and out of his sickness, his advisers did what they could to shield him from any disagreeable news from his kingdom, including even the death of his wife, 'Ismat al-Din. As a result, over that dark Mesopotamian winter Saladin continued to write to her every day until his advisers broke the news to him in March.

Such sadness as he may have felt at this news will have been alleviated by the tidings from Mosul: Saladin's patience had paid off, for the city was willing to capitulate and recognize his authority. By further good fortune, even as the treaty was finally settled on March 4, 1186, Saladin emerged definitively from his illness, a coincidence of grace not lost on his contemporaries. The reenergized Saladin was now master of a sultanate that stretched from the Euphrates to the Nile, from northern Mesopotamia to southern Yemen. It may have seemed that he was at the pinnacle of his career. But the reality was a bit different: his vast lands, for example, were divided among his ambitious and fractious kinsmen and sons.

Saladin's most prominent agenda item as sultan—prosecuting the jihad against the Franks—had been sidelined in favor of his need to eliminate all Muslim rivals for so long that even his close advisers had their misgivings. He badly needed to assert his authority as sultan over his kinsmen and to keep his troops busy in the field to obtain plunder. Dusting off his title as the great mujahid was a solution whose time had come. By the spring of 1186 Saladin had seen to his priorities. Now it was time to see to the Franks.

The Merchant's Tale

The Franks, however, posed more than a simple military problem for medieval Muslims. To illustrate the complexities involved, we might fast-forward to a tale set some years after the death of Saladin, when a prominent amir, who worked for Saladin's successors, met a dark-skinned merchant in Upper Egypt and was surprised to find that he had children with white complexions "who were very handsome." The amir asked the merchant if the children were his, and the man offered the following explanation.[2]

Some time in the past, during the reign of Saladin, he had been a successful flax farmer in his village. Setting off to sell his produce in the region's markets, he stopped in Cairo and Damascus before reaching the Frankish-held town of Acre, where he rented a shop. Acre had been in the possession of the Franks since 1104, but Muslims were still allowed within its walls, especially merchants.

One day a Frankish woman passed through the market in the company of some of her female compatriots, none of whom were wearing the niqab veil. She visited the merchant's shop along with an old woman, apparently her chaperone, to purchase some flax. The merchant recalled, "What I saw of her beauty truly dazzled me, so I showed her indulgence in the price I asked." As a result, and not unnaturally, she came back a few days later, chasing bargains. Upon her return the merchant had to admit to himself that he had fallen in love with this Frankish woman. Speaking aside to the old woman who accompanied her, he declared, "I am destroyed by these feelings of love for her!" Together they arranged a secret meeting, for which the merchant paid the Frankish woman fifteen dinars; she even took note of the payment and then handed the coins to her chaperone. For their meeting he set up a suitably romantic dinner with everything one could want of food, drink, candles, and sweets. They ate and drank, and "when darkness fell, there was nothing more to do except sleep. The woman was furious when he insisted that they do just that, and nothing more. In the morning they went their separate ways."

The next time she came to him, the price of her company had gone up. He paid it, all the while grappling with an inner struggle to obey God's commands and to save himself from hellfire. But again he remained chaste. At their third encounter the price rose again, and she declared, "By the Messiah, you shall not have your pleasure with me except for five hundred dinars—or you can choose to die heartsick!" He returned to Damascus, battered and broken-hearted, but trading now in slave girls to dispel the feelings in his heart that the Frankish woman had stirred up.

A few years later Saladin won back Jerusalem and set about retaking cities along the coast. The merchant was sent to procure a slave girl of sufficient beauty to present to the sultan, and in the process he decided to purchase a slave for himself. When he did so (as the reader may already have guessed), he discovered that he had purchased the same Frankish woman who had so broken his heart. He indulged in a bit of gloating and taunted her about the fact that she had once offered herself to him for five hundred dinars, whereas he had just now bought her outright for ten. In response she converted to Islam on the spot. Since it was a "true conversion," he went to the local qadi to contract an official marriage with her. And then it seemed as if the poor merchant's heart might be dashed to pieces again, for it turned out that she was already married to a Frank. Nevertheless, when questioned by Saladin himself, the woman warmly expressed her love for the merchant over her Frankish husband and remained with him, so far as we know, happily ever after. The End.

Readers of medieval narratives of the Crusades—and quite a few modern ones—may come away with the impression that life in Muslim lands during the era of the Crusades lived up to the image proffered by the ideologies of holy war and jihad: that of two uncompromising archenemies bent on each others' destruction. Given the sources' focus on military matters, this misunderstanding can be forgiven. The reality was quite different. Most Muslims at the time probably never interacted with Franks; of those who did, the vast majority did not do so as combatants but as townspeople, neighbors, and, as in this tale, traders. This did not mean that civilian contacts between Franks and Muslims were always genteel, but it does mean that Frankish-Muslim relations were far richer than a strictly military narrative would allow.[3]

Figure 1. Statue of Saladin, Damascus. Courtesy Olfa Guizani.

Figure 2. World Map of al-Idrisi, ca. 1154. Courtesy of Wikimedia Commons.

Figure 3. The Circle of Equity. From Linda T. Darling, *A History of Social Justice and Political Power in the Middle East* (London: Routledge, 2013), fig. 1.

Figure 4. Jerusalem, al-Haram al-Sharif. © Eve81/Shutterstock.

Figure 5. Crac des Chevaliers. Bernard Gagnon, Wikimedia commons.

Figure 6. Tomb of Nur al-Din. Courtesy of Tekisch, Wikimedia Commons.

Figure 7. Almoravid gold dinar. Courtesy of Wikimedia Commons.

Figure 10. Coin of Baybars, Mamluk sultan of Egypt. Courtesy of University of Pennsylvania Museum of Archaeology and Anthropology.

Figure 8. Crusader coin from Acre, 1230. Courtesy of Wikimedia Commons.

Figure 9. Torre del Oro, Seville. Almohad Watchtower, thirteenth century. © Artur Bogacki/Shutterstock.

Figure 11. Portal of madrasa of al-Nasir Muhammad, from Acre
Cathedral. Courtesy of Martyn Smith/Wikimedia Commons.

Figure 12. Ottoman Miniature of the Battle of Nicopolis. Courtesy of Wikimedia Commons.

Figure 13. Commemorative stone in Latin, Greek, Hebrew, and Arabic from Palermo, 1149. © Nico Traut/ Shutterstock.

Figure 14.
Lucera Cathe-
dral of Santa
Maria della
Vittoria.
©Mi.Ti./
Shutterstock.

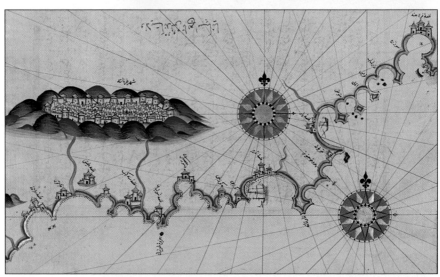

Figure 15. Ottoman map of Granada, from the Kitab-i Bahriye of Piri
Reis (1525). Courtesy of Wikimedia Commons.

The most telling aspect of our merchant's tale is its uncontroversial commercial context: Muslims and Franks were far more economically and commercially integrated than their ideologues liked to let on. The Franks in the Near East did not keep to the safety of their walled urban centers and castles, for example, but settled the land about them, albeit more often in settlements populated by native Christians than by Muslims.[4] And commercial interests often bound Muslim and Frankish communities in ways that made the unilateral claims of holy war inconvenient or easy to ignore. For Muslims who scrupled about such things (and our chaste merchant's behavior suggests that he certainly tried), it helped that Islamic law permitted commerce with infidels, so long as it did not involve prohibited commodities such as wine or the export of war materiel (such as weapons, armor, and, in some interpretations, slaves and horses) that might aid an enemy. The importation of such commodities, however, was certainly permitted, for they generated customs duties for the Muslim polities involved. Judging by the repeated (and hence unsuccessful) attempts by the papacy to criminalize such trade with Muslims, it seems to have been a busy sector of the economy for Christians and Muslims throughout the period. As Ibn Jubayr remarked, speaking of Saladin's Syria in terms applicable to al-Andalus and Sicily, "One of the astonishing things that is talked of is that though the fires of discord burn between the two parties, Muslim and Christian, two armies of them may meet and dispose themselves in battle array, and yet Muslim and Christian travelers will come and go between them without interference."[5]

This was aided no doubt by the fact that Frankish-Muslim exchange made use of ties that existed before the Frankish invasions and that developed and expanded even as the Franks extended their presence across the Mediterranean.[6] Italian merchants, for example, had long been a regular feature of the mercantile scene in Egypt, and Alexandria was one of the most cosmopolitan cities in the medieval world as a result of its ties to Europe, to say nothing of Africa and Asia. Other Muslim commercial hubs, such as Almería in al-Andalus, al-Mahdiya in North Africa, and Palermo in Sicily, were already linked to Christian ports, including Barcelona, Venice, and Constantinople. And pan-Mediterranean institutions, such as merchant hostelries (*funduq* in Arabic; *fondaco* in Italian) ensured that merchants and their commodities would be safely housed (and controlled) wherever they conducted their business. The expansion of the Franks into formerly Muslim territory only heightened a long and comfortable commercial relationship, even if it did require some reorientations, as, for example, with the rise of Acre as a Frankish commercial hub after Saladin's death, or the slow shift of Norman Sicily away from links with Islamic markets to those of southern Europe.[7]

Even the most strident of our military accounts allow for the fact that warfare, even holy war, required the deft use of treaties and alliances, which themselves were often freighted with economic consequences. Many such treaties involved some form of condominium (*munasafa*, in Arabic usage) or division of lands, water sources, or harvests, for example, ratifying the economic interpenetration of the Frankish and Muslim worlds.

As we have already seen, from almost the very beginning the Franks inserted themselves quite seamlessly into the political and diplomatic playing fields of al-Andalus, Sicily, and the Near East. And the use of alliances and treaties of mutual benefit continued even into the reign of Saladin, an era usually taken as a high point of Frankish-Muslim confrontation. Indeed such alliances and truces were produced *despite* the real gulfs that existed between Frankish and Muslim legal cultures that might otherwise have discouraged them; on the Islamic side expedients were even found to circumvent Islamic legal restrictions on, for example, the length of truces. From the first, local politics almost always trumped the needs of ideology. That such diplomatic activity appears to wane after Saladin's time has more to do with the fact that the Muslim states in the region no longer considered the Frankish polities to be equals worth allying with or threatening enough to merit constant diplomatic massaging. Still, as we shall see, this did not prevent Saladin's successors from making use of such diplomacy with their Frankish neighbors when particular circumstances, political or economic, dictated it.[8]

As in the merchant's story, commercial interaction implies cultural interaction of some kind, and it is a relatively easy thing to trace Muslim-Frankish interchange through the commodities that they traded. Western merchants sought out the usual exotic Eastern luxuries, including spices and medicaments (such as pepper, ginger, and, that luxury of luxuries, sugar produced in the Jordan Valley), textiles, ivory, gold, and porcelain. But they also purchased basics like dyes, glassware, metalwork, metal ores, and raw goods like our merchant's flax. In return, buyers in Islamic lands (Muslim or otherwise) purchased woolen cloth, some grains, silver, and above all wood, iron, and, as in our merchant's second career, slaves.

Such interaction is visible in the form of language, traceable most famously in the commercial terms of Arabic origin that entered into various Romance languages. For example, words for "customs" like *douane*, *dogana*, and *aduana* all hail from the Arabic *diwan* (itself a loan-word from Persian), meaning an account book or the office where one is kept. Many of these subsequently found their way into English: think of *cheque/check* (from *sakk*, a letter of credit) or *tariff* (from *ta'rif*, a notification), to say nothing of the vocabulary of exotic commodities like *artichoke, aubergine, caraway, cotton, crimson, mohair, muslin, orange, saffron, satin, syrup*, and *tamarind*. Spanish prices (and tribute) were paid in coins called *maravedí* (from "Almoravid", the dynasty having produced fine gold coins; Fig. 7), and the Venetians minted their own coins at the Zecca, the mint (*sikka*), not too far from the shipyards known as the Arsenale (*dar al-sina'a*). The Franks themselves modeled their coins on Muslim models, sometimes right down to the Arabic inscriptions (Fig. 8). The flow of words seems not to go the other way; when our Arabic sources use Frankish words, it is most often for that arcane hierarchized social vocabulary for which there was no equivalent. These include words like *sarjand* (sergeant), *burjasi* (burgess), *biskund* (viscount), *bayli* (bailli), and even *al-raydafrans* ("le Roi de France," or king of France).

Similarly the transmission of learning that took place between Muslims and Franks went in one direction. Some Frankish lords patronized the composition of new Arabic works, notably the Normans of Sicily, for whom, as we have seen, the geographer al-Idrisi compiled his geographical treatise that contains his famous upside-down map, which is sometimes called *The Book of Roger*; they also gilded their courtly assemblies with Arabic poetry and panegyrics. But the Normans always distinguished themselves as Fatimid wannabes (when not aping the Byzantines), and this patronage was something of an exception to the rule.[9] Most of the translation of scientific and religious works that occurred as a result of the Frankish-Muslim encounter went from Arabic (or Greek) into Latin, and almost exclusively in Spain and Sicily rather than in the Levant. Muslims had little need for what Frankish scholars had to offer. Given the poor impression that Frankish civilization left on Muslims, this unidirectional flow of culture would not have surprised anyone. Nature, they would no doubt have pointed out, abhors a vacuum.[10]

When medieval Muslims learned about the Franks, they did so mostly in their daily interactions with them as erstwhile enemies, consumers, neighbors, and slaves. That our merchant owned Frankish slaves was as common a feature of daily life as his Frankish equivalent owning Muslims, as domestic help and as concubines. In such a context some degree of cultural interaction was a certainty. But pinning down actual examples in our sources has proven frustratingly hard; cultural interaction would have varied in quality and direction in every context. It seems doubtful that our merchant and his new Frankish wife debated the nuances of Aristotelian metaphysics together.

Finally, the merchant's tale reveals something about Muslim attitudes toward intermarriage and sex. Indeed our merchant's story makes sense only in a literary context in which Frankish cities were seen as titillating zones where the social regulations keeping men apart from women would have been lax. As the tale indicates, intermarriage between Muslims and Franks was always a possibility. The amir's befuddlement at the reason that lay behind the fair complexion of the merchant's children, however, suggests it was nevertheless a rarity. The tale's context was also one in which Frankish women were seen as easy and as pernicious temptations to the upright. For all that the merchant might have wished it otherwise, his lady love bore all the hallmarks of a prostitute, with her demands for cash and her aged procuress, to say nothing of her professional sense of outrage at her mark's unyielding chastity. In that respect her final conversion to Islam marks a conquest on par with those of the amir who interviewed her husband.

Living with the Enemy

Of course, Muslims didn't just learn about the Franks as equals; some had plenty of opportunity to observe them firsthand as subjects of Frankish rulers. The situation of Muslim subjects of Frankish lords in Spain, Sicily, and the Near East varied considerably, both across these three zones and within them.[11] Muslim-Christian interaction in these zones was a story neither exclusively of oppression or of tolerant *convivencia* but rather a moving target along a spectrum between these two poles, ever-dependent upon context, locality, and political whim. This perhaps best explains the plight of subject Muslims: the constant sense of unpredictability and the sense that their time as tolerated minorities could, at any moment, run out. But any generalizations about how Muslims fared under Frankish rule are just that and should be understood as tentative; for every anecdote or example adduced about tolerance or intolerance, there usually exists a counterexample.

Every area had its specificities. Christian Spain had the longest history of holding a population of Muslim subjects. As a result there developed new social terms emerging from conquest, immigration, and conversion. There Muslim subjects were known as Mudejars, from *al-mudajjan*, an Arabic term adopted from animal husbandry meaning "domesticated." By contrast, Christian subjects of Muslim rulers (who came to adopt elements of Arabic language and culture) were known as Mozarabs, from *al-musta'rab*, meaning "Arabized." These terms seem to be specific to the Andalusi experience and did not apply in Sicily or the Near East (despite attempts by some modern authors to apply them). The Frankish Near East was unique in being so isolated from the rest of Europe; Franks there were always a minority, and manpower shortages an unshakeable reality for its rulers. Perhaps more than in Spain or Sicily, the Franks in the Near East were heavily dependent upon local methods and the cooperation or at least resignation of the subject population.

For the most part, the Muslim subjects of Frankish rulers inhabited a social class much like Christian and Jewish subjects of Islamic rulers did: subject Muslims were, in effect, dhimmis, a protected religious subject population, but in this case a Muslim majority ruled by a non-Muslim minority. They were thus second-class citizens, exploited but included, with certain protections and rights as well as certain duties, obligations, and humiliations. In this respect it is important to note that no consistent attempt was ever made at the conversion of these subject Muslim populations, despite how hard individual Christians might have prayed for it. Canon law discouraged it. The few outbursts of actual Christian missionary activity directed at Muslims (principally in Spain) were aberrations—and, it bears noting, dismal failures. Pressures on Muslims to convert were generally more complex than simple coercion. For example, according to Ibn Jubayr, who passed through Sicily in 1184–85, it was not unheard of for the sons or daughters of Sicilian Muslims facing the anger of their parents to take refuge with the Church and so convert to escape punishment and recrimination. He further claimed that some Muslim fathers pressed their unmarried daughters upon visiting Muslim men to take them far away from the pressures and temptations of a rapidly Christianizing and Latinizing Sicily. Although some Muslims did convert on their own and even gained status as a result, some Frankish lords actively discouraged it, if only because non-Christian slaves who converted would be entitled to their freedom.[12]

Yet for all that, living under infidel rule posed numerous problems for Muslims, not least for religious reasons. For many, emigrating from infidel territory was an obligation to ensure proper practice of the rituals of Islam and to live as a good Muslim; it was moreover an act in imitation of the Prophet, who himself had emigrated from Mecca to Medina to avoid an infidel environment in what was then pagan Mecca. Even travel to infidel territory for purposes of trade, such as that made unapologetically by our merchant, was for some legists an undesirable act, and commodities like paper and cloth produced in Frankish lands were likewise suspect when considering points of ritual purity. Frankish conquest thus produced not just refugees, as in the earliest days, but also émigrés once the dust settled. North Africa and al-Andalus provided ready destinations for Sicilians seeking new homes in solidly Muslim lands. At the Norman conquest of the island in 1090 it has been estimated that there were about a quarter of a million Muslims, along with Greeks and Jews. A century and a half later there were only twenty thousand left to be exiled to mainland Italy. In the Near East in 1156 the inhabitants of nine Frankish-held villages near Nablus emigrated to Damascus, where the enclave they settled (and scholars and stringent devotees they brought with them) played an important role in the later religious history of the city. Perhaps the most eloquent expression of the situation comes from an Andalusi Muslim voice preserved in a Latin source, an old man among the Muslims evacuating Gibraltar in 1309. He addressed Fernando IV, the Christian king who took his town, with a question: "My lord, why do you drive me hence? When your great-grandfather King Fernando took Seville he drove me out and I went to live at Jerez, but when your grandfather Alfonso took Jerez he drove me out and I went to live at Tarifa, thinking that I was in a safe place. Your father King Sancho came and took Tarifa and drove me out and I went to live at Gibraltar, thinking that I would not be in any safer place in the whole land of the Moors…but now I see that I cannot remain in any of these places, so I will go beyond the sea [to Morocco] and settle in a place where I can live in safety and end my days."[13]

Such emigration tended to be the choice of elite groups, the ruling strata of captured lands and the courtiers who depended upon them, and as such, not very significant as a percentage of the population. Most Muslims were peasant cultivators and craftsmen who could not so easily pick up and leave. Life under Frankish rule for them continued largely as it had under Muslim rule. For economic and practical reasons, the Franks preferred to limit their changes to the existing regime in the lands they conquered, just enough to maintain their status as a ruling minority but without disrupting the fiscal and economic functions of their subjects. Indeed to Ibn Jubayr, despite what he saw on Sicily, it seemed as if Muslim subjects of the Franks in the Near East rather preferred their new lords, who apparently demanded lower taxes than the Muslims: "This is one of the misfortunes afflicting the Muslims. The Muslim community bewails the injustice of a landlord of its own faith, and applauds the conduct of its opponent and enemy, the Frankish landlord, and is accustomed to justice from him."[14] On the other hand, Ibn Jubayr was plainly involved in a critique of the injustice of certain Muslim rulers of his day, so one must take his observations—made while merely passing through Syria, after all—with a grain of salt.[15]

Muslims living under Frankish rule have not left us much in the way of observations of their masters. However, Muslims in Islamic lands still had plenty of opportunities for observations of the Franks in their civilian settings, and one can at least get a sense of common Muslim attitudes toward the Franks, something rather less than the unbiased ethnographic scrutiny one might wish—but then, that is true of their observations of any ethnic group.[16] For the most part, it does not seem that Muslim discussion of the Franks had shifted much from the sorts of things that were said before the first acts of Frankish aggression on Islamic lands (see chapter 1). Ibn Jubayr, as noted, was keen to depict the Franks as a *cultural* threat to Muslims, who turned the heads of the natives with their ready women, frivolous public spectacles, and childish creed, and whose easy ways might tempt otherwise respectable Muslims to embrace their servitude to them or, worse still, convert to Christianity.

For the Syrian mercenary and diplomat Usama ibn Munqidh, the Franks served as living proof that God worked in mysterious ways, for the Franks—even the Franks!—could achieve some victories, despite their bestial qualities, when God so chose.[17] Like some other Muslim observers, Usama noted the difference between Franks who had spent time and settled in Muslim lands and the more oblivious newcomers. It was the latter that you really had to watch out for, as with a newly arrived knight who accosted him while he was attempting to pray (toward Mecca, of course) in Jerusalem during a diplomatic visit. Only the intervention of some of his fellow Franks—friends of Usama's— got him to clear out: "They apologized to me, saying, 'This man is a stranger, just arrived from the Frankish lands sometime in the past few days. He has never before seen anyone who did not pray towards the east.'" He noted that some Franks eventually acclimatized and frequented the company of Muslims: "They are much better than those recently arrived from their lands, but they are the exception and should not be considered representative."[18]

Like most of his contemporaries, Usama didn't really see any of the human virtues at all in the Franks taken as a whole, save courage, and even that, he suspected, was a product of their stupidity, not their wisdom. Indeed they were remarkable people to watch: great fighters but terribly afraid of being caught by tricks in the field; utterly hopeless when it came to the finer side of life; completely devoid of any sense of female honor; fanatical in their approach to their flawed religion; resistant to assimilation; and their systems of law and medicine had little to recommend them.

Of course, individual Franks, even Frankish rulers, might rise above these generalities and prove themselves admirable. The pilgrim and scholar al-Harawi, who worked for Saladin as a bureaucrat and spy, was grateful for Richard the Lionheart's attempt (despite its failure) to return his books and papers to him after they had been seized in the course of a battle. He also notes with genuine awe his meeting with an elderly Frank who had a reputation for piety among his people and who had been inside the Tombs of the Patriarchs in Hebron.[19] Usama, as mentioned, had friends among the Franks in Jerusalem—to be specific, they were Templars garrisoned on the Temple Mount. Another fellow took quickly to Usama, calling him his "brother" and making Usama a signal offer as he was returning to Europe: "My brother [the man said], I am leaving for my country. I want you to send your son…with me to my country, where he can observe the knights and acquire reason and chivalry. When he returns, he will be like a truly rational man."[20] Usama, horrified at the idea, managed to politely fend off the man's offer; one cannot help but wonder what might have happened had the boy spent some of his youth as a guest, and perhaps better observer than his peers, in the land of the Franks.

A century later an Egyptian official name al-Khazandari paused from writing a chronicle of the events of his day to provide a brief ethnographic excursus on the Franks, and the image had not changed much even then.[21] For al-Khazandari, the Franks were, of all the peoples he knew, lamentably provincial. There were five things in particular that Franks laughably seemed to find wondrous about life in Islamdom: black people, whom they have never seen before and whom they secretly think all harbor anger toward them; camels; the mamluk system, in which a slave can become a prince; polygamy; and the formal deposing of witnesses in court proceedings, as opposed to relying upon one's neighbors to testify before priests and monks. All of these were quotidian features of al-Khazandari's world, yet seemed to be sources of continuous fascination for the Franks he knew of. As with al-Bakri's account of Frankish Christianity centuries earlier, one can almost sense al-Khazandari's pity. Many more (if less substantial) such accounts could be adduced, but on the basis of the literary record at least, it seems clear that despite some heightened appreciation of the nuances of Frankish culture and society, the long confrontation of Muslims and Franks did not much alter their initial impressions of each other. Like Usama's dodging the invitation to send his son on study abroad in Europe, it was a history of missed opportunities.

Córdoba Revisited

Just as the Muslim kingdoms of Zangi, Nur al-Din, and Saladin in the Near East were scoring consistent military victories against a divided Outremer, so too in distant al-Andalus the slowdown of Frankish expansion was turning into a new wave of Almohad victories (Map 8). After 1150 the Almohads were making unmistakable progress in consolidating their hold on al-Andalus, capturing towns and fortresses

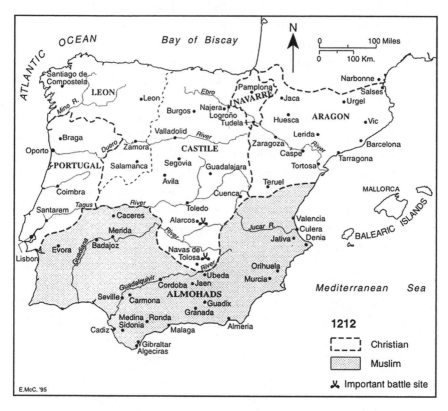

Map 8 Al-Andalus under the Almohads. From O. R. Constable, ed., *Medieval Iberia: Readings from Muslim, Christian, and Jewish Sources*, 2nd ed. (Philadelphia: University of Pennsylvania Press, 2012), 226, map 3.

held by various foes: Christians, old Almoravid loyalists, and independent adventurers. We have seen that the Almohads had tamed the Algarve on the eve of the fall of Lisbon to the Franks, and things progressed from this kernel. In 1154 they took Granada, putting a permanent end to Almoravid rule, though some loyalists held on in the Balearic Islands. In 1157 they delivered a blow to the Franks by recapturing Almería. Alfonso VII, who had captured the city a decade earlier, died during his retreat, which must have been welcome news to the Almohads.[22] Indeed his death resulted in the division of his kingdom into two separate kingdoms, León and Castile, each governed by their own ruler and each a victim to their own rivalries, a situation that only strengthened the hand of the Almohads.

In 1160 the Almohad caliph ʿAbd al-Muʾmin made the gravity of his intentions clear to all when he established a base and palaces at Gibraltar to facilitate the back-and-forth of troops, supplies, and information between al-Andalus and Morocco, the better to keep tabs on both active fronts of his expanding domains. Indeed while still in North Africa after ousting the Normans from Mahdiya, the caliph had raised a large army of Arab nomads to assist in the jihad in al-Andalus, appealing to their specific role in Islamic history: "No one fights [the Franks] like you do. It was through you that the lands were conquered at the beginning of Islam, and now it is through you that the enemy will be driven back."[23]

It was in this context of seemingly ineluctable Almohad triumph that Muslim power in al-Andalus anchored itself once again in Córdoba. Seville, the old Almoravid capital, continued to serve as the Almohad's base in al-Andalus (the main capital remained Marrakesh in Morocco), but ʿAbd al-Muʾmin's new resolve with regard to his empire and to al-Andalus in particular needed a grand gesture to show that the Almohads were no longer simple Berber hirelings who had grown mighty but rather the elite of a new caliphate that was here to stay. Córdoba was ideal for this purpose. An ancient city, Córdoba was long the capital of the Umayyads, the first caliphs of al-Andalus, who held the country together before the period of disunified taifa kings. It was a site rich in meaning. Córdoba had fallen on hard times since the golden age of the Umayyads. The civil wars of the taifa period, the "party kings," had been especially cruel to the place, and when the Almohads came to claim it, it was practically an empty ruin of a town; eyewitnesses mention a population of a few score men and their families making a hardscrabble living farming plots behind the safety of the city walls. But the Almohads rose to the challenge, ordering the transfer of the Andalusi bureaucracy from Seville to the new capital and encouraging its leading citizens to make the move as well. Architects were commissioned to build or repair the fortifications, palaces, and houses for the populace. A garrison was established, ready to prosecute the jihad in al-Andalus at the caliph's command. The Almohads, this move seemed to be saying, were bringing glorious caliphal rule in al-Andalus back to its proper seat.

Of course, such a message would need to be made only if there were people who needed to be convinced of it. 'Abd al-Mu'min died in 1163, and when, after a swift but tense coup d'état, his son Yusuf I succeeded him (though he deferred taking the title of caliph for a few years), he continued his father's policy of bringing the jihad to al-Andalus.[24] This involved Muslim targets, above all the recalcitrant "Wolf-King" Ibn Mardanish, lord of Murcia and Valencia. He had long been a thorn in the side of the Almohads, stymieing nearly all expansion in the east. Yusuf I's armies slowly strangled off the territories belonging to his domains, and co-opted what remained of the Wolf-King's family after his death in 1172. But by now the Christians had returned to the offensive and posed numerous problems. The Portuguese warlord Giraldo Sempavor ("The Fearless") captured Trujillo and Evora and, with the help of the king of Portugal, in 1169 nearly captured Badajoz.

Here the internal rivalries of the Christian courts provided the Almohads with the opening they needed. Fernando II, king of Leon, would not sit idly by while Badajoz fell to his Portuguese rivals. So he offered the Almohads an alliance and sent troops to assist the besieged Almohad garrison. In the fighting the king of Portugal himself was taken prisoner, released only upon relinquishing his recent conquests. So in 1170 Badajoz reverted to the Almohads. Afterward Fernando II renewed his treaty with the Almohads at, of all places, al-Zallaqa, the plain northwest of Badajoz where in 1086 the Almoravids had won their famed victory against Alfonso VI. Perhaps this was another symbolic revisiting on the part of the Almohads; it was certainly suggestive of Almohad fortunes. With Badajoz returned, Giraldo Sempavor was driven out of the region, and the Almohads seemed to be, like the Almoravids decades earlier, the newly anointed saviors of al-Andalus.

It was an illusion. Andalusi enthusiasm for war depended heavily upon the charismatic leadership of the caliph: when he was present in al-Andalus, major losses could be averted; when he was absent, the Franks roamed with impunity. And Yusuf was absent more than he was present. When he left for Morocco in 1176, years of Christian raids and conquests and mostly feeble Andalusi responses followed. An exception was a massive naval battle in 1181 in the Atlantic off of Silves, which was a resounding victory for the Almohad fleet, caliph or no. Still al-Andalus waited. Yusuf returned only in 1184, his goal being Santarem, from whence the Portuguese had been raiding the villages around Seville. Though the Almohads had the city under a tight siege, news that Fernando II, the king of Leon, was on the way to assist the Portuguese struck a chill in Yusuf's camp. As the caliph's troops began to decamp, the Portuguese stormed out of the city and an orderly retreat turned into a chaotic rout. In the melee and panic, the caliph himself was badly injured; during the ignominious return to Seville, he died.[25]

Yusuf's son and successor became caliph with the title al-Mansur. Like his father, al-Mansur was preoccupied with warfare and diplomacy elsewhere—in North Africa and Majorca mostly; when he finally returned to al-Andalus in 1190, it was clear that the Christians had been busy. Thus in 1189 King Sancho of Portugal, with help from some Frankish volunteers who were en route to Syria as part of the Third Crusade, captured Silves after a short siege. This was sufficient provocation for al-Mansur, who crossed over in 1190. After visiting sites of ancient caliphal grandeur in Córdoba, he finally took back the city in 1191. He celebrated this rather minor triumph in grand style in Seville but, not wanting to tempt fate, then returned to Morocco. In 1195 al-Mansur returned to al-Andalus in what would turn out to be the last significant Almohad victories against the Christians. A major victory in a pitched battle against the army of Alfonso VIII of Castile at Alarcos was followed by a series of highly profitable raids on Christian territory, as at Trujillo and even before the walls of Toledo and, less successfully, at Madrid and Guadalaljara. Muslim allies were also present when a Christian coalition invaded Castile. Taken together, these sorties, in their effect and in geographical scope, were the high-water mark of Almohad power.

By 1198 al-Mansur clearly felt it was time to return to Marrakesh and see to the less exciting aspects of running his empire. Upon returning, however, he suddenly took ill and, in 1199, died. Al-Mansur had been a more serious military man than his father, and his successes against his foes in al-Andalus (and elsewhere) reflect that. But for him as for all the Almohads, it is worth putting all this military activity in context. As with the Saljuqs and Ayyubids in the east, jihad was just one aspect of a broader attempt on the part of the Almohads to reform society and legitimize their state. Al-Mansur's campaigns thus went hand in hand with the administrative reforms he enacted from Marrakesh and pious gestures such as building programs, fortification of cities, and, most notably, putting on trial in Córdoba the famous (or perhaps infamous) philosopher Averroes (Ibn Rushd), whose teachings had led to accusations of heterodoxy on the part of some of the Andalusi religious classes. Who could reject a caliph who policed orthodoxy, buttressed justice in his kingdom, and kept the predations of the infidels at bay?[26]

Al-Mansur was succeeded by his son al-Nasir, who, aside from successfully capturing Majorca from its Muslim lords, was not the warrior his father was. Although he came to power in 1199, al-Nasir engaged in no activity against the Franks of al-Andalus until 1211. That at least was a small success at Calatrava in retaliation for Christian raids over the previous years in the Levante. But this triumph was overshadowed by a defeat—perhaps the most significant of all—in 1212. It was in that year that King Alfonso VIII of Castile, assisted by a coalition of Christians from Spain and beyond, marched south to revenge himself against al-Nasir and to reclaim lands and strongholds that had been lost to the Almohads in previous years. Al-Nasir preferred to wait and see, perhaps hoping that scarce supplies would force the Christians to withdraw, as had happened so often in the past. While the Almohad army encamped in waiting at a place called al-ʿIqab, Alfonso marched on them by an unexpected route and, on July 16, caught them unawares. Confounded, it seems, by divisions within the Muslim forces, the caliph fled almost as soon as Alfonso arrived, and the Almohad army was routed. As the chronicler al-Marrakushi (d. 1270) put it, "The main reason for this defeat was the divisions in the hearts of the Almohads. In the time of [the caliph al-Mansur] they drew their pay every four months without fail. But in the time of this [caliph, al-Nasir], and especially during this particular campaign, their payment was in arrears. They attributed this to the viziers, and marched to battle bearing this grudge. I have heard from several of them that they did not draw their swords nor train their spears, nor did they take any part in the preparations for battle. They fled at the first assault of the Franks, having intended to do so from the start."[27] As it happened, supply problems did vex Alfonso, and he was not able to build upon this victory; the major Muslim cities of the area, Córdoba, Granada, and Jaen, remained safe. But the damage was done. Al-Nasir shipped back to Marrakesh, where, in 1213, he was killed by one of his own men. The Battle of al-ʿIqab, or, as it is known in the West, of Las Navas de Tolosa, would emerge as one of the most decisive engagements ever fought on the Iberian Peninsula and marked the end of Almohad power (Fig. 9).[28]

After al-ʿIqab, Almohad collapse came swiftly.[29] The new caliph, al-Mustansir, was a child entirely restricted by the maneuvers of palace factions, and he died shortly after acceding to the throne, the last of the Almohad rulers directly descended from the dynasty's founder. Moreover, despite some moments of mutual distrust, the Christian kingdoms of Leon and Castile were now reunited after some seventy-odd years. In the Almohad civil war—the first of its kind—that erupted after the death of the child al-Mustansir, the Castilians and Portuguese were only too eager to involve themselves. Through offers of alliance, antagonism, or outright conquest, the Christians gained most of Al-Andalus as the Almohads and Andalusis themselves let it slip from their grasp. Indeed many Andalusis were bravely defending their lands against the Christians entirely without Almohad support.

One such Andalusi who gained a reputation for personal heroism was a certain Ibn Hud of Murcia, who in 1228 rose in a widely popular revolt against the feebleness of Almohad rule. Soon the populace of Córdoba rose up and ousted their Almohad governor, and Ibn Hud went so far as to send a message to Baghdad, repudiating Almohad suzerainty and pledging allegiance to the 'Abbasid caliphs of the east. The Almohad caliph, who was himself facing enemies from within the ruling elite, withdrew to Marrakesh to confront his rivals; he and his armies never again confronted the Franks, nor for that matter did they ever again cross the Straits to tend to their former domains in al-Andalus.

The Wheel of Ruin

Almohad failure in the West did not necessarily mean that Saladin's parallel attempts in the Near East to solve his Frankish problems would suffer the same fate. Having set to rights the last of Nur al-Din's legacy, Saladin faced a Frankish problem rather different from the one that had occupied the Almohads in al-Andalus. In Syria the Franks were comparatively isolated from their European sources of support; manpower and supplies were a constant source of weakness for them. Yet Saladin had the backing of the caliph in Baghdad and had methodically crushed or subdued all his Muslim foes in the region. The Almohads never had such luxuries, and so their campaigns against the Franks produced much less satisfying results than did the accomplishments of Saladin.

After touring the last of his newly conquered lands in northern Syria, Saladin was ready to focus on the Franks. He arrived in Damascus in May 1186. On the way, he had summoned his son al-Afdal from

Cairo, who set out for Syria after mustering a small army. He was obliged to pause, however, as Frankish raids on the Egyptian border blocked his passage. Saladin was not particularly concerned. By instigating this raid, the Franks had broken the four-year truce they had once demanded and that had inconveniently tied his hands. If the Franks were going to engage in such practices, "then the wheel of ruin will turn against them," his secretary smugly wrote. In August al-Afdal arrived in Damascus, while other of Saladin's sons were sent to take charge in Aleppo and Cairo.[30]

Much had happened in the Latin kingdom since Saladin first arrived in Syria nearly a decade earlier. By 1186 the leper-king Baldwin IV was dead, succeeded by his nephew Baldwin V, another child, who ruled only under the regency of Raymond of Tripoli. Then, when this Baldwin died a few months later, his mother, Sibyl, took the throne. As queen of Jerusalem, Sibyl came with her husband, Guy of Lusignan, whom she crowned in the summer of 1186 as king.

This reshuffling in the palace at Jerusalem resulted in two changes of direct interest to Saladin. On the one hand, it created a potential new ally in Raymond of Tripoli, the former regent. At court his talents were no longer needed, and he was put out to pasture. As a result he opened negotiations with Saladin and, it appears, entered into a treaty with him, opening passage to the Muslims through his lands around Tiberias. On the other hand, the new situation in Jerusalem also created a new enemy, in the form of Reynald of Châtillon. By 1186 Reynald could not really be called "new" as if he were an unknown quantity. Indeed his problem was that he was all too well known. Formerly prince of Antioch and now lord of Transjordan, Reynald was a hard-liner who came east with the Second Crusade and stayed on to make his name, eventually winding up as a guest in Nur al-Din's prison in Aleppo for seventeen years. Later, as lord of Transjordan, he had outraged Muslims by sending a squadron of ships out on the Red Sea to attack merchants and pilgrims bound for Mecca. From his base at Karak, he followed the same modus operandi on dry land, harassing the caravans that crossed from Syria to Egypt, even while the truce between Saladin and Jerusalem was supposed to be in effect.[31]

In this context Saladin's options seemed fairly clear. He badly needed a victory against the Franks to silence those who criticized him for spending so much time at war with his fellow Muslims. Reynald's actions were provocative, and Transjordan was an important jigsaw piece of territory connecting Saladin's lands in Egypt to those in Syria. In itself the conquest of Transjordan would be a small gain against the

Franks—but perhaps a threat there could lure the rest of the Franks out into the field. When Reynald captured a large Egyptian caravan and its guard, Saladin had his pretext. He demanded the immediate release of the prisoners, but Reynald refused, even (or perhaps especially) when Raymond of Tripoli arrived to serve as an intermediary. In March 1187 Saladin arrived at Karak for retribution and spent the spring harassing the countryside. The peasants fled in droves to Muslim territory. Meanwhile his son al-Afdal was mustering a large army at the Sea of Galilee; he led one impetuous raid to Saffuriya (ancient Sepphoris) in Palestine, where the Muslims overwhelmed a smaller Frankish force. Among the slain was the master of the military order of St. John, or Hospitallers, a valued Frankish commander. By May Reynald's lands in Transjordan were devastated and virtually every stronghold, including Karak, was in Saladin's hands. However, when news reached Saladin that his erstwhile ally Raymond of Tripoli had made peace with his fellow Franks, he knew that now was the time to strike at the Latin kingdom.

All of Saladin's forces that were in the field, from Egypt, Syria, and Mesopotamia, made for Tiberias. Additional troops were on the move from Egypt if needed, and Saladin's nephew in Aleppo made a truce with the Franks of Antioch to ensure his army would not be distracted. The sultan even sent a polite invitation to the Byzantine emperor, but he declined to join in. The Franks, led by King Guy, assembled at Saffuriya and had at their disposal the entire army of the Latin kingdom, including Templars and Hospitallers, assisted by much smaller contingents from Antioch and Tripoli. The exaggerated figures given by our medieval sources on the disposition of the Muslim and Frankish troops are hard to swallow, but Saladin's army, soberly estimated at about thirty thousand, seems to have grossly outnumbered the combined forces mustered by the Franks. Indeed the very size of Saladin's army may have added to his sense of urgency, as it would be very difficult to muster so many soldiers again and to keep them supplied and in the field for very much longer. If Saladin was to act against the Franks, he needed to act then and there.

In late June Saladin camped with his army at Kafr Sabt, to the southwest of Tiberias and the Sea of Galilee. There he controlled access to abundant sources of water and, more important, to the road running east from the Frankish camp at Saffuriya to the town of Tiberias. The city's lord, the once-friendly Raymond of Tripoli, was of course away with most of his men in the camp of King Guy, but a small garrison, and Raymond's wife, remained behind. Rather than stampeding into the Frankish camp, Saladin instead put Tiberias under siege in the hope of drawing the Franks into territory of his own choosing. The plan worked; after much argument, which even the Arabic sources take note of, the Frankish army marched east to relieve Tiberias. As the Franks strung themselves out along the road, a division of Saladin's army maneuvered behind them to prevent their retreat. Other troops harassed them with feints and arrow fire as they traveled. In the heat of the season (now early July 1187) the battle became, at base, a battle about water. Saladin had ready access to his sources, but the Frankish troops were now sealed off from the secure sources at Saffuriya. Such springs that Guy could gain en route were utterly insufficient to the needs of his army; this seems to be what pushed him to make the fateful decision on July 4 to direct his army to the springs near the little village of Hattin.[32]

At the Horns of Hattin, a double hill formed by the basalt rim of an extinct volcanic crater, the Frankish army saw that their progress was blocked even here. Trapped, unable to punch through the Muslim lines to Tiberias, most of the army retreated to the Horns, where Guy pitched his tent and the walls of ancient ruins atop the hill provided some semblance of cover. The Franks mounted numerous charges against the Muslim army, but Saladin's men simply closed up around any men who came through. Only Saladin's former ally Raymond III and a few of his men were allowed to pass through unharmed—a fact that cannot have buoyed Raymond's stock among the few who survived the battle. The Muslim troops had the Franks on the Horns surrounded by fire and smoke, cut off from retreat or water, exhausted and decimated. By the end of the day the Muslims had managed to gain the summit. Saladin's son al-Afdal later provided this dramatic eyewitness account:

> When the king of the Franks was on the hill with that band, they made a formidable charge against the Muslims facing them, so that they drove them back to my father. I looked towards him and he was overcome by grief and his complexion pale. He took hold of his beard and advanced, crying out "Give the lie to the Devil!" The Muslims rallied, returned to the fight and climbed the hill. When I saw that the Franks withdrew, pursued by the Muslims, I shouted for joy, "We have beaten them!" But the Franks rallied and charged again like the first time and drove the Muslims back to my father. He acted as he had done on the first occasion and the Muslims turned upon the Franks and drove them back to the hill. I again shouted, "We have beaten them!" but my father

rounded on me and said, "Be quiet! We have not beaten them until that tent [Guy's] falls." Even as he was speaking to me, the tent fell. The sultan dismounted, prostrated himself in thanks to God Almighty and wept for joy.[33]

The Battle of Hattin left the Frankish military gutted and thereby opened the Frankish kingdoms to reconquest by Saladin's seemingly unstoppable armies. It was celebrated in Saladin's sword-rattling chancery as "a day of grace, on which the wolf and the vulture kept company, while death and captivity followed in turns. The unbelievers were tied together in fetters, astride chains rather than stout horses."[34] Those Franks who did not die that day were taken as captives to be ransomed or sold. The most prized were taken to Saladin's tent to be dealt with personally; Guy and many other lords were eventually ransomed. Reynald of Châtillon did not join them. Instead, following the letter of Islamic law when dealing with dangerous prisoners, Saladin urged Reynald to convert to Islam and, when he refused, personally executed him, as he had twice vowed to do. It was the social implications of the act, not its finality, for which Saladin felt he should apologize, saying to Guy, "It is not customary for one prince to kill another, but this man had crossed the line."[35] The same process attended the execution of the Templars and Hospitallers, who were considered such a danger that Saladin personally ransomed any such prisoners found in the hands of his men, to ensure that they would meet their end. He also had any Turcopoles (Turkish light cavalry in the service of the Franks) executed as traitors.

Throughout Syria, it is said, the price of slaves plummeted as the markets were flooded with Frankish captives. According to one source, one Frankish prisoner was traded in exchange for a shoe. When asked, the captive's seller explained that he insisted on the price because he "wanted it to be talked about."[36] The nonhuman plunder taken was also said to be considerable. Among the treasures was the relic of the True Cross, which the Franks had carried before them in battle. Its capture was precisely as devastating to the Franks as it was thrilling to Saladin's subjects in Damascus, who suspended it upside-down on a spear and paraded it through the streets of the city. It was later sent by Saladin's son al-Afdal as a trophy for the caliph of Baghdad and was never seen again—lost, one presumes, during the Mongol sack of 1258. At Hattin itself Saladin had a "Dome of Victory" constructed to commemorate what was already being seen as a turning point in his life; however, within a few decades, like much Saladin left for his descendants, it was in ruins.[37]

By the end of 1187 Saladin's armies had captured most of the territory that the Franks had taken since they arrived with the First Crusade. The cities of Syria and Palestine fell one by one, in diverse circumstances. In the wake of the debacle at Hattin, the mere sight of Muslim armies was often enough to convince Frankish leaders to surrender their towns, as at Acre. At Nablus the local villagers—almost all of whom were Muslims—blockaded the Franks in the citadel until one of Saladin's commanders arrived and accepted their surrender. Jubayl, on the northern coast, surrendered as ransom for its lord, Hugh Embriaco, who had been captured at Hattin. A similar ploy was attempted in the south, where King Guy and the master of the Templars were trotted out to convince the garrison of Ascalon to surrender, but to no avail. Instead Saladin's armies met fierce resistance, though the Franks there were eventually prevailed upon to surrender. Other cities likewise gave Saladin some serious resistance, as at Beirut and Jaffa. Then again, some places were simply passed over and saved for later, notably the port of Tyre, which Saladin reconnoitered but left untouched not once but twice as he crisscrossed the region. It was an act of expediency he would live to regret.[38]

The Strayed Camel

Needless to say, it is Saladin's reconquest of Jerusalem that ensured his lasting fame.[39] He and his army arrived before the Holy City on September 20, 1187. The Franks were clearly preparing for a long siege, strengthening fortifications, stationing mangonels, deepening the fosse, and sending a guard to keep watch outside the walls. The city's fighting force was now swollen by tens of thousands of refugees from Saladin's conquests, all come in a last bid for security, relying, as one Frankish observer put it, "on the city's sanctity rather than its strength."[40] Five days later, replicating precisely the situation of the Frankish armies in 1099, Saladin decided to move his army to the less-fortified northern wall. From there his archers pelted the walls with covering fire while sappers began undermining the walls, the cavalry prepared to repulse any sorties, and the rest of the army gathered around the siege engines being pushed slowly to the city walls. Despite some feeble resistance, Saladin's engines quickly breached the walls, and the man commanding the defense of the city, Balian of Ibelin, requested a meeting with Saladin to discuss terms. Outnumbered and defeated, Balian had only one thing left to bargain with: he demanded that the Franks be given quarter; that is, none of Saladin's defeated foes were to be killed. If these terms were not accepted, then Balian would kill every Muslim prisoner in the city (several thousand, according to the sources) and destroy every Muslim shrine that stood, including the Dome of the Rock and the al-Aqsa Mosque. These were hijacker's demands, but it was a clever ploy nonetheless. For in doing so Balian gambled, not with Jerusalem exactly (for Saladin could take it with ease if necessary), but with the meaning of Jerusalem in the hearts of his Muslim opponents. With the bloody precedent of 1099 no doubt on their minds, Saladin and his counselors agreed to the terms, not wishing to add more bloodshed for a victory that was already complete. By Friday, October 2, the terms were settled. Muslim banners were hoisted to fly once again over the city walls and, caught up in the moment, a group of Muslims clambered up to the top of the Dome of the Rock and removed the cross that the Franks had placed there so many decades before, the crowds below them cheering, "Allahu akbar!" God is great![41]

Rather than celebrating the capture of the city in blood and rapine, Saladin kept to the terms of surrender and allowed the defeated Franks a forty-day grace period in which to ransom themselves—ten dinars for a man, five for a woman, and one for a child. As was usual in such cases, those who could not pay were to be taken as slaves, though one wonders how many these could have been in the end. Many Franks, for example, donated or raised cash to ransom the poor. Certain Muslim princes, it is recorded, demanded the return of Armenians found in Jerusalem, who (they claimed) had been their subjects. Many other Franks found the officials in charge of recording the ransoms terribly easy to bribe. Others, such as the widow of the despised Reynald de Châtillon, whom Saladin had personally beheaded, Saladin simply let go unhindered. The sultan's generosity evoked worried wincing from his more level-headed advisers, as when he allowed the patriarch of Jerusalem to make off with the treasure stripped from the Holy Sepulcher (valued by a contemporary at some 200,000 dinars). Though the terms of surrender did ensure the safety of Frankish property, it did not cover church property. But Saladin looked the other way, saying, "We shall not leave them to accuse the people of the Faith of breaking faith."[42] Indeed most of the ransom money, it was found, had been given away as soon as the sultan had received it.

Whether intentional or not, these sorts of gestures went far to create a new image of Saladin and to silence any tongues still wagging about his earlier period of relentless campaigning against his fellow

Muslims. It helped that he also now had letters written and distributed throughout Muslim lands that cast those earlier campaigns as an unfortunate necessity to seal his final triumph against the Franks. Saladin, as in all things, had long had his eye on his audience. Certainly Jerusalem was and is no ordinary city, and its reconquest was immediately recognized as a historic achievement, and one full in the public eye. The event thus needed to be handled carefully. In the days after the conquest Saladin paid special attention to purging the city of its long association with infidels, cleaning out the al-Aqsa Mosque compound, which the Templars had made their headquarters, complete with "all that they needed, storerooms, a privy and such like," and ordering the Dome of the Rock, where the Franks had set up an altar, to be "cleansed of filth and impurities."[43] He later had some especially magnificent manuscripts of the Qur'an brought to the al-Aqsa Mosque and established reciters there subsidized by a perpetual endowment. As for the Church of the Holy Sepulcher, on this Saladin and his advisers were divided. Some saw in it the root of the Near East's Frankish problem and wanted to destroy it. However, others pointed out that the Franks "would not stop coming even if the earth [on which it stands] was scattered in the air," and this seems to have persuaded the sultan to leave the church and its functionaries alone.[44] Besides, the pious caliph 'Umar himself had refused to tamper with the church when he conquered the city in the seventh century, and Saladin, ever eager for the mantle of righteousness, could hardly break ranks with the pious forebears. Then, in one final nod to continuity, he had an intricately carved pulpit, which his mentor Nur al-Din had commissioned, brought from Aleppo to Jerusalem, where, it was said, Nur al-Din had originally planned for it to be set up.

The first Friday after the conquest was perhaps the pinnacle of celebration of Saladin's achievement, for this was the first communal prayer to be held in Jerusalem since it was captured in 1099. The Franks had been expelled, the city cleaned up, and the shrines cleansed and repaired. The air of restoration and of jubilation must have been palpable. The religious scholars in Saladin's retinue all vied with one another to win the honor of giving the *khutba*, or Friday sermon, before the sultan and the assembled faithful. It was a historic moment that demanded historic words, and every candidate sent the sultan a copy of his speech to be vetted. In the end Saladin chose Muhyi al-Din ibn al-Zaki for this signal honor. Muhyi al-Din was himself a prominent scholar from a prominent dynasty of scholars from Damascus, the Banu al-Zaki, who established close ties with Saladin's new regime.

Muhyi al-Din, for example, was made chief judge of Aleppo when Saladin finally took the city in 1183 and, later in life, would be named chief judge in Damascus itself, a post held by his father and grandfather before him and his own sons after him.

Muhyi al-Din gave his audience everything they could have hoped for.[45] He began by giving praise to God for the victory, quoting the Qur'an on the matter of praise—not just once but every instance of the concept in the Holy Book where it urges praise unto God, verse after verse, eliding effortlessly into his own invocation of God's might: "Praise be to God, by Whose aid Islam has been exalted, and by Whose might polytheism has been humbled; Whose decrees control all events, and Who rewards gratitude by continuing His favors. He has enveloped the infidels in His toils...and caused His religion to triumph over all others." He then invoked blessings upon the Prophet Muhammad—who had made a miraculous journey to the very spot where they now prayed—and upon the four "rightly guided" caliphs who succeeded him and kept the community whole.

Muhyi al-Din cast the great victory that his audience had enacted as a gift from God in return for their good faith, God making "it easy for your hands to recover this strayed camel [i.e., Jerusalem] from the possession of a misguided people, and to bring it back to the fold of Islam, after it had been abused by the polytheists for nearly one hundred years." Alluding to tropes from the ancient literature that Muslims circulated in praise of Jerusalem, he urged them all to rejoice at the return to Islam of "the dwelling-place of your father Abraham; the spot from which your blessed Prophet Muhammad mounted to heaven; the *qibla* towards which you turned to pray at the commencement of Islam; the abode of the prophets; the place visited by the saints; the cemetery of the apostles; the Holy Land whereof God has spoken in His perspicuous book."

He went on to compare this victory to the great triumphs of Islam's heroic past and to stress how great a gift God had bestowed upon them, "a victory which has opened for you the gates of heaven, and illumined by its light the face of the darkness." Was this not, after all, a site of historic and primordial importance to God, mentioned in the Qur'an in God's very own words? "Is it not the house which all religions honored, towards which the prophets turned themselves in prayer, and in which were read the four books [Torah, Gospels, Psalms, and Qur'an] sent down from Almighty God?" Such a gift demanded gratitude, a gratitude that can best be expressed by maintaining the struggle against evil. "Take care, servants of God, after His having ennobled you by this great conquest, this signal favor...not to commit such deeds as He has forbidden, or show the grievous sin of disobedience....Maintain the jihad: it is the best means which you have of serving God, the most noble occupation of your lives....For now the times cry aloud: 'Vengeance for Islam and the community of Muhammad! God is mighty! God gives victory and aid! God conquers and subdues! He humbles the infidel!'"

Muhyi al-Din then offered up prayers for the 'Abbasid caliph in Baghdad, marking the Holy City's official return to the Sunni fold. He closed by invoking God's favor on Saladin: "Your trenchant sword, Your shining torch; the defender of Your faith, the champion and protector of Your Holy Land...him who gave might to the declaration of the true faith, who vanquished the adorers of the cross; the restorer of the world and of religion. Grant, O Almighty God, that his empire extend over the earth, and that the angels encircle his standards." It was as if the thirty-three months Saladin had spent in the field against his fellow Muslims had never happened.

-7-

From Every Deep Valley

NOT EVERYONE WAS taken in by the theatrics of Saladin's victory at Jerusalem. Shortly after his triumph, the sultan received a snappish message from one Muslim leader who was not at all amused: the ʿAbbasid caliph in Baghdad. As nominal head of the Sunni Muslim community and the figure in whose name Saladin technically made his conquests, one might think the caliph had cause for rejoicing. In fact, though, Saladin's almost transcendent power in Egypt and Syria and his worrisome meddling in northern Iraq were becoming a threat to what little worldly power the caliph himself possessed. The caliph upbraided his servant for a host of petty failings and warned him not to meddle in Iraqi affairs. Saladin and his chancery reacted swiftly with the utmost diplomacy and smoothed the matter over; still, this was not the thank-you note Saladin had been expecting.

To add to the tarnish on Saladin's conquests, the siege of Tyre, whence he had relocated even before affairs were settled in Jerusalem, was dragging on. In part this was the result of support from Conrad of Montferrat, freshly arrived from Frankish lands. Indeed one chronicler suggests that the city, thronged with Frankish refugees but lacking any real leader, was about to surrender to Saladin before Conrad arrived and rallied the defense.[1] But it was also because Tyre posed numerous challenges for any besieger, as Alexander the Great had famously learned. Ibn Jubayr, a Muslim pilgrim who passed through Frankish and Ayyubid Syria in 1184, accurately described the situation that Saladin faced a few years later: "[Tyre] has come proverbial for its impregnability, and he who seeks to conquer it will meet with no surrender or humility. The Franks prepared it as a refuge in case of unforeseen emergency, making it a strong point for their safety."[2] Its outer defenses were considerable, consisting of only two gates, one landward, which could be accessed only after navigating the city's outermost walls, and the other on the sea, which "is flanked by two strong towers and leads into a harbour whose remarkable situation is unique among maritime cities. The walls of the city enclose it on three sides, and the fourth is confined by a mole bound with cement." A chain was stretched between these two seaward towers, which "prevents any coming in or going forth, and no ships may pass save when it is lowered. At the gate stand guards and trusted watchers, and none can enter or go forth save under their eyes."

As Ibn Jubayr noted, it was Tyre's harbor that held the key to the city, and Saladin naturally blockaded the city from both land and sea, positioning five galleys outside the harbor to prevent any supplies reaching the Franks. With the city surrounded, its eventual surrender would be assured. Human error granted another setback to Saladin. At dawn on December 30, 1187, Conrad assembled over a dozen galleys and sailed forth from Tyre to break the blockade; the Muslim sailors on watch had fallen asleep during the night and never knew what hit them. Most were captured, though some jumped ship to escape. The few Muslim ships that fled were beached and their hulls stove in to prevent recapture by the Franks. The biggest casualty was the morale of Saladin's army, which, already exhausted, could not brook another prolonged siege. Ranks were thinning and supplies and funds were low. To counter this ebb in enthusiasm, Saladin capitalized on his popularity and rallied his troops for one final massive assault on the city, the cavalry at times chasing the Franks even into the sea. But it was not enough. Conrad had only to sit tight as the waves of Saladin's troops surged but then broke against Tyre's defenses. On January 1, 1188, Saladin withdrew, and the various armies under his commanders dispersed.

Most of the remainder of 1188 was spent not on besieging the tougher Frankish strongholds on the coast, like Tyre or Tripoli, but on mopping up softer targets. For the most part these were small fry, minor coastal cities like Jabala; little forts and castles in the hills above, such as Yahmur (Chastel Rouge) or Sahyun (Saone) high in the forests above Latakia; or the minor, down-market port of Tartus (Tortosa), which was stormed and, apparently, left nearly in ruins. By the end of the summer one of Saladin's secretaries could write without exaggeration, "We have conquered from the borders of Tripoli to those of Antioch.... Antioch remains but cannot survive."[3] In fact, however, Saladin was forced to agree to a truce with Antioch, a city that would long outlive him and his dynasty. As for Tyre and Tripoli, they would be among the last cities to be taken back from the Franks.

However, there were some small triumphs. Latakia in northern Syria was captured, its superb harbor a welcome addition. Safad, a Hospitaller castle in northern Palestine of some importance, surrendered, as did Karak in Transjordan, the old headquarters of Reynald of Châtillon. There Reynald's widow offered to exchange the castle for the release of her son Humphrey, but the deal was refused. Instead Saladin's commander, his brother al-'Adil, tightened the siege until the castle surrendered. Saladin also put Reynald's nearby castle of Shawbak (Montreal) under siege, though it did not fall until May 1189. Finally, in early January 1189, the massive Hospitaller fortress of Belvoir (Kawkab), whose ruins near the Sea of Galilee still impress the visitor, surrendered to Saladin after a determined defense and amid miserable winter weather. During the remainder of the winter, Saladin rested up and dispersed his troops, planning on returning to the vicinity of Antioch in the spring. It was at this time he also received word of a new Frankish expedition that was setting out from Europe to avenge the loss of Jerusalem—what would become known as the Third Crusade.

The Third Crusade

When spring arrived, Saladin was to have sent troops to complete his conquests by capturing Tripoli and Antioch in the north. However, he was delayed by other targets and was ultimately forced to come to the aid of the Muslim garrison at Acre, which was under siege by a Frankish army led by Guy of Lusignan, who never ceased to be a thorn in Saladin's side. As noted, Guy had once been king of Jerusalem through marriage to Queen Sybil, but at her death, his title was in dispute. It may be that Guy thought a stunning victory against the Muslims would help his claims. Although he had been taken captive at Hattin, Saladin had released him after making him swear a vow to desist from further attacks against Muslims. Be that as it may, Guy seems to have been absolved of his vow in the meantime (if Saladin indeed believed he would ever keep it), and, assisted by reinforcements sent from Italy, Germany, France, and the Low Countries, in late August 1189 he had Acre under siege.

It was Saladin's plan to relieve Acre the old-fashioned way: by attacking the besiegers before their swelling ranks became even more of a worry. It should have been fairly straightforward, as the Franks were dangerously exposed, caught between a Muslim garrison within the city and Saladin's armies and allies mustering on the plain outside. And yet, as in a similar situation at Antioch a century before, the Muslim armies had great difficulty dislodging the Franks. The main battle for Acre, on October 4, resulted in a stalemate, as the Franks, instead of pursuing Saladin's routed troops, stopped to plunder the Muslim camp. Saladin quickly rallied his men, who set upon the Franks, and these, in their turn, now fled to regroup and repulse the Muslim advance, suffering heavy casualties in the process.

At this moment neither side could afford another pitched battle, so both spent the next year strengthening their forces, Saladin unable to effectively commit his troops to any prolonged action by the knowledge that the armies of the Third Crusade were on the way from Europe. Hunger and disease spread rapidly among the Franks encamped at Acre, and also among the Muslim garrison within the city. Saladin was able to briefly cut his way to the city to regarrison it, but the Franks had to wait until March 1190 for supplies to arrive.

With the return of Frankish shipping, and Saladin's Egyptian fleet not in evidence, Acre was cut off once again from Saladin's forces; pigeons and a few intrepid divers were henceforth used to deliver messages. The Franks were now supplied with imported timber, from which they constructed rolling siege towers, covering them in hides steeped in vinegar to repel any Greek fire that might be launched upon them. As the Franks gained tighter control of the city walls, the Muslim garrison within was showing every sign of giving up. It was just at this interval that an entrepreneurial Muslim inventor arrived on the scene, a coppersmith from Damascus, we are told by the Arab chroniclers. Though the troops scorned him, this man concocted his own variety of Greek fire that alone proved effective in destroying the Frankish siege towers, and indeed anything else in its path. The playing field was level again, and Saladin was informed that the fosse ringing the city was now a pool of fire.

News was now reaching Saladin in regular intervals about the progress of the German army under Emperor Frederick Barbarossa, the leader of the new crusade.[4] By late March 1190 the Germans had crossed into Anatolia, a disruption that troubled the Byzantines as much as it did the Muslims.[5] Qilij Arslan, the sultan of the Rum Saljuqs, appealed to Saladin for troops to help him stop the Germans, but

Saladin could do nothing. Qilij Arslan's troops raided and harassed the Germans as they marched east, but in mid-May the Germans defeated Qilij Arslan's son in battle and captured Konya, taking hostages among the leading Saljuq amirs. By the end of the month the Germans were on the borders of Cilicia and well on their way toward Syria. Thanks to the intelligence sent on to him from Qilij Arslan, Saladin could at least prepare for the invasion. He ordered his amirs in Hama and Homs in northern Syria to harvest their grain posthaste and lay it in for safe-keeping. Despite the ingenuity of the coppersmith from Damascus, Saladin saw that he was to be locked into precisely the sort of extended waiting game that his armies loathed.[6]

Then, it seemed, a miracle happened. On June 10, 1190, the elderly German emperor died while bathing in the Göksu River, the victim, evidently, of a stroke. The armies that had followed him so far from home were heartbroken. Of the men who did not return immediately to Germany, some took ship to Antioch and Tripoli, while others struggled on overland. By the time they reached Acre their ranks had thinned from capture, hunger, or disease. Few of them stayed on at Acre past the spring.

By then, too, news arrived that two other Frankish kings, Richard the Lionheart of England and Philip Augustus of France, each with their own armies, were on their way across the sea to Syria. In the meantime both armies at Acre were severely challenged by the problem of supply. During the summer the Muslims even resorted to the sub-terfuge of disguising one of their supply ships from Beirut as a Frankish vessel, shaving the crew's beards and populating the decks liberally with swine. The blustery storms of the Mediterranean autumn thwarted most of Saladin's attempts to resupply the city from Egypt, and when stores did arrive, they rarely lasted very long. Saladin even sent an embassy to Ya'qub, the Almohad ruler in the Maghrib, asking for naval assistance to help break the stalemate at Acre. But the Almohads had long been the victim of Ayyubid raids from Egypt, and so, when Saladin's ambassador refused to address Ya'qub using the caliphal titles he had arrogated to himself, Ya'qub was disinclined to help out the Ayyubids. Even within Saladin's armies, dissent and suspicion were growing as the stalemate stretched on. In early 1191 he sent a letter to the caliph in Baghdad, begging for whatever assistance he could provide, painting a dire picture of entrenched Franks at Acre, a weakened Anatolian front under the Saljuqs of Rum, an approaching crusade, and disunity within the Muslim ranks. It is not known whether the caliph responded at all.

Philip of France arrived at Acre by sea on April 20, 1191, and Richard the Lionheart on June 8, having taken the opportunity to capture Cyprus from a Byzantine adventurer who had seized power there. Of Richard even the Muslim sources noted that, though inferior to Philip in rank (being merely king of England), he was "more famous in war and for courage." With Saladin's troops now probably much diminished and the Frankish camp resupplied and expanded, the odds for holding Acre did not look good. Saladin nonetheless stood his ground. The major fighting broke out within days of Richard's arrival and occupied most of the month of June as the Muslims within and without rebuffed or thwarted repeated attacks on the city, but it was touch-and-go. Saladin was thus elated to receive reinforcements at the end of the month, though also scandalized to learn that political rivalries among his allies kept some amirs from responding to his call. Fortunately the Frankish commitment to holy war was also known to be shaky. "Had the people of Acre prosecuted the jihad that they proposed with the intent of gaining heavenly reward," Saladin's chief secretary speculated ruefully, "no one would have beaten them in the race to paradise."[7]

The siege now entered its final, diplomatic phase. Richard sent envoys, often with promises of gifts (or demands for them), to Saladin's camp, where his brother al-'Adil acted as go-between. In each case Saladin, who was suffering from an unknown illness at the time, shrewdly refused all invitations to meet with Richard in person, seeing these little gestures as what they undoubtedly were: attempts to spy on the Muslim headquarters and assess enemy morale. In one such visit Saladin allowed them to tour the market in his camp, overwhelming them with the amount and quality of his supplies. Frankish entreaties for peace were, in any case, difficult to credit when Richard's armies were at the same time renewing their assaults on the city. On July 3 the Muslim garrison wrote to Saladin to tell him they would soon fall. A coordinated attack on the Frankish camp was tried, but failed; that night several of Saladin's leading amirs quietly slipped out of the harbor, abandoning their men and their sultan. Saladin tried to make the best of it, and reinforcements even arrived a few days later.

But it was not enough to save Acre from the Third Crusade. On July 12 the Franks stormed the city, and the Muslim commander inside negotiated the terms of surrender: the vast sum of 200,000 gold dinars and the return of prisoners and the relic of the True Cross taken at Hattin. A payment schedule of three monthly installments was later agreed upon. Saladin's biographers suggest he did not authorize these

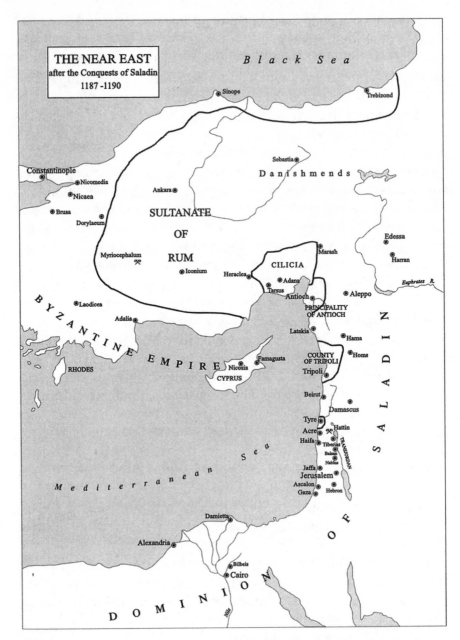

Map 9 The Near East after 1187. From Thomas F. Madden, *A Concise History of the Crusades*, 2nd ed. (New York: Rowman and Littlefield, 2006), 79, map 6.

terms and had planned to send a swimmer out to cancel the deal, but it was too late. Frankish banners were soon raised on Acre's walls, and Saladin's troops broke out in weeping and wailing. His secretary tried to console his lord with the thought that, though Acre had fallen, Islam had not. That day there were undoubtedly some who wondered if that was really so.

The truth is that Acre was not a great loss from a strategic point of view (Map 9). After all, the Franks already controlled important harbors and coastal towns, as at Tyre and Tripoli; Acre added nothing to their hand. The loss of cash, supplies, and men to the fruitless siege was disappointing, but this too was nothing the Ayyubid military could not absorb. However, it was the sting of loss that mattered here, for the real casualties at Acre were Saladin's prestige and Muslim morale. The victor of Hattin and the reconqueror of Jerusalem should have been able to hold on to this one port city. The prolonged siege had brought Muslim rivalries and pettiness out into the open for all to see. And problems with the surrender negotiations put a final, bloody tarnish on the whole episode. As the date by which to pay the first installment of ransom approached (August 12), Saladin sought to renegotiate some of the terms—perhaps as an attempt to buy more time. Richard was pressed for time and would have none of it: on August 20 the Lionheart had some three thousand Muslim prisoners brought out to the plain before Acre and massacred. It was an act of brutality that would not be forgotten even in the final days of the Frankish presence in the Near East.

An ailing Philip had returned to Europe just after Acre fell. The Franks under Richard were on the move, marching south in formation along the coast toward Jaffa. The Frankish fleet shadowed them by sea; more to the point, Saladin and his army shadowed them in the rougher country above them. After so long waiting before the walls of Acre, this at least promised the sort of military engagement his men excelled at. He sent some contingents ahead to intercept the Franks in the open terrain around Caesarea, while the rest stayed behind to harass the Franks as they marched. One of Saladin's secretaries remarked upon their perseverance—all without complaining about pay—in an unfavorable comparison with Saladin's fractious troops at Acre.

At Caesarea, which Saladin had had destroyed lest it become a Frankish stronghold again, the Muslims delayed but did not stop the Frankish march, as Richard and his men managed still to punch through to the south. At Arsuf a tentative attack by Saladin was met with a reckless charge from the Franks, which knocked the Muslim forces off balance, and a number of leading warriors were killed in the melee. The rout that followed forced Saladin to regroup in the forested land above Arsuf, where the Franks dared not follow. Despite other attempts, Saladin was unable to lure the Franks into rashly repeating themselves. The Franks settled in at Jaffa, while Saladin retired inland and camped at Ramla in early September 1191, though he later moved to Jerusalem itself.

Jaffa, which Richard fortified and made his headquarters, is roughly equidistant from Ascalon and Jerusalem, and both were plum targets for the Franks. Saladin was not eager to relive the experience of attempting to rescue the garrison at Acre, so he immediately ordered the withdrawal of the troops stationed at Ascalon and the dismantling of its fortifications, lest Richard use it as a base to threaten Jerusalem and, still worse, Egypt itself. This left Richard with the prospect of marching from Jaffa to Jerusalem, a route that took him through the Judean hills dominated by his enemies. Saladin cannot have been surprised, then, to learn that Richard wanted to negotiate a peace instead. Negotiations commenced, with various dispositions of territory floated, including an offer by Richard to marry his sister Joan to Saladin's brother al-'Adil, the two of them ruling jointly over Jerusalem. Nothing practical resulted from all this. It didn't help that Richard was at the same time sending occasional forays toward Jerusalem to test the waters in case of an assault.[8] In addition—and despite Saladin's exertions—Richard captured Ascalon and began rebuilding it. But these probes led nowhere: one could not hold Ascalon *and* hope to capture Jerusalem.

In late July 1192 Saladin learned that Richard had taken ship for Acre to put Beirut to siege, perhaps thinking that Frankish hopes would be best realized in consolidating control over the northern coast before tackling the south again. Saladin took the opportunity of his absence and struck at Jaffa. Within a few days the town had surrendered, though the garrison in the citadel was still resisting. It too would have fallen, except at the last minute Richard returned from the north and rallied his men, ousting the startled Muslim troops from the city.

This, however, was the last Frankish triumph of the Crusade. In mid-August Richard, like so many others, had fallen seriously ill, and it was clear to all that his crusade had stalled. In September Saladin formally agreed to a truce, to last three years and eight months: the Franks were to hold the entire coast from Tyre to Jaffa; Saladin would retain Ascalon, though its rebuilt walls were to be demolished again (by a combined team of Franks and Muslims), and Christians and Muslims alike were to have free passage within Palestine. When peace was pro-claimed, Saladin put some final touches on Jerusalem, strengthening its walls and establishing some pious foundations, such as the Salihiyya madrasa (formerly the Church of St. Anne), a hospital, and a sufi meet-inghouse. He then quit Jerusalem, and "the two armies fraternized,"[9] presumably at feasting. The markets opened at Jaffa, and Saladin ex-pressly encouraged as many Franks as possible to visit Jerusalem—in the hope that, thus satisfied, they would never return again. The crusad-ing armies were then allowed to disperse, and, on October 9, Richard sailed from Acre for Europe.

As for Saladin, he toyed with the idea of finally making the pil-grimage to Mecca; however, given the caliph's anxieties about his public posturing, his advisers convinced him there were more imme-diate needs. There were plenty of civilian matters to attend to after years of warfare and disruption, the treasury was empty, and, as his secretary reminded him by allusion to the Circle of Equity, "the inves-tigation of the people's injustices is the most important of the ways in which to become close with God."[10] So Saladin remained in Syria, trav-eling briefly to Beirut, where he entertained Bohemond of Antioch, then to Damascus for the first time in nearly three years. In February of the following year he took ill again. This time he did not recover. On March 4, 1193, he was dead.

With Saladin's death, many of his contemporaries must have felt that they had lost an uncommon leader, and that was undoubtedly so. Nonetheless a sober assessment suggests that his achievements varied greatly over the course of his career. As a military man, Saladin showed his mettle on numerous occasions, especially against his Muslim foes early on. His famous victory at Hattin, so often named in this connec-tion, cannot really be considered his finest hour, as the result of that battle had as much to do with Frankish bungling as with any strategic genius on Saladin's part. It was his sense of geopolitics—of who to attack and when—that, with a few notable exceptions, such as Tyre, revealed his gifts. Yet for all that, after Hattin, his military record was miserable—a chain of defeats and prolonged periods in the field that alienated his commanders and, in the worst cases, turned his troops against him. His military career produced his greatest achievement, the reconquest of Jerusalem, which would remain in Muslim hands (more or less) until the end of World War I. However, it also produced the Third Crusade, a bloody and costly exercise in stalemate that even the Crusaders grew weary of. Richard never gained Jerusalem, it is true; nonetheless it is hard to claim that Saladin had therefore "won" the Third Crusade.

He was far more successful in the diplomatic and political realm, in building alliances and negotiating deals, in creating a public image for himself as the pious, otherworldly mujahid, and in surrounding himself with advisers and courtiers who could sustain this image. In this sense, at least, he was a dutiful heir to his master, the Zangid Nur al-Din, whose name he has all but eclipsed in history.

The Heirs to Saladin

In keeping with Saljuq and Zangid practice, Saladin's realm was not a centralized kingdom but rather a collection of appanages ruled by various branches of the Ayyubid house, of which one member might achieve preeminence and rule as sultan. Successions tended to bring out the worst in family relationships, precipitating struggles between various rival princes and the military retinues of amirs that supported them. The amirs were fully aware of their importance in this process, and they were never shy of ousting a prince if he proved unsuitable. Thus, although Saladin had named his eldest son, al-Afdal, lord of Damascus, as his heir as sultan, al-Afdal still needed the support of the dynasty's various powerful amirs, and there were other claimants among Saladin's kin for these same loyalties. The machinations involved need not detain us; suffice it to say that Saladin's brother al-'Adil, after first posing as an avuncular mediator between his family's factions, inserted himself fully into the fray and, by 1200, had been named sultan in Cairo. Amid similar struggles he would be succeeded by his son al-Kamil, and he likewise by his son al-Salih Ayyub. Each would have his own distinct role to play in the Ayyubid dynasty's interactions with Frankish invaders.[11]

Saladin's heirs faced a different kind of Frankish problem than their predecessors had. Zangi's and Saladin's reconquests, combined with the failure of the Third Crusade, meant that the Ayyubids after Saladin never had to face any serious threats from the local Franks of the Near East. These Levantine Franks were easily contained. However, externally launched invasions from Frankish Europe were another matter. And so the Ayyubids spent much less energy attempting to reconquer lands from the kingdom of Jerusalem and much more on diplomacy, commerce, and fending off such crusades as made it to the Near East. The Franks too seem to have shifted their policy in the post-Hattin world. Jerusalem was, as ever, the Franks' goal, but, increasingly, new crusades recognized that the prerequisite for regaining the Holy Land was the conquest of Egypt, the heart of the Ayyubid state.

Once he secured himself as sultan in Egypt, al-ʿAdil set about establishing order internally and externally as best he could. As was typical, within his domains he appointed his sons to rule in the major provinces of the sultanate. Facing devastating drought, famine, and earthquakes early on, he sent soldiers into the Egyptian countryside to work lands that lay fallow and abandoned, and fostered commerce with the Italian city-states; his friendship with one Genoese merchant named William was a source of some consternation, as he was thought to be sending intelligence back to the Franks. Externally, he signed a truce with the Christian kingdom of Georgia in the Caucasus, securing his north-eastern frontier.[12]

Al-ʿAdil's relations with the Franks were more of a mixed bag. In 1197 German troops sent by Emperor Henry VI succeeded in capturing Sidon while al-ʿAdil was vying with his kinsmen for preeminence. At the same time, the Franks captured Beirut, despite al-ʿAdil's efforts at regarrisoning the city, and the Ayyubids were likewise unable to prevent the Franks from raiding around Gaza. In the end, though, the Muslims recaptured Jaffa (a task left undone since the Third Crusade) and secured a three-year truce with Acre.[13]

Then again, in 1198, another crusade, known conventionally today as the Fourth Crusade, was preached, with Ayyubid Egypt its principal target. Yet this crusade famously never made it to the Islamic Near East; it was diverted instead to the Christian capital of Constantinople, where in 1204 it toppled the Byzantine emperor and founded a Latin kingdom on Byzantine soil reminiscent of the Latin states carved out of Muslim lands during the First Crusade. It would seem as if the Fourth Crusade had almost no impact on the Islamic world. The Arabic sources on the Fourth Crusade itself are sparse but relatively well-informed, noting that the Crusade was diverted from its initial course and that in the end Constantinople itself was sacked and burned, and many of the city's relics and precious *objets* were carried off to distant markets, including the Near East. "The Franks," the Syrian chronicler Abu Shama reported, "looted its treasures and all the fixtures and marbles in its churches. They then brought them to the lands of Egypt and Syria, where they were sold. Damascus," he added, "has seen plenty of that marble." The Byzantine ruling house was sent into exile—the Saljuqs of Rum having refused to assist them—but they would eventually regain their empire.[14] Moreover it seems that the sultan al-ʿAdil had clear advance warning of the coming of the Franks, so it is a moot question whether the Fourth Crusade would have succeeded had it even reached Egypt or Syria.

These events did have some indirect consequences on the Islamic world. For the Ayyubids, at least, the threat of an imminent crusade of newcomers could have been a serious motivation to make deals with the Franks of the Levant, whom they knew better. At least, this seems to be what the Hospitallers of Crac des Chevaliers were hoping in 1204, when they arranged through their Templar comrades to open secret negotiations with Mansur, the Ayyubid lord of Hama, whose lands abutted theirs. Unfortunately for the Hospitallers, Mansur was resolute and pointed out that, when the new Crusaders did arrive, they would be so weakened that they would prove no great challenge. He would make no peace with the Hospitallers. And so, with no peace in the offing, the Hospitallers marched on Mansur. His army routed them and took a number of prominent Frankish prisoners back to Hama to parade through the streets. Eventually the Hospitallers got their truce.[15] Yet, in the same year, the Ayyubid lord of Aleppo was badly defeated at Jabala near Tripoli.[16]

Truly resounding victories seemed to elude al-'Adil. In 1203 he did not deign to take part in a campaign by Mansur of Hama against the Franks of Tripoli and the Hospitallers of Crac de Chevaliers, despite the fact that he was in Damascus at the time; he merely ordered other kinsmen in Syria to send help.[17] In 1204 a naval raid on Rosetta in Egypt that was probably connected to the Fourth Crusade was met with an impotent response, as the Ayyubids had no fleet.[18] And when Franks from Acre (assisted by recent arrivals from Constantinople) raided near Nazareth, al-'Adil was grappling with too many Muslim foes on other fronts and could not commit the troops to respond, despite a call for a jihad. He instead arranged a truce by which Lydda, al-Ramla, Nazareth, and Jaffa were granted back to the kingdom of Jerusalem.[19] Moreover a direct Templar attack on Hama that followed (their recent treaty having elapsed) might well have taken the city, but the local populace stoutly resisted and the Franks retired.[20] Finally, in 1207 he assembled a large force in an attempt to settle things definitively with Tripoli and the Hospitallers. Unhappily he could make no progress at Crac and abruptly broke off the siege there and moved to Tripoli, where he too was obliged to give up after a prolonged siege of this most vexing target. He settled instead for a truce, the release of Muslim prisoners, and annual tribute.[21] More successful was a campaign around Acre led by the lord of Damascus, with large numbers of volunteers, culminating in the construction of a fortress at Mt. Tabor from which to keep the Franks at Acre under watch.[22]

The Fifth Crusade, almost a decade later, could have been al-'Adil's moment of redemption. He died, however, just two months into the defense.[23] The first Crusaders, from Austrian and Hungarian contingents led by Duke Leopold VI and King Bela III, respectively, arrived in Acre in late summer 1217. The chronicler Ibn Wasil recognized that these Franks were being directed from Rome, which he called "the lair of their great tyrant, known as the Pope." It was an impressive mustering of Franks, energized by a focused and organized campaign, "the largest assembly of men since the death of the sultan Saladin."[24] In consultation with local Frankish leaders, the crusader leadership floated the idea of smaller-scale raids in Syria to keep their troops busy, raiding Galilee and the mountains around Sidon, as they awaited reinforcements and the preparation of a fleet to sail to Egypt in the following spring. Al-'Adil had encamped with his army in Syria to meet them, but when he saw how hopelessly outnumbered he was, he retreated to Damascus. After further unhindered raiding, the Franks returned to Acre.[25]

In November, however, they emerged again, this time with a clear goal to strengthen their hold on Galilee. To do so the Franks attempted to capture the newly constructed fortress on Mt. Tabor but were unable to breach its defenses. It is said that the Muslim garrison inside had considered surrendering, but, recalling how Richard the Lionheart had treated the Muslims who surrendered to him at Acre, they chose instead to fight to the death. In the end they didn't need to: the Franks gave up and went back to Acre, looking now toward Egypt, the source of Ayyubid power.[26]

In late May 1218 the fleet arrived before Damietta, at the eastern mouth of the Nile Delta. The Crusaders, replenished with German and Frisian troops, set up camp on a cramped wedge of land with the Nile on one side and a canal on the other. It would be a year and a half before they left it.[27] In the meantime the Crusade's leader, King John of Jerusalem, was joined by the papal legate, Pelagius of Albano. The differences that flared between them upset what unity the Frankish camp possessed. The attitude of Cairo was one of alarm, but not yet panic. Even while al-'Adil lived, his son al-Kamil was in charge of the campaign in Egypt, and he was an able commander. Moreover al-'Adil had his son al-Ashraf invade Frankish territory in northern Syria to cause a suitable distraction, while the lord of Damascus laid in supplies and deployed troops across Syria in anticipation of an invasion.[28] Damietta would in any case be a difficult nut for the Franks to crack, and so long as they remained pinned down there and so long as the Nile remained blocked by the Chain Fortress—a fortlet where chains spread across the river to stop traffic—Cairo was not in harm's way. Then disaster: at the end of August the Franks managed to take the fortress, the chains were lifted, and their ships could now prowl the Delta at will. It was bad timing. Al-'Adil, en route from campaigning in Syria, fell ill and died on August 31, 1218.[29]

Here lies a paradox. This Crusade, whose goal had been to strike the Ayyubid dynasty at its heart, in fact caused the normally fractious Ayyubid princes to unite in the defense of Egypt. At the death of al-'Adil, it might normally have been expected that the claim of his son al-Kamil to rule as sultan would, as usual, be violently contested by his kinsmen and their amirs, and the sultanate might become a victim of its own entropy. Instead the Frankish threat to Egypt silenced (almost) all dissent, and al-Kamil's rivals rallied around him. A case in point is his enemy al-Mu'azzam, lord of Damascus, who now did his best to assist al-Kamil against the Frankish threat. His best-known effort in this regard came in 1219, when he ordered the destruction of the walls of Jerusalem, lest this new Crusade capture it and use it as a base for further conquests. "If they take it," he wrote to his reluctant amirs, "they will kill everyone in it and take over Damascus and all the lands of Islam!" It may have seemed a reasonable strategic act, but the religious men who wrote our histories were appalled. Sibt ibn al-Jawzi tells us that when the walls were dismantled, "there arose a clamor throughout the city as if it were Judgment Day," and the citizens flocked to the Dome of the Rock and the al-Aqsa Mosque pulling their hair and rending their clothes, indeed filling the prayer niche of the mosque with their hair; the roads became flooded with refugees who abandoned their unprotected homes and headed for Egypt, Karak, or Damascus, many dying of starvation or thirst on the way.[30] In any other context al-Mu'azzam or al-Kamil would have used this spectacle to great effect against his rival, but the Frankish invasion of Egypt instead rallied the Ayyubid amirs around al-Kamil, and, slowly but surely, they responded to his appeals for aid.

Throughout the spring and summer of 1219, then, al-Kamil, freshly reinforced with al-Mu'azzam's troops from Syria, pummeled the Franks with raids on their position in the Delta, or else attempted to win back the Chain Fortress. Eventually he took the step of sinking ships in the middle of the Nile to thwart any Frankish progress toward Cairo.[31] Damietta remained hemmed in. Practically no one could get in to aid the Muslims save those brave or foolhardy enough to swim through the Nile while Frankish boats patrolled above them.[32] In early November, however, the Franks finally managed to take Damietta, its sick and starving garrison having abandoned part of the city walls. One of their first acts was to turn the town's mosque into a church; according to Ibn Wasil, its wooden pulpit was broken up and pieces of it were sent as gifts to various princes in Europe.[33] As the Muslim forces retreated from Damietta, the Franks followed behind, capturing Tinnis along the way.

And that was it. For more than a year after the taking of Damietta, the Franks did not budge but divided the spoils and awaited reinforcements. They would not have been hard to find: one chronicler, alluding to a Qur'anic verse, notes, "When the Franks in their homelands heard of the conquest of Damietta at the hands of their fellows, they hurried to join them 'from every deep valley.' It became the goal of their emigration."[34]

Al-Kamil was near despair now, for "all the lands in Egypt and Syria were on the point of being overcome and all the people were fearful of [The Franks] and had come to expect disaster at any time."[35] Ibn Wasil reports that the sultan was so hopeless that he was considering giving up Egypt and Syria to the Franks and retiring to Yemen, where the Ayyubids at least could reign without threat of invasion. But his brother al-Mu'azzam talked some sense into him, and al-Kamil brightened up as troops continued to pour in from Syria.[36] Finally, in early July 1221 King John returned from Jerusalem, where he had earlier moved after a disagreement in the Frankish camp. With Pelagius and John at their head, the Frankish troops rolled out of Damietta and made for al-Kamil's recently built fortified encampment, which the sultan named—perhaps with some hubris—Mansura, "The Victorious."[37] The Franks set up camp just opposite Mansura, on a parcel of land surrounded by two branches of the Nile, and remained there.[38]

It was at this juncture, it seems, that al-Kamil decided to trade in the mandate he had won from his kinsmen and to end the conflict with an offer of truce. The terms were as follows: al-Kamil was to cede all the territory that once formed the kingdom of Jerusalem—the Holy City included—back to King John, except the lands west of the Jordan, and to agree to a truce for the next thirty years. Al-Kamil subsequently offered to rebuild the walls of Jerusalem and a few other castles in the north of the kingdom. Finally, he threw in the relic of the True Cross as part of the bargain, though it seems that he did not actually possess it. In return the Franks were to evacuate Egypt forthwith. To sweeten the deal, al-Kamil further agreed to pay rent to King John to retain possession of Karak and Shawbak, two key castles west of the Jordan, linking Egypt to Syria. The offer—generous by any scale—brought Frankish divisions to the fore, with King John counseling acceptance but Pelagius and the Military Orders brooking no compromise. The plan was rejected quicker than it had been offered.[39]

And there the Crusade met its tragicomic end, for "the Franks," Ibn Wasil explained knowingly, "have no experience with the Nile."[40] In the summer the Nile began to flood, as it always did, and so al-Kamil sent in troops to cut off the Franks' escape by land. To hasten nature's plan for the Franks, the Muslims broke the dykes that held back the waters for irrigation and flooded the land around them. On August 30, 1221, as the floodwaters swirled about their campsite, the Crusaders agreed to a truce. The terms were a shadow of what al-Kamil had once offered. The Franks gained nothing save a truce for eight years. Al-Kamil also agreed—again—to hand over the True Cross. In the end he never was able to find the thing.[41]

The Damietta Crusade had as its sequel one of the more unexpected episodes of the entire confrontation between Franks and Muslims. With the threat of Frankish invasion gone, the divisions within the Ayyubid ruling elite that had threatened the sultanate after al-'Adil's death now reemerged. To that end al-Kamil busied himself forging alliances to neutralize threats and maintain dominance over his rivals, principally his brother al-Mu'azzam, lord of Damascus. One such alliance was with the Holy Roman emperor Frederick II, who had been delayed in making his own crusade since he had vowed to do so in 1215 and who had sent reinforcements to Damietta but was unable to go himself. For his part Frederick too needed powerful alliances against his own enemies, among them the pope, who was angered by Frederick's foot-dragging. And so, in 1226, al-Kamil sent an embassy to Sicily offering Frederick roughly the same terms of truce that he had offered Pelagius so many times in the course of the Damietta Crusade. Frederick accepted immediately. It was a classic, pragmatic, Ayyubid approach to the problem, a win-win situation for all involved: Fredrick would get his little crusade and a kingdom in Jerusalem; al-Kamil would get peace from the Franks and, he believed, a powerful regional ally.[42]

Of all the Crusader leaders that set foot in the Near East, none elicited so much fascination from medieval Muslim observers as did the Holy Roman emperor Frederick II. For the Muslim authors who have written about him, Frederick was something of a puzzle. Even his Christianity was passed off as a cover for his evident "materialism" and disinterest in religion. His interest in logic, philosophy, geometry, and mathematics proved he was a civilized man. His apparent knowledge of Arabic and Muslim ritual—gleaned from his youth in Sicily—and his retinue of Muslim pages made him practically one of them. Many stories were told of his not-so-secret admiration for Islam, and his opponents back home had a field day with such rumors. Frederick nonetheless was an emperor, and his Muslim observers were just scholars. For Frederick, this was a simple charm campaign and part of a greater game. His knowledge of Arabic and ostentatiously staged episodes of delight at Islamic culture were valuable tools in his attempt to secure a suitable treaty within the immediate context of the Ayyubid Levant. It was an entirely different story in his own backyard, where he was busy massacring and exiling his Muslims subjects in Sicily.[43]

However, by the time Frederick arrived at Acre, in June 1228, the situation of both leaders had changed, and al-Kamil found that Frederick had lost some of the value as an ally that he had once possessed, and was in fact "an embarrassment." Frederick, for his part, had been excommunicated by the pope; his much-ballyhooed Crusade had managed to raise only a small force, and even that army was unwilling to stay long. With his rival al-Muʿazzam having died in the interval, al-Kamil was now on much firmer ground than before. He thus began to regret the generous terms he had first broached with Frederick in Sicily, and so he now forced Frederick to renegotiate them. The resulting treaty, signed in Jaffa in February 1229, was a far cry from the original: al-Kamil granted Frederick the towns of Bethlehem and Nazareth, the castle of Tibnin in the north, half of the district of Sidon (which the Christians had occupied in 1197), and Jerusalem itself. However, the Temple Mount would remain in Muslim hands and open to Muslim pilgrims, and the city was to remain unfortified (the walls having been previously dismantled). This last point was important since the plain implication was that al-Kamil could easily retake the city should he need to. In return Frederick was obliged to protect the sultan against his enemies (of whatever creed) for the next ten years. This was a diplomatic coup for al-Kamil. Though he had ceded some lands of no great importance, he had rendered Frederick, one of the greatest kings of Christendom, into a pawn.

Naturally it was the status of Jerusalem that stuck in men's throats. For many Christians, having "won" the city by doing a deal with the Muslims was hard to endure—all the more so since the Muslims still retained so much control over it. Indeed the Latin patriarch was so incensed that he put his own city under interdict, forbidding Christians from entering it. For many Muslims, ceding any part of the Holy City was seen as capitulation to the Franks, a vile betrayal of all that previous generations had worked for. And so it was that two medieval kings were able to work out an agreement by which they shared Jerusalem—a goal that eludes modern diplomats—and yet were loathed by their subjects as a result. Frederick had himself crowned in Jerusalem, the last Western politician to make a claim on the city until 1917. Crowned or not, when he left Acre in May to return to Europe, he was met with hostile crowds and pelted with offal. Al-Kamil likewise faced widespread dismay; one chronicler noted that at the news of the treaty, "all hell broke loose throughout all the lands of Islam."[44]

Although al-Kamil's rival al-Mu'azzam was dead, his son and successor in Damascus wasted no time in scoring points at al-Kamil's expense. The lord of Damascus calculatingly arranged a day of public mourning in his city for the "loss" of Jerusalem and hired the equivalent of a rock star to preside over the event: the wildly popular Syrian preacher Sibt ibn al-Jawzi. The prince wanted what amounted to a mirror image of the sermon preached upon Saladin's recovery of Jerusalem decades earlier: "[Sibt, the preacher,] was to recall the pious virtues of Jerusalem, the traditions and legends associated with it, to make people grieve for the loss of it, and to speak of the humiliation and disgrace that its loss brought upon the Muslims. By this means [the lord of Damascus] proposed to alienate the people from [al-Kamil] and to ensure their loyalty when he went to fight him."[45]

It happens that Sibt was also a historian, and he has left a detailed record of these events.[46] Like many of the pious, he was reluctant to entangle himself in political matters; he may also have found all this opportunism distasteful. Nevertheless he dutifully harangued the crowds, depicting the anguish of the Muslim pious in Jerusalem, cut off from the rest of the faithful, and he heaped shame upon "the Muslim kings," a phrasing perhaps not specific enough for his patron.

Calamitous Days

Jerusalem remained in Frankish hands, with one brief interruption, for the next fifteen years. During that time the Ayyubids in Syria enjoyed a few successes against the Franks of the Levant, as in 1230, when the lord of Hama repulsed an attack from Crac des Chevaliers, or in 1231, when the lord of Aleppo made a daring raid on the fortress of Marqab, liberating a large number of Muslim captives who had been imprisoned there, or, more daring still, in 1236, an Aleppine raid against the Hospitaller fortress of Baghras, which opened up the area to further triumphs.[47]

Yet it was the internal affairs of the sultanate that were most active. In 1238 the sultan al-Kamil died. By 1240 his son al-Salih Ayyub had succeeded in establishing himself as sultan only after an obligatory period of fraternal in-fighting. But even while he reigned, he faced challenges from his kinsmen, especially his uncle, the lord of Damascus, al-Salih Isma'il. To counter the threat posed by his uncle, al-Salih Ayyub relied, like his father before him, on a mixture of military pressure and alliances.[48] Prior to becoming sultan, for example, al-Salih Ayyub was granted control of Mesopotamia, where he was responsible for shoring up the Ayyubids' northeastern frontier. There he had made alliances with bands of troops from the kingdom of Khwarizm in Iran. These men, mostly Qipchaq Turks from Central Asia, had fled west when their lands were invaded, and they settled finally in Anatolia and Mesopotamia as mercenaries, just the thing for al-Salih Ayyub's new private army.[49] Al-Salih Ayyub also recruited new men in the traditional fashion, as mamluks, quickly phasing out older divisions of the Egyptian army and replacing them with his own mamluk corps, housed in a fortress he built for them on the island of Rawda in the Nile, whence they became known as Bahri mamluks (*bahr* meaning "river" in Arabic).[50]

With al-Salih Ayyub supported by this new mamluk army in Egypt and powerful Khwarizmian allies in Mesopotamia, his uncle al-Salih Isma'il naturally made a counteralliance with the Franks, promising them "all the lands that Saladin had reconquered." Those lands included the extremely valuable fortresses of Safad and Shaqif Arnun, which the Franks rebuilt and by which "great injury was inflicted upon the Muslims." Perhaps surprisingly the territory also included Jerusalem, which had recently been taken back from the Franks and was now ceded to them by treaty yet again.[51] The chronicler Ibn Wasil passed through the Holy City on his way to Cairo in 1244, just after the Franks took possession, and he noted with sadness that monks and priests were officiating in the Dome of the Rock and bottles of wine stood on the Rock itself. Since the early Crusades, the Rock had served as an altar in what the Franks called the Temple of Our Lord, the Templum Domini, and the Franks seem to have returned it to that state as a result of this treaty.[52]

This diplomatic activity was itself the result of more recent Frankish interventions in Ayyubid politics that had been launched between 1239 and 1241, generally known collectively as the "Barons' Crusade." These two invasions, though small in scale, proved to have great implications for the future of the Levant. Building perhaps on the diplomatic momentum begun under Frederick II, the leaders of these two Crusades profitably exploited the uncertainty prevailing within the Ayyubid house since the death of al-Kamil. With the combined threat of invasion and promises of alliance, they wrested back substantial territories for the kingdom of Jerusalem. With Jerusalem itself back in Christian hands, by 1244 it must have seemed to the Franks that much of the damage done by Saladin was being rolled back. Al-Salih Isma'il's promises of further territories in his treaty would have been irresistible.

The complicated alliance building that had marked the Barons' Crusade soon proved to be its undoing, for it meant that the battle lines were clearly drawn: the Ayyubids of Damascus and their Frankish allies faced the Ayyubids of Cairo and their fierce Khwarizmian supporters. When, in the summer of 1244, al-Salih Isma'il finally sent troops to Gaza to prepare for war with Egypt, the response was more than either side had imagined. Al-Salih Ayyub's Khwarizmian allies, some ten thousand cavalry, came to Egypt's aid by invading Syria from the north, sweeping into Palestine on a path of destruction, while al-Salih Isma'il recalled his troops to simply get out of harm's way—and leaving the Franks squarely in it. On July 11 the Khwarizmian horde reached Jerusalem, which was still unfortified. The Khwarizmians plundered and ravaged the city and its environs for over a month, apparently paying special care to destroy Christian shrines (and the tombs of the Frankish nobles). In August they granted the beleaguered garrison safe conduct and moved on to Gaza, where they stopped and informed al-Salih Ayyub, who hardly needed the reminder, that they were at his disposal.[53]

Before long, in October 1244, the two rival Ayyubids marched against one another, with their allies in tow. Near Gaza, at al-Harbiyya (La Forbie), the sultan al-Salih Ayyub smartly defeated the Franco-Syrian army, the Ayyubids of Cairo winning the day. Many men were lost. For the Franks in particular, the defeat at al-Harbiyya was a blow to their military capabilities second only to that that had occurred at Hattin. For the Ayyubids of Syria, the defeat opened up most of Syria to al-Salih Ayyub's conquests, including many of those lands that they had ceded to the Franks. Although alliances between Franks and Muslims were typical of the Muslim experience of the Crusades, the spectacle of this particular battle saddened some Muslim observers, especially given the sorry state of Jerusalem. Sibt ibn al-Jawzi was scandalized that Muslim troops should be shaded by Christian banners, fighting fellow Muslims: "It was a calamitous day, the like of which had not happened in [early] Islam nor in the time of Nur al-Din and Saladin."[54]

Sibt ibn al-Jawzi was just the first of many to compare Saladin's readiness for jihad to the behavior of his Ayyubid heirs, invariably at the expense of the latter. However, modern observers should see the Ayyubid penchant for diplomacy and compromise in context.[55] After the death of Saladin, the sultanate's decentralized structure came to the fore, in which (as we have seen) different Ayyubid princes ruled their own appanages under the nominal oversight of the sultan in Cairo. This meant that each Ayyubid prince had his own local pressures and interests, and hence his own set of relationships with the Franks. Thus, for example, Damascus and Cairo—both Ayyubid neighbors of the Latin kingdom—consistently adopted conflicting policies toward any new Crusades or Frankish threats. One prince's challenge was the other's moment of opportunity.

Likewise the Franks themselves became willing participants in inter-Ayyubid rivalries, and this usually involved wresting concessions from their Ayyubid allies. As we have seen, this is how Frederick II was able to gain back Jerusalem for the Franks, if only briefly. It also explains why the lord of Damascus, al-Salih Isma'il, was willing to cede back many of Saladin's conquests in Lebanon and the Galilee to the Franks in the 1240s, when he needed their help against his nephew, the sultan al-Salih Ayyub. And when the lord of Homs mourned the death of the Frankish ruler of Antioch, he was not so much betraying his commitment to jihad as noting the passing of a valuable ally.[56]

There is also a familiar reason behind the Ayyubid reluctance to embrace the lesser jihad against the Franks: holy war is bad for business. Peace in the flourishing ports of the Frankish Levant and in the towns and cities of the Ayyubid interior produced enormous profits for all involved. Places like Acre, Tyre, and Beirut were prime depots for the goods of the West to enter the markets of Syria; by the same token, Damascus and Aleppo were hubs for traffic along the pilgrimage roads to Mecca and trade routes farther east. The Ayyubids, particularly those of Syria, had no great mastery of the sea, and so leaving these rich ports in Frankish hands must have been seen as a regrettable necessity. But not too regrettable.

Finally, it should be remembered that there is more than one path of jihad. The Ayyubids after Saladin may not have been proactive devotees of the lesser, external jihad of holy war. They nevertheless never shirked the greater responsibility of struggle against unbelief and support for religious renewal. In this they looked to the model of Nur al-Din, and many were themselves trained in the religious sciences as young men, and, as adults, spent lavishly in establishing religious foundations in their cities. In Damascus alone, the Ayyubids founded sixty-three madrasas, as many as all the dynasties one century before and after their era of rule combined. With these and other architectural forms came associated displays of public devotion such as prayer, recitation, and pilgrimage. As with Nur al-Din and Saladin, the Ayyubids actively promoted their connection to holy war, learning, and justice in their official titles, and if they did not jump to attack the Franks, they were not diffident with regard to heretics in their midst, such as the Nizari "Assassins" of Syria against whom they put increasing pressure. That the Ayyubids adopted policies toward the Franks that were different from that of Saladin does not mean that their commitment to religious struggle was any weaker.[57]

The Frankish defeat at al-Harbiyya, coupled with the horror stories circulating about the Khwarizmian sack of Jerusalem and followed in 1247 by the Ayyubid conquest of Ascalon, were more than enough to spur yet another expedition from the West.[58] Though amply funded, well-supplied, and backed by the pious king of France, Louis IX, this expedition showed a striking resemblance to the Damietta Crusade, and its leaders seem not to have learned much from the failure there. It may be that the Ayyubids were better prepared this time around: Ibn Wasil states that Frederick II, in keeping with his warm relations with Cairo, had sent a secret agent to Egypt to warn the sultan about the French king's intentions.[59] One chronicler related an imaginary conversation between Frederick and Louis, in which the French king responds to Frederick's earnest attempts to dissuade him from his Crusade with a concise summary of a Crusader's position: "Speak no more! By God, by God, and by the truth of my religion, there is no alternative to me but to go to Damietta, Jerusalem, and the lands of Egypt; I will not be dissuaded from this even were I killed, and those with me."[60]

The course of the Crusade was eerily similar. In June 1249 the Franks took Damietta (although this time it was without a siege, as the garrison had fled); the Ayyubids and the Bahri mamluk corps again made al-Mansura their forward base. Moreover, as with the Damietta Crusade, during this campaign the reigning sultan also died (on November 1249), from an illness that had been afflicting him for some years. However, this time a Frankish invasion did not galvanize support for a fledgling Ayyubid successor; this time it gave rise to an entirely new, and (for the Franks) formidable Muslim power: a state controlled by the mamluks themselves.

In order for the Mamluk dynasty (as they are called) to come to power, the Crusade of Louis IX had to be neutralized and the Ayyubid succession dispute quashed. For the moment the household of the dead sultan, led by his chief concubine, Shajar al-Durr, agreed with the army to keep his death a secret until his son and heir could arrive. This was Prince Turanshah, who was governing his father's old dominions in Mesopotamia. However, Turanshah made achingly slow progress to Egypt, and while Egypt waited, divisions in the palace and the army came to the fore. With the help of some of the Bahri mamluks, Shajar al-Durr kept the lid on things until Turanshah arrived. In the interval the Franks seized the moment and finally emerged from Damietta, in November 1249, fighting their way upstream to Mansura, not far from where the Damietta Crusade was flooded out years before. The defenders at Mansura managed to quickly repel a reckless assault in the city but found themselves bogged down in a more protracted battle with the main Frankish force, led by Louis. The Muslims withdrew to Mansura, and a waiting game ensued. Soon, however, Turanshah arrived with his army, on February 24, 1250, and the Franks beat a desperate retreat to the safety of Damietta. In the course of the retreat, Louis himself was captured, and in April Turanshah received the surrender of Damietta, so the Muslim sources claim, from Louis's wife and queen.[61]

In May the Franks finally took their leave of Egypt, the last such invasion until Napoleon returned five and a half centuries later. Turanshah entered Damietta in triumph, and, as often happened, the victory provided an excuse for various kinds of bullying toward local Christians.[62] The town was eventually dismantled and its population moved to prevent any Frankish reconquest. Louis himself was later released and sailed to Acre, where he remained in the Holy Land for several years, seeing to the fortifications and defenses of Frankish lands there. But while he still had the king in captivity, Turanshah sent a letter bearing the good news to his governor of Damascus, and with it King Louis's scarlet cloak, trimmed in ermine. The governor could not resist trying it on himself.[63]

Yet Turanshah's arrival in Egypt during the Crusade's final moments had more long-lasting repercussions. His behavior toward the Ayyubid army, though typical for new sultans, betrayed his naïveté: he tried to replace his dead father's amirs with his own men from Mesopotamia. The Bahri mamluks, who had been within a stone's throw of thwarting the Frankish menace *again*, were having none of it. On May 1, 1250, they murdered him; he was the last of his line to rule in Egypt. Remarkably it was Shajar al-Durr, who was both a woman and of servile origin, who emerged triumphant. She skillfully parlayed her handling of the succession into her own bid for supremacy, ruling as "Queen of the Muslims" for some three months, before marrying the Bahri commander Aybak and ceding the throne to him. The Mamluks would rule in Egypt and much of the Near East until 1517, one of the longest-ruling dynasties in Islamic history, a by-product of inter-Muslim rivalries and Frankish intervention.

– 8 –

Wolves and Lions

NOT LONG AFTER the creation of the universe, a wolf with fur of deepest blue-gray, the color of Heaven, took as his companion and mate a fallow deer. The pair roamed the world and finally settled on the plains before the sacred mountain Burkhan Khaldun. There they had their first child, a human boy, named Batachikhan. From him sprang all the Heaven-touched nomadic peoples known to us today as the Mongols.

Such is the brief account of Mongol origins in a remarkable anonymous work known as the *Secret History of the Mongols*, written just a few years after one of the wolf's descendants, named Chinggis (or Genghis) Khan, had united most of his people into a vast confederation that conquered the largest land empire in human history, extending at its peak from Austria to Korea, and spread terror in the hearts of the settled people of the oikumene.[1] In eastern Europe, Russia, and China the Mongols have remained in the public consciousness as archetypal enemies of civilization since their arrival in the early thirteenth century. In the Islamic Near East, the situation is no different. From 1219 to 1223 the pagan armies of Chinggis Khan subjected Islamic central Asia and Iran to unparalleled destruction. Cities that refused to submit to Mongol rule were, simply, effaced: razed and plundered, their inhabitants massacred or, if they offered some skill, carted off to Mongolia to be put to some useful purpose. The inhabitants of these lands thus quickly learned not to resist.

Further conquests followed these early campaigns of terror. In 1243 the Mongols forced the Saljuqs of Rum to become their vassals; by 1258 the rest of Iran and most of Iraq had been subjugated, including Baghdad, for five centuries the symbolic heart of Islamdom. There the inhabitants witnessed scenes of rapine and massacre far more horrific than even the early invasions of the Franks into Syria. From that moment until the 1330s, the conquered lands of the Near East would be administered as a separate part of the Mongol Great Khan's world empire under a subordinate and, at first, pagan *khan* known as an *il-khan*. Yet even before these developments, the historian Ibn al-Athir saw in the Mongols and their predations in the eastern lands of Islam a disaster of apocalyptic proportions, evoking images of the terrors of Judgment Day: "For several years now I remained loath to report this disaster as it horrified me and I was unwilling to recount it, hesitating again and again. Who would find it easy to write the obituary of Islam and the Muslims? Who would take lightly the recollection of such an event? Oh, would that I had died before it occurred and been a thing forgotten, quite forgotten!…Perhaps humanity will not see such a calamity, apart from Gog and Magog, until the world comes to an end and this life ceases to be. As for the Antichrist, he, at least, will spare those who follow him and destroy only those who oppose him, but these spared no one."[2]

Yet for all the apocalyptic aura surrounding them, the very success of the Mongol invasions indirectly led to their defeat. Among the many peoples that the Mongols displaced by their westward invasions were the Qipchaq Turks, who had settled in southern Russia north of the Caspian Sea. These lands were devastated by the Mongols in the 1220s, and the Qipchaqs who were not killed or taken captive were sold into slavery, thousands of them flooding the markets of the Black Sea and, importantly, Cairo. It was there that the Ayyubid sultan al-Salih Ayyub procured the hardiest of the Qipchaqs to serve in his personal army of Bahri mamluks, and it was these very same Qipchaq mamluk troops who seized power from the Ayyubids in 1250 and, as we have seen, inaugurated their own Mamluk sultanate.[3]

Unlike the Ayyubids, the Mamluk sultans did not rule as a dynasty per se. That is, for the Mamluks, the family did not, as it did for most ruling houses throughout history, define the pool from which the rulers were chosen. Instead the military household produced sultans. In practice, some reigning sultans did fall prey to the dynastic principle, and so occasionally sons did indeed succeed fathers as sultans. But in theory, new sultans were to be drawn from the most ambitious and talented of a given cohort of high-ranking amirs, and in a context like that of the Mamluk palace, talent was measured by one's ability to get ahead by whatever means necessary. Within the upper ranks of the Mamluk state, then, factionalism, diplomacy, intrigue, and dirty tricks were the new normal.

The Mamluks also distinguished themselves from the Ayyubids in their approach toward the Franks, adopting a far more confrontational and militant stance than did the heirs of Saladin. This is not to say that they abandoned the diplomatic and internal approaches to jihad that the Ayyubids started; indeed, as we shall see, they extended, even perfected them. But diplomacy and religious reform were but a small part of an approach to the Frankish threat that, for the Mamluks, was best met with swift and brutal eradication, a policy for which the promised merits of external jihad seemed ready-made.

The Mamluks embraced this approach to the Franks for many reasons. The fact that they were, after all, a military caste drawn from career soldiers altered the tone of the regime for them. As one modern historian put it, a reader of the official biography of the sultan Baybars (about whom much more below) "almost gets a headache from the throbbing drums and the glare of sunlight on armor."[4] But they were also a more centralized regime than the Ayyubids ever were, marking out Egypt and especially Cairo as their inviolable center of power. This meant that, unlike the bickering Ayyubid princes, the Mamluk sultans could follow a unified policy toward the Franks, and, for the most part, the regime could stick with it. Moreover, in the final analysis, from the vantage point of Mamluk Cairo, Syria was merely a province to be governed, not a collection of family appanages to be wooed, and it was a frontier zone to boot. Whereas destructive policies (like warfare) toward Egypt might give a sultan pause, in Syria they were always an option. Finally, the Franks were hardly the only threat they had to face in Syria. A new Mongol invasion of Syria seemed always to be in the offing and the possibility of a Frankish-Mongol alliance a constant source of anxiety.

The first years of Mamluk rule in Egypt were tumultuous ones, in which the sultanate was contested by rival mamluk factions, their amirs, and surviving Ayyubid princes in Egypt and Syria. During these contests the Bahri mamluk faction that had originally seized power in 1250 was expelled from Egypt, and its men found various forms of employment in the courts of the leftover Ayyubid princes who still ruled in Syria. The unofficial leader of these Bahri exiles was the amir Baybars, who had been prominently involved in the coup of 1250 and, through a series of adventures, had ended up in the service of the Ayyubid prince of Damascus, al-Nasir Yusuf. With the Mongols (and a plague) now menacing Syria after their sacking of Baghdad, al-Nasir Yusuf and Baybars appeared to be Syria's best hope. In Egypt meanwhile the Mongol threat empowered one mamluk amir, Qutuz, to brush aside any pretense of deference to protocol and to seize the sultanate for himself. In 1259, whether these new leaders in Syria and Egypt would see each other as potential allies or potential rivals against the inevitable Mongol invasion was anyone's guess.[5]

The first to be tested was al-Nasir Yusuf in Damascus. He first tried diplomacy. Having temporarily neutralized his Frankish enemies with a truce in 1255, this seemed a sensible course of action with the Mongols, and so he sent his son with gifts to propitiate Hülegü, the Mongol il-khan.[6] He was sent back to his father in humiliation, bearing only threats. Al-Nasir Yusuf then assembled an army, but it didn't last. Hülegü crossed the Euphrates and captured Aleppo in January 1260, its wizened Ayyubid prince—a son, no less, of the mighty Saladin—having put up a brave but futile resistance. At this news the army from Damascus broke; al-Nasir Yusuf himself fled into Transjordan, where he was captured by the Mongols and eventually put to death. Baybars, however, kept his head and wrote to the sultan Qutuz, who granted him amnesty and allowed him and his men to return to Cairo, where the sultan was amassing an army to march against the Mongols.

The situation in Syria could not have been more grave. With Aleppo occupied and the Ayyubid princes of Syria in disarray, Damascus itself fell quickly, in March 1260. The local Christians were said to have made much of this, encouraged by the presence of Eastern Christian allies among the Mongol invading force and Hülegü's treatment of all his subjects as equals. Freed of their status as dhimmis, it is said, they indulged themselves in symbolic acts of defiance, even forcing Muslims to stand as they processed through the city bearing the cross, an unintentional rejoinder to the Muslim mockery of the relic of the True Cross after Saladin's victory at Hattin generations earlier.

As for the Franks, their approach to these developments varied. Bohemond VI of Antioch (and count of Tripoli), for example, had unambiguously thrown in his lot with the Mongols, thanks to the persuasion of his father-in-law, the king of Armenia. The leaders of the Latin kingdom, however, were more circumspect. Two decades of observing

Mongol raids into Anatolia and Iraq had shown them just how reliable a threat Hülegü posed and how unreliable the Mongols were as allies. Unlike Bohemond VI, the Franks at Acre maintained a stance of benevolent neutrality as the inevitable contest played out before them.[7]

More worrisome for the Mamluks was the news that bands of men from Hülegü's army were raiding far to the south, occupying Jerusalem briefly and threatening Gaza, as ever a gateway into Egypt. However, just at this juncture, in the late spring of 1260, Hülegü left Syria for China, once news reached him that his brother, the Great Khan, had died. With a Mongol succession dispute in the offing, there were bigger fish to fry for the il-khan, and so he left the field to his trusted commander Kitbuga (himself a Christian) with a greatly reduced force. A pliable Ayyubid prince, the lord of Homs, was given the unenviable position of Mongol governor of Syria to assist him.

The Mamluk sultan Qutuz and his amir Baybars now knew exactly what to do. Earlier Hülegü had sent an embassy to Cairo, demanding the sultan's complete surrender, as was the Mongol custom. Hülegü's letter was admirably blunt, as was also customary:

From the King of Kings in the East and West, the mighty Khan. Let Qutuz, who is of the race of *mamluks* who fled before our swords into this country, who enjoyed its comforts then killed its rulers, let Qutuz know…that we are the army of God on His earth.…Be warned by the fate of others and hand over your power to us before the veil is torn and you are sorry.…For we do not pity those who weep, nor are we tender to those who complain. You have heard that we have conquered the lands and cleansed the earth of corruption and killed most of the people. Yours is to flee; ours is to pursue. What land will shelter you, what road save you? You have no deliverance from our swords, no escape from the terror of our arms. Our horses are swift in pursuit, our arrows piercing, our swords like thunderbolts, our hearts like rocks, our numbers like sand. Fortresses cannot withstand us; armies are of no avail in fighting us. Your prayers against us will not be heard.…Do not debate long, and hasten to give us an answer before the fires of war flare up and throw their sparks upon you. For at that time you will find no dignity, no comfort, no protector, no sanctuary.[8]

Qutuz got the message. He quickly had the Mongol ambassadors executed for their effrontery and, in a final act of defiance, had their heads displayed at the gates of Cairo until they rotted. For the Mamluks too had their customs.

There would be no turning back now. The campaign was cast as a jihad, and Qutuz exhorted all his amirs to earn their keep by joining in. In late July 1260, Qutuz and Baybars, at the head of a large Mamluk army, marched out of Egypt along the coast of Palestine to confront Kitbuga in Syria. From Acre the Frankish leaders offered to add what men they could to assist the Mamluk army. Qutuz politely declined and marched on. The Mongol army, including contingents of Georgian, Armenian, and even Ayyubid allies, was encamped at a spot in eastern Galilee called 'Ayn Jalut (Goliath's Spring), a propitious toponym for a battle between a Mamluk army of rivals and refugees and a Mongol giant that had never yet tasted defeat.[9] On September 3 the two armies finally met in battle. As the Mamluk army approached, Kitbuga attacked, but the Mamluks held firm. A second Mongol assault nearly overwhelmed them, but Qutuz rallied his men and launched a crushing countercharge directly into the Mongol ranks. At a certain point the Syrian Ayyubid troops fighting in Mongol service brazenly switched sides and fled to Mamluk protection. Before the day was over, Kitbuga had been killed in battle, at which his men, badly shaken, fled en masse from the field, eventually crossing the Euphrates. The Mongol occupying forces in the rest of Syria soon followed suit.[10]

In hindsight it is easy to claim that, with this defeat, the Mongols had reached their high-water mark in the Near East. But Muslims who were contemporary to these events could not be so consoled. The Mongols would continue to threaten Mamluk domains for decades before signing a treaty with the sultans of Cairo in 1323. Until then the descendants of Chinggis Khan remained in the background as an ever-present threat even as the Mamluks directed their attention to other matters.

The Mamluk victory at 'Ayn Jalut offered one immediate windfall to Qutuz and the Mamluks: Ayyubid Syria could now be claimed without having to conquer it. The sultan immediately set about arranging the disposition of the various Syrian domains, sending up a Mamluk governor to restore order in Damascus, where vengeful anti-Christian riots had broken out. In his reorganization of Syria, Qutuz naturally made use of the Ayyubid princes who had ruled in Syria before 1260. However, the conduct of these lords during the recent crisis was not always exemplary, and Qutuz had to factor this into his plans. The disparate fates of these amirs is instructive—which was no doubt the point. The lord of Hama, a steadfast Mamluk loyalist, was confirmed in possession of his kingdom and was even granted new lands to add to his domains. The lord of Homs, who had fought alongside the Mongols but cleverly turned coat in the midst of battle, was rewarded for his timely perfidy and was granted his kingdom as well as a pardon for collaborating with the enemy. Aleppo was put under the control of a refugee prince from Mosul, the better to keep an eye on Mongol-controlled Iraq. The lord of Banias, however, had chosen poorly; his unambiguous enthusiasm for Mongol rule gained him only a swift execution.[11]

Left out of this flurry of rewards was Baybars, who had provided valuable men and counsel to Qutuz. The sources suggest he had hoped to be granted Aleppo as his reward and was outraged when he was passed over. But perhaps Baybars needed no new excuse to be angry with Qutuz; the two had been bitter rivals in earlier years, and only the shared threat of Mongol conquest had united them. With that threat gone, the two allies fell back on their accustomed enmity. Qutuz must have felt the awkwardness, for he quickly decamped from Syria for the comparative safety of his base of support in Cairo. But Baybars never let him get that far. In the desert on the border with Egypt, Baybars arranged for Qutuz to be killed and had himself proclaimed sultan in his place.

The Conquering King

Baybars's first priority was to secure Cairo and, importantly, the royal treasury, as ever the central tool for retaining control of the army.[12] No one resisted. On November 25, 1260, he was publicly enthroned, though he was formally invested as sultan only in July 1261. Following standard practice, the Friday sermon was invoked in his name and coins were now minted with his name and his titular, "The Conquering King, Pillar of the World and of the Faith." His coins retained his more common epithet, al-Salihi, which quietly evoked his servile connection to the household of the old Ayyubid sultan, al-Salih Ayyub. Some such coins also bore his chosen emblem, the lion, which also decorated secular and religious buildings and other objects throughout his sultanate (Fig. 10). Especially religious buildings. For the Mamluks, like their Ayyubid and Zangid predecessors, knew well to favor the religious elites of their realm with their patronage.

Baybars's next priority was to secure the Syrian lands that his sultanate had so recently acquired. Partly this involved some final housecleaning. The great fortress of Karak in the Transjordan, for example, was too crucial a connector between Syria and Egypt for anyone but the sultan himself to control. Evidence of its Muslim lord's complicity with the Mongols was soon waved about, and Baybars had the man arrested and the fortress confiscated. He likewise crushed rebellions in Damascus and a more troubling insurrection at Aleppo. This last was interrupted only by the return of a Mongol invasion force to northern Syria. A counterattack by the Ayyubid armies of northern Syria stopped them near the city of Homs in December 1260; by 1261 Aleppo was definitively restored to the Mamluks.[13]

A fascinating component of these events was Baybars's effort to revive the office of caliph, which, as we have seen, was extinguished with the Mongol conquest of Baghdad in 1258. In fact two minor 'Abbasid aristocrats had survived the horrors of 1258 and were making themselves conspicuous in the Mamluk domains; one of them was openly courted by the rebels in Aleppo. Being, after all, a usurper in a very insecure political context, Baybars was quick to see the value of the caliph as a guarantor of his legitimacy in the broader Sunni world, and so he eventually recognized both of these pretenders as caliph in turn. It was a reciprocal arrangement. On July 4, 1261, the first of these caliphs formally conferred upon Baybars the title of sultan amid great pomp in Cairo. This caliph's successor played a similar role, helping to smooth relations between Baybars and Berke Khan, the recently converted Mongol ruler of the Golden Horde in southern Russia. This line of so-called shadow caliphs, powerless in all but symbolic terms, survived on and off in Egypt until the demise of the Mamluks in 1517.[14]

Partly too Baybars secured Syria by applying constant pressure on the Franks. By the early 1260s the Frankish states of the Levant were much reduced in every way from their former days of glory. The rump kingdom of Jerusalem, for example, had neither a king nor Jerusalem: the nominal Hohenstaufen king, Conrad III, known as Conradin, was a child living in Europe, an heir to the reluctant Crusader king Frederick II. During one phase Conrad's regent, Hugh of Cyprus, was also a child, and so required a regent for his regency. Meanwhile the grown-ups were hardly any better. The principality of Antioch and the county of Tripoli were combined under the rule of Bohemond VI, who had unwisely thrown in his lot with the Mongols at 'Ayn Jalut. The Templars and Hospitallers eyed each other suspiciously, and in the cities Genoese and Venetian merchant communities vied for control of the dwindling but still lucrative trade passing through Levantine ports. Soon the Italians declared outright war against one another, which only further divided the loyalties of the ruling elites.

Taken as a whole, the territory under the (nominal) sway of these Frankish lords amounted to a strip of noncontiguous lands from Jaffa to Antioch, with a handful of castles farther inland. Baybars sent raid after raid to harass and threaten the Franks, beginning with the perfidious ally of the Mongols, Bohemond of Antioch-Tripoli. In 1261 Baybars was threatening Antioch itself; in 1262 he sacked its port, Saint Symeon. He then kept to the south, attacking Nazareth and razing the Church of the Virgin there in 1263 and turning up to threaten the very walls of Acre. He followed up with a visit to various holy sites in Palestine, including Jerusalem.[15]

After the death of the Mongol il-khan Hülegü in 1265, however, Baybars could afford to move from mere raids designed to pressure the Franks to a concerted effort designed to oust them for good. Nearly every year saw Baybars leading campaigns into Frankish Syria. The strategy behind these campaigns was clear and part of a broader vision. As one chronicler put it, incidentally putting the Franks in their proper context, "One part of the army uproots Frankish castles and destroys fortresses, while another rebuilds what the Mongols have destroyed in the East."[16] On the one hand, Baybars aimed to capture inland strongholds and regarrison them as bases for further campaigns and to strengthen his borders. Yet so long as their connections to Europe were secure, the Franks could always return in force. Baybars was reasonable enough to realize that Muslim navies could no longer compete against Frankish domination of the Mediterranean. It was their footholds on dry land that needed to go. And so, on the other hand, his goal was to capture coastal towns and demolish them, to prevent any return of the Franks once they were driven out. Along the way the smaller towns and villages that supplied the Franks would be harassed and pillaged, their largely native Christian inhabitants being viewed in Baybars's eyes as fair game.

Thus in 1265 he prepared to lead an army far to the Euphrates frontier to secure al-Bira, which was under threat of a Mongol attack. But when news reached him that the garrison there had already repelled the invaders, he sent his men instead against the Franks, who had been raiding in the vicinity of Ascalon. He made short work of the southern coast. Caesarea fell in late February, the troops jury-rigging siege ladders out of their bridles—a bit of siege-craft that only Qipchaq horse warriors could conceive. The fortifications were demolished and the town burned to the ground. A few days later Haifa was captured and razed, but the fortress of Athlit nearby could not be taken. Baybars instead circled back to what was left of Caesarea and, just south of it, invested the mighty Hospitaller castle of Arsuf. Once his troops had battered their way into the lower town, the garrison within the castle surrendered, provided they be allowed to go free. Baybars agreed and then coldly sent them off into captivity anyway. These were fighting men far too dangerous to let go.[17]

Baybars seemed unwilling to leave Syria. In 1266, perhaps in response to a thwarted Frankish assault on Homs, he sent a massive expedition into Syria. While he encamped near Acre and visited Jerusalem, he sent troops toward Tripoli to menace the various fortresses in the area and toward Tyre to pillage its lands and disrupt trade. It was at this time that he captured the massive Templar fortress of Safad in northern Galilee, treating it quite differently from the other Frankish keeps he had taken. According to an amir present in his army, Baybars was motivated by revenge for a slain companion to kill his Frankish prisoners rather than ransom them, as was usual. When they arrived at the spot of their execution, the Frankish nobles, sensing their fate, ordered the men and women of their households to stand to one side, so that they would not have to meet their deaths amid mere servants, subscribing to the scruple of *pas devant les domestiques* to the bitter end. The fortress was retained, repaired, and manned with a garrison of mamluks, and the town became one of the principal cities of Mamluk (and later Ottoman) Palestine.[18]

In 1268 Jaffa was dismantled, perhaps as a response to the news that Louis IX of France was preparing for another Crusade.[19] Its garrison was allowed to flee to Acre, though Baybars let his men take their right of pillage on the civilian population, many of whom were killed or taken captive. In the context of Louis IX's threatened Crusade, Baybars was even willing to dismantle the fortifications at Ascalon, a Muslim-held town—anything to thwart the arrival of more Frankish visitors. But farther inland the Templar fortress of Beaufort (Shaqif Arnun) was repaired and regarrisoned, as it controlled an important route connecting the kingdom of Jerusalem with the lands of Antioch-Tripoli. Its Templar garrison was sold into slavery, but the noncombatants were released to find refuge in nearby Tyre. Once again Baybars raided in the area of Acre, but this time he left a detachment of troops to keep an eye on the city. The Frankish capital was not yet ready to fall.

It is in the context of Baybars's plans to deprive the Frankish states of options that we must also see his expedition in 1266 to Cilician Armenia, long an ally of the Franks.[20] Its king, Hethum I, was father-in-law to Bohemond VI of Antioch-Tripoli, and, like him, he had been an ally of the Mongols at 'Ayn Jalut. Baybars sent a joint Egyptian-Syrian army with the Ayyubid lord of Hama at its head to exact retribution. It scattered the Armenian army that had assembled and pillaged the kingdom, took the prince and heir captive, and killed his brother. His father, Hethum, remained in the comparative safety of the Mongol court. Baybars sacked all the principal towns of Cilicia: Tarsus, Adana, and Ayas, as well as the capital of Sis. There the cathedral was burned down and the royal palace pillaged. It is said that tens of thousands of captives were taken during the campaign.

Baybars saved his pièce de résistance for 1268. In the spring of that year he marched north after the destruction of Jaffa, pausing to receive the surrender of the Lebanese castle Shaqif Arnun and crossing over the mountains to raid and devastate the lands of Tripoli and the surrounding mountains. By May 14 he was encamped before the walls of his prime target: Antioch. He sent one division of his army to secure the port of Saint Symeon, and another to the north to guard against the possibility that an Armenian or Mongol rescue might interrupt the proceedings. Antioch was trapped.[21]

Bohemond had little to work with for his defense. The massive fortifications that had resisted the First Crusaders were no match for Mamluk siege engines; the undermanned garrison was overwhelmed by Baybars's massive army. On May 18 the Mamluk army attacked from all sides. Near Mt. Silpius, supposedly the city's crowning defense, a breach was made, and the army poured in. The city gates were sealed, and Baybars gave his men free rein to take vengeance on the Franks who had stood side-by-side with Hülegü at 'Ayn Jalut, Franks who had been a thorn in the side of Islamdom for more than a century and a half. Only the garrison in the citadel was granted safe conduct; the others were killed and the loot distributed to Baybars's leading mamluks and their men. Baybars himself used his own share of the plunder to underwrite the construction of a mosque in Cairo. Bohemond, who was in Tripoli at the time, was spared the sight of his city's sacking. But in a letter worthy of the Mongol chancery, Baybars venomously let him know what he missed:

> You would have seen your knights prostrate beneath the horses' hooves, your houses stormed by pillagers and ransacked by looters, your wealth weighed by the hundredweight, your women sold four at a time and bought for a *dinar* of your own money. You would have seen the crosses in your churches smashed, the pages of the false Scriptures scattered, the Patriarchs' tombs overturned. You would have seen your Muslim enemy trampling on the place where you celebrate the Mass, cutting

the throats of monks, priests and deacons upon the altars, bringing sudden death to the Patriarchs and slavery to the royal princes....Then you would have said: "Would that I were dust, and that no letter had ever brought me such tidings!"[22]

The capture of Antioch was more than just an excuse for gloating for Baybars. It also effectively cleared northern Syria of the Franks for good. The Templars in the area abandoned their castles, and Antioch's defenses were rebuilt. The city now became a forward base for operations into Anatolia, but it did not flourish again as a city (now called Antakya) until the modern era. Baybars also took the opportunity to pummel the nearby lands held by the Nizari "Assassins," capturing most of their mountain forts, including their Syrian headquarters, Masyaf.[23]

By now the news of Louis IX's planned second crusade had arrived. This turn of events forced the sultan to halt his operations and prepare for another invasion. In that same year Baybars signed a treaty with the kingdom of Armenia, which could easily have been his next target, and a temporary truce with Acre. Returning to Egypt, he fortified some coastal settlements, such as Alexandria, and laid waste to coastal settlements in Palestine, as we have seen, and saw to the needs of his shipyards.

And yet nothing came of the much-feared Frankish invasion. For all that Louis had himself condemned Baybars's activities, other Frankish leaders near and far had been quick to send the sultan propitiatory letters of goodwill. The crusading lord Edward I of England did arrive in Acre, but this was a mere ripple produced from Louis's failed crusade and had little or no impact upon the Mamluks. Edward did later open negotiations with the Mongol il-khan for joint operations against Baybars, but the plan produced only a minor Mongol raid that Baybars easily dispatched. Nonetheless Edward *was* a Crusader, so Baybars at least tried to have the man assassinated, with Nizari help, it is said.[24]

By the start of 1271 Baybars was back in the field against the Franks of Syria, raiding around Tripoli and capturing the Templar fort of Safitha (Chastel Blanc). By early March he had arrived to encamp around the massive Hospitaller fortress of Hisn al-Akrad (Crac des Chevaliers). In practical terms Crac was the county of Tripoli's early-warning system against any Muslim attack. Its loss would spell doom for the Franks of the coast. Spring rains, usually a blessing in the Near East, bogged down the siege, but Mamluk sappers managed to bring down one critical section of the outer wall. The army then streamed in, filling the outer yard around what was an essentially impenetrable inner citadel. The garrison inside could do nothing but wait; knowing full well that no help would come, however, they soon surrendered. The fate of the military orders at the other fortresses that Baybars had already taken was no doubt prominent in their minds, but Baybars showed uncharacteristic civility and allowed all the Franks to withdraw to Tripoli. Clemency from a sultan like Baybars was perhaps the strongest evidence yet that the Franks of Syria were no longer considered a serious threat. Baybars had the castle refortified and garrisoned, his commemorative inscriptions still visible today. With the subsequent fall of al-Qurayn (Montfort, headquarters of the order of the Teutonic Knights) and ʿAkkar (Gibelacar) by June 1271, Syria was now cleared of all Frankish castles in the interior. Significantly only at the coastal fort of Maraqiyya (Maraclea) did Baybars meet defeat, when Frankish ships arrived to assist the defense.[25]

The capture of Crac des Chevaliers was Baybars's last great victory against the Franks. As Edward I was still in Acre, colluding with the Mongols at the time, Baybars had thought it prudent to make a truce with the miserable Bohemond VI, and so Tripoli was temporarily saved the fate of Antioch. The rest of Baybars's reign was dominated by his intrigues in the affairs of the Saljuqs of Rum in Anatolia, some of whom were hoping to shake off the yoke of Mongol vassalage that had been imposed upon them back in 1243.[26] Baybars agreed with them to a joint campaign against the Mongol il-khan and set out for Anatolia in 1277. At Abulustayn (Elbistan) his army encountered a Mongol force and destroyed it. Baybars's presumed Saljuq allies never appeared, however, and news was circulating that the il-khan was assembling an army of revenge. Baybars left the Saljuqs to their fate and withdrew to Damascus, where, after taking ill, he died on June 30, 1277. He was buried in a richly decorated mausoleum and madrasa complex not far from the tomb of his more famous predecessor, Saladin. Though his tomb did not come to be quite so frequented in later centuries as that of Saladin, Baybars secured for himself a different kind of immortality, becoming the focus of a cycle of oral epics that are sung to this day, joining the ranks of the great heroes whose exploits Saladin never quite matched.

Jihad by Treaty

In March 1274, shortly before Baybars's death, Pope Gregory X convened the fourteenth ecumenical council of the Catholic Church at Lyon to discuss matters of great weight to the Latin faithful. Prime among them was a recent pledge on the part of the Byzantine emperor to reunite the Greek Church of the East with the Latin Church of the West. Given this momentous goal, the council attracted prominent churchmen and nobles from near and far, bishops, abbots, prelates, theologians, scholars, kings, and their representatives. The great scholar Thomas Aquinas himself was due to attend but died en route; his fellow philosopher Bonaventure at least lived long enough to make some of the first sessions. But by far the greatest stir was caused by the arrival of representatives of the Mongol il-khan of Persia, whose leader underwent public baptism to underline the Ilkhanate's commitment to an alliance with the papacy against the Mamluks.

In the end nothing came of this nightmare scenario, though not for want of enthusiasm on the Mongol side. It was rather the Frankish kings who, upon Gregory's death two years later, lost interest in the plan.[27] It may also have helped that, in addition to waging total war on the Franks of the Levant, the Mamluks had inserted themselves in the web of diplomatic relations that the Ayyubids had formed with various Frankish powers, "the first systematic and sustained diplomacy with Christian powers in Islamic history."[28] Since Fredrick II's overtures under the Ayyubids, the Hohenstaufen rulers of Sicily had been fast friends of Egypt, and Baybars made the effort to renew these ties in 1261. When the Hohenstaufen were ousted from Sicily in 1266, Baybars dutifully established ties with Charles of Anjou, who replaced them. Similarly, once the Byzantine emperors regained the empire lost to them in the Fourth Crusade and were restored to Constantinople, Baybars wasted no time in crafting a commercial treaty with them (in 1261) as also with the all-important city-state of Genoa. Baybars's ultimate successor as sultan, Qalawun, renewed the treaties with Genoa and Byzantium and added a new treaty with the Catalan king Alfonso III of Aragon, who had recently added Sicily to his dominion.[29]

The Mamluks also made deft use of treaties closer to home in the Levant, pairing their military actions against the Frankish states with diplomatic overtures to ensure access to commercial revenues, buy time or breathing space to focus on bigger threats, like the Mongols, or finalize the disposition of conquered lands. The fragmented nature of the Frankish leadership in the Levant, combined with disputes over the crown of Jerusalem, made playing one party off the other a simple matter. A prime example of how the Mamluks used diplomacy to subdue the Franks is a series of pacts made in 1261 (a busy year for Mamluk diplomats). In that year Baybars warmly received the envoys of the counts of Jaffa and Beirut but treated the main Frankish envoy from Acre with disdain. Eventually he agreed to a temporary truce with all of them. Nonetheless it is the use of "carrot and stick" during the negotiations that is more revealing than the outcome.[30] It seems that prices, food shortages, and debased coinage were making life difficult for Franks and Muslims alike in Syria. And so, even before showing up in force at the borders of Frankish territory, Baybars "had sent a vast amount of barley and flour by sea from Damietta to Jaffa," the Frankish port. This was an odd way of reducing one's sworn enemy, but it had the advantage of stimulating commerce and of indirectly supplying the Syrians, who imported most of their goods from the Franks anyway.

It also made it impossible for Jaffa to resist Baybars. When the sultan finally did arrive, the grateful count of Jaffa "sent a messenger presenting his obedience and bearing gifts" and then begged permission to appear before the sultan to present his service in person. Baybars "wrote him a decree, covering his lands and then sent him back in safety to his city." One by one other Frankish rulers, including the lord of Beirut, arrived bearing gifts and proffering their obedience. In the end a truce was reached, set on the basis of the status quo during the reign of the last Ayyubid ruler of Aleppo and Damascus, and the sultan sent envoys back with these Franks to their lands "to administer the oaths to them." As one modern scholar has observed, this seems very much as if the sultan "was entering into some sort of semi-feudal relationship" with Jaffa and Beirut. The principal Frankish embassy from Acre, however, was poorly received, and instead of receiving their obeisance, Baybars sent a raiding party into their lands.

The sultan's separate treaties with the Hospitallers suggest that this divide-and-conquer strategy was very effective. In 1265 or 1266 they sent an envoy to confirm the continuation of their existing treaty with the Mamluks and to ask to extend it to protect their lands in the vicinity of Homs and the Nizari lands of the Lebanese highlands that they held. In return Baybars insisted they release various lords from the obligation of paying them tribute. The Hospitallers dithered. However, once Baybars began pillaging the lands outside Acre, a Hospitaller delegation quickly arrived to conclude the truce, in 1267.[31] Even more constricting terms were negotiated in 1271, when Baybars obliged the Hospitallers to cede lands to the Mamluks outright and to share the revenues of others. Similar arrangements were worked out for the lands around Sidon. As we have seen, in 1271 Baybars was planning a campaign against Tripoli. The arrival of Edward I in Acre thwarted those plans, and so he made a strategic truce with Bohemond VI to concentrate on

Edward. When Bohemond VI died before the truce's ten-year limit, Baybars was able to press his claims upon the new lord of Tripoli, a minor, and wrest control of Latakia and 'Arqa from him. Baybars's successors, in particular the sultan Qalawun, likewise made heavy use of treaties with the Franks, treating at various times with Templars, Hospitallers, and indeed nearly every Frankish polity—a prudent policy so long as the Mongols remained an active threat.

The Nation of the Cross Has Fallen

Long before his death, Baybars had arranged for a smooth succession. Alas, this did not guarantee an easy transition. His son and heir, Baraka, was forced by a rival mamluk faction to abdicate, and Baraka's successor was likewise deposed, in 1279. The sons of Baybars were kept on a form of house arrest at Karak in Transjordan, though eventually they were recalled to live their final days in Cairo. A last descendant, a great-great-grandson of Baybars, died in 1488, his connection to the founding of the Mamluk regime all but forgotten. The man who supplanted the sons of Baybars as sultan was an elder statesman, an old Bahri colleague of Baybars named Qalawun (also Qalavun), who was a veteran of the campaigns in Syria and Armenia.[32] Like his former comrade Baybars, Qalawun was a Qipchaq Turk who had been captured, enslaved, and purchased to become a member of Egypt's mamluk corps. His nickname, "al-Alfi" or "Thousand-Coin," alluded to the steep price he was said to have fetched. Once he was recognized as sultan, most of Qalawun's attentions were taken up by the twin threats of rebel amirs in northern Syria and the Mongol il-khan Abaqa, who still hoped to take Syria for the Mongols. The rebels, though, were eventually placated and, with typical Mamluk efficiency, were brought as allies against the Mongols, who met Qalawun in battle near Homs—their second battle there—in October 1281 and were soundly defeated, their second defeat there. When the new il-khan converted to Islam and sent envoys to curry favor with the sultan, his gesture of friendship was rebuffed like that of a whingeing underclassman. In Cairo the Mongol threat was beginning to lose its bite.[33]

Qalawun also prosecuted jihad against the Franks, continuing Baybars's plan to drive them from Syria altogether. They were, in any case, truly just clinging to the coast of Syria. Only Tripoli now remained of the original Frankish capitals, the capital of the kingdom of

Jerusalem having been moved to Acre in Saladin's day. Even at Acre the Frankish crown was in dispute, with the Lusignan Hugh III of Cyprus claiming it against the demands of the king of Sicily, Charles of Anjou. The remaining Frankish holdings at Sidon, Tyre, and Beirut were thus obliged to recognize one claimant over the other. The Frankish states had divided themselves; all Qalawun had to do was conquer them. In May 1285 al-Marqab (Margat) fell to Qalawun, who repaired it and stationed a garrison there, its Hospitaller occupants given safe passage to Tripoli. The coastal fort of Maraqiyya (Maraclea), which had so thwarted Baybars, was now easily taken thanks to a deal worked out with Bohemond VII. Following standard procedure, it was dismantled. In 1287 an earthquake badly damaged the defense of the port of Latakia, and Qalawun wasted no time in snapping it up.[34]

It was at about this time that some Franks begged him to capture Tripoli. This perhaps requires some explanation. Tripoli's last lord, Bohemond VII, had died in 1287; in this vacuum, power in the city was divided among the Frankish nobility, the Italian merchant communes, and the military orders, all of whom were at each other's throats. When it seemed that a sister of the dead Bohemond would be able to take power with Genoese backing, the Venetians implored Qalawun to put a stop to it. And stop it he did. In March 1289 his army began its siege of Tripoli. It was slow going for Qalawun, as a renewed sense of urgency—not to say doom—struck the Franks remaining in Syria. The Italian communes all provided galleys, as did Frankish Cyprus. A corps of knights came from Acre.

After nearly a month of constant bombardment from Mamluk siege engines, however, Tripoli's stout defense began to crumble. The Italians, sensing a turn in fortune, quickly took ship and fled. On April 26, 1289, the city fell in an all-out attack. It is said that every man found in the streets was killed, and everyone else was sold into captivity. Those who could fled to Cyprus. So bent on cleansing the land of Frankish pollution were Qalawun's men that some were reported to have ridden their horses into the sea in pursuit of Franks taking refuge on a nearby island, dragging their mounts by their reins until they reached the place, where everyone in hiding was cut down. The bones of the dead lord Bohemond VII were dug up and scattered to the wind. His city, like all the others on the coast, was demolished. Some few Frankish castles in the vicinity fell soon after Tripoli, and the Italian lord of Jubayl readily handed over his town to Qalawun.[35]

By now three of the four Frankish states, Edessa, Antioch, and Tripoli, had been eradicated. Acre, itself a place-holder for what was left of the old kingdom of Jerusalem, was alone and clearly bound for destruction along with what remained of the orts and crumbs of Crusader Syria. However, Qalawun knew that any siege at Acre would be a long and bitter one, in which the Franks would pull out all the stops to retain their last serious foothold on the Levantine coast. So, to bide his time, he made a temporary truce with Acre and returned to Egypt to rest, resupply, and build up an unstoppable army.

In August 1290 Acre's moment came.[36] A riot in the city, in which some Franks killed a number of Muslim townsmen (possibly merchants), provided Qalawun's pretext for claiming the Franks had broken their truce. He called for jihad against these perfidious Franks and marched at the head of his Egyptian troops, sending word for his Syrian amirs to assemble their men and siege equipment. But fate struck Qalawun before it saw to Acre; just a few miles on the road from Cairo, the aging sultan, ailing from a sickness contracted months earlier, died.

At this surprising turn of events, it might have seemed that the Franks had been blessed with another miracle. In fact the old sultan's death provided only a brief respite. In March 1291 his son and heir, al-Ashraf Khalil, renewed his father's campaign. Qalawun's funeral was used as a pulpit from which to preach the jihad in Egypt; in Syria the sultan's representative launched a carefully planned program designed to spur the populace of Syria to jihad. The preachers were so successful that volunteers were said to outnumber the regular troops, and the whole populace pitched in, despite rain and snow, to help haul the siege equipment overland to be gathered by contingents of the army. Peasants and townsmen were joined by "jurisprudents, teachers, scholars, and the pious" in their heavy lifting.[37] Armies from Hama, Homs, Tripoli, and other fortresses arrived to rendezvous with the Egyptian and Palestinian troops. Few could doubt that the new sultan had managed to mobilize most of his domains for this one, final siege.

Once arrived at Acre on April 6, al-Ashraf's army found a large, well-fortified city, its garrison supplemented by contingents from the Hospitallers and Templars. Frankish ships carrying mangonels fired down upon those Muslim divisions encamped closest to the sea, and Frankish knights rode out daily to harass and provoke the soldiers engaged in the siege. At one point the Templars and Hospitallers led a dangerous sortie that was thwarted only by a last-minute warning to the sultan. Eventually a contingent from Cyprus led by King Hugh himself arrived, though Hugh did not linger. The Mamluks never paused in their bombardment and sapping operations. Finally, their persistence paid off: a tower collapsed, and the army now got clear of the outer walls and confronted the city's inner defenses, where some of the most bitter fighting with the military orders took place. In mid-May a group of Acre's notables emerged to negotiate a truce but were rejected. Al-Ashraf instead offered the Franks safe conduct provided they abandon the city. The deal never got very far, for at this point someone fired a mangonel from the city and the sultan was nearly killed. Negotiations were canceled, and the bombardment began afresh.

At dawn on May 18 al-Ashraf ordered the drums—all three hundred of them—to signal what would be the Mamluk's final offensive. As the doom of Acre was drummed into the morning light, arrow fire denuded the walls of their defenders. Despite intense fighting from the Templars and Hospitallers, the Mamluk troops were finally able to force their way into the city. Al-Ashraf's banners were flying on Acre's walls by midday. The Franks fled to the port to escape or else holed up in the remaining towers and defenses. While al-Ashraf's regular troops were occupied with these remaining defenders, the volunteers who accompanied the army broke ranks and began pillaging the city at will. One man was said to have needed three rows of porters to carry all his plunder back to Cairo. Virtually all the remaining Frankish defenders had surrendered, save in one tower, where a contingent of Templars, Hospitallers, and other knights were cornered with some civilians. They had arranged to surrender too, but some of the Mamluk troops, perhaps worried that the jihad volunteers were taking the best of the plunder, rushed in before the tower could be evacuated and began seizing the women and children as captives. At this the Templars preferred to stand and fight and, closing the gates, killed whatever Muslims they had managed to trap inside their tower. Three days later, however, they agreed to surrender. Again some undisciplined Mamluk troops broke the terms of their agreement, slaughtering the knights that emerged and seizing the civilians for captivity. The surrender turned into the bloodiest fighting of Acre's last hours. In retaliation the Templars took Muslim prisoners and began killing them and attacking any troops that approached the tower. One of the Muslims trapped in the tower lived to tell the tale, perhaps the last Muslim eyewitness voice from Outremer: "I…was among the group who went to the tower and when the gates were closed we stayed there with many others. The Franks killed many people and then came to the place where a small number, including my companion and me, had taken refuge. We fought them for an hour, and most of our number, including my comrade, were killed, but I escaped in a band of ten persons who fled in their path. Being outnumbered, we hurled ourselves toward the sea. Some died, some were crippled, and some were spared for a time."[38]

Al-Ashraf, however, was not about to let these Templar holdouts ruin his victory. He ordered the tower sapped, and the defenders inside quickly evacuated the premises. The dismantling of Acre's other defenses began immediately. Carrier pigeons brought the news of the fall of Acre to Damascus on the same day, and the city broke out in public rejoicing. Saved from the rubble was the Gothic façade of one of Acre's churches. Its handsomely crafted entryway, with its slender columns and triple-lobed recess, was carried off to Cairo, where it serves as an entrance to the madrasa and tomb complex of al-Ashraf's half-brother, the sultan al-Nasir Muhammad (Fig. 11).

At the time, no one seems to have questioned all the slaughter at Acre, estimated in the tens of thousands. Both sides knew what Acre meant and that this was Outremer's last stand. Only one historian, al-Yunini (d. 1326), was able to look back a generation later and put the violence in context: "In my view this was [the Franks'] reward for what they did when they conquered Acre from the martyred sultan Saladin. Although they had granted amnesty to the Muslim inhabitants, they betrayed them after the victory, killing all except a few high-ranking amirs....Thus God requited the unbelievers for what they did to the Muslims."[39] In the wake of al-Ashraf's reconquest of Acre, the Franks remaining in Sidon, Beirut, Tyre, and Haifa soon surrendered their cities, providing the sultan little or no resistance when his men took them. At Tyre, for example, the Muslim commander claimed to have found only a few dozen old men and women. The last Templar forts at Antartus (Tortosa) and 'Atlith were easily taken too. With the goal of nearly every Muslim ruler in the Near East since the coming of the Franks finally realized, al-Ashraf visited Damascus, covered in glory. The city was decorated and illuminated, and the sultan trod upon runners of satin that indicated his path from the city gate to the palace. Before him the sultan paraded 280 Frankish prisoners in chains; one carried an inverted Frankish banner, the other a banner festooned with the hair of some of his slain comrades. People from the city and from miles around lined the streets to view the spectacle: scholars, mystics, peasants, merchants, Christians, and Jews. The satin was rolled out again for al-Ashraf when he finally returned to Cairo in triumph, piously ending his march at the tomb of Qalawun, a gesture of humility meant to suggest that his deed was merely that of finishing a job started by his father.

That the abiding conquest of Frankish Syria was a job started by one party and finished by another was also true of those with longer historical memories, such as the poet who praised al-Ashraf, and indeed the Mamluks in their entirety, with these lines:

> Through al-Ashraf the Lord Sultan, we are delivered from the Trinity,
> and Unity rejoices in the struggle!
> Praise be to God, the nation of the Cross has fallen; through the Turks
> the religion of the chosen Arab has triumphed![40]

A.D. 1292

The fall of Acre in 1291 is traditionally seen to mark the end of the main story of the Crusades. And although most historians today recognize the many subsequent attempts by Christians of Europe to return to the Levant as "Later Crusades," the very designation only confirms that for most observers, it all came to a conclusion before the walls of Acre.

To our Muslim chroniclers, even those who acknowledge the significance of Acre's fall, the victory of 1291 doesn't confer anything like a sense of an ending. Just as our Islamic sources ignore the totemic date of Urban II's Clermont speech in 1095 and see the genesis of Frankish aggression in earlier invasions—in Sicily and Spain—so too does an Islamic history of the Crusades extend, with nary a pause for breath, well beyond 1291. The great Mamluk campaigns against the Franks occurred in the Near East, but the Near East was but one of many fronts in Islamdom's far-flung wars against the Franks, which continued to rage in al-Andalus, eastern Europe, and elsewhere. Even in the Near East the Frankish threat did not magically vanish in 1291. The Italian lords of Jubayl retained a ghostly presence near Tripoli, and until 1302 a garrison of Templars stubbornly clung to the rock of the island of Arwad, just off Tartus.

Of far greater weight was the continued Frankish presence on Cyprus, whence the royal Lusignan family of Jerusalem had long ago fled and lived as royalty in exile.[41] While the Latin states of the Levant still existed, Frankish Cyprus had maintained close social, political, and commercial connections to the mainland. Baybars himself learned not to underestimate these island Franks after a disastrous naval campaign against Cyprus in 1270.[42] After 1291 it remained the Franks' closest outpost in the Mediterranean. From Cyprus the Frankish kings of Jerusalem continued to look across to the desolated ports and coastal towns of the Levant and, over the course of the later Middle Ages, entertained more than a few plans to recapture the Holy Land. Once in a while they acted on them. For the Mamluk sultans, then, the Frankish threat was greatly weakened but did not entirely disappear in 1291; it simply relocated off-shore.

Frankish problems aside, there were also more pressing and proximate concerns facing the sultanate. After all, in the years after 1291 the Mongol il-khans in Persia still hovered at the borders of Mamluk Syria. In 1299 they even defeated the Mamluks in battle and opened up Syria for conquest and devastation, sacking and occupying Damascus in 1300. After a few months the Mongols pulled out of Syria, threatened as they were with invasion from other Mongol rivals. They returned more than once in the fourteenth century, but without any success. Only once, in 1303, did Mongol armies get anywhere close to Damascus again, and they were swiftly repulsed. Their last invasion, in 1312, barely managed to cross the Euphrates before being forced to retreat. With Islam more and more in favor among the Mongol elite in Persia, and with Mamluk prosperity surely suggesting something about the virtues of having good neighbors, the il-khan saw the wisdom in changing his stance and suggested a treaty. And so in 1323, nearly a century after Chinggis Khan's first predations on the lands of Islam, the Mongols and Mamluks finally settled their differences and signed a lasting peace.

During this period, and in the decades that followed, the Franks of Cyprus were eager to avoid any hint of conflict with Mamluk Egypt. When the Cypriots did attack Muslims, it was to deal with the increasing threat posed by Turkish corsairs in the Aegean, far away from Egypt; at times these Aegean campaigns were justified as crusades and involved fleets from across Latin Europe; in one case, in 1344, just such a crusading fleet managed to defeat a Turkish fleet and capture the port of Izmir (Smyrna) from its amir. Other lands in Anatolia were made tributary to Cyprus. In all these campaigns it was essential for Cyprus to avoid a confrontation with Egypt—the king even went so far as to curtail crusade preaching in his kingdom in deference to local sentiment. This was not simply because any Mamluk-Cypriot war would likely result in a Frankish defeat but because by now the fortunes of Cyprus rested upon the steady flow of commerce to and from the Mamluk-controlled ports of the Levant and, above all, Alexandria. It wouldn't do to antagonize such powerful and generous neighbors.

Eventually, however, the live-and-let-live policy ran its course. King Peter I of Cyprus upped the ante, striking targets that threatened Cypriot shipping specifically, as with his capture of the Anatolian port of Antlaya in 1361. His interest in Egypt and his specific goal of capturing Alexandria was thus formed, perhaps unsurprisingly, in this mixed context of crusading and commerce.[43]

Certainly in Egypt his plans came as no great surprise. The chronicler al-Maqrizi, who has left one of the fullest account of Peter's activities, describes how for some months "the Alexandrians had been aware of the Franks' intention to raid them," tipped off perhaps by the assembly of the fleet (including some French, Venetian, Genoese, and Hospitaller forces) off of Rhodes as it waited for Peter's command. The governor of Alexandria dutifully sent word to the sultan in Cairo and an appeal for help, but "the government showed no interest in their affairs." And so the governor went on pilgrimage to Mecca, leaving his deputy to see to the city should the situation develop. It did.

Alexandrians were of course used to seeing Frankish ships sail into harbor; Western merchants had been a steady feature of the local economy for centuries. The Mamluk coast guard thus thought little of the line of Venetian sails that appeared headed for the harbor in early October 1365. But when these few ships were followed "by between seventy and eighty craft, both galleys and warships," the alarm was sounded. The gates of the city were shut, and the guard mounted the city walls: the city was under attack. At first, for days, the Franks seemed to do nothing except linger outside the harbor. Bedouin auxiliaries arrived to assist in the defense, and they headed for the city's famous lighthouse, which jutted out into the sea at some distance from the city. Other fighters followed them in the hopes of baiting the Franks to come in and fight. It all seemed so sporting and remote from the hum of the busy city that "traders and youths went out for amusement, taking no notice of the enemy." Finally "a good number of Muslims, both Bedouin and townspeople, had joined together at the lighthouse," and a Frankish galley sailed against them on intercept. At this the Muslims split up, one group of soldiers and townspeople staying to attack the galley while the other continued on to secure the lighthouse.

It was then that the Alexandrians learned what the Franks had been doing over the past few days: a contingent had slipped ashore under cover of night and secreted themselves in the cemetery outside the gates. These Franks emerged now from their hiding places among the tombs and "made a knavish charge on the Muslims" as the Franks in the ship rained arrows down upon the shore. The Muslims, soldiers and civilians, fled in panic to the city, many of them dying in the crush to get through the gate. Meanwhile the Franks aboard ship disembarked and captured the harbor, bringing their ships up to the city walls. Finding these denuded of guards, they set up ladders and scaled the walls into the city. Once within the walls this scouting force made a quick raid into the city, setting the shipyards ablaze, affixing a cross to one of its gates, and attacking another gate where a large crowd had stopped in a bottleneck in their attempt to escape the slaughter. Then they made their way back to their ships, "leaving the city and its contents open to the Franks."

The governor's deputy, who had been left to run the city, was obviously outmatched. As the Frankish scouting party was marauding through the city, he rounded up a group of Frankish merchants who had been conducting their business in the city and, confiscating the city treasury for safekeeping, fled with his prisoners for a neighboring town in the hope of leveraging a truce from a safe distance. The citizens of Alexandria were not as lucky. Later in the day King Peter himself made a triumphal entrance. This initiated a general plunder of the city and slaughter of its inhabitants. "So they continued, killing, taking prisoners and captives, plundering and burning from the forenoon of Friday to the early morning of Sunday." By then, however, a Mamluk army was approaching from Cairo to bring reckoning. It seems to have been this news that persuaded the Franks to collect their loot and captives and, having gutted the city's naval and commercial capacities, to sail back to Cyprus as quickly as they had come, "to flee like Satan flees when he hears the call to prayer."[44] Their occupation of Alexandria had lasted all of eight days.

The Mamluks did their best to repair the damage, mustering sailors and supplies to rebuild the fleet, for example, though this never seems to have been completed. The rank of the governorship of Alexandria was elevated in an effort to make it a more palatable position, and many of the Muslim prisoners were ransomed (using money confiscated from Frankish and native Christians in Syria and Egypt). But while Alexandria would recover in time, its medieval glory days were effectively over. The Black Death of the 1340s had taken an incalculable toll on the cities of the Near East, as elsewhere in the medieval world, and shifting trade routes made Syria, not Egypt, an ever more attractive destination for Frankish commerce.

If it accomplished anything, the sack of Alexandria at least wakened the Mamluks to the reality that they could not treat the Franks of Cyprus as a problem that could be left out of sight and therefore out of mind. Moreover the Mamluks weren't the only ones discomfited by these events, as the Cypriots' main trading rivals, Genoa and Venice, stood to gain nothing from the new scenario. And so it was upon them that the sultan now exerted all his diplomatic pressure in an attempt to secure a peace from Cyprus. The back-and-forth was a long and drawn-out affair but was not without some successes. The Venetians, for example, managed to convince Peter to redirect an assault on Mamluk-held Beirut toward the Turkish ports of Anatolia, and Peter agreed to receive the sultan's embassies from time to time.

It became clear, however, that Peter was simply buying time, for all the while these negotiations were taking place, the king was also organizing (in 1366) a new campaign against the Mamluk ports of Syria. With assistance from the Hospitallers of Rhodes, a fleet roughly the size of the one that had taken Alexandria was readied and set sail in January 1367. However, a bad winter storm battered the Frankish fleet, and, although a few ships managed to plunder the port of Tripoli, most straggled back to Cyprus without causing any damage. This Frankish debacle was exactly what the Mamluks needed for their negotiations, and so the sultan piled on the embassies to Peter's court to sue for peace. Peter made himself difficult to persuade, leading yet another series of raids on the Syrian coast that summer, in which he attacked Tripoli, Cilician Ayas, and Tartus among other places. At each successive raid, the Mamluk troops of Syria under the sultan's deputy decisively turned the Franks back. At Ayas the "lord of Rhodes"—presumably the leader of the Hospitallers—was killed and the king himself was injured.[45]

At length they returned to Cyprus. Diplomacy might have been expected to improve after 1369, when Peter was murdered in his sleep by three of his own knights, and so it did, but not before his successor sent a series of small raids along the coasts of Anatolia, Syria, and Egypt. But it didn't last. Cyprus had become a reckless rogue state of the sort that the commercially minded notables of Genoa, Venice, and even Hospitaller Rhodes could not abide. The new king was persuaded to rein in his activities against the Muslims and, in 1370, to ratify a peace treaty with Cairo.

For some fifty years the Mamluks and the Lusignans of Cyprus backed off from one another, preferring to enjoy the fruits of their common commercial interests and distracted by other concerns. For the

Mamluks, these included the Christian kingdom of Cilician Armenia, which was finally extinguished in 1375 with the sack of the capital, Sis, and the captivity of its royal family in Cairo. For the Lusignans, they included above all the Genoese, who invaded Famagusta and Nicosia in 1374 and made the island a tributary and Famagusta a Genoese enclave. In the interval Frankish pirates had become the terror of the seas, preying on Muslim and Byzantine shipping across the eastern Mediterranean. It appears that, by the 1420s, many were operating out of Famagusta, on Cyprus.

It was in this context that the Mamluks had their final revenge on Cyprus.[46] In 1424, in retaliation for attacks on Mamluk shipping off Egypt, the Mamluk sultan Barsbay (not to be confused with the earlier conquering sultan Baybars) sent three naval raids against the island. The first two were tentative probes: in the first, the Genoese governor of Famagusta encouraged the Mamluk raiders, and Limassol was sacked; for the second, Barsbay had ships built at Cairo's Nile shipyards at Bulaq and then sent to Tripoli to collect reinforcements. From there they sailed into Famagusta and sent raiding parties overland while the fleet mauled the coast before withdrawing. Finally, in 1426 came a full-scale invasion.

On July 3 they landed at what was left of Limassol, and a land army was dispatched toward the Frankish capital, Nicosia. Ibn Taghribirdi, a contemporary, noted the almost casual attitude of the troops, who wandered about "not in battle-array but like travelers," many unarmed, fully expecting the Franks to be waiting for them near Nicosia. They were thus startled to find a Frankish army led by the Lusignan king Janus bearing down upon them. The Mamluks stood fast. "They fought bitterly. Some of the company backed them up, others lagged behind." King Janus himself was captured and his army routed. The Mamluks pursued the Franks back to Nicosia, which they sacked, looting even the royal palace. A further defeat of a Frankish fleet nearby sealed the victory, and the expedition returned to Cairo. There the army and its captives marched in a triumphal procession to the Cairo citadel, and King Janus was received in humiliating fashion by the sultan. The Frankish merchant leaders resident in Egypt managed to collect enough money to ransom the king, but he was now obliged to become a vassal and his island kingdom a tributary state of the Mamluk sultan.

From this new low, the Lusignan house had farther still to sink. In 1460 the Mamluk sultan became involved in a succession dispute in Nicosia, but in 1489 the throne was ultimately seized by Venice, the last of the Lusignans (by marriage) abdicating in favor of military rule by a Venetian admiral. In 1490 the Mamluk sultan, richly recompensed, officially acknowledged Venice as the new lord of Cyprus, the last of the Crusader states of the east extinguished at the hands of a Frankish merchant republic, an indication perhaps that a new age with new priorities was on its way in Europe. While for those with a historical turn of mind this state of affairs must have generated its share of satisfaction in Egypt (and especially Alexandria), the Mamluk sultanate itself did not long outlast the kingdom of Cyprus. In 1517 the sultan of Cairo became the last medieval victim of an imperial force far greater than anything concocted in the cold and distant land of the Franks: the Ottoman Turks.

- 9 -

Let Them Be Our Eulogists

O SMAN HAD A dream. The chieftain of a small but successful
band of Turcoman warriors in western Anatolia, Osman, like
his followers, styled himself a *ghazi*, or frontier fighter, who
battled against the foes of Islam. These were, in his case, not yet the
Franks of Latin Christendom but first and foremost the Byzantine
Greeks. In 1261 the Greeks had retaken Constantinople from the
Franks, who had occupied it during the Fourth Crusade, and reclaimed
what was left of their ancient empire. By Osman's day the Byzantines
were the only traditional land-based empire in Anatolia, the Saljuq sultans of Rum having been extinguished by their Mongol overlords in
1307. In the vacuum that resulted many claimed power, but few held
onto it. Out there, on the very edge of the Islamic world, Osman
seemed to be just one of many chieftains, or *beys*, fighting the Byzantines
(or one another) to gain plunder to enjoy in this world and religious
merit in the next. Yet there was something special about Osman. One
summer night around 1300, while returning to his people's pasture-
lands after a great battle, "Osman Ghazi prayed, and for a moment he
wept. He was overcome by drowsiness and he lay down and slept. Now
in that vicinity there dwelt a certain holy shaykh named Edebali.... As
Osman Ghazi slept, he saw in his dream that a moon arose out of this
holy man's breast and entered Osman Ghazi's breast. Then a tree
sprouted out of Osman Ghazi's navel, and the shadow of the tree covered the entire world. In its shadow, there were mountains, with streams

issuing from the foot of each mountain. And from these flowing streams some people drank, and some watered gardens, and some caused fountains to flow."[1] Troubled, Osman went to visit the holy man who appeared in his dream and told him all he had seen. "Osman, my son!" the shaykh said, "sovereignty has been granted to you and your descendants." Metaphorically shading the entire world under his dominion, Osman and his progeny were destined to shower its people, its economy, and its civilization with their munificence. Or so at least later generations wanted to think. 'Ashiqpashazade, the chronicler who recorded this imperial creation myth, wrote centuries after the fact—toward the end of the fifteenth century—by which time the dynasty (called Ottoman after its dreaming founder) was close to realizing this vision.

The path to that realization involved transforming the nomadic tribal confederation of ghazi warriors into a sedentary empire. To do so required not just fighting (and defeating) the Byzantines, who fell in 1453, but also other Muslim polities, including the Mamluk sultanate, which fell to Ottoman armies in 1517. In this setting conflict with the Christians of the Balkans and the Franks of Latin Europe—who still entertained plans of crusade to retake the Holy Land—was also part of the equation.[2] But Osman's descendants had first to leave Anatolia.

Into Europe

After the death of Osman Ghazi in 1324, his son Orhan oversaw his house's most crucial territorial gains from the Ottoman capital of Bursa; with these came a new relationship with the Byzantines. During this time Turkish activities on land were aided by what have been called "sea ghazis," Turkish corsairs operating out of the ports of southern Anatolia, who did their best to harass Christian shipping in the Aegean and eastern Mediterranean; these were the same pirates who caused the Franks of Cyprus such grief.[3] Orhan and the Turkish mercenary groups who rallied around him had an even greater ally in the persistent divisions within the Byzantine ruling house. Orhan deftly inserted himself into the conflicts, supporting John VI Cantacuzenus against his rivals in Constantinople.

Even before John gained the throne in 1347, he relied almost exclusively upon the Ottomans as his muscle to use against his foes. In 1346 and again in 1350 he ferried Ottoman troops across the Bosporos Straits into Thrace to thwart Serbian troops who were advancing upon

Byzantine lands in Greece. John is thus usually singled out by historians as the man who opened up Europe to Ottoman conquest, much as Ibn al-Thumna became the fall guy for the loss of Islamic Sicily. That is not really fair: these were brief campaigns, and the Ottomans swiftly returned to Anatolia after defeating their foes and collecting their plunder.

Far more important for Ottoman connections to Europe was the Venetian-Genoese war of 1350–55, during which the Byzantines joined forces with the Venetians and, of all the possible players, the Ottomans allied themselves with Genoa—apparently the first treaty conducted between the Ottomans and a European power. Thanks to Ottoman military assistance, the Genoese were able to wrest concessions from the Byzantines, including a permanent base and trading colony at Pera on the Straits; thanks to Genoese ships, the Ottomans could now cross the Straits safely whenever they needed. Both allies benefited from the commercial links between Genoese Pera and Ottoman Bursa, the latter emerging as a hub for the silk trade from Iran and Central Asia.

In 1352 civil war broke out again between rival Byzantine princes, and Cantacuzenus dropped his Venetian allies for the more reliable military backing of the Ottomans. His rival, John V Paleologus, was supported by the Serbs. Between them, these two rival Byzantine forces tore Thrace apart over the next four years, the Ottomans nearly always dominating their Serbian adversaries. It was in this context that Ottoman troops and their families chose to stay on in Thrace and expand Ottoman control into the Balkans, a province they usually called Rumelia. Among the towns of Rumelia that were captured was Gallipoli (thanks to a timely earthquake that collapsed the city walls), which now gave the Ottomans control of secure landing points on both sides of the Straits. As Ottoman forces occupied more and more Byzantine territory, Cantacuzenus was pilloried as a traitor to Christianity. Soon enough he was ousted from power by his old rival John V Paleologus. The Paleologi would remain in power in Constantinople until that city too fell.

Paleologus wasted no time in taking action against the Ottomans, even agreeing to papal overtures to unite the Greek and Latin Churches in return for military aid to shore up his evaporating empire. The pope dutifully sent letters to all the Frankish principals in the region: Venice, Genoa, Cyprus, and the Hospitallers, based on Rhodes. Everyone had an excuse not to get involved. The Ottoman occupation of Thrace seemed unstoppable, as Orhan sent wave after wave of Ottoman troops into Europe to settle and expand the frontiers. This was Christian

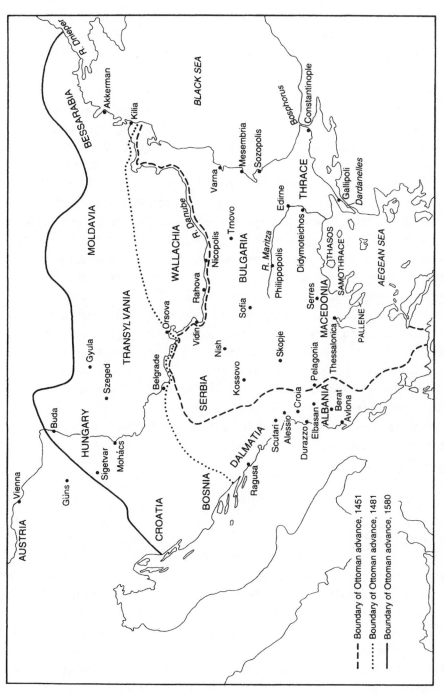

Map 10 Ottoman Campaigns in the Balkans. From Norman Housley, *The Later Crusades: From Lyons to Alcazar, 1274–1580* (Oxford: Oxford University Press, 1992), xiii, map 3.

territory, however, and it would take more than a few garrisons to bring it to heel. As ʿAshiqpashazade put it, quoting Suleiman, the Ottoman prince in charge of the campaigns in Thrace, in a message to his father, "A great number of people of the Islamic faith are needed here so that the conquered fortresses can be settled and the country around them be made to flourish."[4] Orhan was in agreement with this, according to ʿAshiqpashazade, and as a result "Islam was so strengthened that whenever they attacked, the infidels were unable to resist them." It was only when Greek pirates managed to capture Orhan's teenage son and hold him hostage that the sultan was forced into making concessions with the Byzantines, including an end to all hostilities in Thrace.

The peace was short-lived. In 1359 the pope managed to throw together a crusade of sorts. The papal legate arrived with a small contingent of Hospitallers, Genoese, Venetians, and Englishmen. They made a raid on an Ottoman port in the Dardanelles, but the Ottomans had set up an ambush and came close to wiping them out to a man. In Thrace, Prince Murad had taken over command and reenergized the Ottoman campaigns there, still acting ostensibly in the name of the ousted Cantacuzenus. In 1359 he was threatening Constantinople itself, the first Ottoman attack on the city. But the next few years were spent subduing the rest of Thrace, extending Ottoman influence westward along the old Roman highway, the Via Egnatia, which stretched from Constantinople to the Adriatic. The reversal in the regional balance of power could not be better illustrated: the Ottomans were driving westward using the very invasion route favored by the Crusaders when, once upon a time, they had first marched to the east (Map 10).

The Balkan Tangle

At Orhan's death in 1362, his son Murad was named sultan and was obliged to return to Bursa. For the next decade Ottoman ghazis did their best in Thrace, aided by the fractious nature of Christian politics in the Balkans, with Catholic Hungary now emerging as the major Christian power in the region. Indeed Hungary under the Angevin king Louis was endeavoring to create its own Danubian empire, eclipsing the once-mighty Byzantine Empire, which by this point was virtually limited to the city of Constantinople. With the backing of the papacy, Hungary took upon itself the mantle of the defender of Latin Christendom against the Ottoman menace; if the heretic Greeks or others should fall in the process, no tears would be shed. Added to this mix were the Orthodox lands of Bulgaria in the north and the Serbs in the west and the commercial empires of the Venetians and the Genoese in the Aegean, all of which provided the Ottomans with ample opportunities to pit rival against rival and to gain vassals in the process. Thus in 1371, when Ottoman ghazis crushed the Serbs during a surprise attack at Chernomen, the Serbs agreed to pay tribute and to supply troops to the sultan. In the wake of this defeat, rather than join the Hungarians as brother Christians, the Bulgarian czar and finally the Byzantine emperor likewise recognized Ottoman overlordship; a Hungarian crusade was clearly felt to be a greater threat to the Orthodox than was the lighter hand of Ottoman suzerainty.

As for the sultan Murad, his activities at this time were above all focused on securing and expanding Ottoman territories in Anatolia. By 1383 the eastern front appeared sufficiently calmed and the alignment of the various powers in the Balkans was sufficiently favorable that Murad could safely cross the Straits with an army, establishing his headquarters at the old Byzantine city of Adrianople (Edirne). From there, in 1385, the Ottomans advanced into western Thrace and Albania and north into Moravian Serbia, capturing Nis, the birthplace of Constantine the Great. The Serbian prince Lazar surrendered to Murad and agreed to pay tribute and to send a contingent of troops to fight for the sultan.

At this juncture, however, Murad was called back to Anatolia to defend Ottoman lands against a Turkish rival. He soundly defeated them, the new Serbian troops fighting bravely for their Ottoman lord. However, it seems that these Serbian troops, being mere vassals, had not been treated with the honor they felt they deserved. Upon their return to Serbia, Lazar broke his agreement with Murad and renounced his allegiance. Encouraged by his audacity, other local lords joined him, including the rulers of Bulgaria and Bosnia, and Prince Lazar followed this up by becoming a vassal of the king of Hungary.

Murad could not let a recalcitrant vassal like Lazar go unpunished. His actions with Hungary and the other Balkan lords were openly provocative. He would have to be crushed. Supported by Christian and Muslim contingents, Murad's army neutralized Bulgaria and then, on June 15, 1389, poured into Serbia toward Kosovo Field, near Pristina. Murad's army probably numbered about twenty-five thousand to thirty thousand men. To meet them, Lazar brought with him the full strength of the Serbian military, aided by Bosnians, Croatians, Franks, Hungarians, and others: twenty thousand men at the very most. The Ottomans made short work of them. The details of the battle, which assumed epic resonance in later Serbian tradition, are obscure, but the outcome is not. Both Lazar and Murad were killed during the battle, and Serbia submitted to Ottoman suzerainty.[5]

The new sultan, Beyazid, gained a nickname, Yildirim, "The Thunderbolt," as the swift punisher of upstart Balkan kings. But before he did so, he was obliged to tend to Anatolia. The death of his father, Murad, meant that certain Anatolian vassals had an opportunity to exploit, and so Beyazid left Kosovo almost immediately to subdue these rebellious beys in the Ottoman heartlands. In the process he expanded and consolidated Ottoman rule over the western half of Anatolia. In 1393, his rear secured, Beyazid returned to Rumelia to remind his Balkan vassals of their loyalties; some had become overmighty in his absence. Ottoman armies roamed freely through Greece, Hungary, and Wallachia. By 1395 all of Bulgaria had been conquered and Wallachia became a tributary province under a vassal prince. Beyazid garrisoned forts along the Danube, and Sigismund, the king of Hungary, knew they all looked threateningly at him. In such a position, and with crucial Venetian and Byzantine backing, he called upon the papacy for help.

In the spring of 1396 a small crusader army arrived from the west to assist Hungary and its allies. The Ottoman troops in Rumelia were strong, but Beyazid was himself besieging Constantinople to hem in the Byzantines. So, rather than engage the Franks in the open field, the Ottomans delayed them at strongholds and behind city walls until the sultan could come at the head of his army. The Franks made slow progress; by September 12 they were bogged down at Nicopolis (Nikopol), a small but nearly impregnable Bulgarian town on the lower Danube. Its Ottoman garrison kept the crusaders occupied for two weeks without giving way (Fig. 12). Finally, Beyazid the Thunderbolt arrived via Edirne, his Serbian vassals having joined him along the way.[6] The size of the armies on both sides varies wildly in the historical accounts; the most sober estimate puts them roughly evenly matched, at about fifteen thousand men each. The crusaders were probably exhausted, having already been encamped in a two-week siege (even if it was one that, according to contemporary accounts, involved a good deal of feasting and gaming). The Turks, however, were joined by their fresher Serbian allies, and these troops proved crucial in the final phase of the battle. The Hungarian troops were forced into a rout, and Sigismund took refuge in one of the Venetian ships blockading the Danube below the town. From there a formal surrender was negotiated.

By every account it was a cruel little war. Among the Frankish prisoners captured during the final rout was a young Bavarian page name Johannes Schiltberger, who later wrote a memoir of his decades in captivity. His account, though broadly hostile, leaves little doubt about the harshness of the confrontation. The casualties involved were high, many of them prisoners killed on both sides—in open contradiction to the immemorial customs of war. Schiltberger himself survived only thanks to his youth, and he went on to serve (more or less dutifully) as a runner for Beyazid and accompanied him on the rest of his campaigns in Rumelia and Anatolia.[7] Although the Nicopolis crusade was small by comparison to other Frankish invasions, the sting of defeat, combined with other distractions in Europe, kept back for decades any further such coalition against the Ottomans. As for Beyazid, he maintained the pressure on Wallachia, invading it in the following year and again in 1400, but with no success. As it happened, the Ottomans too became distracted with their own struggles, and Hungary, so close to feeling the full force of the Thunderbolt's anger, was saved from an unexpected quarter.

The man who prevented the Ottomans from invading Hungary was, in fact, a Muslim warlord named Timur, or Timur-Lenk (Timur the Lame), as he was known, thanks to an injury he had received to his leg. He is best known in the West as Tamerlane, the very emblem of the conquering Oriental despot in early modern Europe (thanks to the embellishments of Christopher Marlowe and G. F. Handel). That reputation was due in no small part to his dealings with Beyazid, whose dramatic encounter with Timur captured the imaginations of many a librettist, to say nothing of the historians. A man who could single-handedly stop the Turkish Menace must surely be someone to reckon with.

In fact, however, the fledgling Ottoman sultanate under Beyazid was the least of Timur's concerns, at this point a marginal statelet on the margins of his massive empire. Beginning in the 1390s Timur, himself of Turco-Mongol origin, had set out from his capital of Samarqand in central Asia (currently Uzbekistan) with no less a goal than to restore the glory of the Mongol Empire of Chinggis Khan. Given the destruction that Hungary endured under the original Mongol invasions in the thirteenth century, Timur's motives would not have comforted the Hungarians in the fourteenth, had they even known them. But they proved a powerful goad for the Turkish and Mongol tribes who came to form the bulk of Timur's followers. Hardly a year passed when Timur and his troops were not active somewhere on campaign, in Iran, Iraq, India, Syria, Central Asia, and the Caucasus.

In 1400 Ottoman Anatolia's turn came up when Timur captured the Ottoman town of Sivas; in 1401 he was fighting (and defeating) the Mamluks in Syria and being interviewed by the great scholar of the age, the Maghribi philosopher of history, Ibn Khaldun (with Timur doing his own bit of subtle interviewing); in July 1402 he returned to Anatolia to take on the Ottomans and met them at Ankara, where, in a catastrophe, the Ottomans were routed and Beyazid himself was taken prisoner (and with him his redoubtable page Johannes Schiltberger, who went on to serve Timur and Timur's sons). The sultan died in captivity a few months later, perhaps at his own hand in despair at the shame he had brought to the once-proud house of Osman Ghazi.[8]

In the Marketplace of Death

On all these fronts Timur's conquests were visited with terrible destruction and brutality, evoking the massacre and rapine of his Mongol forebears. But as a Muslim, Timur should have known better: terror like this was no way to maintain the Circle of Equity. And indeed his empire, unlike that of Chinggis Khan, did not outlast his death in 1405 but instead disintegrated into various (but glorious) Timurid successor kingdoms or else reverted to powers that had held sway before. Anatolia, never fully absorbed by Timur, returned to Ottoman control, but not easily. It would take nearly two decades of civil war before one Ottoman prince could emerge as undisputed ruler of the Ottoman domains and to once again set Turkish sights on the Balkans and the Frankish lands farther west. This was Murad II (d. 1451).

Murad was keenly aware of the fact that he had inherited a two-front empire. As long as Anatolia occupied his attention, he could not easily fight the Christians in Rumelia; so long as his eastern front was quiet, the Balkans could remain his focus. In their campaigns in the Balkans, the Ottomans had principally to deal with the Byzantines, the Venetians, and Hungary.[9] In March 1429 Ottoman naval raids in the Aegean and attacks on Venetian possessions in Greece culminated when a Turkish fleet appeared before the city of Thessalonica, a major Byzantine city recently occupied by the Venetians. A blockade ensued and the city slowly starved. The Venetians cut off Ottoman shipping across the Straits and even tried to foment rebellions in Anatolia, but it was not enough to distract Murad. Eventually the starving populace of Thessalonica rose up against their foreign Venetian occupiers, and in March 1430 Murad officially took control of the city. The capture of

Thessalonica meant that the Ottomans now had a relatively free hand in the Balkans and could concentrate their attention on Rumelia's northwestern frontiers. Albania in particular became the principal theater of Ottoman-Venetian rivalry, as the Ottomans saw control of the Adriatic shore as a prerequisite for any attacks on Italy. This was a wake-up call for the papacy, whose renewed interest in the crusade was now decidedly less about any high-flying plans to reclaim the Holy Land and more about neutralizing this direct threat to Italy. Although Ottoman control of northern Albania (from 1433) was relatively stable under their vassal John Kastriote, the south was wracked by rebellion and remained a flashpoint for much of the fifteenth century.

By this point Murad seemed to prefer direct Ottoman annexation over the temporary comfort of ruling by vassal. Albania was difficult to rule in any other way, but Serbia, long a subjugated vassal state of the sultans, was ripe for annexation and, moreover, was strategically close to the Ottomans' principal Frankish enemy, Hungary. If the Ottomans were to invade Hungary, Serbia could not be left in the hands of a mere vassal. Murad began not by force but by diplomacy, marrying the daughter of the Serbian king in 1435. In 1439 he took Zvornik and Srebrenica and brought northern Serbia under his direct control. Hungary was next.

The timing could not have been better. With his Muslim foes in Anatolia recently subdued and the Byzantines completely closed up in Constantinople, Murad's rear was secure. And with much of Albania, Serbia, and the rest of the Balkans under his control, there was little to distract him from a full-fledged assault across the Danube into Hungary. Indeed events across the Danube showed that there was every reason to seize the moment: a peasant revolt had recently rocked the kingdom, and the king himself had died, leaving Hungary in the grip of civil war. Yet, despite the propitious timing, Murad could make no ground. In 1440 his siege of Belgrade, the vital gateway to central Europe, failed, and attacks launched into the kingdom in 1441 and 1442 were turned back by the armies under command of the Hungarian lord John Hunyadi.

These Ottoman failures in Hungary set Frankish hearts afire with hopes for a renewed crusade, with Hunyadi the emerging hero. In 1439 the Byzantine emperor, John VIII, had accepted the union of the Greek and Latin Churches in return for military aid from the Franks. Hungary, Venice, and others agreed to the plan as well; the Franks even reached out to one of the Ottomans' Muslim rivals in Anatolia to distract Murad when necessary. But the timing was off: Murad quickly pacified Anatolia and was able to meet Hunyadi and the Hungarian troops as they cut their way across the Balkans. At the Zlatitsa Pass in December 1443 Murad's army stopped the Hungarian advance. It was grim fighting in the snows of Zlatitsa; Murad's cavalrymen deserted him, and he held the pass only thanks to the weariness of the Hungarians and the steadfastness of the Janissaries, a relatively new corps of elite infantry who served as the sultan's bodyguard. It was not so much an Ottoman victory as a retreat on both sides. And it was more than enough to convince both sides to agree to a peace. At Edirne in the gentler summer of 1444, Murad and Vladislav of Hungary signed a ten-year truce and Vladislav ceded a number of frontier forts to Murad's Serbian vassal.

It was therefore at the height of Ottoman influence, their Hungarian foes humbled, that the unthinkable happened. The truce secured, Murad, exhausted and saddened by the recent death of his favorite son, abdicated the throne in favor of his twelve-year-old heir, Mehmed. For the Franks, this was an opportunity that could not be passed up, truce or no truce.[10] The pope gladly absolved Vladislav of Hungary of his oath of truce, arguing that an oath made with an infidel was no oath at all. So emboldened, in mid-September 1444 the Frankish army, led by Vladislav and Hunyadi, crossed into Ottoman territory near Belgrade and made its way across Rumelia toward Varna on the Black Sea coast, the aim being to coordinate the attack with a fleet of Byzantine, Venetian, and Burgundian ships that had gone on ahead to block the Straits. Terror at the advancing Franks spread throughout Ottoman Rumelia. In the capital, Edirne, the palace ordered the digging of a moat, and the viziers began removing their valuables from the city to safer havens. Among the common folk a preacher of a heretical Muslim sect emerged, claiming the superiority of Jesus over Muhammad. While the movement was quickly crushed, it only added to the sense of foreboding in the Ottoman capital.

At this point the viziers in the young sultan's palace realized the gravity of the situation: Ottoman troops from Anatolia would be blocked from providing support in Rumelia, and the Franks would soon have mastery over the Black Sea. They needed Murad back. Without hesitating, Murad returned to the throne to lead the Ottoman army against the Franks. By splitting his army in two and procuring the crucial aid of Genoese ships, he foiled the Frankish blockade. On November 9 the Christians besieged and captured Varna. The next day Murad arrived to confront them. In the principal Muslim account of this battle, King Vladislav soon realized the futility of his position and that, as a breaker of oaths, he was doomed to defeat. He also blamed the Byzantine emperor for leading him on and vowed revenge: "Fine! Whatever happens to us and the Turks, today is the day. We either win or lose. But after this is over, I shall drag the wretch called the Emperor before the Pope of Rome and I shall denounce him to the world. If he resists I shall send an army and bring [Constantinople] crashing about his ears."[11]

Nonetheless Vladislav and his army emerged from their camp, and soon battle lines were drawn. The sultan's Anatolian troops were repulsed and bloodied early on; the Rumelian troops, close as they were to their homelands, were the first to break and run, leaving the Anatolian troops to hold the field. Eventually they rallied and returned to defend Murad, surrounded by his Janissaries. The fighting was, by all accounts, bitter and fierce: "The two armies clashed all along the line, and that day there was a battle such as words cannot describe. As the fight increased in fury, both the troops of Islam and the infidels displayed such zeal that, in the marketplace of death, father could not recognize son nor son father, and the angels in heaven and the fish in the sea wondered at the fury of the fight."[12]

In the fracas John Hunyadi was injured and forced to withdraw, and King Vladislav himself was killed. It was this last action that seems to have caused the Hungarians to rout, and Murad—himself in command of only a few troops by now—was able to win the day. The Ottoman troops pursued the fleeing enemy into the nearby hills to take captives and kill any who resisted, "bringing them down like autumn leaves."[13] Murad urged restraint and called his men back: "They have done enough to prove their manhood. If one or two of the infidels who are as low as dust succeed in extricating themselves from these lands…let them go. Let them return to their own countries and tell of the miracles they encountered at the hands of the community of Muhammad. Let them be our eulogists."[14]

The last survivors barricaded themselves behind their wagons and positioned cannon to decimate anyone who approached, a fine example of a "wagon-fort" (*wagenburg*), or what the Turks called a *tabur-cengi*. Here Murad was calmly advised to avoid a direct onslaught; instead he ringed the encampment with his own men, well out of range. The size of the surrounding army convinced the defenders of the hopelessness of the situation, and they surrendered. Their treasure was sent as a gift to the young Mehmed in Edirne, since the little prince had been obliged to miss the fighting.

The impact of Murad's victory was immediately felt. Letters of good tidings, accompanied by parades of Hungarian captives, were sent throughout the Ottoman domains and to the sultan's peers and neighbors. Hungary plummeted into a succession crisis. Ottoman control in the Balkans was made tighter and more secure than ever before, though raids from Hungary and Wallachia continued to be a nuisance. In 1448 Murad invaded Albania and Serbia, where the Ottomans once again triumphed at Kosovo.

But the clearest victim of Varna was, as King Vladislav had promised, the Byzantine emperor in Constantinople. More and more the Greeks and other Balkan peoples were becoming used to the idea of living under Muslim rule rather than the heavy hand of Venetians or Hungarians. This was a pragmatic sentiment that was to prove immensely useful to the Ottomans in their last great conquest.

The Falcon and the Crow

In 1451 Murad died in Edirne after an illness. His son Mehmed II immediately succeeded him. Things had changed since Mehmed had ruled as a worrisome boy sultan who had to be helped out by his father when the Franks struck at Varna. The young Mehmed was now his own man, and very much a capable sultan, his activities against Ottoman enemies during his long reign (1451–81) gaining him the epithet Fatih Sultan Mehmed, "Mehmed the Conqueror."[15]

It is clear from his actions that Mehmed had the final conquest of Constantinople as his goal from the outset, though the start was not auspicious.[16] Soon after succeeding to the throne, it looked as if it was the overwhelmed boy sultan who had returned, and Ottoman enemies in the Balkans, including the Byzantine emperor Constantine XI (1448–53), made small but successful inroads into Ottoman territory. But Mehmed soon showed his true colors by acting quickly at the diplomatic level, confirming his father's treaties in the Balkans and with Venice, settling his disputes with local rulers in Anatolia, and reorganizing his sometimes fractious army. In 1452 he completed construction of a fortress on the European side of the Bosporos, called Rumeli Hisar, the twin of an older fortress on the Anatolian side, called Anadolu Hisar. Constantinople was thus cut off from supplies from the Black Sea, and Ottoman troops could now cross the Straits as needed. Mehmed's men cleared the area around the city of its villages, causing many to petition the Byzantine emperor, who aptly characterized his relationship to his new neighbor by saying, "Neighborliness between them and us is the neighborliness of the falcon and the crow."[17]

By early April 1453 the city was surrounded and under siege, the Straits were closed, and Mehmed's massive, carefully regimented army and terrifying artillery were plain for all to see. With his target already so nicely trussed, Mehmed sent a messenger to allow Emperor Constantine the easy route of surrender, by offering the security of the inhabitants' lives and property in return. The offer was refused. The Genoese, from their colony of Pera, had no such scruples, however. Their leader eagerly pledged his neutrality, all the while supplying both the sultan and the emperor with men and materiel. The Venetians, no doubt goaded by this display of Genoese backsliding, sided with Byzantium and made much of providing soldiers to help man the walls during what many saw as the last defense of Christendom.

But Constantinople, isolated, surrounded, and out-gunned, was still no simple nut to crack. Mehmed's attempt to mine under the walls near the Blachernae Palace was a dismal failure, and his sappers were burned to death in their tunnels. When he sent a small fleet to intercept some Genoese merchantmen making for harbor in the Golden Horn (no doubt carrying supplies for the Greeks), his own ships proved an embarrassment and found themselves under fire and entangled until the weather changed and the Genoese were able to flee. Even his vaunted cannon were doing little against Constantinople's mighty walls. In the few spots where the original walls collapsed, the defenders were able to repel his soldiers and fill the gaps with earthworks that were almost as impenetrable. The defense of the city was like a knot that could not be untangled. Cannon were unreliable, slow-acting, fickle allies, and where a breach made in one stretch of the wall might distract defenders from another, there was never enough time to take advantage before the distraction passed. The Golden Horn, leading to the city's harbor and sea walls, was blocked by a chain and a fleet of Venetian ships. Though morale among the defenders was clearly at an ebb, the siege was at a standstill.

It was then, in late April, that Mehmed showed his mettle by unbinding the knot of Constantinople's defenses with beautiful simplicity, Gordion-style. While his ships could not sail through the mouth of the Golden Horn, they *could* go around it, if in unconventional fashion. Over the next few weeks Mehmed ordered his men to begin felling trees from his anchorage at Diplokionion clear across the stretch of land north of Pera, clearing an *overland* path from the Bosporos to the inner waters of the Golden Horn. By laying the fallen timber (now greased and oiled) like rollers, he had teams of men drag some seventy ships through this makeshift portage and deposit them in the Golden

Horn; the defenders could only watch in dismay. The Venetian flotilla guarding the mouth of the Golden Horn must have felt especially vulnerable, but the Turkish fleet did not stir. This was not because the fleet was wary of tangling with the Venetians but because it had already accomplished its mission: defenders from the city's land walls now poured into the harbor area to defend the sea walls along the Golden Horn. The defense of Constantinople was now dangerously overstretched. In late May it snapped.

By then the Ottomans had managed to fill in part of the moat that had been dug prior to the siege and had sufficiently pulverized stretches of the land walls so that they could be scaled. Before dawn on May 29, Mehmed sent a first wave of troops—mostly drawn from his Christian allies—to do the ugly business of scaling and clearing the outer land walls, where the defense was known to be hottest. These troops arrived with the unwelcome companion of Ottoman cannon fire from behind them, which must have decimated them as much as it cleared the walls of the enemy. The defense held, even against a fierce assault by Mehmed's Janissaries, and might have continued holding had not the leader of the Venetian troops on the walls been wounded and dragged away from the defense. This was a terrible blow to the morale of the defenders, and when some of Mehmed's men captured a small and little-known gateway that gave them access to the high walls near the Blachernae Palace, it was over.

The siege of the greatest city in Christendom had lasted a mere fifty-four spring days. The defenders, aware now of the loss that overwhelmed them, flooded back to the inner walls, seeking any passage into the city proper and hopefully to the harbor. Many were trampled in the panic. With the Janissaries leading the way, Mehmed's troops tore through the city at their heels. About four thousand were said to have been killed, among them Constantine XI, lost in the crowd, the last emperor of New Rome.

The city was given over to the traditional three days' pillage. Despite the fact that Mehmed had posted guards at the major sites in the city, Ottoman troops made off with piles of Byzantine treasures looted from homes and churches, and thousands of prisoners were taken from those who had not been able to flee or ransom themselves. Once hostilities had ceased, Mehmed made a triumphal procession into the city, ashamed at the level of destruction and pillage. He and his bodyguard made their way to Hagia Sophia, the great domed church that was one of the wonders of Byzantine architecture (though much-neglected at the time), soon to be adapted into a mosque and a jewel of Ottoman religious building. There he prostrated himself in the dust in gratitude to God for procuring this great victory, foretold in prophecies, coveted by kings. On the first Friday after the conquest the Muslims held communal prayers in Hagia Sophia for the first time and invoked the name of Sultan Mehmed from the pulpit. Mehmed and his successors would spend their reigns adorning his city, Istanbul, as it now known, with palaces and mosques and madrasas and repopulating it with Christian, Muslim, and Jewish subjects. By 1500 it was the largest city in Europe, and a true cosmopolis, the final ingredient needed to realize Osman's dream and transform the Ottoman house from a confederation of rough ghazi warriors into a fully fledged world empire.

The Fate of Islam in Sicily

Even as the early Ottomans were opening up a new front against the Franks in the Balkans, the area of the oldest Frankish assaults, Sicily, was definitively lost to Islamdom. After the Normans finalized the capture of the island in 1091, but prior to their short-lived conquests in North Africa, the Muslims of Norman Sicily were a subjected population but a more or less docile one. The pressures of conversion and emigration certainly thinned the ranks of the Muslim population under Norman rule, but Muslims remained a vital part of the local economy and the thriving and diverse society of what is often called Sicily's golden age (Fig. 13). After the Almohad reconquest of Norman North Africa, however, the Muslim subjects of Sicily's kings faced vicious recriminations from elements of the Sicilian Christian elite who found fault with how King William and his eunuchs and familiars handled the whole African adventure. It was the men of the palace in particular who were thought to have lost North Africa, who had ruled it too softly, and who were widely believed to be crypto-Muslims anyway.

In 1161 a mob broke into the prison at Palermo and released the prisoners there, sacking the royal palace. Some leading men of the palace were murdered, and the king was even briefly held captive by his own coreligionists. The mob reserved its fury for the Muslims of the city, and the violence soon spilled outside the walls. Forced by royal decree to disarm in the previous year, the Muslims of Palermo were an easy target for gangs seeking a scapegoat for Norman losses in Africa. Eventually the Muslims under attack abandoned their homes near the palace and fled to a protected suburb, where they fended off their attackers until the violence was quelled. In the east of the island more pogroms were carried out, forcing most of the Muslims out of the area altogether and into the rural southern and western reaches of the island, where the Muslim population became more and more concentrated.[18]

By the mid-1180s, when the Andalusi pilgrim Ibn Jubayr passed through the island, the Muslims of Sicily could be depicted, for all the island's wonders, as a dwindling subject population ground down into poverty and thinned out by conversion, assimilation, and flight.[19] On the one hand, Sicily under the Norman king William II, despite certain discomforts such as taxes, seemed at first glance to be a civilized and tolerant place: "Their King, William, is admirable for his just conduct, and the use he makes of the industry of the Muslims, and for choosing eunuch pages who all, or nearly all, concealing their faith, yet hold firm to the Muslim divine law. He has much confidence in Muslims, relying on them for his affairs, and the most important matters."[20]

On the other hand, we should bear in mind that Ibn Jubayr's most proximate point of comparison was the rather more brutal setting of the Crusader states of the Syrian coast, which he had just left. Moreover, by the end of his three-month stay on the island, he had had the opportunity to experience Muslim life outside the major cities of Messina and Palermo, particularly in the western part of the island at and around Trápani. There he could observe the dire transformations affecting the Muslims of Sicily that were obscured by the pageantry and theater of the Norman court. Here, he claimed with alarm, the delights of Frankish culture were tempting Muslims into conversion, thereby fragmenting families, the true bearers of Muslim identity. Moreover the Normans placed such steep financial and professional demands on Muslim elites that some, he claimed, were effectively forced to convert. One such local notable told Ibn Jubayr he would prefer to be sold as a slave in a Muslim land rather than suffer the humiliations of Christian servitude. The interfaith trappings and suggestions of a thriving and tolerated Muslim population were, it turned out, a mirage. For all that the Normans aped the cultural cosmopolitanism of their Muslim neighbors in the Mediterranean, their Muslim subjects knew exactly what the future promised.[21]

It must have been partly in response to these negative trends that some elements of the Muslim population in the west decided to rise in revolt upon the death of King William II in 1189.[22] Muslim sources are silent on these events, but it appears that after the revolt was quashed by Tancred, William's successor, many of the Muslims abandoned their lands and fled to the hills, from which, under a handful of different leaders, they raided the lowland plains around Palermo and forced Tancred to buy their surrender.

Having reconstituted themselves as a political force on the island, the Muslims of Sicily also made themselves vulnerable to the larger political currents that were sweeping the final days of Norman Sicily, when the island was contested between the Hohenstaufen Holy Roman emperors and the papacy. Thus in 1199, when the imperial seneschal Markward invaded Sicily at Trápani, he gained control of western Sicily by allying himself with the scattered Muslims of the region. His opponent, the Crusade-promoting pope Innocent III, predictably condemned Markward as "another Saladin" and called for a Crusade against him and, by extension, his Muslim allies on Sicily.

Papal forces defeated Markward in battle, but Innocent III was careful to tactfully negotiate the fealty of the now fiercely independent Muslim enclaves of the west and to gain their support for the claims of the new king, Frederick II. Ultimately the Muslims conceded to these political realities, though resistance in the west continued to disturb Hohenstaufen rule on the island. Only after Frederick was crowned as the new Holy Roman emperor in 1220 could he turn his attention to his Muslim problem on Sicily. Despite Frederick's famously cozy reception and Orientalist theatrics before the Muslim elites of the Ayyubid Near East, at home on Sicily he had no need to court opinion. No exchanges of intellectual puzzles with the literati here, no misty-eyed defense of the muezzin's call: just the armies of the Holy Roman emperor hammering at those of his Muslim subjects who resisted. The leader of the resistance was one Ibn ʿAbbad, who styled himself "commander of the Muslims in Sicily" on his coinage—the minting of which was itself a brazen claim for authority. The few Muslim sources that mention his revolt are contradictory, but it appears that the last Muslim strongholds of the resistance had fallen by 1223. Although Ibn ʿAbbad was killed (perhaps by a Frankish ruse, or perhaps beaten and kicked to death by Frederick himself), some sources indicate that his daughter (who is left unnamed) continued the resistance but, in despair, committed suicide without any other Muslim ruler lifting a finger to help the cause. Even as fiction, the anecdote is a telling representation of the political fortunes of Sicily's Muslims under the "enlightened" Emperor Frederick II.[23]

The final blow came in the wake of Ibn ʿAbbad's fall. To Frederick the Muslims had proven themselves untrustworthy as factional pawns on Sicily; moreover their valuable lands were lying unworked. To remove Sicily's Muslims definitively from the scene, then, and replace them with Latin settlers (and, it seems, some Jews from North Africa) he began, starting in the 1220s, deporting them to mainland Italy and settling them at a Muslim colony he established at Lucera. The resettlement continued even after 1243, when a further—and final—Muslim uprising shook the island around Entella. By the time the dust had settled, some twenty thousand Muslims from Sicily and Malta had been relocated to the Italian mainland, and, for all intents and purposes, the island had seen the last of its medieval Muslim inhabitants. A Sicilian survivor took the opportunity presented by his travels while on pilgrimage to approach the Ayyubid sultan al-Kamil in northern Iraq to report to him the horrors of the situation and to beg him to convince Frederick to return them to their homes or, failing that, to settle them among Muslims in Egypt. Al-Kamil dutifully wrote to Frederick, but nothing ever came of the plan.[24]

Lucera itself, surely one of the oddest products of the age of Crusades, was a thriving city of Apulia.[25] As on Sicily, its population was free to practice their religion, and the city possessed a mosque, a qadi, and something referred to as a *gymnasium*, probably a Qur'an school for children rather than a full-fledged madrasa. As expert farmers, the Muslims were expected to work the lands around Lucera and engage in the panoply of other crafts they brought with them. Adult men, moreover, were expected to serve as soldiers for the Hohenstaufens, as they had for the Normans, who valued them especially for their skills in archery. Thus, as a source of taxes and of military manpower, "Lucera of the Saracens," as it was known, was a valued possession of the Holy Roman emperors. Even when Charles I of Anjou besieged and captured the city from the Hohenstaufens during a Crusade in 1268, he retained the Muslims there and restored their tax status, showing how long-range fiscal calculation was weighed separately from religious merit. So it remained for another generation or more.

In 1300, though, it was short-range thinking that spelled the demise of Lucera's Muslims. The new Angevin king, Charles II, was badly in need of cash to cover his war costs, and he calculated that the quick liquidation of Lucera would provide just the windfall he needed. Despite the proven utility and obedience of the Muslim community there, Charles ordered the colony dismantled and its population sold into slavery; their property was likewise seized by the crown. Moreover, compared with his predecessors, Charles was also eager to score religious points. With the fall of Acre in 1291 still clear in people's minds, Charles (who never himself went on crusade) made much of allegations of Saracen wickedness despite the loyalty and utter docility of the city, and he clearly depicted his actions at Lucera as a triumph for Christianity. Once the colony was destroyed, Charles had a new cathedral built on the site of the mosque, the last of medieval Italy, unintentionally linking the town to other sites of Christian triumph and Muslim loss across the Mediterranean, from Toledo to Jerusalem (Fig. 14).

Nasrids and Granada

Thanks to the interventions of the Almoravids and the Almohads after them, al-Andalus was able to fend off the Franks for centuries. But in the end the Muslims of al-Andalus shared in their Sicilian coreligionists' story of conquest, assimilation, and exile, even as they skillfully held on to their autonomy for as long as possible. The post-Almohad period in al-Andalus is hopelessly confused and one of the most difficult periods to analyze as a whole, due in large part to the political fragmentation of the period.[26] The unavoidable truth was that what was left of Muslim al-Andalus was being overrun by Christian armies, and while individual Andalusi notables might step up to defend their cities or even make grander claims for authority, it was, in this setting, military success that drove political fortunes. Thus in 1230, when Ibn Hud, for all his international posturing, was defeated in battle despite possessing a larger army, he lost all credibility. He was soon ousted at his city of Murcia, and a series of local notables rose to take his place, only to be deposed in turn. City by city in the south fell to Christian armies; a Catalan fleet even took Majorca and the rest of the Balearics. The Minorcans at first agreed to become Aragonese vassals to save themselves, but in 1282 the Catalans invaded, and, as would happen at Lucera in Italy, they sold the populace into slavery and repopulated the island with their own settlers.

In Valencia the last Almohad governor still clung to power, sad and isolated. He too was deposed by his subjects and lived in exile as an Aragonese vassal, converting to Christianity before his death and marrying his daughter to a Christian lord. But the lord who replaced him was no more successful, and in 1236 the city was handed over to the king of Aragon. Córdoba fell later that year to the Castilians. With most of the Iberian Peninsula now in Christian hands, there was very little meaning even to the name "al-Andalus." Only Seville and Granada remained of the principal cities formerly ruled by Muslim lords. Seville had bought itself time by becoming a vassal of Fernando III of León-Castile. When his vassal was murdered, Fernando took the opportunity to appear outraged and, in November 1248, grabbed the city for himself. For the next two and half centuries "Muslim Spain" would be a hemmed-in, isolated, and besieged toehold at Granada, ruled with consummate skill by the Nasrid dynasty, the last, but in many ways the greatest, kings of al-Andalus.

The key to Nasrid durability lay in their diplomatic connections. The dynasty's founder, Ibn al-Ahmar, emerged on the Andalusi scene as one of the many local rulers who claimed power in their own settlements after the collapse of the Almohads. While not everyone embraced Ibn al-Ahmar as the best option to provide them with the security they needed against Christian invasion, he gained a following—without hurting a fly—throughout the remaining lands of al-Andalus, as in Guadix, Malaga, Almería, and, from 1237, Granada, which became the capital of his dynasty. Granada's fortress and palace complex, the Alhambra, became the seat and refuge of the Nasrids and, over the centuries of their stewardship, one of the most serene and elaborate medieval palaces in Europe. As was so often the case, Ibn al-Ahmar maintained his power not through the restless pursuit of jihad but rather through the deft (some would say cynical) use of alliances—with his Andalusi rivals, with the Hafsid rulers of Tunis, with the ʿAbbasid caliph in Baghdad, and with the Christian kings of Castile—surrendering contested territories to King Fernando III and even sending soldiers to help him capture Córdoba and Seville. These were unpopular concessions to assure the safety of Granada itself. Unpopular, but highly successful: until the last years of the kingdom's existence, it retained most of the territories that Ibn al-Ahmar had held at its founding. Indeed in the last years of his reign, Ibn al-Ahmar almost had the chance to extend his influence when, from 1264 to 1266, Muslims living under Christian rule, known generically as *mudejars*, revolted against their Christian lords, with some acknowledging the suzerainty of Granada. But the kings of Aragon and Castile were able to crush the revolt, with devastating results for the mudejars, who had played their hand and so were expelled or killed outright. By the late 1260s there were few Muslims remaining in Christian territory. Refugees crowded into the kingdom of Granada (Fig. 15).

After the death of Ibn al-Ahmar in 1273, of particular importance to the kingdom's political fortunes were its relations with the Merinid dynasty of Fez, which had replaced the Almohads as the main power in Morocco. Unlike the Nasrids, the Merinids were much more ideologically inclined toward jihad. Not only did warfare against the infidels bring religious merit and legitimacy to the dynasty, but it also kept their crowded and potentially rebellious army of Zanata Berbers occupied far from home, collecting plunder to keep them sated. But the Merinids were in Morocco, and the infidels were across the Straits. And the Nasrids of Granada stood, rather anxiously, between them both. For the Nasrids, the Merinids provided a source of eager manpower to be used when necessary against the Christians, but at times such an obstreperous neighbor also provided a direct threat to Granada's well-being. It was up to the Nasrids to keep these threats and promises balanced, and, right up to the end of the kingdom, they did, in a fairly stable setting of on-again, off-again warfare with the Christian kingdoms of the North.

The troubled events of the reigns of the Nasrid amirs Nasr (1309–14) and Isma'il (1314–25) should suffice as examples of these challenges and of the delicate situation in which the Nasrids operated. When Nasr took the throne in Granada in 1309, the kings of Castile and Aragon had made a rare alliance, sending a combined fleet into the Straits of Gibraltar—the Castilians capturing Gibraltar, while the Aragonese put the vital port of Almería to siege. Nasr immediately requested a peace treaty with the Merinids in Morocco, with whom the Nasrids had been warring. The sultan agreed and, in return, sent a contingent of his Moroccan troops to assist Nasr and a hectoring letter to the king of Aragon requesting that he make peace with Granada and inviting him to send his Majorcan merchants to trade in Morocco, where they would be welcomed. The Aragonese bowed to the pressure and withdrew; the Castilians took a few towers here and there but in any case remained at bay once their king died in 1312. Although this should have been a moment of triumph, in fact Nasr had made many enemies in his own inner circle, among them his cousin Isma'il. With support from the Berber contingents of the Granadan army, Isma'il rose up and in 1314 deposed Nasr, forcing the old amir to make do as a mere provincial governor under the new administration.

Isma'il would have done better to find a more permanent resting place for his predecessor, for Nasr wasted no time in making an alliance with the king of Castile, or rather with his two coregents since the monarch, Alfonso XI (1312–50), was still a child. Meanwhile, across the Straits, the Merinids watched with suspiciously uncharacteristic aloofness; one wonders what they really thought of Isma'il. In 1319 they might have intervened but didn't: the Castilian army marched on Isma'il in Granada and put the city to siege. In the end Granada didn't need the Merinids and achieved a stunning victory in the plains outside the city, routing the Castilians and killing both of the king's regents then and there. It was a refreshingly decisive victory for the much-beleaguered kingdom. And so, when this action repeated itself some years later, there was no reason to think the outcome would be any different. In 1340 Castilians under Alfonso, now a grown and ambitious man, sent a fleet with their Catalan allies to retake Gibraltar, and, as before, the Muslim navy, this time composed of Moroccan and Tunisian ships, prevailed. Where things went wrong was on land, where Alfonso and the king of Portugal joined forces and easily defeated a joint Nasrid and Merinid army on the banks of the Rio Salado. Yusuf I, the Nasrid amir at the time, escaped to the safety of Granada. The Merinid sultan withdrew to Morocco.

As it turns out, the Merinid withdrawal from al-Andalus in 1340 was permanent; never again would any North African state involve itself significantly in the affairs of the Muslims of al-Andalus. This was partly because the Merinids were distracted by their own internal challenges, and no equivalently powerful state replaced them. But it was also because the defeat at the Rio Salado had opened up the south to Alfonso, greatly limiting the opportunities and indeed the anchorages necessary for any kind of movement of armies across the Straits. For example, Algeciras, where the Muslim defenders made the first recorded use of cannons in the peninsula, fell to Alfonso in 1344, the product of a massive international assault that brought holy-warring noblemen from England, France, and elsewhere in Spain. Even Gibraltar itself was saved only when Alfonso died of the plague in 1350 while besieging it.

By the middle of the fourteenth century, then, Granada was really and truly alone, with no expectation of aid or alliance from North Africa, facing a Christian foe that could rely upon the fervent support of the military and ecclesiastical institutions of all of Christendom. And yet Granada stood, resolute, for another century and a half. Why this should be so is a difficult question to answer, as our sources become increasingly reticent at this point. The answer must surely have something to do with the fact that the Christian kingdoms were themselves facing internal divisions at precisely this time. But it is also true that the kingdom was blessed by some very capable rulers, who knew enough to use diplomacy to enhance the stability of the realm. In other words, they knew enough to make peace with Castile and keep it. Indeed this was also something of a golden age for Granada, whose unusual stability allowed its rulers, most famously Muhammad V (1354–59 and 1362–91), to cultivate and reform the administration, patronize poets and scholars, and, as anyone can now see, embellish the fortresses and palace of the realm, including the Alhambra.

Yet, through all the inward-gazing accounts of alliance, counteralliance, and intrigue that chroniclers loved to dwell upon—some of them being principal actors in these events, after all—there do emerge here and there individual rulers whose need to prove themselves as warriors of the faith disrupted this mutually beneficial peace. On the Nasrid side, this includes Muhammad VII (1392–1408), who launched offensives into Castilian territory starting in 1405, despite the objections of elements within the Granadan ruling elite. On the Christian side must be numbered Henry IV of Castile (1454–74), who took advantage of the power struggles under Muhammad XI and raided deep into the kingdom, as at Malaga and Granada itself; in 1461 he took Gibraltar outright.

The low-level raiding and intermittent warfare that had generally characterized the Nasrids' approach to their Christian foes continued almost to the end. The last Muslim victory in the peninsula took place in late December 1481, when a Nasrid commander led a small force against the fortress of Zahara, captured it, and took its garrison, about a hundred men, as prisoners. Over the next decade the Muslim experience of kingship in the peninsula, which began in 711, would be slowly but decisively extinguished. The kingdom of Granada fell due to the confluence of two common occurrences at the worst possible time: the kingdom became internally divided precisely when the Christian kingdoms were reunited under fiercely militant rulers. In 1479 Fernando V of Aragon (1479–1516), united with his wife, Queen Isabella of Castile (1474–1504), in a planned and protracted war to extinguish the kingdom of Granada. There was little the Nasrids could do to stop them. Indeed in their dynastic struggles they were effectively helping them.

In July 1482 the Nasrid king Abu al-Hasan was ousted from Granada by his son Abu 'Abd Allah (known as Boabdil in most Christian sources). This effectively split the kingdom, with Boabdil and his followers ruling in Granada and his father and his followers scheming in exile from Malaga. In 1483 Boabdil appears to have foolishly embarked on a raid into Castilian territory, perhaps to bolster his standing as king, but those days were long gone. His small force was crushed and he was captured; Ferdinand and Isabella extracted humiliating concessions from him. In Granada his stock plummeted, and he was openly denounced. In 1485 his aging father abdicated in Malaga and was succeeded by his brother, known as Muhammad al-Zaghal, "the Brave," whom even Boabdil was eventually induced to recognize formally as his king, even as he allied with the Castilians to undermine him.

By 1488 only Granada and the eastern lands of the kingdom remained in Muslim hands, and here al-Zaghal continued the fight, while Boabdil remained ensconced in Granada. But al-Zaghal had been unable to stem the tide from Castile. At the end of 1489 he surrendered Almería and Guadix in exchange for a small principality of his own. But then he thought better of it, sold his claims back to the Catholic monarchs, and sailed to Algeria, never to return. Granada had only Boabdil to buoy it. In the end it was the Granadans themselves who fought hardest, as the Christians had the city surrounded and Boabdil was in the field attempting, to no avail, to distract them. As prices rose and famine spread, Boabdil's vizier traveled to the Christian camp at Santa Fe and surrendered the city on November 25, 1491. A few months later this same vizier led the Castilian commander and other grandees to the Alhambra, where Boabdil formally relinquished power. Ferdinand granted Boabdil lands in the Alpujarras, where he briefly established himself. But, like his uncle before him, he had second thoughts and instead crossed over to Morocco and settled in Fez, where, al-Maqqari tells us, "complaining of his unlucky fate, and regretting the kingdom he had lost, he settled with his family and his adherents, and built some palaces in imitation of those in Granada."[27]

This last king of al-Andalus died in Fez in 1538; as late as the 1630s al-Maqqari encountered some of his descendants, who were living off of the Islamic tithe monies in poverty, "nothing more than mere beggars."[28] Although Boabdil and his advisers had worked hard to spell out specific capitulations in their treaty of surrender to safeguard the Muslims who remained behind in al-Andalus, Ferdinand was quick to break the agreement and began forcing Muslims subjects to convert to Christianity. The result was a series of mudejar revolts, which were followed by swift and brutal reprisals and mass emigrations to the cities of North Africa and, for some, to the most successful protector of Muslims of the age: the Ottoman Empire. For others, however, old Andalusi traditions were hard to break. At the close of his long chronicle, al-Maqqari notes that "some entered the service of the Sultan of [Morocco], who formed them into a body, and allotted them for a residence the port of Salé, where they have since made themselves famous by their maritime expeditions against the enemies of God."[29]

Epilogue: Buried Horsemen

THE FIRST FRANKISH invasions of the Near East, we are told, were attended by the usual signs of cosmic foreboding. According to one story in circulation a generation or so after the First Crusade, some workmen in the employ of Yaghi-Siyan, the ill-fated governor of Antioch, discovered a covered stone basin during their repair work on the walls of the city, which had been damaged in an earthquake some years earlier. Peeking inside, they discovered a group of brass figurines of mysterious horsemen, "each dressed in a long coat of chain-mail, grasping a shield and spear."[1] Puzzled, the amir asked a group of the local city elders—native Christians—what they thought these figures could represent.

The elders too were stumped. They didn't know, they said. But the figurines reminded them of something that took place many years before, when the city was still in Byzantine hands. In 1084 the walls of a local monastery had collapsed, and, during the reconstruction work, they discovered a similar stone basin, containing brass figurines of horsemen bearing bows and arrows, which they easily identified as Turks. They thought little of the discovery. Little, that is, until a short time later, when an army of precisely these sorts of horsemen—the Saljuq Turks—captured the city and subjected it to decades of Turkish rule. Perhaps, the elders meekly suggested to the amir, these strange new figurines in chain mail represented some *other* conquering nation still unknown to Antioch? Yaghi-Siyan merely scoffed at them, snorting in disbelief that there were any other infidels left to be worried about. Alas, and as we might have predicted, a short time later word arrived that the Franks, some doubtless clad in long coats of chain mail, had encamped before Constantinople, en route to Yaghi-Siyan's date with destiny.

Another good story. The tale succeeds in explaining the catastrophic loss of Antioch to the Franks as ineluctable, fated from the first, showing that the conquest of the city by the Franks, just like its conquest by the Turks, had been decreed long before, in the legendary age of the city's founding. The story fits into a small genre of medieval Arabic stories in which buried antiquities provide warning of future events, in which the future history of a given city is literally built into its fabric. Like many similar narratives about the First Crusade, the tale also pins the blame for the Frankish conquest on the personal failing of Yaghi-Siyan, whose hubris blinds him to his fate even as he stood, in the face of such clear omens, duly warned.

It is also a good story because of who told it. This was a Syrian Muslim named Hamdan ibn 'Abd al-Rahim al-Atharibi, a man of wide intellectual horizons who also has the distinction of being one of the few Muslim landlords we know of who willingly ruled in service to a Frankish lord. There were doubtless others, but none have left such a traceable profile as Hamdan.[2] Hamdan was born in the 1060s or 1070s in a small village called Ma'aratha near Atharib, not far from Aleppo, but then he and his father moved to the larger town of Atharib itself and settled there. He thus came of age under Saljuq rule and won a post as a tax administrator and bureaucrat based, it seems, in the uncertain context of Ridwan's Aleppo.

It was from there that one day he decided to return to the village of his birth, even though the Franks had captured the area in 1110. While there he learned that the local Frankish lord of Atharib, a certain Sir Manuel, had taken ill, so he went to examine him. His ministrations were successful, and, in gratitude for curing him, Manuel offered him a fiefdom of a small village to the south, which he ruled for the Franks for some thirty years, developing it and settling down there, calling it home. His descendants ruled there for many generations even after the Muslims recaptured the territory. In his service to Franks and Muslims, he was frequently relied upon as a messenger and was involved in diplomatic missions to Egypt (where he was accused of being a *hashishi*, a Nizari "Assassin"), Damascus, and even Baghdad. As a younger man in Saljuq Aleppo, Hamdan had received an excellent liberal education, and he became an accomplished hand in belles-lettres, genealogy, poetry, grammar, astronomy, mathematics, and, as Sir Manuel could have attested, medicine.

Most interesting for us, he was also a historian, and he later wrote a history known under various titles, which was, according to a medieval chronicler who had read it, "a book on the history of Aleppo...including accounts of the Franks and their deeds and their invasion of Syria...and its aftermath." Sadly, only a few fragments survive, such as this tale of buried horsemen. The tale was itself one that Hamdan claimed, as with all good urban myths, to have heard from someone else. But Hamdan added his own contemporary postscript. In the year 1118, Hamdan tells us, Roger of Salerno, the lord of Antioch, found himself in need of marble for a building project, and so he sent some men to a ruined palace in Antioch to strip it of what they could use. It was there that Roger's workmen found (what else?) a covered stone basin containing a figurine of a horseman: "except that the mount had features inconsistent with a horse and the horseman wore a head-wrap such that only his eyes showed." When this figurine was presented to Roger, someone related that story about the Turkish and Frankish figurines, and so he looked into the matter. One of the priests he questioned told him, "Dash it on the ground so that it breaks and breaks its evil with it!"

Roger did so, and at that moment word came that an Egyptian army had arrived before Jerusalem. Roger somewhat reluctantly marched south to the defense of the city, yet to his surprise the Egyptians were routed and Jerusalem was unharmed. Roger returned in triumph to Antioch, having concluded, no doubt, that the curse of the figurines had been broken. But then, a few days later, Roger decided to attack A'zaz, and it was only *then* that the fearful citizens of Aleppo called upon the group apparently fated to be the latest of Antioch's mysterious conquerors: the Turcoman troops of Il-Ghazi, who dutifully defeated Roger and the flower of Antioch's fighting men at the battle of the Field of Blood.

Roger never managed to escape his fate, but the Turcomans never conquered Antioch either, as the Saljuqs and the Franks had done, and so this was Hamdan's chance to make a moral for his tale: "If only the army of Il-Ghazi had continued on to Antioch, he would have taken it. But he was over-cautious in the affair. To God alone belongs the Will!" For Hamdan, the Muslim reconquest of Antioch was simply not to be, no matter what ominous figurines may promise. For so powerful is God's will that it can reverse the fates of all of us, even those laid down in remote antiquity and proven time and again to be written into our history.

That Hamdan felt the need to write this account at all is central to understanding how medieval Muslims, or medieval Muslim historians at least, understood the coming of the Franks to Sicily, al-Andalus, North Africa, and the Near East. Hamdan was manifestly not interested in retailing "truth"; the prophetic archaeological discoveries in his story are purely fictional, and one suspects his readers knew this. What he and the other historians mentioned in this book *were* keen to do, however, was to derive lessons from the tales of Frankish encounters that they related. For Hamdan and so many of his contemporaries, the Frankish successes against Islamdom provided proof of God's inexplicable will. In that respect at least, these observers had much in common with their Frankish counterparts. Over the centuries of Muslim writing about this encounter, they derived other lessons too: the perils of disunity; the evil of pride, oath breaking, and tyranny; the need for administrative reform; the fear of disloyalty from religious minorities; the wisdom of leniency; the imperative of spiritual renewal; the prize of martyrdom; the rewards of upholding the Circle of Equity.

Modern readers might derive other lessons from an Islamic history of the Crusades. Perhaps the most important is that there was no single, shared Muslim experience of the Crusades. It follows, then, that there was no such thing as the "countercrusade," in the sense of a coherent movement against the Franks that shared the same motivations and goals. What we find instead are specific Muslim leaders who, at specific times in their careers, employed the language of jihad against the Franks to mobilize support for their own endeavors, claiming (with various degrees of success) to be acting for the benefit of all (Sunni) Muslims. The optical illusion of a countercrusade results from the fact that the most successfully persuasive of these leaders (Zangi, Nur al-Din, and Saladin) happened to succeed one another. But as we have seen, even with these three, their resort to jihad against the Franks was calculated and intermittent. Their predecessors and successors tried just as hard. A concerted countercrusade remained, if anything, only an ideal to be invoked.

Given the broad and sustained assault on Islamdom's Mediterranean frontiers from the middle of the eleventh century onward, one can understand why some Muslims saw the Franks as a threat to Islamic civilization as a whole, and why some sought to unify Muslim responses to the Franks in their literary and historical depictions of them. Yet this was just one way of dealing with the Frankish problem. It is easy to find medieval Muslims who experienced the Frankish invasions as conquered subjects or as aspiring countercrusaders. It is just as easy to find collaborators, neutral parties, diplomats, and, like the many border-crossers like Hamdan mentioned in this book, inscrutable and long-lived individuals whose motives defy easy summation.

The lasting impact of the Frankish invasions on the Islamic world varied accordingly. Seen from the Jerusalem-centric "traditional perspective," as I noted in the book's introduction, it is easy to dismiss the Crusades as an ephemeral episode; hence any preoccupation with them would be seen as a histrionic overreaction. After all, the Muslims "won" the Crusades in the end, modern writers often tell us. However, seen from the sort of Islamic perspectives offered in this book, the cost was indeed high, and one can appreciate the sense of panic that must have gripped medieval Muslims as news of Frankish conquest after conquest circulated across the Mediterranean. Sicily was taken; al-Andalus lost. For all that the Frankish states in the Levant came and went, these other losses were permanent and ever after shaped the posture of Islamdom toward Christian Europe.

Here too Islamic history can offer some perspective. As much as one might mourn the loss of Muslim Spain and Sicily, subjects and souls were being gained elsewhere as Islamic states, and Islamic culture spread over vast amounts of territory. As we have seen, the Ottoman Turks were relentless in their conquests in the Balkans and in eastern Europe and eventually threatened Italy and central Europe. Elsewhere, in sub-Saharan and East Africa, in Central, South, and Southeast Asia, rulers and their subjects adopted Islam and much of the culture that came with it. Islam's Frankish frontier was just one small part of an otherwise irrepressibly successful global civilization.

Such a perspective also suggests an end-point for this book; other books might choose other endings for an Islamic history of the Crusades. With the conquest of Granada in 1492, the setting for Islamdom's Frankish problem was irrevocably changed. Sicily and al-Andalus were controlled by the Franks now, the Frankish states in the Near East and Cyprus were destroyed, and the Byzantine Empire eliminated. The Mongols and Tamerlane had left the shores of the Mediterranean far behind them. Only the Ottomans and a few Barbary pirates seemed to care about the Franks anymore. The Hospitallers hung about on Rhodes, but the Ottomans caught up with them too, in 1522, and what was left of them relocated to Malta. In the years that followed, the Ottomans focused their attentions on Hungary and the Hapsburgs, but not as foes of crusading Franks so much as a regional power fully integrated into the European monarchic system. The world that Mehmed the Conqueror's successors inherited bore little resemblance to the world of Ibn al-Thumna, the Almoravids, or Saladin.

Other areas of impact are less direct. It has often been maintained that the Crusades resulted in a hardening of attitudes among Muslims toward Christianity and toward Europeans. Yet that seems like something for which cause and effect are nearly impossible to untangle.[3] Muslim responses to the Frankish threat did not lead to "militant Islam," medieval or modern. Rigorist movements of Islamic reform long predate the coming of the Franks and continued well after they were gone. The medieval reformers, like the Mamluk-era firebrand Ibn Taymiyya whom modern jihad enthusiasts like to cite, were far more concerned with what they saw as the spiritual failures of their fellow Muslims; their occasional concern with jihad was more about their criticism of the Muslim regimes of their day than with any specific goal (or desire) of destroying the Franks.[4] It is certainly true that individual Muslim thinkers were motivated by their experiences with the Franks to advocate for a direct and uncompromising stance against them, politically and religiously. And some undoubtedly were driven to preach to, write to, and harangue their coreligionists to that end because of what they saw as a catastrophe befalling Islam. These events cannot have helped but shape the attitudes of some Muslims toward Christians and toward their own religion. They probably also hardened attitudes toward eastern Christians living under Islamic rule.

Nonetheless the most far-reaching factor in the religious history of Islam in this period was not the Crusades but rather that collection of new attitudes of reappraisal and reform in law, theology, and devotion that has been called the "Sunni Revival." Christians, Jews, and heretical innovations in Islam were almost always invoked as targets of such thinking. As we have seen, this revival has its own wellsprings, and these have only little to do with the religious threat of the Crusades.

What the Crusades *did* lead to was Muslim state formation. And even there, their impact is indirect. The presence of a proximate, tenacious Frankish foe in al-Andalus and the Near East provided a pretext for ambitious military commanders like Zangi and Saladin, reformers like the Almoravids, and military juntas like the Mamluks, and all the diverse states that they founded. In each case jihad against the Franks became a plank in their platforms, from which otherwise illegitimate power-grabbers publicly proclaimed themselves to be defenders of the faith and upholders of the Circle of Equity. The post-Saljuq military regimes that held sway over most of the Muslim Mediterranean do not owe their existence to the Frankish threat, but they probably owe something of their longevity to it. The mobilizing power of calls to jihad was something that Muslim statesmen were well aware of; the menacing presence of Frankish armies only made the calls that much easier. The Crusades did not make Islam militant; they did, however, help to justify the dominion of military elites.

It is also often maintained that, in the end, the Crusades did not really matter to Muslims after the Middle Ages. It was only when they were "rediscovered" in the nineteenth century through translations of European historical works and in the context of late Ottoman backlash against European colonialism in the Middle East that these events came to take on meaning again for Muslims. As evidence of Muslims having supposedly forgotten about the Crusades, it is often pointed out that the first modern Muslim-authored biography of Saladin was that of Namik Kemal, written in 1872, and the first historical monograph was that by Sayyid ʿAli al-Hariri, *Al-akhbar al-saniyya fi-al-hurub al-salibiyya* (*Splendid Accounts in the Crusading Wars*), written in 1899. But this is not, strictly speaking, a very good argument. For it was not until the late nineteenth century that Muslims published monographs—printed, focused academic studies—on *any* topic. The form in question is a modern invention and one would not have expected to see such works devoted to the Crusades (or any other period of history) much earlier.

If we put aside our focus on scholarly works for the moment and look to other forms, we can see that the Crusades did live on in Muslim historical memory. We can see it in the evocation of jihad that the Ottomans continued to use in their European campaigns; in the continued copying and circulation of medieval Arabic chronicles in which the Franks featured; in the folk epics about Baybars recited in public fora; in the panegyrics that made comparisons to the Ayyubid and Mamluk past; and in the silent, immovable presence of castles, walls, and ruins linked—sometimes by name—to a region's own experience with the Franks. The details of names and dates of this history thus might be lost, but many of the lessons were not. It is this constant, ambient memory of the Crusades that explains the composition in 1519 of a short treatise on the Frankish wars in the Near East called *Al-Iʿlam wa-al-tabyin fi khuruj al-firanj al-malaʿin ʿala diyar al-muslimin* (*Information and Explanation concerning the Raids of the Franks on the Lands of the Muslims*) by one Ahmad ibn ʿAli al-Hariri; it also explains the mournful reflections on the historical and literary heritage of al-Andalus by al-Maqqari, who died in 1632; it explains how the Ottoman historian

Naʿima in the early eighteenth century could suggest the examples of the Ayyubids and Mamluks (and their willingness to make truces as well as to fight) to his royal Ottoman readers; and it explains why, in 1701, Jerusalemite notables petitioned the Ottoman sultan to prevent a visit to the Holy City from the French consul because "our city is the focus of attention of the infidels," and "we fear that we will be occupied as result of this, as happened repeatedly in past times." And so on. Historical memory does not always abide in scholarly books and articles.[5]

What Islamic history cannot explain is the pervasive modern use of the Crusades as an analogy or birth moment for some allegedly epochal clash between "Islam and Christianity." For all that Frankish and Muslim ideologues liked to cast their conflicts as total war with the enemies of God, and for all that many, maybe most Franks and Muslims wished it to be so, the realities were rather different. This was not a clash of Islam versus Christianity. It was at best a clash of specific Frankish polities warring with specific Muslim ones, where universal claims to religious truth or holy war almost always took a backseat to specific regional and political interests. Lachrymose narratives of victimhood—no less than heroic narratives of triumph—do no justice to the richness of the encounters described in this book, nor to the context and specificity of Islamic experiences of the Crusades. Worse still, they do outright injustice to the more nuanced, less dramatic, but nevertheless authentic decisions made by generations of medieval Christians, Muslims, and Jews involved in this history. The Crusades, understood from any perspective, cannot shed light on modern struggles, and their motivations cannot be legitimately claimed as background or inspiration for contemporary conflicts. Medieval Muslims and Christians went to war for their own motives, not ours.

Viewing the Crusades from an Islamic perspective can, however, give us so much. First, as should be clear by now, it adds raw material to the familiar story that the traditional perspective offers and provides a parallel narrative against which historical details can be checked. It allows us to view these events without the predetermined frame and storyline favored by that perspective. But there is more to it than that. It allows us to understand the contexts of the Muslim populations who were the targets of Frankish conquest from Spain to Syria, the economic, political, and social settings of actors in these events who are poorly represented in the traditional perspective—a history of the crusaded, not just of crusaders. More important, it forces us to contend with medieval Islamic religion and culture, with the ideals that guided medieval Muslims, the meanings they attached to their actions, and how and why these chose to tell their stories in the ways they did. It helps us to understand why the Crusades might matter.

Adopting such a perspective also confronts us with its limits. The Crusades can be seen as an integral part of the history of Islamdom (as I have tried to do here), just as they have been studied for centuries as a part of European history. However, it would seem pointless, save as a thought experiment, to substitute a narrative built largely from one perspective for yet another such narrative. Doing so would be a terribly shortsighted way to treat the rich history offered by this long-lived phenomenon. It may be that the difficult future task of weaving together the traditional perspective and an Islamic perspective will give us a more balanced understanding of the Crusades, but it is only the first step. There are plenty of other voices clamoring to get to the table in what Gibbon (quoting Shakespeare) called "the World's Debate."

For the Crusades offer us not merely a story of military conflict between two enemies of God but a tale of human encounters: of Christians, Jews, Muslims, and heretics; of Normans, Palermitans, Provençals, Granadans, Jerusalemites, Germans, Shayzaris, and Hungarians, to name a few. It is there, in the diverse humanity of the medieval Mediterranean, where the actors in these events emerge most fully as individuals, high-minded and worldly, subject to good decision making and bad. An approach to the Crusades that embraces multiple perspectives recovers medieval people not as heroes or villains but as fellow humans, members of families, products of communities, cultural beings subject to the vagaries of the world they created around them, their grand, civilizational contests just the oscillations of restless populations crowding the shores of an inland sea.

Abbreviations

AA	Albert of Aachen, *Historia Ierosolimitana*, ed. and trans. Susan B. Edgington (Oxford: Clarendon Press, 2007).
Abu al-Fida'	Isma'il ibn 'Ali Abu al-Fida', *Al-mukhtasar fi akhbar al-bashar*, partial edition and translation by P. M. Holt as *The Memoirs of a Syrian Prince* (Wiesbaden: Franz Steiner, 1983).
Abu Shama	Shihab al-Din 'Abd al-Rahman Abu Shama, *Kitab al-Rawdatayn fi akhbar al-dawlatayn*, ed. Ibrahim Zaybaq (Beirut: Mu'assassat al-Risala, 1997).
'Azimi	Al-'Azimi, *Ta'rikh Halab*, ed. Ibrahim Za'rur (Damascus: n.p., 1984).
Baybars al-Mansuri	Baybars al-Mansuri, *Zubdat al-fikra fi ta'rikh al-hijra*, partial edition by D. S. Richards (Beirut: United Distributing, 1998).
Bughya	Kamal al-Din 'Umar ibn al-'Adim, *Bughyat al-talab fi ta'rikh Halab*, 11 vols., ed. Suhayl Zakkar (Damascus: n.p., 1988).
CHESFAME	*Egypt and Syria in the Fatimid, Ayyubid and Mamluk Eras*, various editors (Leuven: Peeters, 1995–ongoing).
CIP	Carole Hillenbrand, *The Crusades: Islamic Perspectives* (London: Routledge, 1999).
EI2	*Encyclopaedia of Islam*, 11 vols. and supplement, ed. H. A. R. Gibb et al. (Leiden: E. J. Brill, 1960–2003).
Fulcher	Fulcher of Chartres, *Historia Hierosolymitana (1095–1127)*, ed. H. Hagenmeyer (Heidelberg: Carl Winters

Universitätsbuchhandlung, 1913). Translated by F. R. Ryan and H. S. Fink as *A History of the Expedition to Jerusalem, 1095–1127* (Knoxville: University of Tennessee Press, 1960).

Gabrieli

Francesco Gabrieli, *Arab Historians of the Crusades* (London: Routledge, 1969).

GF

Gesta Francorum et aliorum Hierosolymitanorum, ed. and trans. Rosalind Hill (Oxford: Oxford University Press, 1962).

IA

'Izz al-Din 'Ali ibn Muhammad ibn al-Athir, *Al-Kamil fi al-ta'rikh*, 13 vols. (Beirut: Dar Sadir, 1965–67). Translated by D. S. Richards as *The Chronicle of Ibn al-Athir for the Crusading Period from al-Kamil fi'l-Ta'rikh*, 3 vols. (Aldershot, UK: Ashgate, 2006). Pre-Crusades material translated by D. S. Richards as *The Annals of the Saljuq Turks* (London: RoutledgeCurzon, 2002).

IAH

'Izz al-Din Muhammad ibn Abi al-Hayja', *Ta'rikh Ibn Abi al-Hayja'*, partial edition by Subhi 'Abd al-Mun'im Muhammad (Cairo: Riyad al-Salihin, 1993).

Ibn Duqmaq

Sarim al-Din Ibrahim ibn Muhammad ibn Duqmaq, *Nuzhat al-anam fi ta'rikh al-islam*, ed. Samir Tabbara (Sidon: al-Maktaba al-'Asriyya, 1999).

Ibn al-Furat

Muhammad ibn 'Abd al-Rahim ibn al-Furat, *Ta'rikh al-duwal wa-al-muluk*, partial edition and translation by U. Lyons, M. Lyons, and J. Riley-Smith, 2 vols. (Cambridge, UK: W. Heffer and Sons, 1971).

Ibn Jubayr

Abu al-Husayn Muhammad ibn Ahmad ibn Jubayr, *Rihla*, ed. W. Wright, revised by M. J. De Goeje (Leiden: E. J. Brill, 1907). Translated by Roland Broadhurst as *The Travels of Ibn Jubayr* (London: Jonathan Cape, 1952).

Ibn al-Mughayzil

Dhayl mufarrij al-kurub fi akhbar Bani Ayyub, ed. 'Umar 'Abd al-Salam Tadmuri (Sidon: al-Maktaba al-'asriyya, 2004).

Ibn Shaddad

Baha' al-Din Yusuf ibn Shaddad, *Al-Nawadir al-sultaniyya wa al-mahasin al-yusufiyya*, ed. Jamal al-Din al-Shayyal (Cairo: al-Dar al-misriyya li-al-ta'lif wa-al-tarjama, 1964). Translated by D. S. Richards as *The Rare and Excellent History of Saladin* (Aldershot, UK: Ashgate, 2002).

Ibn Taghribirdi

Abu al-Mahasin Yusuf ibn al-Taghribirdi, *Al-Nujum al-zahira fi muluk Misr wa-al-Qahira*, 16 vols. (Cairo: Dar al-kutub al-misriyya, 1963–72).

IAZ	Muhyi al-Din ibn ʿAbd al-Zahir, *Al-Rawd al-zahir fi sirat al-Malik al-Zahir*, ed. ʿAbd al-ʿAziz al-Khuwaytir (Beirut: Muʾassassat al-fuʾad, 1976).
IQ	Abu Yaʿla Hamza ibn al-Qalanisi, *Taʾrikh Dimashq*, ed. Suhayl Zakkar (Damascus: Dar Hassan, 1983). Partial translation by H. A. R. Gibb as *The Damascus Chronicle of the Crusades* (London: Luzac, 1932).
IW	Muhammad ibn Salim ibn Wasil, *Mufarrij al-Kurub fi akhbar bani ayyub*, vols. 1–5 ed. Jamal al-Din al-Shayyal et al. (Cairo: various publishers, 1953–77), vol. 6 ed. ʿUmar ʿAbd al-Salam Tadmuri (Beirut: al-Maktaba al-ʿUdriyya, 2004).
Kanz	Ibn Aybak al-Dawadari, *Kanz al-durar wa-jamiʿ al-ghurar*, 9 vols., various editors (Beirut: Deutsches Archäologisches Institut, 1960–94).
Khazandari	Shihab al-Din Qaratay al-Khazandari, *Taʾrikh majmuʿ al-nawadir mimma jara liʾl-awaʾil waʾl-awakhir*, ed. Horst Hein and Muhammad al-Hujayri (Beirut: In Kommission bei Klaus-Schwarz Verlag, 2005).
KI	Usama ibn Munqidh, *Kitab al-Iʿtibar*, ed. Philip K. Hitti (Princeton, NJ: Princeton University Press, 1930). Translated by Paul M. Cobb as *The Book of Contemplation: Islam and the Crusades* (London: Penguin Classics, 2008).
LA	Usama ibn Munqidh, *Lubab al-Adab*, ed. A. M. Shakir (Cairo: Maktabat Luwis Sarkis, 1935). Partial translation by Paul M. Cobb in Usama ibn Munqidh, *The Book of Contemplation: Islam and the Crusades* (London: Penguin Classics, 2008).
Malaterra	Geoffrey Malaterra, *De rebus gestis Rogerii Calabriae et Siciliae comitis et Roberti Guiscardi ducis fratris eius*, ed. Ernesto Pontieri (Bologna: Nicola Zanichelli, 1925–28). Translated by Kenneth Baxter Wolf as *The Deeds of Count Roger of Calabria and Sicily and of His Brother Duke Robert Guiscard* (Ann Arbor: University of Michigan Press, 2005).
Al-Maqqari	Ahmad ibn Muhammad al-Maqqari, *Nafh al-tib min ghusn al-Andalus al-ratib*, 8 vols., ed. Ihsan ʿAbbas (Beirut: Dar Sadir, 1988). Partial translation by Pascual de Gayangos as *The History of the Mohammedan Dynasties in Spain*, 2 vols. (London: W. H. Allen, 1840–43).
Al-Marrakushi	*Al-Muʿjib fi talkhis akhbar al-Maghrib*, ed. M. S. al-Uryan (Cairo: n.p., 1949).

Sibt	Sibt ibn al-Jawzi, *Mir'at al-zaman fi ta'rikh al-a'yan*, vol. 8, in two parts (Hyderabad: Da'irat al-Ma'arif al-'Uthmaniya, 1952).
Suluk	Ahmad ibn 'Ali al-Maqrizi, *Kitab al-suluk li-ma'rifat duwal al-muluk*, ed. Muhammad Mustafa Ziadeh and S. 'Abd al-Fattah 'Ashur (Cairo: Lajnat al-ta'lif wa-al-tarjama wa-al-nashr, 1956–72).
TM	Muhammad ibn 'Ali ibn Nazif al-Hamawi, *Al-Ta'rikh al-Mansuri*, ed. Abu al-'Id Dudu (Damascus: Majma' al-lugha al-'arabiyya bi-Dimashq, 1981).
TMD	Abu al-Qasim 'Ali ibn 'Asakir, *Ta'rikh madinat Dimashq*, 80 vols., ed. 'Umar al-'Amrawi (Damascus: Dar al-Fikr, 1998).
Yunini	Qutb al-Din Musa al-Yunini, *Dhayl mirat al-zaman*, 4 vols. (Hyderabad: Da'irat al-Ma'arif al-'Uthmaniya, 1955).
Zubda	Kamal al-Din 'Umar ibn al-'Adim, *Zubdat al-halab min ta'rikh Halab*, 3 vols., ed. Sami Dahhan (Damascus: Institut Français de Damas, 1951–68).

Notes

Prologue

1. For an overview of the mythical image of Saladin, see Carole Hillenbrand, *The Crusades: Islamic Perspectives* (London: Routledge, 1999), 592–600, which includes photos of the statue described here. On Saladin's image in the West, see Margaret Jubb, *The Legend of Saladin in Western Literature and Historiography* (New York: Edwin Mellen Press, 2000). On Saladin's image in the Islamic world, see the superb biography by Anne-Marie Eddé, *Saladin*, trans. Jane Marie Todd (Cambridge, MA: Belknap Press, 2011), 472–92.

2. On Saddam's identification with Saladin, see Ofra Bengio, *Saddam's Word: Political Discourse in Iraq* (Oxford: Oxford University Press, 1998), 82–84.

3. The notion that modern Muslims had to be "reminded" of Saladin has deep roots in the modern literature on the Crusades, but it has been effectively demolished recently by Diana Abouali, "Saladin's Legacy in the Middle East before the Nineteenth Century," *Crusades* 10 (2011): 175–89.

4. Eddé, *Saladin*, 492–502.

5. Steven Runciman, *A History of the Crusades*, 3 vols. (Cambridge: Cambridge University Press, 1951), I: xi.

6. The reasons why Arab scholarship is not well-known in the West are complicated, not least because of the different standards of academic publishing and scholarship at play in the Arab world and the West. It should also be noted that philological approaches—the editing and publishing of medieval texts—are generally held in much greater esteem in Arab academic culture than in the West, so that many of the works of some Arab scholars (Zakkar being a prime example) are editions or studies of medieval

texts. For a survey of the contributions of Western Orientalists to the study of the Crusades, see Robert Irwin, "Orientalism and the Early Development of Crusader Studies," in P. Edbury and J. Phillips, eds., *The Experience of Crusading*, 2 vols. (Cambridge: Cambridge University Press, 2003), II: 214–30.

7. For the best attempt to classify the various approaches taken by traditional Crusades historians, see Giles Constable, "The Historiography of the Crusades," in A. E. Laiou and R. P. Mottahedeh, eds., *The Crusades from the Perspective of Byzantium and the Muslim World* (Washington, DC: Dumbarton Oaks, 2001), 1–22. It should be stated from the outset that my own use of the adjective *traditional* to include all of these approaches should not be confused with Constable's own specific category of "traditionalist" historians of the Crusades. Nor are all traditional surveys entirely one-sided: one of the standard overviews, Jonathan Riley-Smith's *The Crusades: A Short History*, 2nd ed. (New Haven, CT: Yale University Press, 2005), endeavors to be inclusive, and Christopher Tyerman's *God's War: A New History of the Crusades* (Cambridge, MA: Harvard University Press, 2006) is admirable in its scope.

8. An idea realized with some success in one massive project, Kenneth M. Setton, ed., *A History of the Crusades*, 6 vols. (Madison: University of Wisconsin Press, 1958–89), but one worth reviving.

9. A small number of books have also related a perspective on the Crusades based largely on Arabic sources, although I have framed the subject matter at hand differently from my predecessors. See the Bibliographical Sketch at the end of this book.

Chapter 1

1. Harun's journey is recounted in the geography of Ibn Rustah: Abu ʿAli Ahmad ibn ʿUmar ibn Rustah, *Kitab al-aʿlaq al-nafisa*, ed. M. J. de Goeje (Leiden: E. J. Brill, 1892), 119–30. On Harun more generally, see *EI2*, s.v. "Harun b. Yahya."

2. Abu ʿUbayd al-Bakri, *Kitab al-Masalik waʾl-mamalik*, ed. A. P. van Leeuwen and A. Ferré, 2 vols. (Tunis: Dar al-ʿArabiya liʾl-Kitab, 1992), II: 477–81 (Rome).

3. On Idrisi and his maps, see S. Maqbul Ahmed, "Cartography of al-Sharif al-Idrisi," in J. B. Harley and D. Woodward, eds., *The History of Cartography*, vol. 2, book 1: *Cartography in the Traditional Islamic and South Asian Societies* (Chicago: University of Chicago Press, 1992), 156–74. Another twelfth-century world map has recently been discovered in the remarkable *Book of Curiosities*. See Jeremy Johns and Emilie Savage-Smith, "*The Book of Curiosities*: A Newly-Discovered Series of Islamic Maps," *Imago mundi* 55 (2003): 7–24.

4. On Muslim attitudes toward Europe and Europeans in the Middle Ages, see Bernard Lewis, *The Muslim Discovery of Europe* (New York: Norton,

1982); *EI2*, s.v. "Ifrandj"; Aziz al-Azmeh, "Barbarians in Arab Eyes," *Past and Present* 134 (1992): 3–18; *CIP*, 267–74 (for the period before the Crusades).

5. Mas'udi's comments are in his *Kitab al-tanbih wa'l-ishraf*, ed. 'Abd Allah Isma'il al-Sawi (Cairo: Al-Maktaba al-Ta'rikhiya, 1938), 21–23.

6. On Ibrahim and his travels, see André Miquel, "L'Europe occidentale dans la relation arabe d'Ibrahim b. Ya'qub (Xe s.)," *Annales* 21 (1966): 1048–64.

7. The best discussion of demography in the medieval Islamic world and its debates can be found in Maya Shatzmiller, *Labour in the Medieval Islamic World* (Leiden: E. J. Brill, 1995), 55–68.

8. Ihsan 'Abbas, ed., *'Ahd Ardashir* (Beirut: Dar Sadir, 1967), 98. The definitive study of this concept is Linda T. Darling, *A History of Social Justice and Political Power in the Middle East* (London: Routledge, 2013).

9. For example, the Syrian historian Ibn Wasil, who glosses the pope as "the Caliph of the Franks" (Gabrieli, 277).

10. The literature on jihad and holy war is vast. An excellent place to start is Asma Afsaruddin, *Striving in the Path of God: Jihad and Martyrdom in Islamic Thought* (Oxford: Oxford University Press, 2013). On the mobilization of people to jihad, see Daniella Talmon-Heller, "Islamic Preaching in Syria during the Counter-Crusade (Twelfth-Thirteenth Centuries)," in I. Shagrir et al., eds., *In Laudem Hierosolymitani*. (Aldershot: Ashgate, 2007), 61–76.

11. Here I am borrowing a concept identified in another context by Deborah Tor, "Privatized Jihad and Public Order in the Pre-Seljuq Period: The Role of the Mutatawwi'a," *Iranian Studies* 38 (2005): 555–73.

12. IA, X: 453/I: 133–33 (the veteran in question is Fakhr al-Mulk ibn 'Ammar, lord of Tripoli).

13. *KI*, 94/108 (martyrs), 37–38/46–47 (Malik al-Ashtar).

14. On the sacredness of Syria, and the preceding quotations, see Paul M. Cobb, "Virtual Sacrality: Making Muslim Syria Sacred before the Crusades," *Medieval Encounters* 8 (2002): 35–55. On the interfaith cults of medieval Syria, see Josef W. Meri, *The Cult of Saints among Muslims and Jews in Medieval Syria* (Oxford: Oxford University Press, 2002).

Chapter 2

1. Ibn al-Thumna's story appears in IA, X: 132, but his dating of 444/1052 is clearly a mistake for 454/1061. The poet is Ibn al-Khayyat (d. ca. 1120): *Diwan ibn al-Khayyat*, ed. Khalil Mardam Bey (Damascus: Matbu'at al-Majma' al-'Ilmi al-'Arabi, 1958), 184.

2. The surviving fragments of al-Sulami's *Kitab al-Jihad* have been edited (albeit poorly) and published in Suhayl Zakkar, ed., *Arba'a kutub fi al-jihad min 'asr al-hurub al-salibiya* (Damascus: al-Takwin, 2007), 41–182. The passages translated

here are from 45. A new scholarly edition and translation by Niall Christie is forthcoming.

3. Muslim views of Frankish motives have been analyzed most recently in Carole Hillenbrand, "The First Crusade: The Muslim Perspective," in Jonathan P. Phillips, ed., *The First Crusade: Origins and Impact* (Manchester, UK: Manchester University Press, 1997), 130–52, reprised in *CIP*, 50–54; Niall Christie, "Religious Campaign or War of Conquest? Muslim Views of the Motives of the First Crusade," in Niall Christie and Maya Yazigi, eds., *Noble Ideals and Bloody Realities: Warfare in the Middle Ages* (Leiden: E. J. Brill, 2006), 57–72.

4. ʿAzimi, 353.

5. IA, X: 272/I: 13 (slightly modified).

6. IA 10: 272/I: 13. A specific context for the account is suggested in David Abulafia, "The Norman Kingdom of Africa and the Norman Expeditions to Majorca and the Muslim Mediterranean," in R. Allen Brown, ed., *Anglo-Norman Studies VII* (Woodbridge, UK: Boydell Press, 1985), 26–49, especially 29–30.

7. ʿAzimi, 356. Ibn al-Athir, for his part, also says he had heard that the Fatimids may have put the Franks up to it all—but this is likely just Sunni calumny (IA, X: 273/I: 14).

8. The account, from the *Annales Altahenses Maiores*, is translated in James A. Brundage, ed., *The Crusades: A Documentary Survey* (Milwaukee, WI: Marquette University Press, 1962), 3–7.

9. Jonathan P. Berkey, *The Formation of Islam: Religion and Society in the Near East, 600–1800* (Cambridge: Cambridge University Press, 2003), 143.

10. In fact Sunnis also use the term *imam* as a synonym for *caliph*, but this is usually in philosophical or theological writings. The term is of course also used generically by all Muslims to indicate the leader of prayer in a mosque and, by extension, an especially prominent scholar or spiritual guide.

11. For example, Marshall G. S. Hodgson, *The Venture of Islam: Conscience and History in a World Civilization* (Chicago: University of Chicago Press, 1977), II: 153.

12. On Fatimid empire and economy, the classic study is S. D. Goitein, *A Mediterranean Society: The Jewish Communities of the Arab World as Portrayed in the Documents of the Cairo Geniza* (Berkeley: University of California Press, 1967–94), especially vol. I. The entire work can now be appreciated in an abridgement revised and edited by Jacob Lassner (Berkeley: University of California Press, 1999). For political history, see the excellent synthesis of Paula A. Sanders, "The Fatimid State, 969–1171" in Carl F. Petry, ed., *The Cambridge History of Egypt* (Cambridge: Cambridge University Press, 1998), I: 151–74, and the overview of Paul Walker, *Exploring an Islamic Empire: Fatimid History and Its Sources* (London: I. B. Tauris, 2002), 40–64. On the rerouting of Persian Gulf traffic to the Red Sea, see Bernard Lewis, "The Fatimids and the Route to India," *Revue de*

la Faculté de Sciences Économiques de l'Université d'Istanbul 11 (1949–50): 50–54. On Tunisian trade, see S. D. Goitein, "Medieval Tunisia—The Hub of the Mediterranean," in his *Studies in Islamic History and Institutions* (Leiden: E. J. Brill, 1966), 308–28.

13. On the Zirids, see Hady Roger Idris, *La Berbérie orientale sous les Zirides, Xe–Xiie siècles* (Paris: Maisonneuve, 1962). On the highly controversial issue of the Hilalian invasions, see Michael Brett, "Fatimid Historiography: A Case Study—The Quarrel with the Zirids, 1048–58," in D. O. Morgan, ed., *Medieval Historical Writing in the Christian and Islamic Worlds* (London: SOAS, 1982), 47–59.

14. On the controversial letter documenting the alleged appeal of Pope Sergius IV, see Aleksander Gieysztor, "The Genesis of the Crusades: The Encyclical of Sergius IV," *Medievalia et Humanistica* 5 (1949): 3–23 and 6 (1950): 3–34.

15. The reign of al-Hakim has attracted a large body of scholarship. The new biography by Paul Walker, *Caliph of Cairo: Al-Hakim bi-Amr Allah, 996–1021* (Cairo: American University in Cairo Press, 2009), is the essential starting point. On the destruction of the Holy Sepulcher and its limited impact in Western Christendom, see John France, "The Destruction of Jerusalem and the First Crusade," *Journal of Ecclesiastical History* 47 (1996): 1–17 and, more generally, Colin Morris, *The Sepulchre of Christ and the Medieval West: From the Beginning to 1600* (Oxford: Oxford University Press, 2005), 134–39.

16. For the period of the end of Islamic rule on Sicily, the monumental collection of excerpts from the Arabic sources by Michele Amari is still fundamental: *Storia dei musulmani di Sicilia*, ed. C. A. Nallino, 3 vols. (Catania, Italy: R. Prampolini, 1933–39). Ibn al-Athir, al-Nuwayri, and Ibn Khaldun are best informed; however, all are late, and all appear to derive their information from the same (now lost) source. It thus seems that there is really only *one* Muslim narrative on the loss of Sicily.

17. The somewhat patchy history of Islamic Sicily before the coming of the Normans can be surveyed in Aziz Ahmad, *A History of Islamic Sicily* (Edinburgh: Edinburgh University Press, 1975).

18. On the Norman conquest of Sicily, see Graham Loud, *The Age of Robert Guiscard: Southern Italy and the Norman Conquest* (London: Longman, 2000). Most recently, see the study by Paul Chevedden, "'A Crusade from the First': The Norman Conquest of Islamic Sicily, 1060–1091," *Al-Masaq* 22 (2010): 191–225, which situates the conquest as part and parcel of the broader crusading enterprise.

19. Amatus, *The History of the Normans by Amatus of Montecassino*, trans. Prescott N. Dunbar, rev. with introduction and notes by G. A. Loud (Woodbridge : Boydell Press, 2004), V.10/137.

20. Malaterra, 2.6/88.

21. Malaterra, 2.11/91.

22. Malaterra, 2.46/126–27.

23. The literature on Islamic Spain is comparatively vast, most of it in Spanish and French. An accessible and consistently rewarding overview can be had with Richard Fletcher, *Moorish Spain* (New York: Henry Holt, 1992). A shrewd survey of political history is Hugh Kennedy, *Muslim Spain and Portugal: A Political History of al-Andalus* (London: Longman, 1996). Various aspects of the rich history of al-Andalus are treated by the experts in Salma Khadra Jayyusi, ed., *The Legacy of Muslim Spain*, 2 vols. (Leiden: E. J. Brill, 1994). On the Umayyads, see Pierre Guichard, *La España musulmana: Al-Andalus omeya (siglos VIII–XI)* (Madrid: Temas de Hoy, 1995).

24. The standard work is David Wasserstein, *The Rise and Fall of the Party-Kings: Politics and Society in Islamic Spain 1002–1086* (Princeton, NJ: Princeton University Press, 1985).

25. On Ibn Hazm, see the studies in Camilla Adang, Maribel Fierro, and Sabine Schmidtke, eds., *Ibn Hazm of Cordoba: Life and Works of a Controversial Thinker* (Leiden: E. J. Brill, 2013).

26. On Sa'id and his works, see the translation of his *Book of the Categories of Nations*: Sa'id al-Andalusi, *Science in the Medieval World: "Book of the Categories of Nations,"* trans. S. Salem and A. Kumar (Austin: University of Texas Press, 1991).

27. Fletcher, *Moorish Spain*, 98.

28. M. Asin Palacios, "Un códice inexplorado del cordobes Ibn Hazm," *Al-Andalus* 2 (1934): 42, cited in MacKay, *Spain in the Middle Ages: From Frontier to Empire, 1000–1500* (London: Macmillan, 1977), 27.

29. *The Tibyan: Memoirs of 'Abd Allah b. Buluggin, Last Zirid Emir of Granada*, trans. Amin T. Tibi (Leiden: E. J. Brill, 1986), 103.

30. On El Cid, Richard Fletcher, *The Quest for El Cid* (Oxford: Oxford University Press, 1989) is the place to start. On Sisnando, see Ramón Pidal Menéndez and E. García Gómez, "El conde mozárabe Sisnando Davídez y la política de Alfonso VI con los taifas," *Al-Andalus* 22 (1947): 27–41.

31. On the eleventh-century "reconquest," see Bernard F. Reilly, *The Contest of Christian and Muslim Spain, 1031–1157* (Cambridge, UK: Blackwell, 1992); Brian A. Catlos, *The Victors and the Vanquished, Christians and Muslims of Catalonia and Aragon, 1050–1300* (Cambridge: Cambridge University Press, 2004), especially 71–120; Joseph F. O'Callaghan, *Reconquest and Crusade in Medieval Spain* (Philadelphia: University of Pennsylvania Press, 2003), especially 1–32. Derek W. Lomax, *The Reconquest of Spain* (London: Longman, 1978), offers a blow-by-blow account.

32. On the siege of Barbastro, see Alberto Ferreiro, "The Siege of Barbastro, 1064–65: A Reassessment," *Journal of Medieval History* 9 (1983): 129–44, which reviews most of the literature. On the rather controversial *qa'id khayl ruma*, see Paul Chevedden, "The Islamic Interpretation of the Crusades: A New (Old) Paradigm for Understanding the Crusades," *Der Islam* 83 (2006): 134–35, n90.

33. The account of Ibn Hayyan is preserved in the later collection of al-Maqqari (d. 1632). See al-Maqqari, IV: 449–54/II: 265–70 (slightly modified). It is also substantially preserved by Ibn Bassam: ʿAli ibn Bassam al-Shantarini, *Al-Dhakhira fi mahasin ahl al-jazira*, ed. Ihsan ʿAbbas, 2 vols. (Beirut: Dar Sadir, 1975–79), I.3: 181–85. See also the contemporary account of our old friend the geographer al-Bakri: al-Bakri, *Kitab al-Masalik*, II: 910.

34. On the career of Alfonso VI, see Bernard F. Reilly, *The Kingdom of León Castille under King Alfonso VI, 1065–1109* (Princeton, NJ: Princeton University Press, 1988). On the conquest of Toledo, the classic study is E. Lévi-Provençal, "Alphonse VI et la prise de Tolède (1085)," *Hespéris* 12 (1931): 33–49; see also al-Maqqari, IV: 352–54, 455/II: 262–64.

35. Abu Muhammad al-Ghassal, quoted in Ibn Saʿid, *Al-Mughrib fi hula al-Maghrib*, ed. S. Dayf, 2 vols. (Cairo: Dar al-Maʿarif, 1953–55), II: 21, #336.

36. On early Muslim-Byzantine warfare on the Anatolian frontier, see John F. Haldon and Hugh Kennedy, "The Arab-Byzantine Frontier in the Eighth and Ninth Centuries: Military Organization and Society in the Borderlands," *Recueil des Travaux de l'Institut d'Etudes Byzantins* (Belgrade) 19 (1980): 79–116; Michael Bonner, *Aristocratic Violence and Holy War: Studies in the Jihad and the Arab-Byzantine Frontier* (New Haven, CT: AOS, 1996).

37. The medieval sources use the term *turkuman* ("Turcoman") not in the modern ethnic sense of the term, but much like the term *bedouin*, that is, for any Turkish-speaking nomad.

38. On the Saljuqs of Rum, a classic work is that of Mehmed Fuad Köprülü, originally published in 1943 but translated and updated by Gary Leiser as *The Seljuks of Anatolia: Their History and Culture According to Local Muslim Sources* (Salt Lake City: University of Utah Press, 1992). For the state of the field, see Sara Nur Yildiz and A. C. S. Peacock, eds., *Court and Society in the Medieval Middle East: The Seljuks of Anatolia* (London: I. B. Tauris, 2012). On the diversity of Saljuq interactions with Byzantium, see the revealing study of Alexander D. Beihammer, "Defection across the Border of Islam and Christianity: Apostasy and Cross-Cultural Interaction in Byzantine-Seljuk Relations," *Speculum* 86 (2011): 597–651.

39. AA, 1.19/39.

40. ʿAzimi, 358. He, like other Muslim sources, is aware that the Franks were working for Alexios, noting that in the year 1097 "The Frankish fleet appeared in the port of Constantinople amidst 300,000 [*sic!*] troops. They had six kings and they had all made an oath to the king of the Romans [i.e., the Byzantine emperor] to cede to him the first fortress they captured, but they did not uphold it." Ibn al-Qalanisi (IQ, 219/43), in much the same language, notes that Franks had made oaths to Alexios to cede the first fortress they captured, but that they refused to comply in the end. Compare IA, X: 273/I: 14, who specifies Antioch.

41. On the siege of Nicaea, see the recent synthesis based on Frankish sources in Thomas Asbridge, *The First Crusade: A New History* (Oxford: Oxford University Press, 2004), 118–31. Only al-ʿAzimi (358) and Ibn al-Qalanisi (IQ, 219/43) mention the conquest of Nicaea by name, and then only in the briefest terms.

42. IQ, 218/41.

43. Ibid. The "brother" mentioned here is unidentified but is usually taken to mean the Danishmend, as he is expressly named by al-ʿAzimi (358) as fighting alongside Qilij Arslan.

44. IQ, 218/42.

45. ʿAzimi, 258.

46. On the multiple agendas behind Armenian interactions with Franks and Muslims during these years, see the study of Christopher MacEvitt, *The Crusades and the Christian World of the East: Rough Tolerance* (Philadelphia: University of Pennsylvania Press, 2008), 54–65.

47. On Baldwin's "liberation" of Edessa, MacEvitt, *Rough Tolerance*, 65–73 is most enlightening.

Chapter 3

1. Alp Arslan's activities in Syria are detailed in *Bughya*, IV: 1972–79; IA X: 63–64/*Annals*, 168–70; Suhayl Zakkar, *The Emirate of Aleppo, 1004–1094* (Beirut: Dar al-Amana, 1971), 175–83.

2. *Bughya*, IV: 1974–75.

3. *Bughya*, IV: 1972.

4. For all their importance, the Saljuqs still do not have their book, though there is a recent survey of the politics of the Great Saljuqs: Osman Aziz Basan, *The Great Seljuqs: A History* (London: Routledge, 2010). A recent edited volume, Christian Lange and Songül Mecit, eds., *The Seljuqs: Politics, Society, and Culture* (Edinburgh: Edinburgh University Press, 2012), can give some sense of the variety of questions one can ask, mostly about the Great Saljuqs in Iran and Iraq. Their entry into Syria and interactions with the Franks are still poorly studied. For now, see Claude Cahen, "The Turkish Invasion: The Selchükids," in Setton, *A History of the Crusades*, I: 135–76. On their institutions relevant to the Near East, see also P. M. Holt, *The Age of the Crusades* (London: Longman, 1986), 67–81.

5. IA, X: 369/I: 76–77 (slightly modified).

6. The locus classicus for the idea of the "Sunni Revival" subsequently much-elaborated, is George Makdisi's critique, "The Sunni Revival," in *Islamic Civilization, 950–1150*, ed. D. S. Richards (Oxford: Bruno Cassirer, 1973), 15–57. For some rethinking on the subject, see Berkey, *The Formation of Islam*, 189–202; Omid Safi, *The Politics of Knowledge in Premodern Islam* (Chapel Hill: University of North Carolina Press, 2006).

7. The literature on al-Ghazali is vast. For starters, see Eric Ormsby, *Al-Ghazali: The Revival of Islam* (Oxford: Oneworld, 2007).

8. According to Ibn al-Athir's anti-Shi'i explanation of the Crusades, it was because of Atsiz's attacks at this time that the Fatimids called upon the Franks to invade Palestine (IA, X: 273/I: 13–14). On Atsiz's adventure and the coming of the Turks to Syria more generally, see the excellent study of Taef Kamal El-Azhari, *The Saljuqs of Syria during the Crusades, 463–549 A.H./1070–1154 A.D.* (Berlin: Klaus Schwarz Verlag, 1997).

9. On Malikshah's visit to Syria, see *Zubda*, 100–103; IA, X: 148–50/*Annals* 225–26.

10. Ibn Taghribirdi, 5: 139.

11. On this devastating sequence of events, see especially Carole Hillenbrand, "1092: A Murderous Year," in *Proceedings of the 14th Congress of the Union Europeénne des Arabisants et Islamisants* (Budapest: Eötvös Loránd University, 1995), II: 281–97; *CIP*, 33.

12. An excellent survey of Nizari history and theology, despite its dreadful title, can be had in Marshall G. S. Hodgson, *The Secret Order of the Assassins: The Struggle of the Early Nizari Isma'ilis against the Islamic World* (The Hague: Mouton, 1955). For a more up-to-date sketch, focusing on the origins and early phases of the movement, see Farhad Daftary, "Hasan-i Sabbah and the Origins of the Nizari Isma'ili Movement," in Farhad Daftary, ed., *Medieval Isma'ili History and Thought* (Cambridge: Cambridge University Press, 1996), 181–204; Carole Hillenbrand, "The Power Struggle between the Saljuqs and the Isma'ilis of Alamut, 487–518/1094–1124," in Daftary, ed., *Medieval Isma'ili History and Thought*, 205–20.

13. *Zubda*, II: 109.

14. *Zubda*, II: 128; IA, X: 269–70/*Annals*, 294.

15. *Zubda*, II: 129.

16. *Zubda*, II: 130. For the siege of Antioch, the recent detailed synthesis of Thomas Asbridge, *The First Crusade*, 153–240, is superb.

17. On Yaghi-Siyan's call to jihad, see *Zubda*, II: 130. The scholarly discussion of the limits of jihad took place among some Shafi'i scholars "when the Franks encamped around Antioch—may God destroy them" ('*inda nuzul al-Ifranj—ahlakahum Allah—'ala Antakiya*), according to a marginal note in al-Sulami's manuscript. See al-Sulami, *Kitab al-Jihad*, 47, n2 (text of notation on 170).

18. Numerous Frankish sources mention the arrival of Egyptian envoys in the Frankish camp in February 1098. For the details, see Asbridge, *First Crusade*, 186–87, n41.

19. *Pace* Asbridge, *First Crusade*, 156, who is aware of Yaghi-Siyan's successful call to jihad yet goes on to state, "In short, faction and instability weakened northern Syria, leaving the Turkish garrison of Antioch in isolation, without immediate recourse to any potent, unified military support." In fact this sizable army was drawn up at a moment's notice *despite* the endemic rivalries among the Saljuq military elite and their men.

20. *Zubda*, II: 131.

21. *Pace* Asbridge, *First Crusade*, 166, who states, "This story [from the Latin chronicler Raymond of Aguilers] is not confirmed by any other sources." See *Zubda*, II: 130, which depicts twenty-two ships arriving via Cyprus to capture Latakia.

22. *Zubda*, II: 130–32.

23. *Zubda*, II: 133–34.

24. IQ, 220/44. See also *Zubda*, II: 135.

25. The fate of poor Yaghi-Siyan is described in IQ, 220/44; 'Azimi, 359. The most sympathetic is the tragic account in IA, X: 275/I: 15.

26. IA, X: 276/I: 16.

27. IA, X: 276/I: 16.

28. IA, X: 276–78/I: 15–17.

29. The only Muslim account is that of IA, X: 277/I: 16–17. Asbridge, *First Crusade*, 221–32, carefully questions the role the Lance would have had in motivating the Franks.

30. IQ, 221/46.

31. IQ, 221/46.

32. IA, X: 278/I: 17.

33. IA, X: 276/I: 16; X: 277/I: 17.

34. IA, X: 279/I: 19.

35. Peter Tudebode, *Historia de Hierosolymitano Itinere*, edited by J. and L. Hill (Paris: Librairie Orientaliste Paul Geuthner, 1977). Translated by J. and L. Hill (Philadelphia: American Philosophical Society, 1974), 92-93; *GF*, 73–74; Ibn al-'Adim, the primary Muslim source for this phase, only has a contingent from Aleppo defending (*Zubda*, II: 138).

36. *Zubda*, II: 141. For a discussion of the Frankish sources that record this, see Thomas S. Asbridge, "Knowing the Enemy: Latin Relations with Islam at the Time of the First Crusade," in Norman Housley, ed., *Knighthoods of Christ: Essays on the History of the Crusades and the Knights Templar, Presented to Malcolm Barber* (Aldershot, UK: Ashgate, 2007), 21–22.

37. *Zubda*, II: 141.

38. *Zubda*, II: 141.

39. *Zubda*, II: 142.

40. On the capture of Ma'arra, see *Zubda*, II: 142–43.

41. Peter Tudebode, *Historia*, 94; Raymond d'Aguilers, *Historia francorum qui ceperunt Iherusalem*, trans. J and L. Hill (Philadelphia: American Philosophical Society, 1968), 73.

42. Fulcher, 112.

43. The most vivid accounts of the siege of Ma'arrat al-Nu'man are found in Raymond, *Historia*, 76–79; Peter Tudebode, *Historia*, 98–102; and *GF*, 77–80.

44. *Zubda*, II: 142; Peter Tudebode, *Historia*, 101.

45. *Zubda*, II: 143.

46. Peter Tudebode, *Historia*, 102. See also Fulcher, 112.

47. *Zubda*, II: 142.

48. *Zubda*, II: 143.

49. Raymond, *Historia*, 81–83; *Zubda*, II: 143.

50. Ibn al-ʿAdim claims that the *only* survivors of Maʿarra were those who happened to have been at Shayzar and other towns (*Zubda*, II: 143).

51. The terror that the Crusaders and the reports of their cannibalism and brutality inspired in the Muslim ranks is described in Raymond, *Historia*, 81.

52. Raymond, *Historia*, 93.

53. Peter Tudebode, *Historia*, 104.

54. Raymond, *Historia*, 83–84; Tudebode, *Historia*, 104–5.

55. Raymond, *Historia*, 83–84. On the Crusaders at Shayzar, see also *GF*, 81–82.

56. The path of the Crusaders into Syria is related in succinct detail in Tudebode, *Historia*, 98–111. Compare Raymond, *Historia*, 75–92, 104–15; Fulcher, 112–16; *GF*, 77–87.

57. IQ, 222/47.

58. On the siege and negotiations at ʿArqa, see Asbridge, *First Crusade*, 282–94.

59. IA, X: 283/I: 21.

60. The precise date of the Fatimid recapture of Jerusalem from the Saljuqs is a matter of some controversy. Ibn al-Qalanisi and al-ʿAzimi, who were both closest to the event in time and place, give the date as Shawwal 491/ September 1098. Ibn al-Athir, by contrast, explicitly places it much earlier, in Shaʿban 489/July 1096, but this is impossible as Suqman had just arrived in Syria at this point and was entangled in affairs in Aleppo. Ibn al-ʿAdim makes no mention at all of the event.

61. Naser-e Khosraw, *Book of Travels (Safarnama)*, trans. W. M. Thackston (Albany: State University of New York Press, 1986), 21. His account can be found on 21–38. The Andalusi scholar Ibn al-ʿArabi passed through Palestine on the eve of the Frankish invasion, and describes a similarly thriving Muslim intellectual life. See Joseph Drory, "Some Observations during a Visit to Palestine by Ibn al-ʿArabi of Seville in 1092–1095," *Crusades* 3 (2004): 101–24.

62. On Jerusalem, see Adrian J. Boas, *Jerusalem in the Time of the Crusades* (London: Routledge, 2001); Joshua Prawer, "The Jerusalem the Crusaders Captured: A Contribution to the Medieval Topography of the City," in P. W. Edbury, ed., *Crusade and Settlement* (Cardiff: University College Press, 1985), 1–16.

63. IQ, 222/47.

64. Thus IQ, 222/47–48.

65. Thus IA, X: 283/I: 21.

66. IA, X: 283/I: 21.

67. IQ, 222/48; ʿAzimi, 360. This is not recorded in any Frankish source.

68. The letters from concerned Jews seeking funds to ransom their coreligionists held captive at Ascalon have been edited and translated in S. D. Goitein, "Contemporary Letters on the Capture of Jerusalem by the Crusaders," *Journal of Jewish Studies* 3 (1952): 162–77.

69. IQ, 222/48.

70. IA, X: 283–84/I: 21.

71. IA, X: 284/I: 22.

72. Ibn Taghribirdi, 151–52, cited in Hillenbrand, "The First Crusade," 140–41.

73. On this point, see the thorough study of Konrad Hirschler, "The Jerusalem Conquest of 492/1099 in the Medieval Arabic Historiography of the Crusades: From Regional Plurality to Islamic Narrative," forthcoming in the journal *Crusades*.

74. IA, X: 286/I: 22. On the significance of Fatimid attempts to take the lead against the Franks, see Michael Brett, "The Battles of Ramla (1099–1105)," in *CHESFAME* I, 17–38.

75. IQ, 223/48, and, more broadly, Brett, "The Fatimids and the Counter-Crusade, 1099–1171," in *CHESFAME* V, 15–26.

76. On the debacle at Ascalon, see IA, X: 286/I: 22. IQ, 223/48–49 mentions the coastal fleet. Al-'Azimi, 360 specifically mentions the death of Jalal al-Mulk.

77. Al-Harawi's harangue is described in IA, X: 285/I: 22.

78. IA, X: 285/I: 22.

Chapter 4

1. On Shayzar, the Banu Munqidh, and Usama's career, see Paul M. Cobb, *Usama ibn Munqidh: Warrior-Poet of the Age of Crusades* (Oxford: Oneworld, 2005). For the *Book of Contemplation*, the standard edition is that of Hitti, *KI*, translated by Paul M. Cobb as *The Book of Contemplation: Islam and the Crusades* (Harmondsworth, UK: Penguin Classics, 2008).

2. IQ, 223–24/49–50; 'Azimi, 360; IA, X: 300/I: 32. *Zubda*, II: 145.

3. IA, X: 300/I: 32, X: 343–44/I: 59; 'Azimi, 361. The most detailed account of this "crusade of 1101" is from the Frankish chronicler Albert of Aachen: AA, book VIII in its entirety. Albert (VIII: 7/595) claims that some of the Franks had planned to march even on to Baghdad—a Frankish threat suspected in other contexts. See *LA*, 132/255.

4. IQ, 232/60–61; 'Azimi, 361; IA, X: 373–75/I: 79–80; Claude Cahen, *La Syrie du Nord à l'epoque des croisades et la principauté franque d'Antioche* (Paris: P. Geuthner, 1940), 237–38; T. S. Asbridge, *The Creation of the Principality of Antioch, 1098–1130* (Woodbridge, UK: Boydell Press, 2000), 55–56.

5. IQ, 226–27/53–54.

6. IQ, 229/55–56; 'Azimi, 361–62; IA, X: 345–46, 364–65/I: 61, 73–74.

7. IQ, 231/58–59; 'Azimi, 362; Ibn Muyassar, *Akhbar Misr*, published as *Choix de passages de la chronique d'Égypte d'Ibn Muyassar*, ed. Ayman Fu'ad Sayyid (Cairo: IFAO, 1981), 74.

8. IQ, 240–41/71; 'Azimi, 362–63; IA, X: 394–95/I: 93; Ibn Muyassar, *Akhbar Misr*, 75.

9. IQ, 226/51–53; 'Azimi, 361. Ibn Sulayha was welcomed in Damascus, where his conspicuous wealth was much commented upon, and then proceeded to Baghdad. There the sultan Barkiyaruq had him arbitrarily arrested and his wealth seized.

10. IQ, 226/53; IA X: 310–12/I: 38–40.

11. Naser-i Khursraw, *Safar-nama*, ed. M. Dabir-Siyaki (Tehran: n.p., 1956), 14–15; Naser-e Khosraw, *Book of Travels (Safarnama)*, trans. W. M. Thackston (Albany: State University of New York Press, 1986), 12–13.

12. 'Azimi, 361; IA, X: 343–44/I: 59–60.

13. IQ, 228/55.

14. IA, X: 365–66/I: 74.

15. 'Azimi, 362, suggesting his son continued the siege directly after him (which is not quite correct); IA, X: 411–12/I: 104–5.

16. IQ, 257/85.

17. 'Azimi, 363; IA, X: 452–54/I: 132–33.

18. IQ, 261–63/88–92; 'Azimi, 364; IA, X: 475–77/I: 148–50.

19. IQ, 225/51; 'Azimi, 360–61.

20. IQ, 228/54–55.

21. IQ, 231/60; 'Azimi, 362.

22. IQ, 232–33/61–62; 'Azimi, 362; IA, X: 372–73/I: 78–79; Ibn Muyassar, *Akhbar Misr*, 75.

23. IQ, 260/87; IA, X: 455–56/I: 134.

24. IQ, 260–61/87–88; IA, X: 467–69/I: 142–43.

25. IQ, 268–69/99–101; 'Azimi, 364.

26. IQ, 273–74/106–8; 'Azimi, 365; IA X: 479–80/I: 152.

27. IQ, 275–76/108–10; IA, X: 480–81/I: 152–53.

28. IQ, 284–91/119–30; 'Azimi, 366; IAH, 168–69.

29. IQ, 233–36/62–65; IA, X: 375–77/I: 80–81.

30. IQ, 239/69; 'Azimi, 362–63; IA, X: 399–400/I: 96–97.

31. IQ, 306/150–51; 'Azimi, 367.

32. IQ, 258–59/86–87; IA, X: 467/I: 142.

33. IQ, 307–13/151–53. Gibb, Ibn al-Qalanisi's translator, has left the difficult text of this important document out of his translation.

34. IA, X: 467/I: 142.

35. IQ, 263–64/92.

36. IQ, 264–65/93; IAH, 163.

37. IQ, 273/106; IAH, 165.

38. IQ, 277–78/113.

39. *Zubda*, II: 148–49.

40. IQ, 239–40/69–70; ʿAzimi, 362; *Zubda*, II: 150–51.

41. IA, X: 460–66/I: 138–42; *LA*, 132–34/255–57; *Zubda*, II: 153; IAH, 158–59; Cahen, *Syrie du Nord*, 247–51.

42. ʿAzimi, 365.

43. *Zubda*, II: 145.

44. IQ, 230, 242, 302/57–58, 72–73, 145; IA, X: 345, 408–10, 499/I: 60–61, 102–4, 164; *Bughya*, VII: 3354–59; *Zubda*, II:145–47, 151–52. On the Nizaris in Syria more generally, see Farhad Daftary, "The Syrian Ismailis and the Crusaders: History and Myth," in F. Daftary, ed., *Ismailis in Medieval Muslim Societies* (London: I. B. Tauris, 2005), 149–70; see also his *The Ismaʿilis: Their History and Doctrines* (Cambridge: Cambridge University Press, 1990), 324–434, 669–99, with thorough bibliography.

45. IQ, 265–66/93–96; IA, X: 452–54/I: 132–33.

46. IQ, 270–71/101–5; IA, X: 485–86/I: 156; *Zubda*, II: 154–56.

47. IQ, 276–77/110–12; IA, X: 482–83/I: 154; *Zubda*, II: 157.

48. IQ, 278–79/114–15; ʿAzimi, 365; IA, X: 486–87/I: 156–57; *Zubda*, II: 158–61.

49. IQ, 280–82/116–17.

50. IQ, 283/118–19; *KI*, 68–69/80–81; IA, X: 487–88/I: 157; *Zubda*, II: 161.

51. IQ, 293–96/133–37; IA, X: 495–96/I: 162; *Zubda*, II: 163–64; IAH, 169–70. It was at this point, according to Ibn al-Qalanisi and others, that Tughtakin transferred an ancient copy of the Qurʾan of the early caliph ʿUthman from Tiberias to Damascus, where it became a special object of devotion in times of trouble.

52. IQ, 298–300/139–42; ʿAzimi, 366; IA, X: 496–97/I: 162–63; IAH, 170–71.

53. IA, X: 501–2/I: 166–67.

54. ʿAzimi, 367; IA, X: 509–11/I: 172–73; *Zubda*, II: 174–75. Significantly Ibn al-Qalanisi does not mention this rebellion of his hero Tughtakin, nor anything about the failed campaign of Bursuq. Usama ibn Munqidh, however, was involved in the siege of Kafartab and was one of the Muslims left behind to guard the prisoners. His own detailed account of the siege differs in some particulars from that of Ibn al-Athir: *KI*, 73–77/85–89. For a Frankish perspective, the eyewitness account of Walter the Chancellor is especially valuable: *Galetrii Cancellarii, Bella Antiochena*, ed. H. Hagenmeyer (Innsbruck, Verlag der Wagner'schen universitäts-buchhandlung, 1896). Translated by T. S. Asbridge and S. B. Edgington as *Walter the Chancellor's The Antiochene Wars: Translation and Commentary* (Aldershot, UK: Ashgate, 1999), I.2–I.7/84–108. Asbridge and Edgington also include translations of relevant excerpts from other Frankish sources, as well as one Armenian text. See also Asbridge, *The Creation of the Principality of Antioch*, 70–73.

55. On the historical geography, see René Dussaud, *Topographie historique de la Syrie antique et médiévale* (Paris: P. Geuthner, 1927), 220–23. The site is located near the modern Bab al-Hawa crossing at the Turkish-Syrian border. On the battle itself, see T. S. Asbridge, "The Significance and Causes of the Battle of the Field of Blood," *Journal of Medieval History* 23 (1997): 301–16; Asbridge, *The Creation of the Principality of Antioch*, 73–81.

56. IQ, 319–21/159–61; 'Azimi, 369–70; IA, X: 553–55/I: 203–5; KI, 118–21/131–32; *Zubda*, II: 187–90; the Frankish account alluded to in Walter, *Bella Antiochena*, II.5/125–29; Cahen, *Syrie du Nord*, 284–87.

57. *Zubda*, II: 190. On the impact of the Field of Blood on Antioch, see Asbridge, *The Creation of the Principality of Antioch*, 80–81.

Chapter 5

1. Abu Bakr Muhammad al-Turtushi, *Siraj al-muluk*, ed. M. Fathi Abu Bakr, 2 vols. (Cairo: al-Dar al-Misriya al-Lubnaniya, 1994). The work remains untranslated into English. There is likewise little scholarship on him in English; for now, see *EI2*, s.v. "al-Turtushi" (A. Abdesselem).

2. On Aleppo after Ridwan, see *Zubda* II: 167–82. On Il-Ghazi's tenure, see *Zubda* II: 185–206.

3. On Artuqid Aleppo, see *Zubda* II: 209–38; 'Azimi, 372–77; IA, X: 531–32, 591–92, 604, 611, 619/I: 187, 231, 240, 245. On wars with the Franks, see especially Asbridge, *The Creation of the Principality of Antioch*, 81–87.

4. On these events, see *Zubda*, II: 220–38; Ibn al-'Adim's account of the Frankish siege is especially valuable as his grandfather was involved in much of the negotiations that took place: IQ, 337–38/172–74, 341/177–78, 344–47/181–83; IA, X: 623–24, 633–34, 649–51/I: 253–54, 261–62, 272–73; IAH, 187–88; Asbridge, *The Creation of the Principality of Antioch*, 87–90. One cannot help noting that it was really Zangi, not the Nizaris, who most benefited from Aqsunqur's death.

5. On Zangi, see the perceptive sketch by Carole Hillenbrand, "Abominable Acts: The Career of Zengi," in Jonathan Phillips and Martin Hoch, eds., *The Second Crusade: Scope and Consequences* (Manchester, UK: Manchester University Press, 2001), 111–32; Coksun Alptekin, *The Reign of Zangi, 521–541/1127–1146* (Erzurum: Atatürk University Press, 1978).

6. The quotations are from IA, X: 658–59/I: 282–83.

7. *Zubda*, II: 241–47; IA, X: 658–59, 662–63/I: 279, 282–83; 'Azimi, 381–83. The exact chronology of the fall of al-Atharib is uncertain.

8. IQ, 342–43/179–80.

9. On the anti-Nizari pogrom in Damascus, see IQ, 351–56/187–95; IA, X: 656–57/I: 277–78; IAH, 185–86.

10. IQ, 339–40/174–77; IA, X: 639/I: 265–66, who comments upon this odd double-rout; IAH, 181–82.

11. On this "Damascus crusade" of 1129, which, among other things, was instrumental in the formation of the Templars, see Jonathan Phillips, "Hugh of Payns and the 1129 Damascus Crusade," in Malcolm Barber, ed. *The Military Orders: Fighting for the Faith and Caring for the Sick* (Aldershot, UK: Variorum, 1994), 141–47; IQ, 356–60/195–200; 'Azimi, 382; *KI*, 114–16/127–28; IA, X: 657–58/I: 278–79; IAH, 187.

12. Ibn al-Qalanisi and Ibn al-Athir claim the Franks planned the attacked only after Tughtakin's death (IQ, 356/195; IA, X: 657/I: 278).

13. IQ, 360/199.

14. Zangi's activities in northern Syria are described in IQ, 386–405/228–40; *Zubda*, II: 260. Usama was involved in one of Zangi's reconnaissance missions toward Damascus in 1135: *KI*, 150–51/163–64; *Zubda*, II: 257–59; IA, XI: 20–22/I: 313–14.

15. Ba'rin: IQ, 407–8/242–43; *Zubda*, II: 261–62; IA, XI: 50–53/I: 335–37.

16. The Byzantine invasion: IQ, 406–7, 412–13, 415–20/240–41, 244–46, 248–52; 'Azimi, 393–94; *Zubda*, II: 262–68; IA, XI: 53, 56–60/I: 337, 339–42. For Usama's insider account of the siege at Shayzar, see *KI*, 2–3/11–12, 113–14/125–26.

17. Zangi's conquests and overtures toward Damascus: IQ, 418–28/252–62; *Zubda*, II: 268–70, 272–74; 'Azimi, 394–95; IA, XI: 55, 68–70, 73–75/I: 339, 349–50, 352–53; IAH, 199–201.

18. The quip is from William of Tyre, *A History of Deeds Done beyond the Sea*, trans. E. A. Babcock and A. C. Krey (New York: Columbia University Press, 1943), 2: 142.

19. On the fall of Edessa, see IQ, 436–38/266–69; IA, XI: 98–100/I: 372–73 (who stresses that Zangi's Artuqid adventures were all a ruse and that most of the plunder taken was returned to its rightful owner); *Zubda*, II: 278–80 (in which it is the governor of Harran who urges Zangi to attack); IAH, 204–7.

20. IQ, 436/266–67.

21. IQ, 437/267–68.

22. On the death of Zangi, see *Zubda*, II: 281–86; IA, X: 110–12/I: 382–83; Abu Shama, I: 154–57; IAH, 207–8.

23. The classic study of Nur al-Din is the older but detailed work of Nikita Elisséeff, *Nur al-Din, un grand prince musulman de Syrie au temps des Croisades, 511–569 H./1118–1174*, 3 vols. (Damascus: Institute Français de Damas, 1967). For an important corrective, see the valuable essay by Yaacov Lev, "The *Jihad* of Sultan Nur al-Din of Syria (1146–1174): History and Discourse," *Jerusalem Studies in Arabic and Islam* 35 (2008): 227–84.

24. IA, XI: 114/II: 8. See also IQ, 449–50/274–75; *Zubda* II: 290–91.

25. For example, IQ, 540–42/275–79; IAH, 210–11.

26. On the Second Crusade and all its fronts, see the excellent study by Jonathan Phillips, *The Second Crusade: Extending the Frontiers of Christendom*

(New Haven, CT: Yale University Press, 2007). Muslim accounts: IQ, 460–66/280–87; IA, XI: 129–31/II: 21–22; *Zubda*, II: 291–93; Abu Shama, I: 175–95; IAH, 211–13.

27. IQ, 460/280–81 (slightly modified).

28. IQ, 462/281.

29. IQ, 462/281.

30. IQ, 462/281–82.

31. On this decision, and the logic thereof, see Martin Hoch, "The Choice of Damascus as the Objective of the Second Crusade: A Re-evaluation," in *Autours de la Première Croisade*, ed. M. Balard (Paris: Publications de la Sorbonne, 1996), 359–69.

32. IQ, 463–64/283.

33. On the siege at Damascus, see IQ, 462–66/282–87; A. J. Forey, "The Failure of the Siege of Damascus," *Journal of Medieval History* 10 (1984): 13–23.

34. IQ, 466–75/287–94; IA, XI: 134/II: 24–25; IAH, 214–15.

35. On Nur al-Din's activities after the Second Crusade and Muslim victories in the north, see IQ, 471/289; IA, XI: 144–45, 149, 154–56, 163–64/II: 31–32, 36, 39–40, 45–46; *Zubda* II: 298–303; Abu Shama, I: 195–257; IAH, 216–17.

36. On Nur al-Din at Damascus, see IQ, 503–9/318–22; IA, XI: 197–98/II: 71–72; *Zubda*, II: 303–5; Abu Shama, I: 241–43, 259–64, 301–6; IAH, 217–22, 229–30.

37. Lev, "The *Jihad* of Sultan Nur al-Din," 275, citing Elisséeff, provides the stunning statistic: "Prior to Nur al-Din's rise to power, in the territories he eventually ruled, there were only 16 law colleges and one *zawiya* (a lodge for mystics). During Nur al-Din's rule, 56 law colleges and five *zawiyas* were established."

38. The quote is from *TMD* 57: 120. Ibn al-'Adim, *Zubda*, II: 293 goes into some detail about the building programs and religious posts Nur al-Din created in Aleppo.

39. On Ibn 'Asakir and his *History*, see James E. Lindsay, ed., *Ibn 'Asakir and Early Islamic History* (Princeton, NJ: Darwin Press, 2002). On his treatise on jihad and the Zangid context, see Suleiman A. Mourad and James E. Lindsay, *The Intensification and Reorientation of Sunni Jihad Ideology in the Crusader Period* (Leiden: Brill, 2013).

40. *TMD*, 57: 121.

41. IAH, 235.

42. IQ, 519/329.

43. On these campaigns in the Hawran and associated public spectacles, see IQ, 519–25/330–37; IAH, 238–39.

44. On the Greek menace, see IQ, 544–46/353–55, Abu Shama, I: 380, 385. On the relative stasis in the north, see IA, XI: 208–9/II: 79–80; *Zubda*, II:

305. On the sectarian violence, Ibn al-'Adim is a vital source, as his grandfather was the qadi of Aleppo at the time (*Zubda*, II: 309–11).

45. On the Almoravids, the best survey is in French: V. Lagardère, *Les Almoravides jusqu'au règne de Yusuf b. Tafšin (1039–1106)* (Paris: L'Harmattan, 1989); Kennedy, *Muslim Spain and Portugal*, 154–88; Ronald Messier, *The Almoravids and the Meanings of Jihad* (Santa Barbara, CA: Praeger, 2010), an accessible read that also incorporates recent archaeological data.

46. On this decision, see al-Maqqari, IV: 359–61/II: 273–75; al-Marrakushi, 130–31.

47. On the coming of the Almoravids and their early activities in al-Andalus, see al-Maqqari, IV: 361–77/II: 279–302; al-Marrakushi, 131–35.

48. J. M. Viguera, "Las cartas de al-Gazali y al-Turtusi al soberano almorávid Yusuf b. Tasufin," *Al-Andalus* 42 (1977): 341–74.

49. On the Almohads, the classic study is Ambrosio Huici Miranda, *Historia política del imperio almohade*, 2 vols. (Tetouan, Morocco: Editora Marroqui, 1956–57). An excellent short survey can be had in Maribel Fierro, "The Almohads (524–668/1130–1269) and the Hafsids (627–932/1229–1526)," in M. Fierro, ed., *The New Cambridge History of Islam*, vol. 2: *The Western Islamic World, Eleventh to Eighteenth Centuries* (Cambridge: Cambridge University Press, 2010), 66–86.

50. The various accounts of the coming of the Almohads to al-Andalus are contradictory; compare IA XI: 115/II: 9; al-Maqqari, IV: 377–78/II: 308–10; al-Marrakushi, 178, especially 208–13. I have relied upon the reconstruction of Kennedy, *Muslim Spain and Portugal*, 202–3 (itself citing Huici, *Historia política del imperio almohade* I: 156–58).

51. As carefully demonstrated in Phillips, *Second Crusade*, 140.

52. For a detailed description of the siege, see Phillips, *Second Crusade*, 156–67.

53. On this correspondence, mentioned only in a Latin source, the remarkable *De expugnatione Lyxbonensi*, see Phillips, 159–60.

54. On these eastern Iberian conquests, see Philipps, *Second Crusade*, 261–68. On Tortosa, see especially Nikolas Jaspert, "*Capta est Dertosa, clavis Christianorum*: Tortosa and the Crusades," in Phillips and Hoch, *The Second Crusade*, 90–110.

55. IA, XI: 136/II: 26.

56. On the Normans in Africa, see Abulafia, "The Norman Kingdom of Africa,"; Michael Brett, "The Normans in Ifriqiya," in his *Ibn Khaldun and the Medieval Maghrib* (Aldershot, UK: Variorum, 1999), 1–26, an updated and recast version of an earlier article published in 1991; Jeremy Johns, "Malik Ifriqiya," *Libyan Studies* 18 (1987): 89–101; and especially Alex Metcalfe, *The Muslims of Medieval Italy* (Edinburgh: Edinburgh University Press, 2009), 160–80.

57. IA, XI: 124/II: 16–17.

58. According to IA, XI: 120–21/II: 13–14, the citizens of Gabès rose up against their governor, allowing the Zirids to take him prisoner and torture him. His kinsmen then called upon Roger and the Normans to revenge him.

59. On the Normans at Mahdiya, etc., see IA, XI: 125–29/II: 18–20.

60. On these uprisings, see IA, XI: 203–5/II: 76–77.

61. On the Almohad conquest of Mahdiya, see IA, XI: 241–45/II: 103–6.

62. On the Frankish strategy toward Ascalon, see Martin Hoch, "The Crusaders' Strategy against Fatimid Ascalon and the 'Ascalon Project' of the Second Crusade," in Michael Gervers, ed., *The Second Crusade and the Cistercians* (New York: St. Martin's Press, 1992), 119–30. On the Frankish conquest, see for example, IQ, 497/314–17; IAH, 225–26.

63. On Saladin's early career in Egypt, the standard work is Yaacov Lev, *Saladin in Egypt* (Leiden: E. J. Brill, 1999). See also Ibn Shaddad, 36–47/40–49; Abu Shama, I: 401–14, II: 10–16, 46–140, 143–47, 180, 184–203; M. Lyons and P. Jackson, *Saladin: The Politics of Holy War* (Cambridge: Cambridge University Press, 1982), 31–80; Eddé, *Saladin*, 26–64.

Chapter 6

1. Saladin's diplomatic wrangling and campaigns against his Muslim rivals are detailed in Lyons and Jackson, *Saladin*, 71–253; *CIP*, 171–95; Ibn Shaddad, 50–74/51–71; IA, XI: 405–43/II: 223–54, XI: 472–503/II: 277–98, XI: 511–25/II: 304–15; Eddé, *Saladin*, 67–89.

2. Taqi al-Din Abu Bakr ibn Hijja al-Hamawi (d. 1434), *Kitab thamarat al-awraq* (Cairo, 1921), 120–23. The story, set in 1207, undoubtedly comes from an earlier work, but I have not been able to trace it.

3. Indeed in certain respects, the military activities of Franks and Muslims could actually be seen as some of the clearest examples of long-term cultural interchange in which each "side" developed in constant dialogue with the other over matters of tactics, technology, and fortification, a point made most forcefully for the Near East in Ronnie Ellenblum, *Crusader Castles and Modern Histories* (Cambridge: Cambridge University Press, 2007), but applicable to other fronts such as al-Andalus. On comparisons and influences on tactics and technology, see especially David Nicolle, *Fighting for the Faith: The Many Fronts of Crusade and Jihad, 1000–1500 AD* (Yardley, PA: Westholme, 2007) and his *Crusader Warfare*, 2 vols. (Hambledon, UK: Continuum Books, 2007), especially vol. 2 on Islamic warfare. See also Yaacov Lev, "Infantry in Muslim Armies during the Crusades," in John H. Pryor, ed., *Logistics of Warfare in the Age of the Crusades* (Aldershot, UK: Ashgate, 2006), 185–208; and John France, "Warfare in the Mediterranean region in the Age of the Crusades, 1095–1291: A Clash of Contrasts," in C. Kostick, ed., *The Crusades and the Near East: Cultural Histories* (London: Routledge, 2011), 9–26.

4. On this finding, which revises earlier models of Frankish "colonialism" and the like, see Ronnie Ellenblum, *Frankish Rural Settlement in the Latin Kingdom of Jerusalem* (Cambridge: Cambridge University Press, 1998).

5. Ibn Jubayr, 287/300.

6. On the Mediterranean commercial economy during these centuries, see Eliyahu Ashtor, *Levant Trade in the Later Middle Ages* (Princeton, NJ: Princeton University Press, 1983); David Abulafia, "The Role of Trade in Muslim-Christian Contact during the Middle Ages," in D. Agius and R. Hitchcock, eds., *The Arab Influence in Medieval Europe* (Reading, UK: Ithaca Press, 1994), 1–24; David Abulafia, "Trade and Crusade, 1050–1250," in M. Goodich et al., eds., *Cross-Cultural Convergences in the Crusader Period* (New York: Peter Lang, 1995), 1–20; *CIP*, 394–406.

7. On *funduqs*, see Olivia R. Constable, *Housing the Stranger in the Mediterranean World: Lodging, Trade, and Travel in Late Antiquity and the Middle Ages* (Cambridge: Cambridge University Press, 2003). On the broad trends in commerce in the medieval Mediterranean, see David Abulafia, *The Great Sea: A Human History of the Mediterranean* (Oxford: Oxford University Press, 2011), especially part III.

8. For a superb analysis of Frankish-Muslim treaties and alliances until the reign of Saladin, see Michael A. Köhler, *Alliances and Treaties between Frankish and Muslim Rulers in the Middle East: Cross-Cultural Diplomacy in the Period of the Crusades*, trans. P. M. Holt, ed. Konrad Hirschler, revised ed. (Leiden: E. J. Brill, 2013). See also Hadia Dajani-Shakeel, 'Diplomatic Relations between Muslim and Frankish Rulers, 1097–1153 A.D.," in M. Shatzmiller, ed., *Crusaders and Muslims in Twelfth-Century Syria* (Leiden: E. J. Brill, 1993), 190–215. On later Ayyubid and Mamluk diplomacy, see chapters 7 and 8 below, respectively.

9. Jeremy Johns, "The Norman Kings of Sicily and the Fatimid Caliphate," *Anglo-Norman Studies* 15 (1993): 133–60. For an (often rosy) account of literary activity in the Norman court, with translations, see Karla Mallette, *The Kingdom of Sicily, 1100–1250: A Literary History* (Philadelphia: University of Pennsylvania Press, 2005).

10. On translation, see Charles Burnett, *The Introduction of Arabic Learning into England* (London: British Library, 1997); Charles Burnett, "The Translating Activity in Medieval Spain," in Jayyusi, ed., *Legacy of Muslim Spain*, II: 1036–58; Thomas E. Burman, *Reading the Qur'an in Latin Christendom, 1140–1560* (Philadelphia: University of Pennsylvania Press, 2007). But see now Emilie Savage-Smith, "New Evidence for the Frankish Study of Arabic Medical Texts in the Crusader Period," *Crusades* 5 (2006): 99–112.

11. A thought-provoking set of essays on all these zones can be found in James M. Powell, ed., *Muslims under Latin Rule, 1100–1300* (Princeton, NJ: Princeton University Press, 1990).

12. Ibn Jubayr, 342/359–60.

13. Cited in Joseph F. O'Callaghan, "The Mudejars of Castile and Portugal in the Twelfth and Thirteenth Centuries," in Powell, *Muslims under Latin Rule*, 54.

14. Ibn Jubayr, 301–2/317.

15. As pointed out by Benjamin Kedar, "The Subjected Muslims of the Frankish Levant," in Powell, *Muslims under Latin Rule*, 166–70. For some demographic considerations of the Muslim peasantry, see Benjamin Z. Kedar and Muhammad al-Hajjuj, "Muslim Villagers of the Frankish Kingdom of Jerusalem," in *Itinéraires d'Orient. Hommages à Claude Cahen. Res Orientales* 6 (1994): 145–56. An Arabic text detailing the history of one such refugee family from Nablus is fruitfully examined (with editing and translation) in Daniella Talmon-Heller, "The Cited Tales of the Wondrous Doings of the Shaykhs of the Holy Land ..." *Crusades* 1 (2003): 111–54.

16. On Muslim perceptions of the Franks in the Near East, see *CIP,* 257–327, 329–80.

17. On Usama and the Franks, in addition to Hillenbrand, see Cobb, *Usama ibn Munqidh*, 93–114.

18. *KI*, 134–35, 140/147, 153.

19. 'Ali ibn Abi Bakr al-Harawi, *Kitab al-Isharat ila Ma'rifat al-Ziyarat*, ed. J. Sourdel-Thomine (Damascus: IFAO, 1953). Edited and translated by Josef W. Meri as *A Lonely Wayfarer's Guide to Pilgrimage* (Princeton, NJ: Darwin Pres, 2004), 4 (Richard), 78–80 (Hebron).

20. *KI*, 132/144.

21. On al-Khazandari's fascinating passage, see Khazandari, 154–55. For general discussion, see Robert Irwin, "The Image of the Byzantine and the Frank in Arab Popular Literature of the Late Middle Ages," in B. Arbel et al., eds., *Latins and Greeks in the Eastern Mediterranean after 1204* (London: Frank Cass, 1989), 226–42.

22. On Granada and Almería, see IA, XI: 223–24/II: 91; al-Maqqari, IV: 378.

23. On these events, see Kennedy, *Muslim Spain and Portugal*, 200–216; Fierro, "Almohads and Hafsids," 70–73. As it happened, many abandoned the cause, fearing the Almohads would seize their lands in their absence (IA, XI: 245–46/II: 106). The activities of the Almohads under 'Abd al-Mu'min and his successors are abundantly documented in the "official" chronicle of the Almohad scribe Ibn Abi Sahib al-Salat, *Ta'rikh al-mann bi-al-imama*, ed. 'Abd al-Hadi al-Tazi (Baghdad: Wizarat al-Thiqafa wa-al-Funun, 1979).

24. Kennedy, *Muslim Spain and Portugal*, 216–36; Fierro, "Almohads and Hafsids," 73–86.

25. On Yusuf in al-Andalus, see al-Maqqari, IV: 378–80/II: 318–19; al-Marrakushi, 236–37, 243–61.

26. On al-Mansur's campaigns, see al-Maqqari, IV: 380–83/II: 318–23; al-Marrakushi, 261–88.

27. Al-Marrakushi, 322.

28. On al-Nasir, see al-Maqqari, IV: 383/II: 323–24; al-Marrakushi, 307–23.

29. On the last days of the Almohads, see Kennedy, *Muslim Spain and Portugal*, 237–66; O'Callaghan, *Reconquest and Crusade*, 78–98; Al-Maqqari, IV: 383–84/II: 324–25; al-Marrakushi. 335.

30. The quote comes from al-Qadi al-Fadil, cited in Lyons and Jackson, *Saladin*, 244. On Saladin's campaigns against the Franks, see Holt, *The Age of the Crusades*, 53–59; Lyons and Jackson, *Saladin*, 242–53; Eddé, *Saladin*, 187–202; Ibn Shaddad, 74–98/71–91; IA, XI: 529–58/II: 318–39, XII: 5–23/II: 344–57, XII: 27–32/II: 360–63; Abu Shama, III.

31. On Reynald, see Bernard Hamilton, "The Elephant of Christ: Reynald of Châtillon," in D. Baker, ed., *Religious Motivation: Biographical and Sociological Problems for the Church Historian* (Oxford: Oxford University Press, 1978), 97–108, which attempts to dispel his bad press. Hillenbrand explores how his treatment as a prisoner of war may have shaped his career in "The Imprisonment of Reynald of Châtillon." On the Red Sea expedition, Gary Leiser, "The Crusader Raid in the Red Sea in 578/1182–83," *Journal of the American Research Center in Egypt* 13 (1976): 87–100 provides a thorough review of the Arabic sources. And see Marcus Milwright, "Reynald of Châtillon and the Red Sea Expedition of 1182–83," in Christie and Yazigi, *Noble Ideals and Bloody Realities*, 235–60, which speculates on the question of motive.

32. On the battle of Hattin, see Lyons and Jackson, *Saladin*, 255–66; Benjamin Kedar, "The Battle of Hattin Revisited," in B. Z. Kedar, ed., *The Horns of Hattin* (Jerusalem: Yad Izhak Ben-Zvi, 1992), 190–207; Eddé, *Saladin*, 203–18.

33. IA, XI: 536/II: 323.

34. C. P. Melville and M. C. Lyons, "Saladin's Hattin Letter," in Kedar, *The Horns of Hattin*, 208–12, quote on 212.

35. Ibn Shaddad, 79/75 (slightly modified).

36. Abu Shama, III: 299.

37. On the victory dome, see Z. Gal, "Saladin's Dome of Victory at the Horns of Hattin," in Kedar, *The Horns of Hattin*, 213–15.

38. On Saladin's conquests in Syria in the wake of Hattin (excepting Jerusalem), see Eddé, *Saladin*, 227–37.

39. Lyons and Jackson, *Saladin*, 267–77; Eddé, *Saladin*, 218–27.

40. Lyons and Jackson, *Saladin*, 273, citing the anonymous Latin *Continuation* of William of Tyre.

41. IA, XI: 551/II: 334.

42. 'Imad al-Din al-Isfahani, *Kitab al-fath al-qussi fi al-fath al-qudsi*, ed. C. Landberg (Leiden: E. J. Brill, 1888), 60.

43. IA, XI: 551/II: 334.

44. 'Imad al-Din, *Kitab al-fath al-qussi fi al-fath al-qudsi*, 69.

45. The complete text of Muhyi al-Din's victory sermon can be found in Ibn Khallikan, *Wafayat al-a'yan*, ed. Yusuf 'Ali Tawil and Maryan Qasim Tawil,

6 vols. (Beirut: Dar al-kutub al-'ilmiya, 1998). Translated by W. M. de Slane as *Ibn Khallikan's Biographical Dictionary*, 4 vols. (Paris: Oriental Translation Fund of Great Britain and Ireland, 1842–71), IV: 69–73/II: 633–43 (slightly modified).

Chapter 7

1. IA, XI: 544/II: 328–39.
2. Ibn Jubayr, 304–5/319–20.
3. 'Imad al-Din, *Kitab al-fath al-qussi fi al-fath al-qudsi*, 153.
4. The Third Crusade awaits its book. For now, see Lyons and Jackson, *Saladin*, 295–363; Tyerman, *God's War*, 375–474; and especially Eddé, *Saladin*, 238–70. Arabic sources: Ibn Shaddad, 123–239/113–236, which mostly duplicates and renders accessible the purple prose of his contemporary, 'Imad al-Din al-Isfahani; IA, XII: 32–87/II: 363–402; Abu Shama, IV.
5. But not enough to push them into an alliance, as has often been maintained. For a sound debunking of this idea, see Savvas Neocleous, "The Byzantines and Saladin: Opponents of the Third Crusade?" *Crusades* 9 (2010): 87–106.
6. IA, XII: 50/II: 376.
7. Abu Shama, IV: 216.
8. It was on one of these forays that Richard's men happened to raid the traveling party of the ascetic and diplomat al-Harawi, making off with his notes and manuscripts. As al-Harawi mentions in passing in his guide to pilgrimage sites, Richard offered to meet with him to return his belongings, but it couldn't be arranged. See al-Harawi, *Kitab al-isharat*, 5/4, 79/78.
9. Ibn Shaddad, 236/232.
10. Al-Qadi al-Fadil, cited in Abu Shama, IV: 332–33.
11. On the Ayyubid dynasty after Saladin, see Holt, *The Age of the Crusades*, 60–81; R. Stephen Humphreys, *From Saladin to the Mongols: The Ayyubids of Damascus, 1193–1260* (Albany: State University of New York Press, 1977), which concentrates on the Ayyubids of Syria even after the fall of the dynasty in Egypt; and, more generally, Michael Chamberlain, "The Crusader Era and the Ayyubid Dynasty," in Carl F. Petry, ed., *The Cambridge History of Egypt* (Cambridge: Cambridge University Press, 1998), I: 211–41.
12. The reign of al-'Adil has so far received only the unwonted attention of a German dissertation: F. J. Dahlmanns, "Al-Malik al-'Adil: Ägypten und der Vordere Orient in den Jahren 589/1193 bis 615/1218," PhD diss., Justus Liebig University, Giessen, 1975. See also Humphreys, *From Saladin to the Mongols*, 132–37; Sibt, VIII/2: 471, 474 (plague, famine), 477–78 (earthquake); *TM*, 65–66 (William).

13. IW, III: 71, 74–76, 78; IA, XII: 126–29/III: 28–31.

14. On the Fourth Crusade, see Jonathan Phillips, *The Fourth Crusade and the Sack of Constantinople* (London: Viking Penguin, 2004). On the Muslim coverage of these events, see Taef El-Azhari, "Muslim Chroniclers and the Fourth Crusade," *Crusades* 6 (2007): 107–16, whence I have taken the quote from Abu Shama.

15. On this intriguing episode, in which the Templars openly shared intelligence on the course of the Crusade with Mansur, see IW, III: 145–50, 152, 154.

16. IW, III: 166–67.

17. IW, III: 143–44. This is a battle that took place *before* the Hospitallers opened negotiations with Mansur.

18. IA, XII: 198/III: 81–82; IW, III: 135, where the aggressors are called "the Franks of Sicily" (*firanj Siqiliya*).

19. IW, III: 159, 162; IA, XII: 194–95/III: 79.

20. IW, III: 162–63. Ibn Wasil tells a ripping yarn of one of Hama's ulema, who had taken up a new career as a warrior. Captured by the Templars, he was taken to Frankish territory, presumably to be sold. But he made his escape by jumping into the sea, and eventually made his way on foot back to Hama and his family. Sibt, VIII/2: 523–24, adds the detail that the Franks captured washerwomen on the banks of the Orontes outside the city; IA, XII: 195/III: 79; TM, 44.

21. IW, III: 173–74; IA, XII: 273–74/III: 136–37.

22. Sibt, VIII/2: 544–45, with a detailed account of the public jihad sermon he gave, during which he cut his hair in order to fashion leads and hobbles for the warriors' horses.

23. On the Fifth, or Damietta, Crusade, see James M. Powell's excellent *Anatomy of a Crusade, 1213–1221* (Philadelphia: University of Pennsylvania Press, 1986); Humphreys, *From Saladin to the Mongols*, 155–70; IA, XII: 320–31/III: 174–82 provides a relatively seamless narrative.

24. IW, III: 254.

25. On these Syrian escapades, see IW, III: 254–57; Sibt, VIII/2: 583–86, claiming only three Franks survived to make it back to Sidon.

26. IA, XII: 322–23/III: 175.

27. On the arrival in Egypt, see IW, III: 258–61; Sibt, VIII/2: 592–93.

28. IW, III: 265–66; Sibt, VIII/2: 593.

29. IW, III: 270, 276. Sibt, VIII/2: 593 says the shock of the news killed him.

30. Sibt, VIII/2: 601–2; IW, IV: 32.

31. IW, IV: 16.

32. Ibn Wasil tells us of just such a fellow, a soldier from a village in the Delta who swam into Damietta to assure the Muslims that they had not been forgotten (IW, IV: 19–20).

33. IW, IV: 18–19, 32–33, 104 (pulpit).

34. IA, XII: 327/III: 179, alluding to Qur'an 22: 27.

35. IA, XII: 327/III: 179.

36. IW, IV: 17–18, 92–95 (troops from Syria). Sibt, VIII/2: 652 also notes a successful Muslim raid outside Sidon.

37. IW, IV: 33.

38. IW, IV: 94.

39. IW, IV: 95.

40. IW, IV: 96.

41. On the final course of events in Egypt, see Sibt, VIII/2: 620–21; IW, IV: 96–107, with much celebratory verse.

42. Or perhaps this was just wishful thinking on Frederick's part, since the Arabic sources have him claiming these treaty terms on the dubious supposition that what was offered to Pelagius at Damietta was by right offered to Frederick, since Pelagius was, as papal legate, ultimately beholden to Frederick as emperor. On the original treaty and al-Kamil's subsequent embarrassment, see IW, IV: 206–7; TM, 163–64, 176–77.

43. Muslim accounts of Frederick are well-known and conveniently collected in Gabrieli, 267–83. Gabrieli appears to have been as charmed by Frederick as were the Ayyubids; see his fulsome study, "Frederick II and Muslim Culture," *East and West* 9 (1958): 53–61. See *CIP*, 337–40; IW, IV: 233–35. On the propaganda value of all this, see James M. Powell, "Frederick II and the Muslims: The Making of an Historiographical Tradition," in Larry J. Simon, ed., *Iberia and the Mediterranean World of the Middle Ages* (Leiden: E. J. Brill, 1995), I: 261–69. On Frederick's campaigns against the Muslims of Sicily, see David Abulafia, "The End of Muslim Sicily," in Powell, *Muslims under Latin Rule*, 103–33; *TM*, 194–95.

44. On Frederick II's crusade, see David Abulafia, *Frederick II: A Medieval Emperor* (Oxford: Oxford University Press, 1988), 164–201. IA, XII: 477–80/III: 289–92, XII: 482–83/3: 293–94. The quote is from Sibt, VIII/2: 654.

45. IW, IV: 241–51; the quote about Sibt is on 245/Gabrieli, 272 (slightly modified).

46. Sibt, VIII/2: 653–57. The account of his sermon is on pp. 654–55.

47. IW, IV: 303–5 (Hama), 310–11 (Aleppo); IW, V: 131–33 (Baghras, etc.). The raid culminated in a confrontation with the Hospitallers and the lord of Jubayl, which resulted in a resounding victory for Aleppo.

48. On this effort, see Humphreys, *From Saladin to the Mongols*, 271–74.

49. On the presence of Khwarizmians in the west, see IW, IV: 325; IW, V: 134–35; Ibn Duqmaq, 83, 109; Khazandari, 16, 18–20, 30–32.

50. Ironically the Rawda fortress was built using Frankish captives as labor: Ibn Duqmaq, 137. On their purchase and their early commanders, see Khazandari, 4–5, 26.

51. Ibn Duqmaq, 130, 135 (with more specific territories, including the right to enter Damascus to buy arms, despite opposition of prominent ulema);

IW, V: 301–2 (Safad and Shaqif); IW, V: 332–33 (Jerusalem, Tiberias, and Ascalon). Rumor also had it that the Franks had been promised part of Egypt too (IW, V: 338; Khazandari, 40).

52. Likewise Ibn Wasil spotted a bell hanging in the al-Aqsa Mosque. These areas had been explicitly excluded from the Franks in the earlier agreement with Frederick II (IW, V: 333). His account is also quoted in Ibn al-Furat, 2/1–2.

53. On the Khwarizmian sack of Jerusalem, see IW, V: 337–38; Ibn al-Furat, 3/2–3; Khazandari, 39; *Kanz*, VII: 353; *Suluk*, 316 Humphreys, *From Saladin to the Mongols*, 274–75. The Khwarizmian troops would eventually be destroyed by an Ayyubid coalition near Homs in 1246 (Sibt, VIII/2: 760; IW, V: 358–59).

54. On this battle, see Sibt, VIII/2: 746. The quote is from *CIP*, 222. Sibt's coverage of the battle is fairly detailed, as he was in Jerusalem at the time (VIII/2: 745–47). See also IW, V: 337–40; Ibn al-Furat, 5/4–7; Khazandari, 40–41; *Kanz*, VII: 354; *Suluk*, 317. On the Barons' Crusade, see Michael Lower, *The Baron's Crusade: A Call to Arms and Its Consequences* (Philadelphia: University of Pennsylvania Press, 2005) and also Peter Jackson, "The Crusades of 1239–41 and Their Aftermath," *BSOAS* 50 (1987): 32–60.

55. I am indebted here to the ruminations of R. Stephen Humphreys, "Ayyubids, Mamluks, and the Latin East in the Thirteenth Century," *Mamluk Studies Review* 2 (1998): 1–17.

56. *TM*, 257.

57. R. Stephen Humphreys, "Politics and Architectural Patronage in Ayyubid Damascus," in C. E. Bosworth et al., eds., *The Islamic World from Classical to Modern Times: Essays in Honor of Bernard Lewis* (Princeton, NJ: Darwin Press, 1989), 151–74; Daniella Talmon-Heller, *Islamic Piety in Medieval Syria: Mosques, Cemeteries and Sermons under the Zangids and Ayyubids (1146–1260)* (Leiden: E. J. Brill, 2007).

58. The Franks had surrendered Ascalon to Saladin in 1192 but then recaptured it during the Barons' Crusade in 1239–41. The Muslim conquest of 1247 would be, it turns out, final. Sibt, VIII: 766; IW, V: 378; Ibn al-Furat, 10/8, 12–13/10–11; Khazandari, 54–55; *Suluk*, 328.

59. IW, IV: 247; Ibn al-Furat, 15/13.

60. Khazandari, 58. He also includes a longer (imaginary) text of Frederick's warning to al-Salih Ayyub (58–59) and also Louis's letter demanding al-Salih Ayyub's surrender (59–60).

61. On Louis IX's crusade to Egypt, see Claude Cahen, "St. Louis et l'Islam," *Journal Asiatique* 258 (1970): 3–12; William C. Jordan, *Louis IX and the Challenges to the Crusade: A Study in Rulership* (Princeton, NJ: Princeton University Press, 1979); Jean Richard, *Saint Louis: Crusader King of France*, trans. J. Birrell (Cambridge: Cambridge University Press, 1992); and the revealing collection of sources (Christian and Muslim) in Peter Jackson,

The Seventh Crusade, 1244–1254: Sources and Documents (Aldershot, UK: Ashgate, 2007).; For a discussion of most of the Arabic sources, see Anne-Marie Eddé, "Saint Louis et la Septième Croisade vus par les auteurs arabes," *Cahiers de Recherches Médiévales (XIIIe–XVes)* 1 (1996): 65–92. Arabic sources: IW, VI: 73–77, 100–28, 133–35 is most detailed, including eyewitness insights; Sibt, VIII/2: 773–75, 778–79; Ibn al-Furat, 14–46/12–38; Ibn Duqmaq, 184–87, 191–92 (largely reproducing Sibt); Khazandari, 57–60, 62–63; *Suluk*, 333ff.

62. Ibn Duqmaq, 192–93. In Damascus a celebratory mob with musicians entered the Church of Mary bent on tearing it down; the story was also told that in Baalbek, the Muslim governor punished some Christians there because they had blackened the faces of their icons in mourning (employing Jews to do the punishing).

63. On the dismantling of Damietta and the foundation of nearby Manshiya, see IW, VI: 145–46; Ibn al-Furat, 46–47/38–39. On Turanshah's letter to Damascus, see Ibn Duqmaq, 191–92.

Chapter 8

1. On the *Secret History*, the standard scholar's translation is the monumental *The Secret History of the Mongols: A Mongolian Epic Chronicle of the Thirteenth Century*, trans. Igor de Rachewiltz, 2 vols. (Leiden: E. J. Brill, 2006). For a less informative but rather more beautiful version, see the "adaptation" by Paul Kahn, *The Secret History of the Mongols: The Origin of Chingis Khan* (Boston: Cheng and Tsui, 1998). The best introductory overview of the Mongol enterprise remains David O. Morgan, *The Mongols*, 2nd ed. (Oxford: Blackwell, 1990).

2. IA, XII: 358/III: 202.

3. On the place of the Qipchaq Turks in the medieval world, and in Mongol-Mamluk relations in particular, see Charles J. Halperin, "The Kipchak Connection: The Ilkhans, the Mamluks and Ayn Jalut," *BSOAS* 63 (2000): 229–45. A complete modern account of the Mamluk sultanate has yet to be written, though it is hoped that Jo van Steenbergen's forthcoming synthesis will do just that. The early phase of Mamluk rule is best served for now by Robert Irwin, *The Middle East in the Middle Ages: The Early Mamluk Sultanate, 1250–1382* (Carbondale: Southern Illinois University Press, 1986).

4. Humphreys, "Ayyubids, Mamluks, and the Latin East," 11–12. Humphreys's comments have informed much of my discussion comparing Ayyubid and Mamluk policies.

5. On the first decade of Mamluk rule, see in particular Irwin, *Middle East in the Middle Ages*, 26–36. For a narrative highlighting Baybars's role in all this, see IAZ, 51–74.

6. On the truce with the Franks, see Ibn al-Furat, 49/40.

7. Frankish dispositions toward the Mongols are masterfully presented in Peter Jackson, "The Crisis in the Holy Land in 1260," *English Historical Review* 376 (1980): 481–513, from whom I have also taken the apt phrase "benevolent neutrality." Mongol conquests in Syria are given some prominence in the contemporary chronicle of Ibn Wasil: IW, VI: 265–66 (Aleppo and A'zaz), 268–70 (Aleppo again), 271–72 (Nablus), 274–75 (Gaza, Damascus, Jerusalem, Ba'alabak).

8. The text, from the chronicle of Ibn al-Furat (d. 1405), is preserved in *Suluk*, 427–29, and a truncated version in various other sources, such as Khazandari, 92–93. The translation is adapted from that of Bernard Lewis, *Islam: From the Prophet Muhammad to the Capture of Constantinople*, vol. 1: *Politics and War* (Oxford: Oxford University Press, 1974), 84–89.

9. Technically the Mongols had already felt defeat at Parwan near Kabul in 1221, but that was a minor setback. More important, it seems that the underdog Mamluks actually outnumbered the Mongols.

10. The best examination of Mongol-Mamluk relations, including this famous battle and its consequences, is Reuven Amitai-Preiss, *Mongols and Mamluks: The Mamluk-Ilkhanid War, 1260–1281* (Cambridge: Cambridge University Press, 1995), 26–48. See also David Morgan, "The Mongols in Syria, 1260–1300," in Edbury, *Crusade and Settlement*, 231–35. For an assessment of tactics and so on, see Peter Thorau, "The Battle of 'Ayn Jalut: A Reexamination," in Edbury, *Crusade and Settlement*, 236–41.

11. On these arrangements, see IW, VI: 295–97; Ibn Duqmaq, 265–66; Baybars al-Mansuri, 52.

12. The standard work on the life and time of Baybars is Peter Thorau, *The Lion of Egypt: Sultan Baybars I and the Near East in the Thirteenth Century*, trans. P. M. Holt (London: Longman, 1992). Like Saladin, Baybars was the subject of a contemporary biography, the *Rawd al-Zahir* of Ibn 'Abd al-Zahir (referred to in these notes as IAZ).

13. On these Syrian troubles, see IW, VI: 302–5; Ibn Duqmaq, 274–75; IAZ, 96–99.

14. On these events, see P. M. Holt, "Some Observations on the 'Abbasid Caliphate of Cairo," *BSOAS* 47 (1984): 501–7, and the thorough study of Stefan Heidemann, *Das Aleppiner Kalifat (A.D. 1261): Vom Ende des Kalifates in Bagdad über Aleppo zu den Restaurationen in Kairo* (Leiden: E. J. Brill, 1994).

15. On these last campaigns, see IW, VI: 336–37 (Antioch), 365–66 (Nazareth), 367–71 (Acre). On holy sites, see IW, VI: 368 (Al-Dahi and Tiberias), 371 (Jerusalem); Ibn al-Furat, 54–80/44–65; IAZ, 113–19, 132–33, 148–62; Baybars al-Mansuri, 76 (Antioch), 81 (Acre and Jerusalem).

16. Ibn al-Furat, 99/79 (slightly modified).

17. On these various Syrian campaigns in the mid 1260s, see Ibn al-Furat, 84–100/68–82; IAZ, 223–47; al-Khazandari, 129; *Kanz*, VIII: 11; Yunini, II: 318; Baybars al-Mansuri, 95–96; *Suluk*, 526.

18. On this campaign, see Ibn al-Furat, 107–10/84–87; al-Khazandari, 134. On Safad, see Ibn al-Furat, 112–19/88–96; IAZ, 250–65; Khazandari, 140; *Kanz*, VIII: 117; Yunini, II: 337; Baybars al-Mansuri, 103–4; Ibn al-Mughayzil, *Dhayl mufarrij al-kurub*, 63; *Suluk*, 545.

19. Muslim sources provide only passing information on Louis's disastrous crusade to Tunis (sometimes called the Eighth Crusade), which resulted in his death by disease in 1270. Ibn al-Furat, 179/141–42; IAZ, 373–74; Khazandari, 150–53; *Kanz*, VIII: 101; Yunini, II: 454; *Suluk*, 502. Ibn Khaldun, *Ta'rikh Ibn Khaldun*, ed. M. A. al-Baydun (Beirut: Dar al-Kutub al-'Ilmiya, 2003), VI: 374–78, is by far the meatiest.

20. On Mamluk campaigns against Armenia, see Angus Donal Stewart, *The Armenian Kingdom and the Mamluks: War and Diplomacy during the Reigns of Het'um II (1289–1307)* (Leiden: Brill, 2001), 43–53 for Baybars's campaigns.

21. On Jaffa and associated conquests in Syria, see Ibn al-Furat, 133–43/105–18; IAZ, 292–306; Khazandari, 142–43; Baybars al-Mansuri, 110–11. On Antioch itself, see Ibn al-Furat, 149–60/118–26; IAZ, 307–25; *Kanz*, VIII: 124; Yunini, II: 374; Baybars al-Mansuri, 111–14 (the author was an eyewitness); Ibn al-Mughayzil, *Dhayl Mufarrij al-Kurub*, 64–69; *Suluk*, 564.

22. The translation of this famous letter is that of Gabrieli, *Arab Historians of the Crusades*, 311 (slightly modified). The full text, worthy of a separate study, can be found in IAZ, 309–13, and Baybars al-Mansuri, 112–14, who provided copies of it himself while in the field.

23. On Baybars's conquests of Nizari lands, see IAZ, 365, 411; Khazandari, 144; Yunini, II: 473, III: 6; Baybars al-Mansuri, 124; *Suluk*, 608.

24. On the slight impact of Louis's Tunisian debacle, see note above. On the preparations of Baybars, see Ibn al-Furat, 177–80/140–42. On Frankish embassies to Baybars after the fall of Antioch, see Ibn al-Furat, 166–67/131–32; Baybars al-Mansuri, 114–15. On Edward in Acre, see Ibn al-Furat, 201/159; IAZ, 401; S. Loyd, "The Lord Edward's Crusade, 1270–72," in John Gillingham and J. C. Holt, eds., *War and Government in the Middle Ages: Essays in Honour of J. O. Prestwich* (Woodbridge, UK: Boydell Press, 1984), 120–33. On anxieties about a Frankish-Mongol alliance, see Reuven Amitai-Preiss, "Mamluk Perceptions of the Mongol-Frankish Rapprochement," *Mediterranean Historical Review* 7 (1992): 50–65.

25. On these campaigns, see Ibn al-Furat, 180–88/143–49, 191–92/151–52 (al-Qurayn); IAZ, 374–82, 385–88 (al-Qurayn); Khazandari, 145, 153; *Kanz*, VIII: 155; Yunini, II: 444; Baybars al-Mansuri, 120, 124, 127–29; Ibn al-Mughayzil, *Dhayl Mufarrij al-Kurub*, 72–73; *Suluk*, 591.

26. On Baybars's intervention in Anatolia and the battle of Abulustayn, see Amitai-Preiss, *Mongols and Mamluks*, 157–78.

27. A fascinating, if fanciful, reflection of this plan and its failure can be found in Khazandari, 153–57, who suggests that Baybars's diplomacy with England saved the day. Reflected also (it seems) in *Suluk*, 364.

28. Humphreys, "Ayyubids, Mamluks, and the Latin East," 14.

29. On Mamluk diplomacy with Christendom, see, with recent bibliography, P. M. Holt, *Early Mamluk Diplomacy (1260–1290): Treaties of Baybars and Qalawun with Christian Rulers* (Leiden: Brill, 1995).

30. On this diplomatic activity, see IAZ, 117–19; Baybars al-Mansuri, 67; Ibn al-Furat, 52–54/43–44, from which the quotes are taken. The suggestion of a feudal relationship was made by Riley-Smith in his notes to these translated excerpts of Ibn al-Furat's chronicle.

31. This truce is discussed in great detail in Holt, *Early Mamluk Diplomacy*, 32–41.

32. Qalawun too received biographies by his contemporaries. One was by the biographer of Baybars, Ibn ʿAbd al-Zahir, entitled *Tashrif al-ayyam wa'l-ʿusur fi sirat al-malik al-mansur*, ed. M. Kamil (Cairo: Turathuna, 1961). Another, shorter work was published as Paulina B. Lewicka, *Safi Ibn ʿAli's Biography of the Mamluk Sultan Qalawun* (Warsaw: Academic Publishing House, 2000). The standard modern biography is Linda Northrup, *From Slave to Sultan: The Career of al-Mansur Qalawun and the Consolidation of Mamluk Rule in Egypt and Syria (678–689 AH/1279–1290 AD)* (Stuttgart: Franz Steiner, 1998).

33. On this battle and its aftermath, see Khazandari, 178–80; *Kanz*, VIII: 241; Yunini, IV: 93; Baybars al-Mansuri, 196–201; *Suluk*, 691. On the il-khan Ahmad Sultan's embassy, see Khazandari, 185–89.

34. On the buildup to his campaign against Tripoli, see Khazandari, 196–98, 202–4 (against rebel-held Sahyun); *Kanz*, VIII: 268; Yunini, IV: 96; Abu al-Fidaʾ, 12–13; Ibn al-Mughayzil, *Dhayl mufarrij al-kurub*, 111–15, 118 (with detailed insights on chancery affairs); Baybars al-Mansuri, 252; *Suluk*, 727.

35. On the reconquest of Tripoli, see Robert Irwin, "The Mamluk Conquest of the County of Tripoli," in Edbury, *Crusade and Settlement*, 246–49, which shows that Qalawun had been actively intervening in Tripolitan affairs even before his campaign. See also Khazandari, 207–8; *Kanz*, VIII: 283; Baybars al-Mansuri, 266–69; Ibn al-Mughayzil, *Dhayl mufarrij al-kurub*, 120–24; Abu'l-Fidaʾ, 14–15; *Suluk*, 747.

36. On the reconquest of Acre and a guide to most of the extant Arabic accounts, see David Little, "The Fall of ʿAkka in 690/1291: The Muslim Version," in M. Sharon, ed., *Studies in Islamic History and Civilization in Honour of Professor David Ayalon* (Leiden: E. J. Brill, 1986), 159–81.

37. Al-Jazari, cited in Little, "Fall of ʿAkka," 169n64.

38. An anonymous combatant, cited in Little, "Fall of ʿAkka," 176.

39. Cited in Little, "Fall of ʿAkka," 176–77 (slightly modified).

40. Quoted by Ibn al-Furat, cited in Little, "Fall of ʿAkka," 180–81.

41. On Cyprus and the Crusades, see Peter W. Edbury, *The Kingdom of Cyprus and the Crusades, 1191–1374* (Cambridge: Cambridge University Press, 1991).

42. On this debacle, see Ibn al-Furat, 203/160; IAZ, 386, 430; Khazandari, 145–49; *Kanz*, VIII: 162; Yunini, II: 453, III: 85; Baybars al-Mansuri, 130; *Suluk*, 593, 615.

43. Arabic accounts: *Suluk*, III: 105–7; al-Nuwayri al-Iskandarani, *Kitab al-il-mam bi al-I'am fima jarat bihi al-ahkam wa-al-umur al-maqdiyya fi waq'at al-Iskandariyya*, ed. E. Combé and A. S. Atiya (Hyderabad: Da'irat al-Ma'arif al-'Uthmaniyya, 1968), II: 137–66; al-'Ayni, *'Iqd al-juman fi ta'rikh ahl al-zaman*, MS Cairo, Dar al-Kutub, 1584 Ta'rikh, vol. XXIV/1, folios 138–39; Ibn Taghribirdi, XI: 29–30; Ibn Iyas, *Bada'i al-zuhur fi waqa'i al-dhuhur*, ed. M. Mustafa (Wiesbaden: F. Steiner, 1974), I/2: 21–23. These are discussed in detail in Jo van Steenbergen, "The Alexandrian Crusade (1365) and the Mamluk Sources: Reassessment of the *Kitab al-Ilmam* of an-Nuwayri al-Iskandarani," in K. Ciggaarr and H. Teule, eds., *East and West in the Crusader States: Context-Contacts-Confrontations*, III (Leuven: Peeters, 2003), 123–37. Peter's motives are explored in Peter W. Edbury, "The Crusading Policy of King Peter I of Cyprus, 1359–1369," in P. M. Holt, ed., *The Eastern Mediterranean Lands in the Period of the Crusades* (Warminster, UK: Aris and Phillips, 1977), 90–105. In what follows, all translations are based upon that of al-Maqrizi's account in Holt, *The Age of the Crusades*, 125–26.

44. Ibn Kathir, *Kitab al-ijtihad fi talb al-jihad*, in S. Zakkar, ed., *Arba'at kutub fi al-jihad min 'asr alhurub al-salibiya* (Damascus: Dar al-takwin, 2007), 424, a wholly ignored source on the Cypriot raids.

45. Ibn Kathir, *Kitab al-ijtihad*, pp. 424–27 has a detailed account.

46. On the Mamluk campaigns against Cyprus, see Holt, *The Age of the Crusades*, 184–86. The main Arabic account is that of Ibn Taghribirdi, XIV: 292–95.

Chapter 9

1. 'Ashiqpashazade, *Tawarikh-i al-i 'Uthman*, edited by F. Giese as *Die altos-manische Chronik des 'Asikpasazade* (Leipzig: Harrasowitz, 1929), 6–35. Translation of this excerpt by Robert Dankoff, published in Barbara H. Rosenwein, ed., *Reading the Middle Ages* (Toronto: Broadview, 2006), 492–93.

2. For general histories of the Ottomans, Colin Imber, *The Ottoman Empire 1300–1481* (Istanbul: Isis Press, 1990) is especially good for this early period. On the Ottomans and the Crusades, see Halil Inalcik, "The Ottoman Turks and the Crusades, 1329–1451," in Setton, *A History of the Crusades*, VI: 222–75. See also Norman Housley, *The Later Crusades: From Lyons to Alcazar, 1274–1580* (Oxford: Oxford University Press, 2001), 49–117. For the latest word, see Housley's *Crusading and the Ottoman Threat, 1453–1505* (Oxford: Oxford University Press, 2012), which extends beyond the chronological frame of this book and does not, in any case, make use of Ottoman sources.

3. On these, and the subsequent entanglements with Byzantium, see Halil Inalcik, "The Rise of the Turcoman Maritime Principalities in Anatolia, Byzantium, and Crusades," *Byzantinische Forschungen* 9 (1985): 179–217.

4. 'Ashiqpashazade, 124. Translation cited by Inalcik, "The Ottoman Turks and the Crusades," 236 (modified slightly).

5. On the Battle of Kosovo, see Wayne S. Vucinich and Thomas A. Emmert, *Kosovo: Legacy of a Medieval Battle* (Minneapolis: University of Minnesota Press, 1991).

6. The classic, but in most aspects outdated, study of the Crusade of Nicopolis is Aziz Atiya, *The Crusade of Nicopolis* (London: Methuen, 1934), which does not use any Ottoman sources. For matters of alliances, supply, and tactics, see more recently David Nicolle, *Nicopolis 1396: The Last Crusade* (London: Osprey, 1999); Housley, *The Later Crusades*, 76–81. For an Arabic eyewitness account, see Ilker Evrim Binbaş, "A Damascene eyewitness to the Battle of Nicopolis: Shams al-Din Ibn al-Jazari (d. 833/1429)," in N. G. Chrissis and M. Carr, eds., *Contact and Conflict in Frankish Greece and the Aegean, 1204–1453* (Aldershot, UK: Ashgate, 2014).

7. On Schiltberger's remarkable memoirs, see *The Bondage and Travels of Johann Schiltberger*, trans. J. Buchan Telfer (London: Hakluyt Society, 1879), especially 2–6 (Nicopolis).

8. On the career of Timur, see Beatrice Forbes Manz, *The Rise and Rule of Tamerlane* (Cambridge: Cambridge University Press, 1989).

9. On Murad's endeavors in the Balkans, especially involving Hungary, see John Jefferson, *The Holy Wars of King Wladislas and Sultan Murad: The Ottoman-Christian Conflict from 1438–1444* (Leiden: E. J. Brill, 2012).

10. On the Crusade of Varna, see Martin Chasin, "The Crusade of Varna," in Setton, *A History of the Crusades*, VI: 276–310; more recently, the rich array of translated Muslim and non-Muslim sources in Colin Imber, *The Crusade of Varna, 1443–45* (Aldershot, UK: Ashgate, 2006). The principal Ottoman account (including much information on other campaigns) is the anonymous *Gazavat-i Sultan Murad ibn Mehemmed Han*, translated in Imber, 41–106.

11. *Gazavat*, 95.

12. *Gazavat*, 99.

13. *Gazavat*, 100.

14. *Gazavat*, 103.

15. On Mehmed II, the classic study is Franz Babinger, *Mehmed the Conqueror and His Time*, trans. R. Mannheim (Princeton, NJ: Princeton University Press, 1978). On the conquest of Constantinople, an excellent if idiosyncratic detailed military study with a collection of some of the Western sources is Marios Phillippides and Walter Hanak, *The Siege and the Fall of Constantinople in 1453: Historiography, Topography, and Military Studies* (Aldershot, UK: Ashgate, 2011). For the context, see the sober and updated

study of Donald M. Nicol, *The Last Centuries of Byzantium, 1261–1453*, 2nd ed. (Cambridge: Cambridge University Press, 1993), 369–94. A more readable survey is that of Jonathan Harris, *The End of Byzantium* (New Haven, CT: Yale University Press, 2010).

16. Though it was an epochal moment for Christendom, the fall of Constantinople did not overtax Ottoman or other Muslim writers of the day. The principal account is that of one of Mehmed's inner circle, the *Tarikh-i Abu'l-Fath* of Tursun Beg, which is badly underserved by the curt summary English translation accorded it by Inalcik and Murphey: Tursun Beg, *The History of Mehmed the Conqueror*, ed. and trans. Halil Inalcik and Rhoads Murphey (Chicago: Bibliotheca Islamica, 1978). To this one can supplement 'Ashiqpashazade's account translated by Lewis in *Islam*, I: 144–48, and the section from Khojah Efendi's *Taj al-tawarikh* translated as *The Capture of Constantinople, from the Taj ut-tevarikh*, "The Diadem of Histories," trans. E. J. Gibb (Glasgow: T. Murray and Son, 1879). Although the chronicler Michael Kritovoulos was a Greek Christian, he was very much Mehmed's creature, and his detailed account of the conquest is in many ways the official Ottoman narrative: Michael Kritovoulos, *History of Mehmed the Conqueror*, ed. and trans. Charles T. Rigg (Princeton, NJ: Princeton University Press, 1954).

17. 'Ashiqpashazade, in Lewis in *Islam*, I: 145.

18. On this phase in Sicily's history, see Alex Metcalfe, *The Muslims of Medieval Italy* (Edinburgh: Edinburgh University Press, 2009), 181–208.

19. For a perceptive analysis of Ibn Jubayr's evidence, see Sarah Davis-Secord, "Focusing on the Family: Ibn Jubayr on the Conversion of Muslims in Norman Sicily," unpublished manuscript.

20. Ibn Jubayr, 297–98/341.

21. Metcalfe, *Muslims of Medieval Italy*, 209, also stresses that William had granted vast tracts of Muslim-occupied lands to his new monastic foundation at Monreale.

22. Metcalfe, *Muslims of Medieval Italy*, 275–98.

23. On these rebellions, *TM*, 99–100 is the most complete, and that is not saying much. For more details, see James M. Powell, "Frederick II and the Rebellion of the Muslims of Sicily," in *Uluslararasi Haçlı Seferleri Sempozyumu* (Ankara: Türk Tarih Kurumu, 1999), 13–22, reprinted in his *The Crusades, the Kingdom of Sicily, and the Mediterranean* (Aldershot, UK: Ashgate, 2007), chapter 14; Metcalfe, 275–87. The tale of Ibn 'Abbad's daughter (from al-Himyari's *Rawd al-mi'tar*) is translated in Mallette, *The Kingdom of Sicily, 1100–1250. A Literary History* (Philadelphia: University of Pennsylvania Press, 2005), 151–53. On Frederick's cynical approach to courting Muslim favor, see Powell, "Frederick II and the Muslims," 261–69.

24. On the deportations, see Metcalfe, *Muslims of Medieval Italy*, 275. The account of the Sicilian petitioner in the east comes from *TM*, 194–95. According to his (rather exaggerated) claim, Frederick "expelled them

from their homes, confiscated their property—170,000 people—and killed a like number of the poor and homeless, so that the mountains were emptied."

25. On the colony at Lucera, see Julie Taylor, *Muslims in Medieval Italy: The Colony at Lucera* (Oxford: Lexington Books, 2003); Metcalfe, *Muslims of Medieval Italy*, 287–94.

26. For some syntheses, see O'Callaghan, *Reconquest and Crusade*, 99–123; Kennedy, *Muslim Spain and Portugal*, 273–304; Fernando Rodríguez Mediano, "The Post-Almohad Dynasties in al-Andalus and the Maghrib," in M. Fierro, ed., *The New Cambridge History of Islam*, vol. 2. *The Western Islamic World, Eleventh to Eighteenth Centuries* (Cambridge: Cambridge University Press, 2010), II: 106–43, especially 131–37; L. P. Harvey, *Islamic Spain, 1250–1500* (Chicago: University of Chicago Press, 1990).

27. On the surrender generally, see al-Maqqari, IV: 523–28/II: 384–90. The quote is from IV: 529/II: 390.

28. Al-Maqqari, IV: 529/II: 391.

29. Al-Maqqari, IV: 529/II: 392.

Epilogue

1. *Bughya*, VI: 2926.

2. Cahen, *Syrie du Nord*, 41–42, 343–44, was the first to draw attention to Hamdan. Others, notably Bernard Lewis, misrepresented him and his work, because it was thought entirely lost. But a few fragments, such as this tale, survive in some later sources. See *Bughya*, VI: 2926.

3. On this question, see the careful discussion in *CIP*, 407–19.

4. On the redoubtable Ibn Taymiyya, see Yossef Rapoport and Shahab Amhed, eds., *Ibn Taymiyya and His Times* (Oxford: Oxford University Press, 2010) for the latest word.

5. Ahmad ibn ʿAli al-Hariri, *Al-Iʿlam wa-al-tabyin fi khuruj al-firanj al-malaʿin ʿala diyar al-muslimin*, ed. Suhayl Zakkar (Damascus: Maktabat Dar al-Mallah, 1981). Al-Maqqari's work is cited throughout this book. On Naʿima, see Lewis V. Thomas, *A Study of Naima*, ed. Norman Itzkowitz (New York: New York University Press, 1972); Lewis, *Muslim Discovery*, 164–66. On panegyrics, see, for example, Abouali, "Saladin's Legacy." The Jerusalemite petition can be found in K. J. al-ʿAsali, ed., *Wathaʾiq Maqdisiya Taʾrikhiya*, 2 vols. (Amman: Jamiʿat al-Urdunniya, 1983), I: 286–91.

Bibliographic Sketch

The modern scholarly studies on the Crusades and Islamic history that have informed this book are produced in many different European and Middle Eastern languages. However, as this book is intended for nonspecialists, unless absolutely necessary, I have tried to limit myself in my notes and in this bibliographical sketch (which is not meant to duplicate the notes) to works appearing in English. For the same reason, I have also indicated when a primary source appears in English translation. In the notes, references to translations appear after a slash.

Compared with the field of Crusades studies, Islamic history has nothing like the number of well-researched and accessible general histories available to the interested reader. The best way to understand the Crusades in the context of Islamic history is to understand that history's broad sweep, not just one particular period or region. M. G. S. Hodgson's classic three-volume opus, *The Venture of Islam: Conscience and History in a World Civilization* (Chicago: University of Chicago Press, 1977) has been of direct influence to me, especially his concept of the oikumene and the clever coinage of "Islamdom." An updated and rather less idiosyncratic survey can be had in Ira M. Lapidus, *A History of Islamic Societies*, 2nd ed. (Cambridge: Cambridge University Press, 2002). The monumental *New Cambridge History of Islam*, edited by Michael Cook, 6 vols. (Cambridge: Cambridge University Press, 2010) is another fruitful place to start, though some chapters are stronger than others. The standard reference for Islamic studies generally is *The Encylopaedia of Islam* published by E. J. Brill, currently in its third edition, though there is much to be found in the first and second editions. On the religious culture of the premodern Islamic world, see Jonathan P. Berkey, *The Formation of Islam: Religion* and *Society in the Near East, 600–1800* (Cambridge: Cambridge University Press, 2003) to start.

Other books have examined Islamic perspectives on the Crusades. The best-known is Amin Maalouf's popular *Les Croisades vues par les Arabes* (Paris: J. C. Lattès, 1983), translated by Jon Rothschild as *The Crusades through Arab Eyes* (New York: Schocken Books, 1987). It is a skillfully written account of the coming of the Franks to the Near East and their final expulsion. It is also, it must be said, not a serious historical study of the period, though it is a "good read." The second is *The Crusades: Islamic Perspectives* by Carole Hillenbrand, originally published in 1999. This is a remarkable work, which explores a wide range of Arabic sources to investigate in depth certain facets of the Islamic experiences of the Crusades in the Levant. Exacting as it is, however, it does not pretend to offer a narrative account of the Crusades nor extend its coverage much after 1291. A similar framework informs the crisp surveys of the late P. M. Holt, *The Age of Crusades: The Near East from the Eleventh Century until 1517* (London: Longman, 1986) and its quasi-abridgement, *The Crusader States and Their Neighbours* (London: Longman, 2004).

For specific dynasties and other issues, readers should consult the notes. However, there are some regional overviews that provide further background. On al-Andalus, the best survey of the Islamic context is Hugh Kennedy's *Muslim Spain and Portugal: A Political History of al-Andalus* (London: Routledge, 1996). On the Maghrib, see Jamil M. Abun-Nasr, *A History of the Maghrib in the Islamic Period* (Cambridge: Cambridge University Press, 1987). On Sicily, see Alex Metcalfe, *The Muslims of Medieval Italy* (Edinburgh: University of Edinburgh Press, 2009). On Anatolia, see Claude Cahen, *Pre-Ottoman Turkey* (New York: Taplinger, 1968), a dry but thorough narrative. On the early years of the Ottoman dynasty, Halil Inalcik, *The Ottoman Empire: The Classical Age, 1300–1600* (London: Praeger, 1973) is still the best overview.

Just as Islamic history is underserved by general histories, so too are the Islamic primary sources not readily available to readers not versed in the relevant original languages. They can be rough going even so. For a fairly comprehensive list of such translations that exist (including those in German and French), see Carole Hillenbrand, *The Crusades: Islamic Perspectives* (London: Routledge, 1999), 619–21. Arabic sources tend to dominate; Persian sources are of only occasional importance; for Ottoman activities, the early narratives in Ottoman Turkish are few and far between but crucial.

For more than a century most historians have made do with the sources collected in the *Recueil des historiens des croisades: Historiens orientaux*, 5 vols., edited by Academie des Inscriptions et Belles-Lettres (Paris, 1872–1906), but neither the editions nor (especially) the translations therein are reliable, and they have long been superseded by more recent editions.

But whereas many good scholarly editions of texts, especially Arabic ones, now exist, and new sources are often brought to light, the pace of translation is very slow. Many of the older translations are accordingly due for an update themselves. A popular anthology of excerpts from many of the main Arabic narratives is Francesco Gabrieli, *Arab Historians of the Crusades* (London: Routledge, 1969), although this itself is a translation from the Italian, so the reader is at two removes from the Arabic originals. Excerpts of Ibn al-Qalanisi's Damascene chronicle can be had in H. A. R. Gibb's partial translation, *The Damascus Chronicle of the Crusades* (London: Luzac, 1932). Ibn Jubayr's account of his travels can be found in Roland Broadhurst's smooth translation, *The Travels of Ibn Jubayr* (London: Jonathan Cape, 1952), though based upon an imperfect Arabic text. Selections from Ibn al-Furat's chronicle can be sampled in *Ayyubids, Mamlukes, and Crusaders*, edited and translated by U. and M. Lyons, with annotations by: J. Riley-Smith, 2 vols. (Cambridge: W. Heffer and Sons, 1971). The autobiographical sections of one Ayyubid prince's chronicle have been collected and translated by P. M. Holt in Abu al-Fida, *The Memoirs of a Syrian Prince—Abu'l-Fida, Sultan of Hama* (Wiesbaden: Harrasowitz, 1983). Usama ibn Munqidh's autobiographical musings can be found in my own new translation, *The Book of Contemplation: Islam and the Crusades* (London: Penguin Classics, 2008).

The series Crusade Texts in Translation published by Ashgate has made recent and magnificent strides in producing new and accessible scholarly translations from texts in a variety of languages. These include (and are not limited to) Colin Imber's most useful collection *The Crusade of Varna, 1443–45* (Aldershot, UK: Ashgate, 2006) and D. S. Richards's clear translations of the relevant parts of Ibn al-Athir's chronicle, *The Chronicle of Ibn al-Athir for the Crusading Period from Al-Kamil fi'l-Ta'rikh* (Aldershot, UK: Ashgate, 2006–) in three volumes ending in 1231, as well as his translation of a biography of Saladin by his secretary Ibn Shaddad, *The Rare and Excellent History of Saladin or al-Nawadir al-Sultaniyya wa'l-Mahasin al-Yusufiyya* (Aldershot, UK: Ashgate, 2002). Richards also produced a translation of Ibn al-Athir's coverage of the coming of the Saljuq Turks as *The Annals of the Saljuq Turks* (London: RoutledgeCurzon, 2002). As with so many aspects of this field, there is much work yet to be done.

Index